Tourism and Development in Tropical Islands

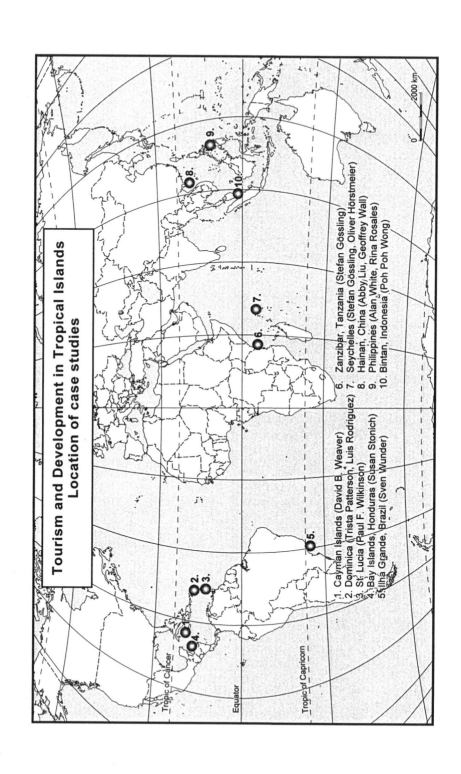

Tourism and Development in Tropical Islands
Location of case studies

1. Cayman Islands (David B. Weaver)
2. Dominica (Trista Patterson, Luis Rodriguez)
3. St. Lucia (Paul F. Wilkinson)
4. Bay Islands, Honduras (Susan Stonich)
5. Ilha Grande, Brazil (Sven Wunder)
6. Zanzibar, Tanzania (Stefan Gössling)
7. Seychelles (Stefan Gössling, Oliver Hörstmeier)
8. Hainan, China (Abby Liu, Geoffrey Wall)
9. Philippines (Alan White, Rina Rosales)
10. Bintan, Indonesia (Poh Poh Wong)

Tropic of Cancer

Equator

Tropic of Capricorn

2000 km

Tourism and Development in Tropical Islands

Political Ecology Perspectives

Edited by

Stefan Gössling

Lecturer, Department of Service Management,
Helsingborg Campus, Lund University, Sweden

Edward Elgar
Cheltenham, UK · Northampton, MA, USA

Published by
Edward Elgar Publishing Limited
Glensanda House
Montpellier Parade
Cheltenham
Glos GL50 1UA
UK

Edward Elgar Publishing, Inc.
136 West Street
Suite 202
Northampton
Massachusetts 01060
USA

A catalogue record for this book
is available from the British Library

Library of Congress Cataloguing in Publication Data
Tourism and development in tropical islands : political ecology perspectives /
    edited by Stefan Gössling.
        p. cm.
    1. Tourism—Tropics. 2. Tourism—Environmental aspects—Tropics. 3.
    Political ecology—Tropics. I. Gössling, Stefan.

    G155.T73T68 2004
    338.4'791'09142—dc22

                                                                      2003049379

ISBN 1 84376 257 9

Printed and bound in Great Britain by MPG Books Ltd, Bodmin, Cornwall

Contents

List of figures   vii
List of tables   viii
List of contributors   ix
Preface   xi

1. Tourism and Development in Tropical Islands: Political Ecology
    Perspectives   1
    Stefan Gössling

2. The Political Ecology of Tourism in the Cayman Islands   38
    David B. Weaver

3. The Political Ecology of Tourism in the Commonwealth of
    Dominica   60
    Trista Patterson and Luis Rodriguez

4. Tourism Policy and Planning in St. Lucia   88
    Paul F. Wilkinson

5. The Political Ecology of Marine Protected Areas: The Case of
    the Bay Islands   121
    Susan C. Stonich

6. Native Tourism, Natural Forests and Local Incomes on Ilha
    Grande, Brazil   148
    Sven Wunder

7. The Political Ecology of Tourism in Zanzibar   178
    Stefan Gössling

8. 'High-value Conservation Tourism': Integrated Tourism
    Development in the Seychelles?   203
    Stefan Gössling and Oliver Hörstmeier

9. Human Resources Development for Tourism in a Peripheral
    Island: Hainan, China   222
    Abby Liu and Geoffrey Wall

10. Community-oriented Marine Tourism in the Philippines: Role in
    Economic Development and Conservation   237
    Alan T. White and Rina Rosales

11. Tourism Development and the Coastal Environment on Bintan
Island   263
Poh Poh Wong

Index   *283*

Figures

Location of case studies   ii
1.1 Groups of actors   13
2.1 Cayman Islands   40
3.1 Dominica   62
4.1 St. Lucia   89
5.1 Bay Islands, Honduras   126
6.1 Ilha Grande, Brazil   151
6.2 Hostel and bed numbers on Ilha Grande   155
7.1 Zanzibar, Tanzania   179
8.1 Seychelles   205
9.1 Hainan, China   225
10.1 Trends in tourist arrivals from 1995 to 2001 for the
     Philippines and Cebu   238
10.2 The Philippines   240
11.1 Bintan Island, Indonesia   264
11.2 Average marine water quality of Bintan Beach International
     Resort, May 1996–November 2000   274

Tables

4.1 St. Lucia tourism statistics   96
6.1 Tourism cash flow in Aventureiro   165
8.1 Distribution of beds in accommodation establishments   207
9.1 Estimation of required tourism workforce by sectors 1995–2010   228
10.1 Potential user fees for marine tourism activities   259
10.2 Present values of coral reefs, beaches and marine waters for
       marine protected areas   259
11.1 Explanation of water quality parameters   273
11.2 Marine water quality of the resorts on the north coast of Bintan,
       April 2001–October 2002   275

Contributors

Dr. Stefan Gössling
Dept. of Service Management
Box 882
251 08 Helsingborg
Sweden
E-mail: stefan.gossling@msm.hbg.lu.se

Oliver Hörstmeier
Dept. of Economic Geography and
Tourism Research
Paderborn University
33095 Paderborn
Germany
E-mail: oliverurlaub@hotmail.com

Dr. Abby Y. Liu
ECOPLAN China Project Office
Faculty of Environmental Studies
University of Waterloo
Waterloo, Ontario N2L 3G1
Canada
E-mail: ayliu@fes.uwaterloo.ca

Trista Patterson
Department of Science, Chemical
Technology and Biosystems
University of Siena
Via della Diana 2/A
53100 Siena
Italy
E-mail: trista@wam.umd.edu

Luis Carlos Rodriguez
Depto. de Ciencas Ecologicas
Casilla 653
Santiago
Chile
E-mail: luis@abulafia.ciencas.uchile.cl

Rina Rosales
Environmental and Natural Resource
Economics (REECS)
Unit 405, Tower at the Emerald Square
J.P. Rizal and P. Tuazon Sts., Project 4
Quezon City 1109
Philippines
E-mail: rinaoct11@yahoo.com

Professor Dr. Susan C. Stonich
Environmental Studies Program
Department of Anthropology
Interdepartmental Graduate Program in
Marine Science
University of California
Santa Barbara, CA 93106
USA
E-mail: stonich@anth.ucsb.edu

Professor Dr. Geoffrey Wall
Graduate Studies and Research
Faculty of Environmental Studies
University of Waterloo
Waterloo, Ontario N2L 3G1
Canada
E-mail: gwall@watserv1.uwaterloo.ca

Professor Dr. David B. Weaver
Dept. of Health, Fitness & Recreation
Resources
George Mason University
PW1 - Mail Stop 4E5
10900 University Blvd.
Manassas, VA 20110-2203
USA
E-mail: dweaver3@gmu.edu

Dr. Alan T. White
Coastal Resource Management Project
5th Floor, CIFC Towers
J. Luna Cor. Humabon Streets
North Area, Cebu City
Philippines 6000
E-mail: awhite@mozcom.com

Professor Dr. Paul F. Wilkinson
York University
Faculty of Environmental Studies
339 Leonard G. Lumbers Building
4700 Keele Street
Toronto, Ontario
Canada M3J 1P3
E-mail: eswilkin@yorku.ca

Professor Dr. Poh Poh Wong
Department of Geography
National University of Singapore
10 Kent Ridge Crescent
Singapore 119260
E-mail: geowpp@nus.edu.sg

Dr. Sven Wunder
Jalan CIFOR
Center for International Forestry
Research
P.O. Box 6596 JKPWB
Jakarta 10065
Indonesia
E-mail: s.wunder@cgiar.org

Preface

This is the finest place I have known in all of
Africa to rest before starting my final journey.
An illusive place where nothing is as it seems.

David Livingstone, 1866

When David Livingstone stayed in Zanzibar, he was, as an ever increasing number of tourists in the early 21st century, fascinated by this tropical island. Even though Zanzibar has fundamentally changed since 1866, Livingstone's suggestion that 'nothing is as it seems' is still valid to a political ecologist concerned with the discourses surrounding tourism development in small islands – too obvious are the multifaceted conflicts between the various groups of actors concerned with tourism. The idea for this book was born out of these observations. Who initiates and controls tourism development, for whom, for what purpose, at what cost, to what end? Who has the power to create and control the narratives related to development issues? And, for fragile island environments, how are ecosystems affected by development processes? It felt as if such questions were inadequately addressed in the existing literature, not only in the context of Zanzibar.

A review of the literature on tourism development in tropical islands revealed two things. First, political ecology, an emerging field of interdisciplinary research addressing the politics of environmental change, is an insufficiently used conceptual framework to analyze tourism development. Susan Stonich's (1998) article on tourism, water resources and environmental health in the Bay Islands of Honduras remains, up to now, the only study explicitly using a political ecology approach in the context of tourism. Second, none of the many books analyzing tourism development in islands has consistently used one methodology, and case studies are usually chosen from very different geographical settings, including arctic, temperate and tropical islands. Comparison thus becomes difficult. Hence the political ecology perspectives of this anthology, which only encompass case studies of tropical islands. These are located between the Tropics of Cancer and Capricorn or 22° 30' northern and southern latitude, representing island states, territories and autonomous parts of continental states. Most case studies are small islands; Hainan, China with its size of 15 500 km^2 is a notable exception.

The authors of the case studies have various academic backgrounds, including economics, biology, geography and anthropology, and the chapters thus cover a wide range of perspectives. This, in combination with the in-depth analysis of the various groups of actors, their motivations and role in development processes and the resulting impacts on the environment, has made it possible to provide new insights into the tourism phenomenon in tropical islands. Political ecology thus deserves our attention as a framework to study tourism-related development processes.

Many people have supported this book and the chapters within. I am indebted to Tom O'Dell for encouraging and supporting this project in its early stages, to Dymphna Evans for being open to the idea and giving its publication a chance, to Matthew Pitman for his patience with my inquiries, to Suzanne Mursell for proof-reading the manuscript, to Thomas Krings, Angelo P. Molinaro and Robert Richardson for their critical advice, to Sven Wunder for vivid discussions, and to Kerstin Schmitt, Birgitt Gaida and Veronica Scheuring for creating the maps contained in this book. Nadine Heck has enthusiastically become engaged as the copy editor, providing me with the freedom to work on the book's content. Many others deserve to be mentioned, including Graham Dunn, Ian Boxill, Mathias Gößling, Peter Häußler, Timo Kunkel and Meike Rinsche. Without their support, this book would not exist.

Stefan Gössling
Freiburg and Helsingborg, May 2003

1. Tourism and Development in Tropical Islands: Political Ecology Perspectives

Stefan Gössling

INTRODUCTION

Tropical island ecosystems are fragile, vulnerable and under increasing stress as a result of forces stemming from coastal development, use of coastal resources and global environmental change. Island economies, on the other hand, are generally in great need of foreign exchange earnings and they are often highly dependent on tourism as a source of income. This raises the question of how to achieve development in harmony with the interests of various stakeholder groups and the environment. While tourism-related development processes in developing countries have been the subject of a range of publications, the relationship of politics and environment has seldom been investigated. In particular, the reasons for and the outcome of the cooperation of governments with international organizations, as well as the consequences of such cooperation for the environment of local stakeholder groups have remained little analyzed. The political ecology perspectives presented in this book thus seek to evaluate the dynamics of material and discursive struggles over natural resources, entitlements and power in tropical islands. In particular, the ways in which conflicts over access to environmental resources are linked to systems of political and economic control, or, in other words, the unequal power relations in politicized tourism environments are the focus of this book.

The Fascination of Islands

Islands have fascinated human beings since historical times. As Hoyle and Biagini (1999) have pointed out, the very idea of an island conjures the image of a microcosm, solitude and isolation. Clear physical borders also constitute psychological borders, which can be seen as an attraction in its own right for tourists seeking to escape routine and responsibility. The often limited size of islands makes it also possible to encompass space mentally, and thus to feel oriented and secure. Abundant beaches and a limited number of attractions invite to rest, creating counter-worlds to those perceived in industrialized countries.

Ultimately, island images refer to the quest for Paradise on Earth that came into being during Romanticism and still persists today (Fagan 1998). In particular, the Pacific expeditions of Louis Antoine de Bougainville (1766–1769) and James Cook (1768–1779) contributed to the creation of the myths still surrounding islands. De Bougainville (1772, p. 225, quoted in Fagan 1998, p. 132) wrote, for instance:

> I thought I was transported into the Garden of Eden; we crossed a turf, covered with fine fruit trees, and intersected by little rivulets, which kept up a pleasant coolness in the air, without any of those inconveniences which humidity occasions . . . We found companies of men and women sitting under the shade of their fruit trees . . . [E]verywhere we found hospitality, ease, innocent joy, and every appearance of happiness among them.

Tales of free love reinforced the romantic image of the tropical paradise: 'the great plenty of good and nourishing food, together with the fine climate, the beauty and unreserved behavior of their females, invite them powerfully to the enjoyments and pleasures of love' (George Forster 1777, p. 231, quoted in Fagan 1998, p. 144). Tropical islands still represent individual freedom, peaceful environments, abundance of food and free sex, and are thus often perceived as happier, better places. Extensive beaches, clean blue waters, lush vegetation and smiling island inhabitants are the corresponding symbols that frequently appear in travel catalogues. Islands have also been popularized by writers, famous novels being, for example, *Treasure Island* and *Robinson Crusoe*. Painters such as Paul Gauguin and Henri Matisse have depicted island life, and films such as *Taboo*, *Blue Lagoon* and *Rapa Nui*, as well as a range of more recent advertisement campaigns, have all contributed to the fascination of islands (cf. di Castri et al. 2002).

Island Characteristics

Islands have been commonly defined as land surfaces totally surrounded by water and smaller in size than the smallest continent. While such a definition implies a certain degree of generalization, islands may in fact be characterized by great differences. Politically, they may be independent (Comoros, Kiribati), self-governing in association with a nation (Zanzibar) or a non-self governing territory administered by a state, often as an overseas territory (US Virgin Islands). With respect to topography, islands can be one single land mass (Sri Lanka, St. Lucia) or be composed of groups or archipelagos of a few (Seychelles) or thousands of islands (Indonesia). Islands can be low lying, entirely consisting of atolls and reefs (Maldives), or mountainous with elevated peaks (Dominica, La Réunion). Geologically, they can be former parts of a continent, separated through tectonic plate movement (Madagascar) or they can be a result of volcanic activity (Hawaii). Islands also have very different sizes. The largest tropical islands are New Guinea, Borneo and Madagascar, each extending over more than 500 000 km^2. In comparison, Tokelau, a non-self governing territory administered by New Zealand, has a land area of 10 km^2. Population size varies accordingly. In 2002 Indonesia had a population of more than 230 million (CIA 2003a), while the population of Tokelau totalled 1 431 (CIA 2003b).

Trade and Economy

Even though some tropical islands have themselves been centers of early 'world economies', such as Zanzibar in the Arab-controlled trade covering the entire Indian Ocean more than 2000 years ago (Sheriff 1987), most have existed in isolation, being islands both in physical and metaphorical senses. It was not before the nineteenth century that 'islands and oceans became frontier spaces of commercial, strategic and scientific expansion at worldwide level' (Biagini and Hoyle 1999, p. 5; see also Houbert 1999), providing world markets with raw materials, usually commodities such as minerals, spices, sugar, copra or bananas (cf. Milne 1997; Wilkinson 1997a). Consequently, colonial empires sought to control and exploit the resources of islands. This often caused the disruption of existing patterns of land use and land ownership, for example through the introduction of plantation crops in the Caribbean (Lockhart 1997).

While islands are different in terms of size and population, they often share characteristics of remoteness and mono-structured economies, limited natural resource endowments and dependence on imports. Many islands have thus sought to diversify their economies towards other activities generating foreign exchange earnings. Industrial development is usually severely constrained by the lack of local financial capital, human resources, small domestic markets, poor infrastructure, high transport costs, and the dependence on single commodities and export markets (King 1999; Lockhart 1997; Milne 1992). Dependence on foreign aid and remittance payments further constrains development processes (Milne 1992), with many islands being characterized by outward migration, dependence on remittances, overseas aid and reliance on bureaucracy for job generation (MIRAB economies; Bertram and Watters 1985). Consequently, tourism development has become the favored option to generate employment, income and foreign exchange earnings, to initiate regional development, to finance infrastructure, and to restore and protect cultural sites (cf. Apostolopoulos and Gayle 2002a).

The Age of Tourism

Even though many islands had already seen substantial tourist arrivals in colonial times, it was generally not before the advent of civil aviation in the 1960s that visitor numbers became significant. Following the construction of international airports and the extension of a global network of air-connections, island tourism has grown rapidly. Often, this happened in terms of a 'plantation tourism model', with tourism replacing the traditional cash-crop based economies (Weaver 1988). In the 21st century, most islands have become part of the globalized world economy, primarily through their involvement in tourism. Visitor arrivals have generally increased as a result of promotion efforts, infrastructure development financed by foreign development aid and foreign capital attracted by tax holidays (cf. Apostolopoulos and Gayle 2002b). The economic importance of tourism for tropical islands has grown accordingly. For example, tourist numbers reached almost 3 million in the Dominican Republic in 2000, generating almost 15 per cent of the GDP (US$2.9 billion) (WTO 2003). Revenues generated from tourism also contributed to a Human Development Index (HDI) value of 0.727 in the Dominican Republic (HDI values range between 0.275 for Sierra Leone and 0.942 for Norway; UNDP 2003). In the Seychelles, 130 000 tourists generated US$112 million in 2000, corresponding to 20 per cent of GDP and 60 per cent of foreign exchange earnings (Shah 2002). The islands have, also through the contribution of tourism, become one of the wealthiest nations in Africa, reaching a HDI value of 0.811 in 2000 (UNDP 2003). Barbados, another destination with a substantial income from tourism, has even advanced to a HDI value of 0.871 in 2000, which is not far short of that of European Islands such as Malta (0.875) or Cyprus (0.883) (UNDP 2003). However, most tropical islands have still comparably low per capita GDPs and HDI values, despite their efforts to attract tourists. For example, GDP per capita has remained less than US$500 in Comoros, with a corresponding HDI value of 0.511 (all values in 2000; UNDP 2003).

In terms of dependency, the islands of the Caribbean and Pacific have been affected most by tourism (cf. Beller et al. 1990; Briguglio et al. 1996). The Caribbean is the most tourism-dependent region in the world, with over 25 per cent of all earnings being derived from tourism, and in the South Pacific, tourism revenues account for almost half of the GDP in most destinations (Kakazu 1994; Tewarie 1997, quoted in Apostolopoulos and Gayle 2002b). In the South Pacific, tourism is also a relatively important source of employment with some islands having more than 15 per cent of their labour force employed in tourism and related sectors (Milne 1997). However, populations of remote islands may also depend on subsistence economies involving fishing, agriculture and animal husbandry. Tourism can be a major factor modernizing these economies, and few islands seem to wish to follow alternative development paths. As Wilkinson (1989, p. 158) notes, tourism is often considered an 'obvious' economic policy choice. In consequence, examples of islands restricting tourist numbers are few. In Huahine and Tuamotu islands (French Polynesia), locals are reported to be afraid of losing their identity because of too many visitors (di Castri 2002a; Salvat and Pailhe 2002). In most cases, however, governments argue in favor of tourism, rendering prominent its many benefits, such as higher profits in comparison to traditional economic activities, greater demand for local produce and thus increased agricultural production, employment opportunities, infrastructure development, foreign exchange earnings and welfare among the population at large (Wilkinson 1997b). In order to maximize the income from tourism, governments of most islands thus follow strategies intended to spur continued (and often unlimited) growth. Even large parts of the local population may often vote in favor of more tourists (cf. Dann 1996), expecting greater economic benefits from growing tourist numbers.

Tourism Dependence

Countries in the transition towards a service economy based on tourism usually require external technical, budgetary and capital assistance. Their modernization demands the subsidized upgrading of transport infrastructures, sewage treatment systems, telecommunications, and water or power supplies. In consequence, a major proportion of the tourism-related gross revenue is usually repatriated owing to expenditures on tourism-related imports and services, the ownership or financial involvement of the international tourism industry, or credit loans (Britton 1982; Milne 1992). Wilkinson (1987) reported first-round leakages of 30–45 per cent and second-round leakages of 15–20 per cent for Antigua, Aruba, St Lucia and US Virgin Islands, which he sees as representative for Caribbean destinations in general. In some Caribbean countries, however, recent development plans may attempt to prioritize local business development (Milne 1997). When capital and support are sought from international organizations such as the World Bank, EU, UNDP and WTO, development is often based on master plans and follows structural adjustment programs (cf. Holm-Petersen 2000; Wilkinson 1997b). In such cases, governments are usually forced to fundamentally re-structure the economy. Commonwealth Caribbean governments, for example, had to implement wage cuts, reduce the size of the public workforce, remove subsidies and import controls, and, in some cases, devalue the currency in order to address the debt problem (Wilson 1996). Such structural changes usually have consequences for the socio-economic situation of large parts of the population.

Tropical islands are also characterized by a process of increasing competition, with travel choices increasingly being made on the basis of two factors, flight duration and hotel standard (also representing a proxy for the price of a vacation). Destinations only offering the 3 to 5 Ss (sun, sand, sea, sex and shopping) have thus become replaceable. Tourism is also highly susceptible to influences beyond the control of destinations, such as rising oil prices, currency exchange rate fluctuations, natural disaster, recession in the source countries, and, more recently, epidemics, political instability, terrorism and war. For example, following the Luxor attack in Egypt in 1996, occupancy rates dropped to 18 per cent nationwide and to 10 per cent in Luxor itself (Poirier 2000). In Kenya, blacklisting by tour operators as a result of political instability caused declining bed occupancy rates, which fell to 24 per cent in April 1998 as compared to 52 per cent in the previous year (Sindiga 2000). Immediately after 11 September 2001, 40–50 per cent of tourist reservations were canceled, and after three months international tourism had dropped by about 30 per cent on average (di Castri 2002b). Tourists also seem increasingly to become the target of terrorists as seen in Tunisia, Indonesia and Kenya in 2001 and 2002. All these factors reflect a situation of instability that may gain importance in the years to come. Alternative development options have thus already been suggested in the early 1990s, including an extension of pelagic fisheries, dairy industries, small livestock production and local agro-industries (cf. McAfee 1991).

TOURISM IN ISLAND ENVIRONMENTS

Islands often have small terrestrial areas, and ecosystems are thus characterized by low species diversity and small populations (MacArthur and Wilson 1967). Nevertheless, islands tend to possess high numbers of endemic species contained in often unique marine and terrestrial ecosystems, a result of biotic isolation and oceanicity (Cronk 1997). A recent study identifying biodiversity hotspots thus included tropical islands and island groups such as the Caribbean, Madagascar, the Philippines, Indonesia and Polynesia/ Micronesia (Myers et al. 2000). Considering the biogeography of islands, oceanic islands have more unique characteristics than continental ones because the latter do not differ as much from the landmasses to which they were earlier related (Salvat and Pailhe 2002). Island ecosystems and their endemic species are generally closely adapted to the specific conditions in a given environment and thus are vulnerable to environmental change. When subject to extrinsic disturbance, island ecosystems may even suffer catastrophic change (Cronk 1997; Liew 1990).

Fundamental alterations of island environments have usually occurred in historical times (cf. Watts 1993). Colonial powers have introduced alien species, often with detrimental consequences for indigenous species, and they have used natural resources in ways that were not sustainable. For example, plantations of commercial crops, such as bananas, cane, coconuts and cotton in the West Indies, have contributed to the large-scale conversion of island ecosystems. As Dolman (1985, pp. 55–6) notes, colonialism also upset traditional patterns of subsistence farming, resulting in a decline in the varieties of crops grown, and changes in the intensity of cultivation systems and the range of farming systems used. All these factors have influenced island environments long before the advent of tourism.

Impacts of Tourism on Island Ecosystems

In the 21st century, tourism is one of the major factors contributing to environmental change in islands, often competing with traditional activities for scarce natural resources, such as land, fresh water, timber or marine edible species. Tourism-related changes of the physical environment include land conversion for infrastructure development (airstrips, ports, roads and accommodation establishments); excessive fresh water use; high energy use and emissions; physical degradation of reefs through jetty construction and trampling, buying and collecting reef species; overexploitation of marine species; erosion caused by infrastructure developments; deforestation of mangroves for construction materials; alteration of coastal wetlands; lake, lagoon and marine pollution; and reef damage through anchoring, sedimentation, sewage discharge, sand mining and dredging (cf. Archer 1985; Biagini 1999; Buchan 2000; Gössling 2001a; Gössling et al. 2003; Liew 1990; McElroy and de Albuquerque 1998; Milne 1990; Wong 1998; Wong 2003). Furthermore, cruise ships have been depicted as polluters of the marine and coastal environment through the dumping of rubbish and plastic (cf. Buchan 2000; Wilson 1996). All these environmental changes may contribute to or add on existing threats to island ecosystems. In the Caribbean, about 30 per cent of the reefs are now reported to be at risk because of runoff and sedimentation, as well as discharges of untreated municipal and hotel waste (Bryant et al. 1998). In the Pacific, deforestation rates are among the highest in the world, and the region also has the largest number of documented bird extinctions in the world, with seven times more endangered species than the Caribbean (UNEP 1999). It should also be noted that seasonality may lead to peak pressures. For example, tourist-related fresh water consumption is usually highest in the dry season, when the recharge of aquifers by rainfall can be very limited (Gössling 2001a).

Environmental change may not always be obvious, which makes the application of environmental impact assessments or the definition of ecological thresholds difficult. For example, local populations in coastal areas in Zanzibar, Tanzania reported that the number of mosquitoes had dramatically increased after the construction of large hotels (Gössling 2001b). While these observations are not obviously interconnected, evidence suggests that the irrigation of hotel gardens (leading to small puddles) as well as the dumping of plastics (with water remaining in thousands of plastic bags) have provided new breeding grounds for the insects. This may in turn impact on the health of locals and tourists, as anopheline mosquitoes are the vectors carrying *Plasmodium spp.*, the parasite causing malaria. Furthermore, the tourism industry may often not respect the ecological limits of small, fragile and often scarce resources in islands because scarcity can be overcome by purchasing at higher prices, turning to imports, or technical solutions such as desalination in case of water scarcity.

Global Environmental Change

From a global point of view, the most important impact of tourism on ecosystems might be indirect. Travel to tropical islands from the industrialized countries (the main source markets) generally involves great travel distances, which are usually covered by aircraft. This entails substantial energy use. In one attempt to grasp and visualize this impact, ecological footprint analysis (EFA) was used as an assessment tool (Gössling et al. 2002). EFA, a concept developed by Wackernagel and Rees (1996), measures the amount of space that would theoretically be required to provide resources and accommodation and to absorb waste, particularly the greenhouse gases produced by air travel. The study revealed that during a typical vacation in the Seychelles (which on average lasts 10.4 days) more than 1.8 ha of biologically productive land is appropriated. This can be compared to roughly two hectares of land annually available to each human being for all-encompassing living space. The major part of the tourist footprint (more than 90 per cent) resulted from transportation to the destination, rendering prominent both the environmental importance of air travel and the fact that tourism to tropical islands contributes over-proportionally to global warming. These insights are of importance given the chronic dependence of islands on aviation and their susceptibility to global environmental change, including global warming and sea level rise. Increasing water temperatures, as observed during El Niño Southern Oscillation (ENSO) phenomena, have been more frequent and intense in recent decades (IPCC 2001). The 1997–98 ENSO, for example, had severe impacts on the climate of the Indian Ocean. In March and April 1998, seawater temperatures increased on average by 1.5°C above values measured during the same period in 1997. Following the event, coral mortality ranged from 50–90 per cent over extensive areas of shallow reefs in the Seychelles (Lindén and Sporrong 1999). With respect to sea level rise, particularly low-lying islands could be seriously affected. The IPCC (2001) calculates that the global mean sea level will rise by 0.09–0.88 metres between 1990 and 2100. This is primarily a result of the thermal expansion of the oceans and the melting of glaciers and ice caps. Sea level rise may also lead to land submergence, beach erosion, increased storm flooding, changes in the tidal range, higher seawater tables and reduced fresh water supplies (cf. Leatherman 1997).

Human–environmental Relations

Tourism may also contribute to environmental change in socio-cultural terms, as it is a potent force turning subsistence economies into service industries, often with complex consequences for the environment (cf. Britton 1991; Gössling 2002). To some authors, 'tourism is now the main vector of the worldwide diffusion of the modern, Western, capitalist economy, which is uprooting and replacing other modes of economic and social relationships' (Greiner 2002, p. 241). Indeed, tourism has often rapidly displaced agriculture, fishing and other traditional economic activities (cf. McElroy et al. 1990). For instance, Rochoux (1999) reports that, in 1946, employment in La Réunion was concentrated in agriculture, forestry and fisheries (66 per cent), while services accounted for only 15 per cent. In 1990, 73.3 per cent of the jobs were in the services sector (mostly tourism-related), while the island's agricultural sector had declined to 7.6 per cent. Similar trends were reported for coastal communities in Zanzibar. A study of the village Kiwengwa found that, within five years (1994 to 1999), tourism had become the sole source of income for 10 per cent of the households, while 50 per cent of households had become economically involved in (and often dependent on) tourism (Gössling 2001b). Such micro-economic changes go along with changes in what could be termed the 'ecological identity' of people and places. For example, in remote tropical islands, people may often still depend on subsistence economies. Such subsistence activities are generally based on (i) a complex knowledge of the environment that has been passed on from generation to generation and thus evolved over large time-horizons (Liew 1990; Tobisson et al. 1998), (ii) diversified production strategies to cope with uncertainty, unpredictability, and risk of the economic and ecological systems (Andersson and Ngazi 1998) and (iii) efficient property rights to regulate access to exploitation of resources (Jiddawi 1998; Msuya 1998; Tobisson et al. 1998). Tourism development may often initiate a process of modernization that alters these elements of ecological identity (see also Patterson and Rodriguez, this volume). In this context, it is interesting to note Dolman's (1985, p. 55) claim that:

> In small island developing countries it will prove impossible to overcome growing food and energy dependence without the reconstitution of local food systems, the rediscovery of the sea, and the imaginative integration of marine and land-based resources. If small island countries are to invent a future that has one leg in the sea and the other on land, then many of them have to reinvent their past.

Environmental Conservation

In most tropical countries, tourism is directly dependent on natural assets, such as scenic landscapes, coastlines and beaches, coral reefs, rainforests or savannahs, and colourful, dangerous or unique animals. Often, tourism contributes directly and indirectly to the preservation of ecosystems in protected areas, such as State-, Nature-, Game-, Special- and Shell Reserves, Conservation Areas, National Parks, Historic Sites, Private Sanctuaries, World Heritage Sites and Man & Biosphere Reserves (cf. Gössling 1999; Langholz et al. 2000). These are also important tourist attractions, generating substantial revenue through admission fees, donations or taxes. In consequence, tourism may often create an interest in the maintenance or implementation of protected and natural areas (Wunder 2000). Tourism has also been depicted in many surveys as an alternative, non-consumptive development option preferable to other, more destructive economic activities (Cesar et al. 1997; Dixon et al. 1993; Pet-Soede et al. 1999).

POLITICAL ECOLOGY PERSPECTIVES

Political ecology applies methods of political economy in ecological contexts and can thus, in short, be understood as the study of ecological distribution conflicts (Martinez-Alier 2002, p. vii). Central to this approach is the insight that economic and political contexts need to be understood to encompass the complexity of human–environment interactions linked to the alteration of the environment (Blaikie 1995; Bryant 1997). Political ecology thus seeks to investigate the interaction of international, national, regional and local actors at the interface of environmental change, economics and politics. Considering the historical context, political ecology focuses on the actors' interests and ideologies in order to understand their role in the observed developments.

In developing countries, environmental change is often rapid, including deforestation and other land conversions (Laurance et al. 2002), topsoil erosion (Mantel and van Engelen 1999), soil salinity (Datta and de Jong

2002), declining bush-meat resources (Stephens et al. 2002), loss of biodiversity (cf. Chapin III et al. 2000), decreasing fish stocks (Ruddle 1998) and the spread of diseases (Rodriguez-Garcia 2001). Tropical environments may also suffer from global environmental change, for example through ENSO phenomena, sea level rise or, more generally, variations in temperature and rainfall (IPCC 2001).

Political ecology has proved to be a powerful tool to understand conflicts surrounding environmental conflicts. In particular, it has provided new insights of how local resource use policies and practices are driven by national and international political, social and economic institutions. The development of political ecology in the contexts of developing countries has been an emerging research field since the 1970s (cf. Wolf 1972), including analyses of global climate change (Geist 1999), large dams (Nüsser 2003), emerging infectious diseases (Mayer 2000), tropical deforestation (Bates and Rudel 2000; Bryant 1997; Dauvergne 1998; Geist 1994; Krings 1996; Montagu 2002), land degradation (Krings 2003a), protected areas, biodiversity and wildlife utilization (Bryant 2000; Bates and Rudel 2000; Escobar 1998; Logan and Moseley 2002; Vorlaufer 2002), mining (Müller 1999), water distribution (Mustafa 2002) and tourism (Stonich 1998).

More recently, there has also been an increasing number of publications evaluating the political ecology of developmental and environmental discourses (Escobar 1995; Fairhead and Leach 1995), providing insights into the social construction of environmental problems (cf. Blaikie 1995; Bryant 1998). For example, Stott and Sullivan (2000) point at the crucial role that books such as *The Population Bomb* (Ehrlich and Ehrlich 1969) or *The Limits to Growth* (Meadows et al. 1972) have played in shaping today's concerns about the state of the environment. Global environmental problems such as deforestation, desertification, biodiversity use and climate change are thus surrounded by narratives about their existence, severity and appropriate solutions (Adger et al. 2001). Consequently, poststructuralist writers such as Forsyth (2003) criticize the use of 'orthodox' language in environmental science ('degradation', 'desertification'). However, as Bryant (1998, p. 88) points out, the objective can rarely be 'to suggest that problems and crises do not exist. Rather, it is to show how their selective identification and representation is a political process'. Political ecology is in such cases concerned with tracing the history of narratives, including the power relationships supported by these narratives (Stott and Sullivan 2000).

Obviously, the perception of the environment is a product of social and cultural experiences and values, thus representing particular human–environmental relations. In consequence, imperatives of development and the appropriate use of the environment change in time and space, as they develop simultaneously with the culturally constructed images of nature (cf. Norton

1996; O'Rourke 2000). Acknowledging these temporal, spatial and cultural dimensions, it is clear that 'the environment' and its use or preservation is 'both a concept and an issue' (Montagu 2002, p. 22). This becomes even more evident in the context of tourism, as images of 'nature' and 'environment' are formed and come into existence through travel. Tourism may both be a result of and an influencing factor of particular human–environmental relations (Gössling 2002). Islands in particular can be seen as places that create and foster ideas of 'ideal' environments.

ACTOR ANALYSIS

A basic methodological principle of political ecology is to investigate all groups of actors that are directly or indirectly involved in environmental change. As will be explained in the following section, political ecologists have usually distinguished place-based and non place-based actors (Blaikie 1995) even though place-based actors can also become relevant as non place-based actors.

In the following – incomplete – overview, local, national and international actor groups are distinguished (Figure 1.1). It becomes obvious that a great variety and number of actor groups are involved in planning, decision-making, monitoring, etc. At the local level, actor groups include villagers, local governments, tourists, managers (such as those working in accommodation establishments and restaurants), staff, migrants, non-governmental organizations (NGOs) and the police (place-based actors). At the national level, the dominant groups are the government and its ministries and departments, as well as the national tourism industry (non-place based actors). Finally, a wide range of international actor groups – some of them being 'supra-national' in that they represent global institutions – can be distinguished. These are usually non-place based, consisting of (i) the international tourism industry and its organizations, including the World Tourism Organization (WTO), airlines and airline associations, international hotel corporations and tour operators, as well as the International Hotel and Restaurant Organization (IHRA), the Tour Operators Initiative for sustainable development (TOI), the International Hotel Environment Initiative (IHEI), and Green Globe, (ii) international political, economic and environmental organizations, including various organizations of the United Nations, World Bank, International Monetary Fund (IMF), Inter-American Development Bank (IDB), Caribbean Development Bank (CDB), European Union (EU), Conservation International (CI), Ecotourism Society, Global Environment Facility (GEF), The World Conservation Union (IUCN), the Center for Tropical Conservation (RARE), the International Coral Reef Initiative

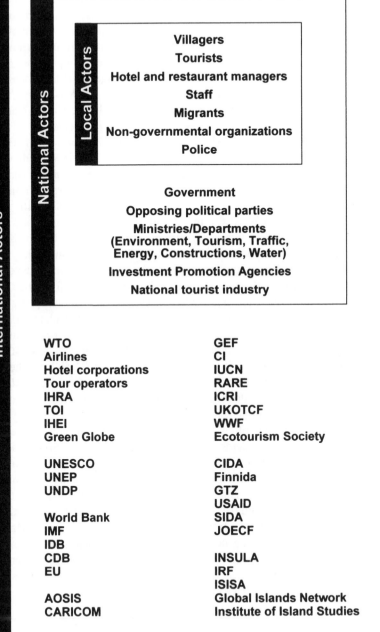

Figure 1.1   Groups of actors

(ICRI), the UK Overseas Territories Conservation Forum (UKOTCF) and the World Wide Fund for Nature (WWF), and (iii) bilateral development aid donor agencies, including, for example, the Canadian International Development Agency (CIDA), the Finnish Department for International Development Cooperation (Finnida), the German Gesellschaft für Technische Zusammenarbeit (GTZ), Japan's Overseas Economic Co-operation Fund (JOECF), the Swedish International Development Agency (SIDA) and the United States Agency for International Development (USAID). Groups of actors often work in a cooperative manner. For example, the United Nations Environment Programme (UNEP) supports the implementation of the Convention on Biological Diversity (CBD), the Convention on International Trade in Endangered Species (CITES) and the United Nations Framework Convention on Climate Change (UNFCCC), all of which affect islands. UNEP works in partnerships with other UN and intergovernmental organizations, including the United Nations Educational, Scientific and Cultural Organization (UNESCO), the World Tourism Organization (WTO) and other arms of the tourism industry such as IHRA, IHEI and Green Globe. Cooperation with NGOs includes, for example, the Ecotourism Society, CI, RARE, IUCN and WWF. Activities related to the implementation of the CBD by developing countries are also eligible for financial support from the GEF. For example, the GEF funded the Caribbean Planning for Adaptation to Global Climate Change Project for small island states (cf. Volonte 1997). Another group of actors that needs to be mentioned are organizations facilitating and promoting studies of islands. For example, UNESCO's International Scientific Council for Island Development (INSULA), the US Virgin Islands based Island Resources Foundation (IRF), the Global Islands Network (Isle of Skye, Scotland) and the International Small Islands Studies Association (ISISA) are organizations with the aim to promote the study and sustainable development of islands. There are also several university departments focusing on islands. For example, the Centre for South Pacific Studies forms part of the University of New South Wales in Australia and coordinates research on Pacific Islands. In Japan, the University of Ryukyus (Okinawa) has a Centre for Asia-Pacific Island Studies, and in Canada, there is the Institute of Island Studies at the University of Prince Edward Island. The Islands and Small States Institute is part of the University of Malta's Foundation for International Studies. Politically, small islands are organized in the Alliance of Small Island States (AOSIS), which consists of 42 member states. There are also several regional island organizations such as the Caribbean Community (CARICOM).

ENVIRONMENT AND SUSTAINABLE DEVELOPMENT

It is beyond the scope of this book to provide a more comprehensive discussion of 'development' and theories of development. It should be noted, though, that any development discourse is implicitly based on personal values and personal conceptions of needs and wants, as well as the perception of the 'right' way to achieve (global or individual) wealth and fulfilment. The dominant position currently presented by neoclassical economists suggests that the spatial globalization of the economy will reduce poverty even in the remotest areas of the world, and subsequently lead to high standards of material wealth for all human beings. The preconditions to be met in order to achieve this goal are largely seen in free, globalized markets, in which all human beings should be integrated and actively participate. This view largely corresponds to that of the international tourism industry and that of many governments in developing countries.

The neoclassical position also implies that sustainable development can be achieved through ecological modernization and is thus technological optimist in character. While it is not the aim to criticize this position, it should be acknowledged that this is only one of several possible theories of development (Söderbaum 2001) and that such neoclassical perspectives on sustainable development have been questioned (Hornborg 2001). It also deserves mention that the supra-national actors driving global development processes, such as the World Bank and the IMF, are characterized by neoclassical economic worldviews. This is of importance because attempts to solve problems of 'underdevelopment', 'poverty' and 'resource depletion' through international organizations have often failed. Adger et al. (2001, pp. 683, 701) suggest one possible explanation:

> The global environmental crises implied in global environmental change discourses require global solutions. The discourses are therefore top-down, interventionist and technocentrist in that solutions to the alleged global environmental problems can and should be devised. The solutions are defined at the global level. Hence, international action is necessary. This action should be co-ordinated by multi-lateral agencies and regulatory frameworks.
>
> . . . [S]ince global discourses are often based on shared myths and blueprints of the world, the political prescriptions flowing from them are often inappropriate for local realities.

When development strategies implemented by international organizations fail, proximate reasons are usually made responsible, including the lack of institutional capacity and political commitment, or discrepancies in the technical approach chosen – the neoclassical development paradigm itself is seldom questioned (cf. Holm-Petersen 2000). It might also be worth noting that a recent publication by the World Bank has shown that the gap between rich and poor countries is widening (Dollar and Collier 2001), while resource use and the loss of ecosystems seem to accelerate (UNDP/UNEP/World Bank/WRI 2000). While this is not to question neoclassical economic development approaches per se, it is argued here that those concerned with development should be aware of their ideological orientation and of its implications for local realities in developing countries.

Sustainable Development, Sustainable Tourism

Butler (1993) defined sustainable tourism in small islands as a state in which tourism is:

> . . . developed and maintained in an area (community, environment) in such a manner and at such a scale that it remains viable over an indefinite period and does not degrade or alter the environment (human and physical) in which it exists to such a degree that it prohibits the successful development and well-being of other activities and processes.

While most people involved in island development will agree to this definition (and the very fact that development should be sustainable), the question of how to achieve 'sustainable development' – a term implying social, environmental, economic and political dimensions as well as continuous change – remains an object of debate. So far, recommendations have mainly been technical and managerial in character, which is also reflected in the terminology used in master plans and guidelines. Keywords include, for instance, 'integrated coastal zone management', 'multiple-use planning', 'non-resource dependent development', 'capacity building', 'multi-agency involvement', 'community involvement', 'environmental impact assessment', 'resource preservation', 'resource restoration' and 'resource enhancement' (cf. di Castri 2002a; Sasidharan and Thapa 2002; Timothy and Ioannides 2002).

Even though 'state-of-the-art' development approaches seem to encompass all dimensions of 'sustainability', they may in reality still primarily be economic and ecological in character, and little concerned with social and cultural aspects (cf. Wilson 1996). However, problems have been recognized in persisting socio-economic inequality and unevenness, large-scale planning, marginalization of people, dependency, government corruption and ineffectiveness, which are to be better addressed in the future. Improved concepts will for example include the proliferation of ecotourism, the use of information technology to empower local communities, and geographic information systems to map island biodiversity and disturbance patterns (cf. the volumes edited by Apostolopoulos and Gayle 2002a; di Castri and Balaji 2002). Hence, the need to 'make tourism sustainable' is usually emphasized, but it is generally not questioned if the fundamental problems underlying sustainable tourism development can be resolved.

Development – for Whom?

As pointed out above, 'sustainable development' is promoted within the discursive framework of 'ecological modernization', while tourism development often seems to be implemented in top-down approaches by international and private sector organizations in cooperation with national governments. Local communities are rarely consulted about their wishes to engage in this economic activity and are poorly informed about the cultural, economic and environmental changes they are likely to face in the course of the development process (cf. Dann and Potter 1997). Wilkinson (1989, p. 159) suggests that:

> . . . [T]he decision whether to encourage or discourage tourism is mostly in the hands of multinational companies (such as airlines, hotels, travel agents, and tour operators), with their relative economic strength often greater than many developing countries. For example, there have been few, if any, cases of an island government blocking tourism development when an international airline decides that it wants to include a particular island on its regular schedule.

Similarly, McElroy and de Albuquerque (2002, p. 26) conclude that:

> . . . [E]xperience indicates that the political directorate in many small islands routinely bypasses the local development authority to approve of major development projects despite community opposition and highly negative impact assessments.

In order to justify tourism development under such conditions, governments and tourism industry seek to communicate about the benefits of tourism in terms of 'the greater social good' (cf. Bryant 1997, p. 87). The result is that tourism development often satisfies the economic interests of international and national groups of actors, while local development needs are 'only partially and too often inappropriately' (Britton 1987, p. 132) met. While these insights are recognized in recent books on tourism and development in islands (di Castri and Balaji 2002; Apostolopoulos and Gayle 2002b), contributions in this volume add depth in illuminating the underlying mechanisms and drawing a more comprehensive and balanced picture of tourism-related development processes in tropical islands.

POLITICAL ECOLOGY PERSPECTIVES

Tourism development initiates complex, interrelated and interacting changes with respect to economics, culture, environment and politics. As outlined earlier, it is the aim of this anthology to analyze the underlying dynamics of material and discursive struggles over power, entitlements and natural resources in tropical islands, and to identify winners and losers in the development process. The following sections highlight the political ecology insights gained through the case studies.

Actors

Benedict (1967) noted 35 years ago that face-to-face personalism and kinship ties among the leaders in small territories would lead to conflicts of interest, and render objective decision-making difficult. A recent workshop on 'Wise Coastal Practices for Beach Management' held by UNESCO in the eastern Caribbean islands concluded that the major conflicts in the coastal zone occurred between traditional beach-user groups, coastal landowners, developers, the public, sand mining operators, and persons dumping solid and other waste (UNESCO 2002). The chapters contained in this book identify similar conflicts, but also highlight cases of successful communication and cooperation. For example, Weaver (this volume) reports that tourism development in the Cayman Islands has been characterized by good communications between all groups of actors (environmentalists, developers and government), allowing to maintain a balance between environmental conservation and development. However, he predicts that with increasing tourist numbers this balance will be in question, which is likely to result in conflict. Of particular interest in the Cayman case is perhaps the fact that the islands, as a United Kingdom Overseas Territory, are bound to international commitments of Great Britain, including the Convention on Biological Diversity, the Protocol concerning Specially Protected Areas and Wildlife (SPAW) in the Wider Caribbean Region, and the United Nations Conference on the Law of the Sea (UNCLOS). Furthermore, the islands are obligated to develop 'appropriate, applicable and affordable environmental policies, legislation and standards' (Weaver, this volume, p. 57). Hence, the Cayman Island's environmental legislation (and, indirectly, tourism development) is strongly influenced by external actors.

In St. Lucia, the government continues to encourage the expansion of foreign-owned, large-scale hotels with the effect of dependency on a few multinational corporations, contradicting the nation's stated policy of small-scale development (Wilkinson, this volume). While the environmental impacts of tourism development in St. Lucia are not quantified as yet,

Wilkinson notes that planning is uncoordinated, increasing the risk of user conflicts and adverse impacts. Local communities are largely excluded from decision-making and planning. Nevertheless, it seems difficult to distinguish winners and losers. While multinational companies and the government belong to the more obvious winners, tourism also generates some 10 000 jobs in this country with few alternative development options.

In their analysis of Dominica, Patterson and Rodriguez (this volume) show that the island's poorest community, the Carib territory, is an important tourist attraction, also constituting an important part of the image promoted in international advertisement campaigns. Paradoxically, the Carib are dissociated from tourism earnings, while more powerful (national and international) tourism actors appropriate commodity-, amenity- and marketing values from the territory, thus contributing to the disempowerment of the community. More generally, large-scale foreign financiers and aid organizations are an important source of funding for tourism development on the island. As they tend to operate in institutionalized networks, they usually cooperate with the more 'visible' groups of local entrepreneurs and exclude actor groups such as women, communities and landowners. Patterson and Rodriguez also note that powerful national actors such as the government may themselves be in weak negotiation positions against even more powerful international actors such as the cruise tourism industry and foreign investors.

In the Bay Islands, Honduras, biodiversity and environmental health are important parameters to sustain and enhance tourism development. As environmental degradation is accelerating in the region, protected areas, specifically Marine Protected Areas (MPAs), have been established to preserve vulnerable ecosystems – also with the goal to increase tourist numbers. In her analysis of the situation, Stonich (this volume) shows how poor groups of local stakeholders are those receiving the least benefits from tourism in terms of income, patterns of consumption, food security and nutritional status, while simultaneously losing entitlements and livelihoods through the implementation of protected areas. This needs to be seen in the light of the fact that the groups of actors controlling the discourses on 'environmental conservation' and lobbying for the establishment of protected areas are those profiting most from tourism development. Ironically, these groups of actors are also responsible for the large-scale degradation of ecosystems through commercial pelagic fisheries, over-fishing of shrimp and lobster, road building, mangrove destruction and dredging of the reefs – activities often related to tourism development. Overall, Stonich shows how the successful management of protected areas ultimately becomes impossible because of the indispensability of integrating different scales of social, cultural and economic aspects and their dynamics into the design, management and evaluation of these areas.

In the case of Ilha Grande, Wunder (this volume) describes a conflict between the owners of 'upmarket' hostels attracting 'high-spending' tourists, and native residents profiting from low-value mass tourism through the provision of camping grounds. In this particular case, hostel owners, park authorities and municipalities push for limiting access to the island. Based on the carrying capacity concept, they have brought into life a 'science'-based discourse to foster the notion that the capacity of the island to accommodate visitors is exceeded. In deconstructing this discourse, Wunder shows that claims of physical degradation and social deprivation do not fit reality because the broad majority of the locals actually profit from tourism, with limited conflict in guest–host relations. In conclusion, claims to limit access to Ilha Grande seem to primarily serve the goal of increasing the benefits of certain – already more wealthy – groups of actors.

Tourism development processes in Zanzibar are top-down, with little or no involvement of local communities (Gössling, this volume). They have been initiated by international actors such as the World Bank, IMF, USAID and the international tourist industry, and are accompanied by structural adjustment programs. The discourses about the benefits of tourism are created and controlled by the government – also the major recipient of foreign exchange earnings. In contrast, local benefits have remained minor on a per capita basis and are generally very unequally distributed, which has caused multifaceted conflicts. The chapter also shows how the contradicting views of the political parties in Zanzibar have magnified the problems surrounding tourism development.

In the Seychelles, tourism development is dominated by a powerful, government-led discourse on environmental conservation. Environmental conservation is made possible on the basis of this discourse, largely ignoring local views. Commitment to the environment is rewarded with increasing tourist numbers and funds from international donor organizations, the latter being important for prosperous islands such as the Seychelles that have become ineligible for foreign aid. However, virtually all groups of actors in the Seychelles seem to profit directly or indirectly from tourism development.

In Hainan, China tourism development is implemented in a large-scale, top-down approach (Liu and Wall, this volume). State planning has largely concentrated on the provision of infrastructure, neglecting human resources development with the notion that local involvement in tourism 'is frustrated and job opportunities in tourism bypass those with the greatest need to benefit from tourism employment' (Liu and Wall, this volume, p. 223). This situation is further complicated through socialist political worldviews, playing down the role of individualism and local participation.

In the Philippines, tourists are warmly welcomed and conflicts between hosts and guests are few. In their contribution, White and Rosales (this volume) present several case studies that show how small-scale, community-based projects can be successful in providing social, economic and environmental benefits. Cooperation with international actors is also positive. For example, White and Rosales report that the WWF had an important role in turning Pamilacan whale hunters into whale watching entrepreneurs. In Boracay, it was possible to address problems of contaminated waters through a sewage treatment plant funded by Japan's Overseas Economic Co-operation Fund. Overall, White and Rosales (this volume, p. 260) conclude that 'successful Philippine tourism examples all represent partnerships among local governments, resorts and the communities living adjacent to the resources of tourism interest'.

Wong (this volume) describes how state-linked companies, government agencies, and private concerns from Singapore and Indonesia have implemented a large-scale tourism development project in Bintan, Indonesia. The Bintan Beach International Resort is the largest of its kind in Asia, consisting of several integrated resorts and occupying an area of 230 km^2. However, the implementation of this project involved the resettlement of several thousand Indonesians and the insufficient monetary compensation for land has resulted in social unrest. More recently, programs have thus been launched to strengthen local stakeholders and to distribute part of the economic benefits among the local population.

In summary, tourism development and the associated discourses on its benefits are usually initiated, maintained and controlled by national governments, often in cooperation with the international tourism industry and international economic and environmental actors. Local communities seem to have little influence in most case studies (cf. chapters by Gössling, Gössling and Hörstmeier, Liu and Wall, Patterson and Rodriguez, Stonich, Weaver, Wilkinson, Wong). However, several island governments have acknowledged the need to increase the participation of local actor groups. Such moves towards more democratic decision-making can be observed in the Seychelles (Gössling and Hörstmeier, this volume) and in the Philippines: 'the classic tourism model of enclosed resorts is present in the Philippines but does not dominate and thus the potential for involvement of local people through community-models is starting to thrive' (White and Rosales, this volume, p. 241).

Economics

In most case study settings, reasons for involvement in tourism appear to be similar: there is a perceived need to diversify the economy, often coupled with reduced levels of foreign exchange earnings as a result of declining world-market prices for cash crops, and rising workforce pressure. Even though tourism has become a broad-scale phenomenon only recently in most islands, its economic importance is highlighted in all case studies. For example, tourism accounts for almost 9 per cent of the GDP in the Philippines (White and Rosales, this volume) and 20 per cent of the GDP in the Seychelles, where it also generates 60 per cent of the foreign exchange earnings (Gössling and Hörstmeier, this volume). In St. Lucia, tourism expenditures represent almost 64 per cent of the GDP (Wilkinson, this volume), and in the Cayman Islands, tourism accounts for about 70 per cent of GDP and 75 per cent of foreign exchange earnings (Weaver, this volume). Employment opportunities may also be substantial, with for example 3 300 jobs being generated in Bintan, 10 000 in St. Lucia and 5 million in the Philippines (Wong, Wilkinson, White and Rosales, this volume).

The distribution of economic wealth generated through tourism is an important aspect of tourism development, but has so far remained insufficiently addressed (cf. Wunder 2000). Hence, the question remains of how benefits are distributed, and if the distribution is considered equitable by the population. Basically, it can be distinguished between groups of actors that profit from tourism (directly, for example through income, or indirectly, for example through improved health services financed with tourism-derived tax money), and those who do not profit at all. Within the group of those profiting directly, benefits may vary considerably. Staff wages may often be low in relative and absolute terms (for example, less than US$30 per month in large hotels in Zanzibar), while the monthly salary of managers can be in the order of several thousand dollars. When a large proportion of the benefits accrue to certain groups of actors, this can, in a subsequent cycle of development, result in a tourism oligopoly. The case studies reveal clear differences between the islands. For example, in Dominica, Bay Islands and Zanzibar, benefits from tourism development seem unequally distributed between different groups of actors (Gössling, Patterson and Rodriguez, Stonich, this volume). In the Seychelles, Ilha Grande and the Cayman Islands, on the other hand, a majority of the local population profits directly or indirectly from tourism (Gössling and Hörstmeier, Weaver, Wunder, this volume). It should also be noted that domestic tourism could gain importance in tropical islands. As shown by the example of Ilha Grande (Wunder, this volume), domestic tourists may spend low per capita amounts of money in absolute terms that may nevertheless be of crucial importance for local economies in relative terms given low income levels in developing countries.

Several case studies show that the economic income from tourism can outweigh the income from traditional extractive activities, and may thus lead to the rapid replacement of these activities. This can be positive, as in the case of the Philippines and Ilha Grande, where pressure on the environment is reduced, or questionable, as in cases where economies become mono-structured and dependent on tourism (as for example in Zanzibar). Wilkinson (this volume, p. 113) thus argues in favour of small-scale, low-density tourism. Tourism markets seem to cater for this more lucrative form of tourism, which is also less vulnerable to political pressures and more socially acceptable, less stressful to human and natural environments, and tends to require resource management policies which preserve options for future development.

Tourism and Environment

Common to all case study settings is the fact that ecosystems have already been substantially altered long before the advent of tourism. However, the impact of tourism on ecosystems is often substantial. For example, in the Cayman Islands, tourism-related development has led to the large-scale conversion of wetlands and mangroves, and turbidity plumes from the use of hydraulic dredges (to obtain fill from the sea floor for land reclamation) have resulted in the damage of reefs through sedimentation. Diving pressure is now such that it has started to affect the reefs (Weaver, this volume). In St. Lucia, the construction of a new pier caused serious erosion problems, and alteration of coastal configurations, discharge of untreated sewage wastes and the removal of beach sand for construction are reported to have a detrimental impact on ecosystems (Wilkinson, this volume). In Dominica, soil brought to a tourism-construction site contained the seeds of two particularly persistent grasses with adverse effects for biodiversity, and constructions of harbours, marinas, airports and hotels have had severe environmental consequences for the island. Sand quarrying for tourism infrastructure, as well as draining estuaries and wetlands for hotels has changed the ecology of several areas (Patterson and Rodriguez, this volume). In the Bay Islands, tourism development has caused environmental degradation through the construction of roads and accommodation establishments, over-exploitation of marine edible species and fresh water use/waste water discharge, as well as the additional demand of natural resources by thousands of poor migrants attracted to the islands through tourism and its employment opportunities (Stonich, this volume). In the Seychelles, the selling of souvenirs such as corals, ornamental shells and other marine species is of concern. Where species are locally protected, imports from other developing countries have brought into existence 'souvenir hinterlands' (Gössling and Hörstmeier, this volume). In Zanzibar, the use of marine resources has increased to such an extent that exploitation is beyond the capacity of ecosystems to recover. The tourism-related curio trade with marine species is also substantial, adding on problems such as fresh water use, untreated sewage discharge and the large-scale conversion of coastal environments (Gössling, this volume). In the

Philippines, various impacts of tourism-related developments affect beaches, coral reefs and wetlands (White and Rosales, this volume). In Bintan, despite the sheer size of tourism infrastructure developments, continuous monitoring of ecological parameters is regularly executed to ensure that environmental quality is maintained (Wong, this volume).

With respect to the global environmental consequences of tourism, particularly the vast amount of energy needed for air travel (see p. 8), it is encouraging that domestic tourism is increasing in many island states. For example, White and Rosales (this volume) show that middle and upper income Filipinos have started to substantially add to tourism revenues, and they outnumber foreign visitors in some areas. Similar trends are reported by Liu and Wall (this volume) for Hainan, where millions of Chinese spend their vacation, and by Wunder (this volume) for Ilha Grande, where tourist arrivals are almost entirely domestic. As Wunder notes, the trend of increasing domestic tourist numbers has gone widely unnoticed by tourism researchers, even though it can be assumed to have profound consequences for these countries and for tourism development in general.

While tourism may often have detrimental consequences for the environment, it can also contribute to conservation. First, protected areas have become important tourist attractions in many tropical countries, and tourism thus increases the interest of governments to safeguard ecosystems or to preserve areas in a natural state. Countries such as the Seychelles already engage in conservation-based tourism development with the ultimate goal to increase visitor arrivals (Gössling and Hörstmeier, this volume). It deserves mention, though, that the implementation of protected areas (and global networks of protected areas; cf. Myers et al. 2000) demands the cooperation of national and international actors (often global institutions; cf. Adger et al. 2001). For example, the Mesoamerican Biological Corridor can only be implemented trans-nationally and with the support of international donor organizations as it stretches over several national borders and involves substantial costs. As the example of the Bay Islands shows, such top-down conservation approaches may often fail because they do not grasp the complexity of the economic, social and environmental changes occurring with the implementation of protected areas at the local level. Ultimately, this might be due to the fact that the design of protected areas has given precedence to ecological criteria while paying scant attention to social, cultural and economic criteria (Stonich, this volume). Second, in cases where the environment is already under serious pressure, tourism may be an alternative development option that can alleviate ecological problems. For example, coral reefs in the Philippines with tourism potential produce net revenues ranging from US$29,400 to US$113,000 per km^2, thus providing alternative income opportunities to exploitative economic activities (White and Rosales, this volume). Similarly, tourism may be less harmful to the environment than banana plantations and other agro-businesses (Wilkinson, this volume). In Ilha Grande, tourism has even enabled the re-growth of forest cover, as it has decreased the pressure of traditional extractive uses on these ecosystems (Wunder, this volume). Third, tourism can also provide income through entrance fees and donations, making the implementation of protected areas feasible from a financial point of view. Tourists may even be willing to pay substantial amounts of money over and above entrance fees in order to conserve the environment they have visited (White and Rosales, this volume). Fourth, the opportunity to experience 'nature' may foster general environmental interest and awareness (Gössling and Hörstmeier, this volume), even though this does not necessarily translate into more sound environmental behavior. Finally, in some exceptional cases, the tourism industry may even lobby for stricter environmental legislation. For example, in the Cayman Islands, the tourism industry was amendable to, and often took the leadership role, in implementation of protected areas and environmental legislation, including building height restrictions, quotas on cruise ship passengers and regulations to protect coral reefs (Weaver, this volume).

However, the interest of the government to protect certain areas or to implement strict environmental legislation is often ambiguous because governments are usually proactive forces for economic growth and development. In consequence, the subsequent chapters produce divergent insights with respect to environmental legislation. For example, in the Cayman Islands and St. Lucia, a range of governmental laws and regulations have minimized the impacts on ecosystems (Weaver, Wilkinson, this volume). In the Seychelles, national environmental law protects species and limits the use of coastal resources (Gössling and Hörstmeier, this volume). In other cases, however, national law may not be well-suited for local realities. For example, in Zanzibar, local environmental legislation was better adapted to local ecosystems, but disappeared through tourism-related development (Gössling, this volume). In some countries such as the Philippines, steps have thus been taken to support devolution of authority to local governments, reflecting the insight that local government and non-government managed marine protected areas perform best (White and Rosales, this volume). Most complex, perhaps, is the situation in the Bay Islands, where the implementation of protected areas by national and international actors has enhanced environmental conflicts (Stonich, this volume).

Dialogue, Discourse and Power

The case studies reveal that tourism development usually generates conflicts between different groups of actors. Such conflicts can be hidden or open, violent or peaceful, and perceived or not perceived by the actors. Generally, conflicts involve aspects of power, identity, entitlements, and natural or financial resources.

Dialogue, it has often been claimed, is a key factor in achieving sustainable development. However, as the chapters contained in this book show, such dialogues involving all groups of actors are rare. In most cases, communication is unidirectional, built on discourse rather than dialogue. It is thus important to understand how certain groups of actors can create or shape discourses that lead to the use or conservation of the environment. On a national level, tourism-related discourses usually promote tourism, rendering prominent its advantages. In such cases, discourses are created, maintained and controlled by political and economic elites, which generally represent the groups of actors profiting most from tourism development. For example, in the Bay Islands and Seychelles, the debate over environmental conservation is led by political and economic elites, justifying stricter environmental legislation and the establishment of protected areas (Gössling and Hörstmeier, Stonich, this volume). The implementation of protected areas, however, reflects a process of nationalizing natural resources and can thus be seen as a means to allocate entitlements (and thus power) to the state (cf. Krings 2003b; Neumann 1998; Peluso 1993). Discourses based on the notion of a 'greater common good' or 'intergenerational equity' are thus part of a rhetoric necessary to create public and international support for environmental conservation. Ultimately, these discourses will also help to attract increasing visitors, and are thus important to maintain the level of income available to the political and economic elites. However, discourses can also be created with the aim to limit tourism development. Wunder's (this volume) analysis of the influential, 'scientific' discourse on the carrying capacity of Ilha Grande serves as an example of such a process. In this case, relatively wealthy groups of actors try to restrict tourism development against the wish of the native population purportedly to increase or maintain visitor numbers.

Other aspects of tourism development related to power deserve attention. Richter (1980, p. 257) predicted more than 20 years ago that the 'new governmental function of tourism promotion will be a potential source for expanding power'. In fact, the ways in which tourism can enhance state power can be intricate. In general, tourism increases the amount of financial resources available to the government, thus increasing its options to extend its power, for example through employing a greater number of policemen or soldiers. Tourism has also been shown to be a means to re-allocate entitlements. In the case of Zanzibar, coastal zones in possession of local communities are leased to the tourist industry and handed back to the government after 33 years, which represents a shift of control from local communities to the government (Gössling, this volume). Of interest in the Zanzibar case is also the fact that local law, which is complex and generally better adapted to local conditions, was replaced by national law. This was a result of tourism growth; once the government became interested in formerly peripheral areas of little economic value, it began to apply the administrative forms regulating the institutional center to the formerly independent periphery. In other cases, the continuing marginalization of local communities may be in the interest of the government. For example, in Dominica, images of the traditional lifestyle of the Carib population constitute an important part of the image of the island promoted in international advertising campaigns (Patterson and Rodriguez, this volume). In consequence, it is in the government's interest to maintain the status quo of these communities.

The Importance of Time

Several aspects of tourism development related to time deserve attention. From a cultural point of view, island populations may have conceptions of time that are fundamentally different from those in western societies. For example, while the international tourism industry economizes time ('time is money'), people in islands may be orientated toward tasks rather than toward time (cf. Gössling 2002). In communities making a living from artisanal fisheries, for example, it is the rhythm of the tides that determines when the fishermen have to leave the village (often during the night). When western conceptions of time are implemented, local human–environmental relations may be disrupted, contributing to the loss of ecological identity. As shown, this may be detrimental to the achievement of sustainability. Another important observation is that local conceptions of time may be focused on the present rather than the future, which makes it more difficult, if not sometimes impossible, for local communities to grasp the medium- and long-term consequences of development. In Zanzibar, for instance, payments by the tourism industry for plots of land were not re-invested to generate an annual rent. Instead, the money disappeared rapidly and locals found themselves in a situation where they had lost access to land and financial resources (Gössling, this volume). Even with respect to the tourism industry, several issues related to time emerge. First of all, investments by the tourism industry are usually planned so as to pay off in a few years. Patterson and Rodriguez (this volume, p. 74) describe this as a situation where immediate profits are coupled with delayed or latent costs. In consequence, the long-term economic and environmental interest in a given destination may be low. Second, the management of many hotels may be frequently replaced in some destinations. In Zanzibar, for instance, the management in most resort hotels changes at least once a year. Under such circumstances, it is unlikely that managers are concerned with sustainability, which can only be achieved through a long-term interest in a place and a profound – usually evolving – understanding of the processes impacting the environment. From the tourists' point of view, the limited period of stay may render a long-term perspective on sustainability equally impossible, and they may even 'see it as their right to use the resource by virtue of the financial outlay they have made to visit the resource' (Butler 1991, p. 204).

TOWARDS SUSTAINABLE TOURISM DEVELOPMENT

The case studies presented in this book provide several insights with respect to sustainable tourism development that deserve mention. First, tourism development in tropical islands is a process driven by certain groups of actors, usually governments in cooperation with the international tourism industry, and with the support of external actors such as economic and environmental organizations. The interests of these actors may often differ from those of local stakeholders, because the groups of actors meeting in the development process may generally have very different conceptions of development, environment, place, time, wealth and social relationships, even though development aspirations of local stakeholder groups may generally also follow a broader 'western' pattern of modernization. Second, the case studies have shown that tourism can either enhance or alleviate problems of poverty and environmental degradation (with all possible options between the two extremes). While results should not be generalized, it seems possible to draw two basic conclusions: i) the greater the differences between hosts and guests in terms of income levels, lifestyles, cosmologies, etc., the greater is the likeliness of conflict, and ii) the better the traditional (local) social and ecological system is adapted to local conditions, the greater is the danger for tourism to produce undesirable outcomes. For example, if tourism is introduced or expanded into a society where traditional social and ecological systems work fairly well, the social and environmental 'costs' may be greater than the benefits (cf. chapters by Gössling, Stonich, this volume). In contrast, where natural resource bases are in decline and where poverty in absolute terms is increasing, tourism may provide benefits that can help to alleviate economic and ecological problems (cf. chapters by White and Rosales, Wunder, this volume). Third, particularly undesirable forms of tourism may develop in those cases where local populations remain uninformed about tourism development and excluded from the decision-making and development process. The conceptual differences in the understanding of what constitutes desirable development are illustrated by the observation that political and economic elites may often seek to establish top-down, large-scale, high-volume tourism while locals may favor bottom-up, small-scale, though not necessarily low-volume tourism. Recent contributions to the internet-based forum Small Islands Voice reflect this view:

> Now tourism is one of our country's main revenue earners. But still 95% of the tourism industry is locally owned. Our government is encouraging investors to come to the island, although we locals have worked hand in hand with government to lay down the rules for investment that have resulted in low-key, locally managed development. Still 81% of our land is traditionally owned with the rest in private or government ownership. We have two structures working hand in hand, our traditional Matai or Chiefly system, which is selected by individual families, and our democratic government selected by the people. So our system has an internal control. Please do not make the mistake of thinking we have no problems. Our main problem is to voice our concern and see that the government listens to us. . . . While many of us are determined to declare Samoa an environmental and cultural destination, others prefer mass tourism. . . . I think the best thing happening to our country is the good flow of dialogue among stakeholders in tourism in Samoa (Jackson 2003).

> There are enough stereotype large resorts which are all inclusive, and also very exclusive, in almost every corner of small islands around the world. I think that we need to take more action to preserve what local, natural resources we have before we bring in the big operators whose interest inevitably is self-interest (Lutchman 2003).

More generally, the observation that proactive planning, acceptance of limitations on growth, education of all parties involved and commitment to a long-term viewpoint are essential for sustainable tourism development (Butler 1991, p. 207) is reconfirmed by the case studies in this volume. This needs to be seen in the light of the fact that tourism dependence is high and increasing in many islands. Often, traditional economic activities are given up in favour of tourism-related income opportunities, which is contrary to beliefs that economic diversification is central to sustainable development (cf. di Castri 2002a). Patterson and Rodriguez (this volume) thus suggest that economic changes should maintain the structure and function of the ecological and social systems that also support local well-being, reminding us of the fact that wealth cannot entirely be measured in economic terms and that non-market contributions to welfare can be great in tropical islands.

Insights provided in this volume also reveal that the state's interests in tourism development may often coincide with the interests of international actors – a dilemma when government intervention is vital to set constraints on the development processes forced by international actors (cf. Butler et al. 1996, p. 8). It is thus encouraging to see recent trends towards local empowerment and involvement. Information technologies (IT) may play an important role in this process. Even though only a minor proportion of the population in islands has currently access to the internet, IT could revolutionize bottom-up tourism development. Small guesthouses, for example, are put in the position of marketing themselves globally, and IT-based advertisement has proved to be a means to increase accommodation occupancy rates (di Castri 2002a). Through IT, islanders are also able to discuss development processes or to seek external advice. Apart from the Small Islands Voice forum mentioned earlier, another important platform is the Wise Coastal Practices for Sustainable Human Development (WiCoP) forum (UNESCO 2001). WiCoP was launched as part of the UNESCO 'Environment and Development in Coastal Regions and in Small Islands' (CSI) initiative to achieve 'environmentally sound, socially equitable, culturally respectful and economically viable development in coastal regions and in small islands' (UNESCO 2001, p. 13). Towards the end of 1999, WiCoP had already more than 10 000 recipients. Another encouraging trend are Local Area Management Authorities (LAMAs), which represent partnerships between government agencies and stakeholder groups. These are established to manage the use of particular resources, and to meet problems of limited human/financial resources and inadequate enforcement of legislation (UNESCO 2002). In combination with coastal management projects and scientific research and data distribution, such as the Caribbean Coastal Marine Productivity Program (CARICOMP), the South Pacific Regional Environment Programme (SPREP) and the Global Coral Reef Monitoring Network (GCRMN), such initiatives could contribute to a major change in tourism development. Overall, many tropical islands seem on the move towards sustainable development. The case studies have shown that political ecology can play an important role in supporting this process.

REFERENCES

Adger, N.W., T.A. Benjaminsen, K. Brown and H. Svarstad (2001), 'Advancing a political ecology of global environmental discourses', *Development and Change*, **32**, 681–715.

Andersson, J. and Z. Ngazi (1998), 'Coastal communities' production choices, risk diversification, and subsistence behavior: responses in periods of transition', *Ambio*, **27** (8), 686–93.

Apostolopoulos, Y. and D.J. Gayle (2002a), *Island Tourism and Sustainable Development. Caribbean, Pacific and Mediterranean Experiences*, Westport, Connecticut: Praeger.

Apostolopoulos, Y. and D.J. Gayle (2002b), 'From MIRAB to TOURAB? Searching for sustainable development in the Maritime Caribbean, Pacific, and Mediterranean', in Y. Apostolopoulos and D.J. Gayle (eds), *Island Tourism and Sustainable Development. Caribbean, Pacific and Mediterranean Experiences*, Westport, Connecticut: Praeger, pp. 3–14.

Archer, E. (1985), 'Emerging environmental problems in a tourist zone: The case of Barbados', *Caribbean Geography*, October, 45–55.

Bates, D. and T.K. Rudel (2000), 'The political ecology of conserving tropical rain forests: a cross-national analysis', *Society & Natural Resources*, **13**, 619–34.

Beller, W., P. d'Ayala and P. Hein (eds) (1990), *Sustainable Development and Environmental Management of Small Islands*, Paris: Parthenon/UNESCO.

Benedict, B. (1967), *Problems of Smaller Territories*, London: Athlone.

Bertram, I.G. and R.F. Watters (1985), 'The MIRAB economy in South Pacific microstates', *Pacific Viewpoint*, **26** (3), 497–519.

Biagini, E. (1999), 'Island environments', in E. Biagini and B. Hoyle (eds), *Insularity and Development. International Perspectives on Islands*, London and New York: Pinter, pp. 17–41.

Biagini, E. and Hoyle, B. (1999), 'Insularity and development on an oceanic planet', in E. Biagini and B. Hoyle (eds), *Insularity and Development. International Perspectives on Islands*, London and New York: Pinter, pp. 1–14.

Blaikie, P. (1995), 'Changing environments or changing views?', *Geography*, **80** (3), 203–14.

Briguglio, L., R. Butler, D. Harrison, W. Leal Filho (eds) (1996), *Sustainable Tourism in Islands and Small States Case Studies*, London and New York: Pinter.

Britton, S.G. (1982), 'The political economy of tourism in the third world', *Annals of Tourism Research*, **9**, 331–58.

Britton, S.G. (1987), 'Tourism in Pacific Island states: constraints and opportunities', in S.G. Britton and W. Clarke (eds), *Ambiguous Alternatives: Tourism in Small Developing Countries*, Suva: Institute of Pacific Studies, University of the South Pacific, pp. 113–39.

Britton, S.G. (1991), 'Tourism, capital and place: towards a critical geography of tourism, *Environment and Planning D: Society and Space*, **9**, 451–78.

Bryant, R.L. (1997), 'Beyond the impasse: the power of political ecology in third world environmental research', *Area*, **29** (1), 5–19.

Bryant, R.L. (1998), 'Power, knowledge and political ecology in the third world: a review', *Progress in Physical Geography*, **22** (1), 79–94.

Bryant, R.L. (2000), 'Politicized moral geographies. Debating biodiversity conservation and ancestral domain in the Philippines', *Political Geography*, **19** (6), 673–705.

Bryant, D., D. Nielson and L. Tangley (1998), *The Last Frontier Forests: Ecosystems and Economies on the Edge*, Washington DC: World Resources Institute.

Buchan, K.C. (2000), 'The Bahamas', *Marine Pollution Bulletin*, **41** (1–6), 94–111.

Butler, R. (1991), 'Tourism, environment, and sustainable development', *Environmental Conservation*, **18**, 201–209.

Butler, R. (1993), 'Tourism – an evolutionary perspective', in J.G. Nelson, R. Butler and G. Wall (eds), *Tourism and Sustainable Development: Monitoring, Planning, Managing*, Publication Series no. 37, Waterloo: University of Waterloo, Department of Geography.

Butler, R., D. Harrison and W. Leal Filho (1996), 'Introduction', in L. Briguglio, R. Butler, D. Harrison and W. Leal Filho (eds), *Sustainable Tourism in Islands and Small States, Case Studies*, London and New York: Pinter, pp. 1-10.

Central Intelligence Agency (CIA) (2003a), The World Factbook 2002: Indonesia, available at: http://www.cia.gov/cia/publications/factbook/geos/id.html.

Central Intelligence Agency (CIA) (2003b), The World Factbook 2002: Tokelau, available at: http://www.cia.gov/cia/publications/factbook/geos/tl.html.

Cesar, H., C.G. Lundin, S. Bettencourt and J. Dixon (1997), 'Indonesian coral reefs – an economic analysis of a precious but threatened resource', *Ambio*, **26** (6), 345–50.

Chapin III, F.S., E.S. Zavaleta, V.T. Eviner, R.L. Naylor, P.M. Vitousek, H.L. Reynolds, D.U. Hooper, S. Lavorel, O.E. Sala, S.E. Hobbie, M.C. Mack and S. Diaz (2000), 'Consequences of changing biodiversity', *Nature*, **405**, 234–42.

Cronk, Q.C.B. (1997), 'Islands: stability, diversity, conservation', *Biodiversity and Conservation*, **6**, 477–93.

Dann, G.M.S. (1996), 'Socio-cultural Issues in St Lucia's Tourism', in L. Briguglio, R.W. Butler, D. Harrison, W. Leal Filho (eds), *Sustainable Tourism in Islands and Small States, Case Studies*, London and New York: Pinter, pp. 103-21.

Dann, G.M.S. and R.B. Potter (1997), 'Tourism in Barbados: rejuvenation or decline?', in D.G. Lockhart and D. Drakakis-Smith (eds), *Island Tourism, Trends and Prospects*, London and New York: Pinter, pp. 205–28.

Datta, K.K. and C. de Jong (2002), 'Adverse effect of waterlogging and soil salinity on crop and land productivity in northwest region of Haryana, India', *Agricultural Water Management*, **57** (3), 223–38.

Dauvergne, P. (1998), 'The political economy of Indonesia's 1997 forest fires', *Australian Journal of International Affairs*, **52** (1), 13–7.

de Bougainville, L.A. (1772), *A Voyage Round the World*, London: Nourse and Davis.

di Castri, F. (2002a), 'Diversification, connectivity and local empowerment for tourism sustainability in South Pacific Islands – a network from French Polynesia to Easter Island', in F. di Castri and V. Balaji (eds), *Tourism, Biodiversity and Information*, Leiden, The Netherlands: Backhuys Publishers, pp. 257–84.

di Castri, F. (2002b), 'Tourism revisited after 11 September 2001', in F. di Castri and V. Balaji (eds), *Tourism, Biodiversity and Information*, Leiden, The Netherlands: Backhuys Publishers, pp. 483–8.

di Castri, F. and V. Balaji (eds) (2002), *Tourism, Biodiversity and Information*, Leiden, The Netherlands: Backhuys Publishers.

di Castri, F., J. McElroy, P. Sheldon and V. Balaji (2002), 'Introduction to geographic regions: the islands' in F. di Castri and V. Balaji (eds), *Tourism, Biodiversity and Information*, Leiden, The Netherlands: Backhuys Publishers, pp. 139–50.

Dixon, J., L.F. Scura and T. van't Hof (1993), 'Meeting ecological and economic goals: marine parks in the Caribbean', *Ambio*, **22** (2-3), 117–25.

Dollar, D and P. Collier (2001), *Globalization, Growth, and Poverty: Building an Inclusive World Economy*, Oxford: Oxford University Press.

Dolman, A.J. (1985), 'Paradise lost? The past performance and future prospects of small island developing countries', in E. Dommen and P. Hein (eds), *States, Microstates and Islands*, London: Croom Helm, pp. 70–118.

Ehrlich, P.R. and A. Ehrlich (1969), *The Population Bomb*, New York: Ballantine.

Escobar, A. (1995), *Encountering Development: The Making and Unmaking of the Third World*, Princeton, New Jersey: Princeton University Press.

Escobar, A. (1998), 'Whose knowledge, whose nature? Biodiversity, conservation and the political ecology of social movement', *Journal of Political Ecology*, **4**, 53–82.

Fagan, B.M. (1998), *Clash of Cultures*, London: Alta Mira Press.

Fairhead, J. and M. Leach (1995), 'False forest history, complicit social analysis: rethinking some west African environmental narratives', *World Development*, **23**, 1023–35.

Forster, G. (1777), *A Voyage Round the World in His Brittanic Majesty's Sloop, Resolution, Commanded by Captain James Cook, During the Years 1772, 3, 3 and 5*, London: White, Robson, Elmsly and Robinson.

Forsyth, T. (2003), *Critical Political Ecology. The Politics of Environmental Science*, London and New York: Routledge.

Geist, H. (1994), 'Politische Ökologie von Ressourcennutzung und Umweltdegradierung', *Geographische Rundschau*, **46** (12), 718–27.

Geist, H. (1999), 'Exploring the entry points for political ecology in the international research agenda on global environmental change', *Zeitschrift für Wirtschaftsgeographie*, **43** (3–4), 158–68.

Gössling, S. (1999), 'Ecotourism – a means to safeguard biodiversity and ecosystem functions?', *Ecological Economics*, **29**, 303–20.

Gössling, S. (2001a), 'The consequences of tourism for sustainable water use on a tropical island: Zanzibar, Tanzania', *Journal of Environmental Management*, **61** (2), 179–91.

Gössling, S. (2001b), 'Tourism, environmental degradation and economic transition: interacting processes in a Tanzanian coastal community', *Tourism Geographies*, **3** (4), 230–54.

Gössling, S. (2002), 'Human–environmental relations with tourism', *Annals of Tourism Research*, **29** (4), 539–56.

Gössling, S., C. Borgström-Hansson, O. Hörstmeier and S. Saggel (2002), 'Ecological footprint analysis as a tool to assess tourism sustainability', *Ecological Economics*, **43** (2–3), 199–211.

Gössling, S., T. Kunkel, K. Schumacher and M. Zilger (2003), 'Use of marine species by tourism', *Biodiversity and Conservation*, submitted.

Greiner, C. (2002), 'How tourism reduces geodiversity and how it could be different: the cases of the Galápagos Archipelago and Easter Island', in F. di Castri and V. Balaji (eds), *Tourism, Biodiversity and Information*, Leiden, The Netherlands: Backhuys Publishers, pp. 233–55.

Holm-Petersen, E. (2000), 'Institutional support for tourism development in Africa', in P.U.C. Dieke (ed.), *The Political Economy of Tourism Development in Africa*, New York: Cognizant Communication Corporation, pp. 195–207.

Hornborg, A. (2001), *The Power of the Machine. Global Inequalities of Economy, Technology, and Environment*, New York: Alta Mira Press.

Houbert, J. (1999), 'Colonization, decolonization and changing geopolitics: the Creole Islands of the Indian Ocean', in E. Biagini and B. Hoyle (eds), *Insularity and Development. International Perspectives on Islands*, London and New York: Pinter, pp. 290–321.

Hoyle, B. and E. Biagini (1999), 'Islands, insularity and development strategies', in E. Biagini and B. Hoyle (eds), *Insularity and Development. International Perspectives on Islands*, London and New York: Pinter, pp. 358–70.

Intergovernmental Panel on Climate Change (IPCC) (2001), '*Climate change 2001: the scientific basis*', edited by J.T. Houghton, Y. Ding, D.J. Griggs, M. Noguer, P.J. van der Linden, X. Dai, K. Maskell and C.A. Johnson, Contribution of Working Group I to the Third Assessment Report of the Intergovernmental Panel on Climate Change, Cambridge: Cambridge University Press.

Jackson, V.M. (2003), *Local Approaches to Tourism Development in Samoa*, available at: http://www.sivglobal.org/?read=26.

Jiddawi, N. (1998), 'The reef dependent fisheries of Zanzibar', in R.W. Johnstone, J. Francis and C.A. Muhando (eds), *Coral Reefs: Values, Threats, and Solutions, Proceedings of the National Conference on Coral Reefs, Zanzibar, Tanzania, 2–4 December 1997*, Zanzibar: Institute of Marine Sciences, pp. 22–36.

Kakazu, H. (1994), *Sustainable Development of Small Island Economies*, Boulder, Colorado: Westview.

King, R. (1999), 'Islands and migration', in E. Biagini and B. Hoyle (eds), *Insularity and Development. International Perspectives on Islands*, London and New York: Pinter, pp. 93–115.

Krings, T. (1996), 'Politische Ökologie der Tropenwaldzerstörung in Laos', *Petermanns Geographische Mitteilungen*, **140** (3), 161–75.

Krings, T. (2003a), 'Zur Kritik des Sahel-Syndromansatzes aus der Sicht der Politischen Ökologie', *Geographische Zeitschrift*, **90**, forthcoming.

Krings, T. (2003b), 'Politische Ökologie', in D. Böhn (ed.), *Handbuch des Geographieunterrichts*, Vol 8, 'Entwicklungsräume', Cologne: Aulis Verlag, forthcoming.

Langholz, J.A., J.P. Lassoie, D. Lee and D. Chapman (2000), 'Economic considerations of privately owned parks', *Ecological Economics*, **33** (2), 173–83.

Laurance W.F., A.K.M. Albernaz, G. Schroth, P.M. Fearnside, S. Bergen, E.M. Venticinque and C. Da Costa, (2002), 'Predictors of deforestation in the Brazilian Amazon', *Journal of Biogeography*, **29** (5–6), 737–48.

Leatherman, S.P. (1997), 'Sea-level rise and small island states: an overview', *Journal of Coastal Research*, **24**, 1–16.

Liew, J. (1990), 'Sustainable development and environmental management of atolls', in W. Beller, P. d'Ayala and P. Hein (eds), *Sustainable Development and Environmental Management of Small Islands. Man and the Biosphere Series*, Volume 5, Paris: Parthenon/UNESCO, pp. 77–86.

Lindén, O. and N. Sporrong (1999), *Coral Reef Degradation in the Indian Ocean. Status Reports and Project Presentations*, Stockholm: SAREC Marine Science Program, Department of Zoology, Stockholm University.

Lockhart, D.G. (1997), 'Islands and tourism: an overview', in D.G. Lockhart and D. Drakakis-Smith (eds), *Island Tourism. Trends and Prospects*, London and New York: Pinter, pp. 3–20.

Logan, B.I. and W.G. Moseley (2002), 'The political ecology of poverty alleviation in Zimbabwe's Communal Areas Management Programme for Indigenous Resources (CAMPFIRE)', *Geoforum*, **33**, 1–14.

Lutchman, I. (2003), Cook Islands: untapped paradise?, available at: http://www.siv global.org/?read=31.

MacArthur, R.H. and E.O. Wilson (1967), *The Theory of Island Biogeography*, Princeton, New Jersey: Princeton University Press.

Mantel, S. and V.W.P. van Engelen (1999), 'Assessment of the impact of water erosion on productivity of maize in Kenya: An integrated modelling approach', *Land Degradation and Development*, **10** (6), 577–92.

Martinez-Alier, J. (2002), *The Environmentalism of the Poor: A Study of Ecological Conflicts and Valuation*, Cheltenham, UK and Northampton, MA, USA: Edward Elgar Publishing.

Mayer, J.D. (2000), 'Geography, ecology and emerging infectious diseases', *Social Science & Medicine*, **50**, 937–52.

McAfee, K. (1991), *Storm Signals: Structural Adjustment and Development Alternatives in the Caribbean*, London: Zed Books.

McElroy, J. and K. de Albuquerque (1998), 'Tourism penetration index in small Caribbean islands', *Annals of Tourism Research* , **25** (1), 145–68.

McElroy, J. and K. de Albuquerque (2002), 'Problems for Managing Sustainable Tourism in Small Islands', in Y. Apostolopoulos and D.J. Gayle (eds), *Island Tourism and Sustainable Development. Caribbean, Pacific and Mediterranean Experiences*, Westport, Connecticut: Praeger, pp. 15–31.

McElroy, J., B. Potter and E. Towle (1990), 'Challenges for sustainable development in small Caribbean islands', in W. Beller, P. d'Ayala and P. Hein (eds), *Sustainable Development and Environmental Management of Small Islands. Man and the Biosphere Series*, Volume 5, Paris: Parthenon/UNESCO, pp. 299–316.

Meadows, D.H., D.L. Meadows and J. Randers (1972), *The Limits to Growth: a Report for the Club of Rome's Project for the Predicament of Mankind*, London: Pan.

Milne, S. (1990), 'The impact of tourism development in small Pacific Island States: an overview', *New Zealand Journal of Geography*, April, 16–21.

Milne, S. (1992), 'Tourism and development in South Pacific microstates', *Annals of Tourism Research*, **19**, 191–212.

Milne, S. (1997), 'Tourism, dependency and South Pacific microstates: beyond the vicious cycle?', in D.G. Lockhart and D. Drakakis-Smith (eds), *Island Tourism. Trends and Prospects*, London and New York: Pinter, pp. 281–301.

Montagu, A.S. (2002), 'Forest planning and management in Papua New Guinea, 1884 to 1995: a political ecological analysis', *Planning Perspectives*, **17**, 21–40.

Msuya, F.E. (1998), 'Socioeconomic impacts of coral destruction on Unguja Island, Zanzibar, Tanzania', in R.W. Johnstone, J. Francis and C.A. Muhando (eds), *Coral Reefs: Values, Threats, and Solutions, Proceedings of the National Conference on Coral Reefs, Zanzibar, Tanzania, 2–4 December 1997*, Zanzibar: Institute of Marine Sciences, pp. 52–62.

Müller, B. (1999), 'Goldgräbergeschichten. Eine politisch-ökologische Betrachtung des Gold- und Diamantenabbaus in den Wäldern Südost-Venezuelas', *Zeitschrift für Wirtschaftsgeographie*, **43** (3–4), 229–44.

Mustafa, D. (2002), 'Linking access and vulnerability: perceptions of irrigation and flood management in Pakistan', *The Professional Geographer*, **54** (1), 94–105.

Myers, N., R.A. Mittermeier, C.G. Mittermeier, G.A.B. da Fonseca and J. Kent (2000), 'Biodiversity hotspots for conservation priorities', *Nature*, **403**, 853-8.

Neumann, R. (1998), *Imposing Wilderness: Struggles over Livelihood and Nature Preservation in Africa*, Berkeley, California: University of California Press.

Norton, A. (1996), 'Experiencing nature: the reproduction of environmental discourse through safari tourism in East Africa', *Geoforum*, **27** (3), 355–73.

Nüsser, M. (2003), 'Political ecology of large dams: a critical review', *Petermanns Geographische Mitteilungen*, **147** (1), 20–7.

O'Rourke, E. (2000), 'The reintroduction and reinterpretation of the wild', *Journal of Agricultural and Environmental Ethics*, **13**, 145–65.

Peluso, N. (1993), 'Coercing conservation? The politics of state resource control', *Global Environmental Change*, **3** (2), 199–217.

Pet-Soede, C., H.S.J. Cesar and J.S. Pet (1999), 'An economic analysis of blast fishing on Indonesian coral reefs', *Environmental Conservation*, **26** (2), 83–93.

Poirier, R.A. (2000), 'Tourism in the African economic milieu: a future of mixed blessings', in P.U.C. Dieke (ed.), *The Political Economy of Tourism Development in Africa*, New York: Cognizant Communication Corporation, pp. 29–36.

Richter, L. (1980), 'The political use of tourism: a Philippine case study', *Journal of Developing Areas*, **14**, 237–57.

Rochoux, J.Y. (1999), 'The development of services in Réunion Island: evolution of a service economy', *International Journal of Island Affairs*, **8** (3), 58–62.

Rodriguez-Garcia, R. (2001), 'The health–development link: travel as a public health issue', *Journal of Community Health*, **26** (2), 93–112.

Ruddle K. (1998), 'The context of policy design for existing community-based fisheries management systems in the Pacific Islands', *Ocean & Coastal Management*, **40** (2–3), 105–26.

Salvat, B. and C. Pailhe (2002), 'Islands and coral reefs, population and culture, economy and tourism: world view and a case study of French Polynesia', in F. di Castri and V. Balaji (eds), *Tourism, Biodiversity and Information*, Leiden, The Netherlands: Backhuys Publishers, pp. 213–31.

Sasidharan, V. and B. Thapa (2002), 'Sustainable coastal and marine tourism development: a Hobson's choice?', in Y. Apostolopoulos and D.J. Gayle (eds), *Island Tourism and Sustainable Development. Caribbean, Pacific and Mediterranean Experiences*, Westport, Connecticut: Praeger, pp. 93–112.

Shah, N.J. (2002), 'Bikinis and biodiversity: tourism and conservation on Cousin Island, Seychelles', in F. di Castri and V. Balaji (eds), *Tourism, Biodiversity and Information*, Leiden, The Netherlands: Backhuys Publishers, pp. 185–96.

Sheriff, A. (1987), *Slaves, Spices & Ivory in Zanzibar. Integration of an East African Commercial Empire into the World Economy, 1770–1873*, Oxford: James Currey.

Sindiga, I. (2000), 'Tourism development in Kenya', in P.U.C. Dieke (ed.), *The Political Economy of Tourism Development in Africa*, New York: Cognizant Communication Corporation, pp. 129–53.

Söderbaum, P. (2001), *Ecological Economics*, London: Earthscan.

Stephens, P.A., F. Frey-Roos, W. Arnold and W.J. Sutherland (2002), 'Sustainable exploitation of social species: a test and comparison of models', *Journal of Applied Ecology*, **39** (4), 629–42.

Stonich, S.C. (1998), 'Political ecology of tourism', *Annals of Tourism Research*, **25** (1), 25–54.

Stott, P. and S. Sullivan (eds) (2000), *Political Ecology: Science, Myth and Power*, London: Arnold.

Tewarie, B. (1997), *A Strategic Approach to the Development of a Sustainable Tourism Industry Across the Countries of the Association of Caribbean States*, St. Augustine, Trinidad and Tobago: University of the West Indies.

Timothy, D. J. and D. Ioannides (2002), 'Tour-operator hegemony: dependency, oligopoly, and sustainability in insular destinations', in Y. Apostolopoulos and D.J. Gayle (eds), *Island Tourism and Sustainable Development, Caribbean, Pacific and Mediterranean Experiences*, Westport, Connecticut: Praeger, pp. 181–98.

Tobisson, E., J. Andersson, Z. Ngazi, L. Rydberg and U. Cederlöf (1998), 'Tides, monsoons and seabed: local knowledge and practice in Chwaka Bay, Zanzibar', *Ambio*, **27** (8), 677–85.

United Nations Development Programme (UNDP) (2003), *Human Development Report*, available at: http://hdr.undp.org/.

United Nations Development Programme, United Nations Environment Programme, The World Bank, The World Resources Institute (UNDP/UNEP/World Bank/WRI) (2000), *World Resources 2000–2001*, Washington DC: World Resources Institute.

United Nations Educational, Scientific and Cultural Organization (UNESCO) (2001), 'Wise coastal practices: Towards sustainable small island living', results of a workshop on 'Wise coastal practices for sustainable human development in small island developing states', Apia, Samoa, 3–8 December 2000, *Coastal Region and Small Island Papers*, **9**, Paris: UNESCO.

United Nations Educational, Scientific and Cultural Organization (UNESCO) (2002), 'Wise practices for conflict prevention and resolution in small islands', results of a workshop on 'Furthering coastal stewardship in small islands', Dominica, 4–6 July 2001, *Coastal Region and Small Island Papers*, 11, Paris: UNESCO.

United Nations Environment Programme (UNEP) (1999), *Environmental Outlooks for the Island Countries of the Caribbean, Indian Ocean and South Pacific*, Nairobi, Kenya: United Nations Environment Programme, available: http://www.unep.ch/earthw/sidsgeo.htm.

Volonte, C.R. (1997), 'Caribbean Planning for Adaptation to Climate Change project (CPACC)', in G. Cambers (ed.), *Managing Beach Resources in the Smaller Caribbean Islands*, Mayaguez, Puerto Rico: UNESCO, pp. 258–65.

Vorlaufer, K. (2002), 'Campfire – the political ecology of poverty alleviation, wildlife utilisation and biodiversity conservation in Zimbabwe', *Erdkunde*, 56, 184–206.

Wackernagel, M. and W. Rees (1996), *Our Ecological Footprint: Reducing Human Impact on Earth*, Philadelphia, Pennsylvania: New Society.

Watts, D. (1993), 'Long-term environmental influences on development in islands of the Lesser Antilles', *Scottish Geographical Magazine*, 109 (3), 133–41.

Weaver, D.B. (1988), 'The evolution of a 'plantation' tourism landscape on the Caribbean island of Antigua', *Tijdschrift voor Economische en Sociale Geografie* 79, 313-19.

Wilkinson, P.F. (1987), 'Tourism in small island nations: a fragile dependence', *Leisure Studies*, 6, 127–46.

Wilkinson, P.F. (1989), 'Strategies for tourism in island microstates', *Annals of Tourism Research*, 16 (2), 153–77.

Wilkinson, P.F. (1997a), 'Jamaican tourism: from dependency theory to a world-economy approach', in D.G. Lockhart and D. Drakakis-Smith (eds), *Island Tourism. Trends and Prospects*, London and New York: Pinter, pp. 181–204.

Wilkinson, P.F. (1997b), *Tourism Policy and Planning: Case Studies from the Commonwealth Caribbean*, New York: Cognizant.

Wilson, D. (1996), 'Glimpses of Caribbean tourism and the question of sustainability in Barbados and St Lucia', in L. Briguglio, R.W. Butler, D. Harrison and W. Leal Filho (eds), *Sustainable Tourism in Islands and Small States Case Studies*, London and New York: Pinter, 75–102.

Wolf, E. (1972), 'Ownership and political ecology', *Anthropological Quarterly*, 45, 201–205.

Wong, P.P. (1998), 'Coastal tourism development in Southeast Asia: relevance and lessons for coastal zone management', *Ocean & Coastal Management*, 38, 89–109.

Wong, P.P. (2003), 'Where have all the beaches gone? Coastal erosion in the tropics', *Singapore Journal of Tropical Geography*, 24 (1), 111–132.

World Tourism Organization (WTO) (2003), *Tourism Highlights 2002*, available at: http://www.worldtourism.org.

Wunder, S. (2000), 'Ecotourism and economic incentives – an empirical approach', *Ecological Economics*, 32 (3), 465–79.

2. The Political Ecology of Tourism in the Cayman Islands

David B. Weaver

GEOGRAPHICAL AND HISTORICAL SYNOPSIS

The Cayman Islands, consisting of Grand Cayman Island, Cayman Brac and Little Cayman Island, occupy a relatively isolated but strategic location in the Caribbean Sea south of Cuba and west of Jamaica. Of the 262 km^2 land area, Grand Cayman Island accounts for 197 km^2, or about 75 per cent of the total. During the 17th century, plantation economies were being established throughout the Caribbean, and the region's sugar islands were prized trophies that changed hands frequently among the European Great Powers of the era. Such a transformation, however, was prevented in the Cayman Islands by the presence of extensive mangrove swamps and contorted limestone rock formations that inhibited large-scale agriculture and denied potential settlers a reliable source of fresh water. The archipelago, therefore, languished as an uninhabited backwater visited periodically by buccaneers and other fugitives who took advantage of their isolation, sheltered harbors, and the readily available food source offered by the abundant sea turtle population (Blume 1974).

Originally claimed by Spain, the Cayman Islands were ceded to Great Britain in 1670 as a corollary to the British conquest of Jamaica. By 1734, the suppression of pirating allowed the archipelago to be permanently settled, and a diverse population of artisans, shipwrecked mariners, refugees, slaves and other arrivals subsequently emerged. The absence of a well-articulated plantation system meant that residents of African descent constituted a relatively small share of the population. However, they were for the same reason also more likely to intermarry with white residents. Mixed race individuals consequently came to form a majority (about 60 per cent) of the native Caymanian population, with African-Caymanians and European-Caymanians each comprising an equal portion of the remainder. With agricultural options limited, this population of a few thousand residents relied for their modest but not impoverished livelihoods on a combination of fishing, turtling, boat building and rope making. In the early 20th century this marine-based economy was reinforced by employment opportunities in the merchant marine industry (Johnson 2001). Politically, the islands have remained a British dependency since 1670. They were administered from Jamaica between 1863 and 1959, and then became a separate colony. As discussed below, an extremely important event in the history of the Cayman Islands was the decision to remain under British rule when Jamaica became independent in 1962.

Employment in the merchant marine provided the Cayman Islanders with a secure and comfortable livelihood during the first half of the 20th century, but subsequent changes in the seafaring industries, including the replacement of labor-intensive vessels by supertankers and the recruitment of low cost sailors from Asia, stimulated efforts to find more sustainable economic alternatives (Wilkinson 1997). Manufacturing was quickly rejected as an option, and tourism and offshore finance were the two activities identified and cultivated to sustain the economic development of the Cayman Islands during the latter half of the 20th century, as described in the two sections that follow. The economic transformation that occurred in the Cayman Islands during this period is nothing short of remarkable in every respect, and attests to the dependency's success as an innovative 'entrepreneurial island' in which geographic size or natural resource endowment are essentially irrelevant to the attainment of economic prosperity (Roberts 1995). By 2002, tourism accounted for about 70 per cent of GDP and 75 per cent of foreign currency earnings, with most of the remainder generated from activities related to offshore finance. The primary and secondary sectors, in contrast, together contributed no more than 5 per cent to the economy (EIU 2002a). More remarkably, the revenues from tourism and offshore finance produced a per capita GDP of US$30,000, thereby positioning the Cayman Islands among the wealthiest of the world's states and dependencies.

THE DEVELOPMENT OF TOURISM

The serious pursuit of tourism in the Cayman Islands as a policy directive is a recent phenomenon, but this sector has historical antecedents that probably reach back to the era of the first permanent settlement, when the provision of basic transportation infrastructure and the elimination of piracy facilitated a small number of social and business visits from Jamaica, Great Britain and elsewhere. In contrast, descriptions of Columbus, the buccaneers or other early opportunistic visitors as the first 'tourists', sometimes made by marketers and publicists, are at best facetious. Anything other than anecdotal or incidental information about tourism or its pursuit in the Cayman Islands prior to World War Two is lacking. The Commissioner's Report of 1913, for example, makes the following comments:

> It is hoped also that tourists in search of peace and quiet will be induced to visit the island, which, though possessing few attractions to offer, is yet entirely free of dust, with good sea-bathing in parts and wild duck shooting (Cayman Islands 1914).

Primitive and irregular steamship connections to other destinations, which were not standardized until 1928, help to account for the apparent paucity of tourist activity in the early 1900s (Weaver 1990). Specialized tourist accommodation was also rare. It was reported as recently as 1947 that just one 'very primitive inn', located in the capital of George Town, was available to inbound visitors (Clark 1952), while the Anglo-American Commission (1945) cited the availability of a few 'primitive cottage sites' for visitors at Grand Cayman Island's Seven Mile Beach (Figure 2.1).

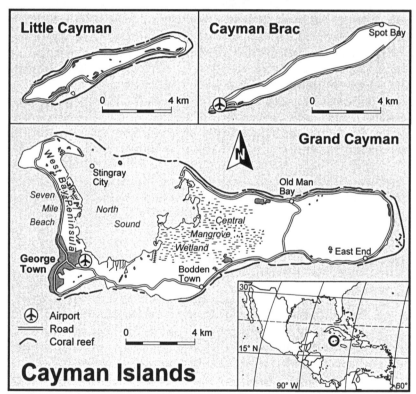

Figure 2.1   Cayman Islands

Early Initiatives and Trends

The first significant indications of what Butler (1980) terms the 'involvement' stage of destination development are evident in 1950. In that year, the 40-room Galleon Beach Club was opened on Seven Mile Beach, inaugurating the era of resort-based 3S (sea, sand, sun) tourism in the Cayman Islands. An early indicator of government involvement was the passing of the Hotel Aid Law of 1955, which like similar legislation in other Caribbean islands, provided incentives for entrepreneurs willing to establish hotels with a minimum number of rooms. Other small hotels and guesthouses soon joined the Galleon Beach Club along the incipient 'tourist strip' of Seven Mile Beach and in George Town, and by 1960 the Cayman Islands boasted an inventory of 300 units of accommodation distributed among eight hotels (Wilkinson 1997). Another significant initiative was the 1961 formation of the Tourist Board as a mechanism for developing the tourism industry, collecting tourism-related data, and promoting the Cayman Islands as an inbound tourist destination. Prior to this, tourism 'promotion' was haphazard and unprofessional, and included a cheap 1956 mimeographed sheet from the Commissioner's Office which cheerfully refers to indifferent roads and a cable office that was usually closed. Potential visitors are told that 'you must console yourself with the thought that life anywhere is impossible without a little healthy frustration' (Gerrard 1956).

Accelerated Growth

Weaver (1990) infers an annual intake of between 1 000 and 1 500 inbound tourists in the Cayman Islands from 1950 to 1960, while Blume (1974) estimates 2 000 arrivals for 1962. Tourist Board statistics for 1964 (the first year for which precise tourism-related statistics are available) reveal a substantially larger intake of 4 834 stay-over tourists and an unknown number of cruise ship excursionists. Arrivals by air quickly dominated this intake following the opening of an airport near George Town in 1953 and the subsequent introduction of flights by the Costa Rican carrier LACSA and British West Indies Airways (BWIA). With regard to available attractions, the Cayman Islands were well known by the early 1960s as a diving destination par excellence, due to the proximity of unspoiled coral reefs located within crystal clear waters uncontaminated by offshore runoff or other sediments and pollutants. The first recreational diving business on Grand Cayman Island was established in 1957, and a diving shop soon became a requisite feature of any self-respecting Cayman Islands hotel. Emphasizing these diving opportunities and the white powder sands of Seven Mile Beach, the well-funded Tourist Board began an aggressive campaign of overseas marketing with the opening of its Miami office in 1965. Fuelled largely by the promotional efforts in the American market, stayover arrivals increased exponentially to 14 460 in 1968, 30 646 in 1972, 64 875 in 1976 and 120 241 in 1980, almost all of which accrued to Grand Cayman Island (Weaver 1990). Over this same 12-year period, cruise ship arrivals increased from none reported to 60 869. Important institutional initiatives of the 1970s included the elevation of the Tourist Board to a full Department in 1974, and the introduction of an annual Pirates Week festival in 1977 as a device for diversifying the Caymanian tourism product. To accommodate the rapidly increasing tourist flow, the inventory of hotel, apartment and condominium rooms increased to 1 702 units in 1975 and 4 030 in 1984, concentrated along the western coast of Grand Cayman Island from George Town to West Bay. The opening of the 250-room Holiday Inn in 1971, moreover, marked the advent of a more sophisticated and 'up-market' tourism product.

The tourism strategy of the Cayman Islands government from the mid-1960s to the mid-1980s, therefore, was characterized by an emphasis on aggressive growth, the US market, marine-based attractions centered around the diving industry and Seven Mile Beach of Grand Cayman Island, the development of the cruise ship industry to augment the well-established overnight market, and the cultivation of an up-market, sophisticated destination image. All of these characteristics were reinforced in subsequent years, and by 2001 the stayover and cruise ship excursionist intakes reached a remarkable level of 334 100 and 1 214 800 respectively, compared with a permanent resident population of about 42 000 (Department of Tourism 2002). The core stay-over market, in concert with the above strategy, is described as consisting of affluent, repeat-visit middle-aged American couples with a primary interest in diving and other water sports (The Tourism Company 2002). The tourism sector performed well against the regional benchmark in terms of visitation growth rates, with stay-over arrivals increasing by an average of 8.9 per cent per year between 1983 and 1995 compared with an overall Caribbean rate of 6.1 per cent (George and Clark 1998). As a contributor to the Cayman Islands GDP, tourism increased from 6.2 per cent in 1967 to 34.8 per cent in 1993 (Wilkinson 1997) and the aforementioned level of 75 per cent by 2000. Direct tourism-related expenditures in that year were in excess of US$600 million, obtained largely through the revenues generated from more than 5 400 units of accommodation (The Tourism Company 2002). The Cayman Islands could be at least ostensibly described at the turn of the 21st century as one of the world's most successful inbound tourist destinations, characterized by an impressive pattern of sustained growth, a high quality tourism product, and a highly satisfied clientele.

THE DEVELOPMENT OF OFFSHORE FINANCE

No discussion of tourism development in the Cayman Islands is complete without mentioning the concurrent development of the dependency as an offshore finance center (OFC). This is due in part to the close and mutually reinforcing relationships between the two sectors. For example, Johnson (2001) estimates that 40 per cent of inbound visitors to the Cayman Islands in the mid-1980s were there mainly for business purposes, even though just 5 per cent of stayovers formally list 'business' as their primary purpose of visit (The Tourism Company 2002). The discrepancy is not surprising when the essentially clandestine nature of offshore finance is taken into consideration. A second aspect of the relationship is that much of the superstructure associated with tourism represents investments associated with offshore finance interests. Third, the granting of 'free port' status to George Town in 1965, an early initiative intended to stimulate the OFC strategy, provided an important foundation for the town's later development as a cruise ship destination (Johnson 2001). The line between the tourism and OFC sectors therefore is often fuzzy, as illustrated by the example of an American businessman who spends two months in his Cayman Islands second home investment, dividing his time between attending to his offshore accounts, and diving. Other relationships include the possibility that any tarnishing of the Cayman Islands image due to perceived improprieties in the OFC sector could translate into reduced visitation levels.

The pursuit of the OFC option in the Cayman Islands was facilitated by a variety of internal and external factors. First, the decision to remain a British dependency since 1962 has conveyed an image of stability and legitimacy (for example being backed by the United Kingdom) in an era when many Third World ex-colonies emerged as economically and politically unstable dictatorships. Second, this decision has also meant that the United Kingdom has retained responsibility for foreign relations and defense, thereby allowing the local government to focus on economic development. A third factor is the passage of extensive enabling financial legislation since the 1960s by this highly autonomous government to formalize and promote the OFC sector. Fourth, the OFC sector has been recently rejuvenated through the introduction of new activities such as mutual fund and insurance management to augment the more traditional banking and company registration areas. Fifth, the government has maintained a policy of importing large numbers of foreign workers in order to provide the OFC industry (as well as tourism) with an adequate skilled as well as menial labor force. Sixth, government has invested heavily in the establishment of the transportation and communication infrastructure necessary to accommodate OFC and tourism-related activity (Amit 2001). Seventh, Roberts (1995) contends that government and business leaders have responded to growing regional OFC competition by successfully marketing the Cayman Islands as an up-market and exceptionally stable OFC sustained by an elite coalition of public and private interests. Eighth, the availability of a tropical climate as well as world-class coral reefs and beaches make the Cayman Islands an aesthetically pleasing destination for visitors needing to travel to this destination for OFC purposes (see above). Finally, the Cayman Islands OFC initiatives were propelled externally by innovations in the global financial sector throughout the 1970s and 1980s that increased the mobility of capital. The fact that the Cayman Islands were one of the first geopolitical entities to capitalize on this trend conferred numerous advantages to the dependency that were not available to many of the more recently established OFCs.

Just four banks and 132 companies conducted business in the Cayman Islands in 1966, but these figures increased respectively to 200 and 6 516 by 1975, and to 527 and 18 263 by 1988 (Ebanks and Bush 1990). At the end of 2001, the Cayman Islands hosted 545 banks and trust companies, 64 495 registered companies, and 3 648 registered mutual funds (EIU 2002a), thereby positioning the dependency as one the world's largest financial centers. This status, and the status of the tourism industry, is sustained by an expatriate worker component that accounts for at least 40 per cent of the entire Cayman Islands labor force. Concerns over this high non-local component have been addressed by a policy of denying expatriates any citizenship rights, thereby allowing 'native' Caymanians to dominate the political decision-making process while simultaneously enjoying the high standard of living that has been made possible by the presence of such workers (Amit 2001).

ENVIRONMENTAL AND SOCIAL IMPACTS OF TOURISM AND OFC-RELATED ACTIVITY

The first significant environmental modifications associated (at least indirectly) with tourism in the Cayman Islands occurred when the Mosquito Research and Control Unit (MRCU) was established in the mid-1960s to suppress the swarms of mosquitoes and sand flies that were then plaguing the western part of Grand Cayman Island and discouraging tourism-related activity. Subsequent suppression attempts have been described as 'very effective' (Ebanks and Bush 1990), but it is unclear whether this suppression, undoubtedly beneficial to the tourism industry and local residents, was positive or negative from an ecological perspective. Johnson (2001), on one hand, contends that the targeted species are not indigenous to the Cayman Islands and may have arrived with the buccaneers and other early arrivals.

However, even if this is true, it is possible that the local ecosystem may have adapted to the arrival of such exotics, and therefore experienced stress as a result of the eradication efforts. A clearly less benign environmental aspect of these efforts was the process most commonly employed to control insect populations, which involved the construction of canals and dykes in wetlands along the western shore of the North Sound to eliminate mosquito-producing habitat (Johnson 2001).

Although the earliest manipulations of the mangrove swamp by the MRCU did not intentionally provide new land for tourism development, subsequent efforts were more deliberate in this regard. By 1975, six major reclamation projects were underway as the strategic and financial value of Grand Cayman Island's West Bay Peninsula became more apparent due to the reduced insect population, its proximity to Seven Mile Beach as well as the airport and George Town, and the shelter from inclement weather provided by the North Sound. Fuelling the reclamation boom was the absence of any obligation on the part of developers to erect buildings within a specified time frame following the completion of the land filling process. Accordingly, many of the areas reclaimed by speculators sat empty for years, serving no other purpose than to violate the scenic quality of the landscape, promote the establishment of invasive weed populations, and encourage erosion. It was estimated in the late 1990s that more than 80 per cent of all canal lot developments built on speculation since the late 1970s were still not occupied (UNESCO 1998). Another significant negative impact of these reclamations was associated with the use of hydraulic dredges to obtain fill from the floor of the adjacent North Sound. This process created turbidity plumes in the mid-1970s that extended all the way to the coral reefs off Seven Mile Beach, prompting divers to report 'massive' damage to these reefs from sedimentation (Ebanks and Bush 1990). Nevertheless, large-scale reclamation projects continued to be approved during the 1980s, including the Cayman Island Yacht Club site (a 30-acre site which additionally required dredging for the establishment of a yachting basin), the Safehaven project (a 280-acre site that included the construction of an artificial beach), and an additional privately owned parcel of 176 acres (Johnson 2001).

By the late 1990s, it was reported that two-thirds of the mangrove forests on the eastern side of the West Bay Peninsula had been lost to dredging, more than 200 ha of marl had been removed from the shallow lagoon to provide landfill and construction material, and large areas of offshore water continued to be impacted by the resultant sediments (UNESCO 1998). A recent report by the Economist Intelligence Unit (EIU 2002a, p. 56) states that 'the pace of property development and the demand for fill have environmental implications for Grand Cayman's North Sound and one of the island's top tourism attractions, Stingray City'. Geographically, most tourism and OFC-related development on Grand Cayman Island has occurred in the West Bay Peninsula, which accounts for 2 133 of 2 812 hotel rooms in the dependency (The Tourism Company 2002). Here, the basic landscape pattern includes (1) an almost continuous strip of hotel, condominiums and other commercial tourist accommodations along Seven Mile Beach, (2) a parallel and adjacent strip of estate housing developments and other amenity land uses along the eastern shore of the peninsula, and (3) growing residential areas to the north (West Bay) and south (George Town). These and other residential areas are not for the most part directly used by the tourism industry, but they must be cited along with the concomitant consumption of land and other resources as an important indirect and induced environmental impact of the tourism sector, since many of the dwellings are occupied by expatriate workers who fill most of the dependency's 7 000 tourism-related jobs (The Tourism Company 2002). It is no coincidence that population growth in the Cayman Islands has mirrored tourist arrivals in its exponential pattern, increasing from 8 500 in 1960 to 16 700 in 1977, 25 900 in 1988 and 42 000 in 2001 (95 per cent of which reside on Grand Cayman Island).

Tourist Activities

Various environmental impacts have also been associated with tourism-related activities such as scuba diving, Stingray City and cruise ships. With regard to the former, it is estimated that 2 400 000 dives are made each year in the Cayman Islands, the vast majority of them at a few sites off Seven Mile Beach (The Tourism Company 2002). Recent scientific research by Tratalos and Austin (2001) indicates that scuba diving is having an adverse impact on these coral reef colonies, in that areas of heavy diver use are more likely to have an abnormally high incidence of dead coral, as well as decreases in hard coral populations and colonies of the main reef-building coral species. These impacts are associated with overuse as well as the carelessness of certain categories of divers such as novices and underwater photographers. According to Ebanks and Bush (1990), damage from anchors, and especially those of cruise ships, was also a major threat to Caymanian coral reefs. In one infamous instance in the mid-1980s, 3 150 intact square meters of reef near George Town were destroyed by one cruise ship in one day (Smith 1988). Anchor damage apparently continued in the 1990s, along with the discharge of sewage (Wilkinson 1997). Shackley (1998) argues that tourism is also having negative impacts on the North Sound's Stingray City, where up to 500 humans at any given time touch and feed stingrays attracted to the site by baiting. With no visitor quota in effect, this unique attraction now draws approximately 700 000 tourists each year, making Stingray City by far the most important named attraction in the Cayman Islands (The Tourism Company 2002).

While most tourism-related impacts are associated with the West Bay Peninsula and adjacent waters, development is also gradually spreading into the eastern two-thirds of Grand Cayman Island due to cheaper real estate prices and good infrastructure (for example roads, electricity and telephone service). Furthermore, as with the West Bay Peninsula, anyone can buy land in the Cayman Islands, and the purchase of property is facilitated by a sophisticated land registration system that simplifies title searches and minimizes risk. No property tax, moreover, is charged on developed or undeveloped land, most of which is held in private hands and is available for development. Among the concerns related to this diffusion of development is the presence in these new areas of endemic bird, plant and reptile species or races (UNEP 1998).

Social Impacts: 'Caymanian' vs. Expatriate Perspectives

In contrast to the environmental impacts cited above, there is little evidence of direct negative social impacts of tourism within the local Caymanian community. This may be due in part to widespread community awareness of the tourism industry's role in fostering the exceptionally high standard of living. As well, the anomalous character of Caymanian society has given rise to a more equitable distribution of wealth as compared with the 'plantation' islands of the Caribbean. More problematic is the large share of the resident population that consists of expatriate workers and their families. While again there is no clear evidence of negative social impacts within this group, there is a basis for suspecting that some of these may exist due to the high portion of menial laborers (many of whom are Jamaican), the tenuous nature of their residency status, the absence of political rights, and the fact that expatriate workers are normally tied to a specified employer and therefore have little or no employment mobility. Expatriate workers are therefore inconvenienced by a system that promotes external mobility (labor can easily be imported or exported in concert with the mobility of international capital requirements) but not internal immobility (expatriate labor cannot easily move to another job within the Cayman Islands that may provide better pay or working conditions). The expatriate labor force may also be associated with indirect negative social impacts within the 'native' Caymanian community, despite the role of the latter in creating the high standard of living. These impacts are associated with growing local insecurity about the large size of the expatriate labor force (notwithstanding its lack of political power) and its purported contribution to congestion, crime and the erosion of traditional Caymanian culture (Amit 2001).

THE POLICY CONTEXT

Despite the litany of negative impacts described above, concern for the natural and social environment of the Cayman Islands is evident in some of the dependency's earliest tourism-related policy. The Tourist Board, for example, was mandated in 1961 to 'develop the tourism of the Cayman Islands without destroying the fragile island environment or placing undue stress upon the island infrastructure and the local labor force' (Wilkinson 1997, p. 124). The Land Development Law of 1969 was an early attempt to regulate the growth of tourism and other activities involving construction, and this was followed in 1971 by the creation of a Central Planning Authority charged with preparing a development plan for the Cayman Islands that would be updated every five years.

Critically, none of these initiatives was intended to curtail tourism growth (as evidenced by visitation statistics for subsequent years), but rather to impose at least some constraints on this process to avoid haphazard physical developments that could undermine the tourism industry itself. Otherwise, the dominant attitude toward tourism development in the Cayman Islands at least until the late 1980s is suggestive of what Jafari (2001) calls the 'advocacy' or pro-growth platform, which is perhaps not surprising considering the crucial role of this sector in sustaining the late 20th century prosperity of the resource-starved dependency. Pro-environmental sentiments in this climate could go only so far. The 1975 Development Plan, for example, was ultimately withdrawn as being too controversial because of its perceived over-emphasis on preserving the natural environment (Wilkinson 1997). Among other proposals, this Plan sought to protect from tourism and other development the Central Mangrove Wetland, a 50 km^2 area on the east side of the North Sound that is critical to the health of the North Sound system and an important habitat for a variety of species. This sweeping proposal was made without any prior public consultation, leading those with land claims in the area to vigorously oppose what they perceived to be the looming seizure of their property. The entire area was soon afterwards registered under private ownership, and an atmosphere of mistrust was created that would help to delay for at least a decade the implementation of land protection measures here and elsewhere (see below).

Yet, for the same reasons of enlightened self-interest that are implicit in the stated 1961 mandate of the Tourist Board, the powerful pro-advocacy tourism industry was itself an instrumental factor in the passing of incipient environmental legislation in the Cayman Islands. Most notably, the Marine Conservation Law of 1978 was passed in part because of lobbying from dive operators wishing to preserve the relatively unspoiled coral reefs and waters upon which their success depended. This legislation prohibited the taking of marine life by scuba divers and the use of poison or explosives to extract marine resources. The destruction of coral during dredging operations was banned (except if licensed by government) along with the discharge of raw sewage and other harmful effluence, while size and catch limits and closed seasons were implemented for species such as conch and spiny lobster. The collection of coral and sponges was outlawed, and Executive Council (the highest legislative body in the Cayman Islands) was given the authority to establish marine parks (Ebanks and Bush 1990). This progressive legislation clearly indicates that the environmental impacts of the rapidly growing tourism sector were not all negative, and that support for environmental legislation was not the sole province of obvious lobby groups such as the Cayman Islands National Trust, a non-profit non-governmental organization established to protect the natural and cultural heritage of the dependency. Another example of positive tourism influence on the natural environment is the fact that sewage control was brought into effect along Seven Mile Beach to protect the tourism industry, after divers complained in the early 1980s of encountering floating human waste at popular dive sites (Johnson 2001).

Indeed, the story of tourism development policy in the Cayman Islands throughout the 1980s and 1990s is a curious and somewhat paradoxical mixture of support for unbridled tourism expansion and the continuing implementation of pro-environmental tourism policies intended at least in part to mitigate the consequences of this expansion – policies, moreover, that continued to receive support in many cases from the tourism industry. For example, the establishment of protected areas under the Marine Conservation Regulations of 1986 was facilitated by support from a broad-based coalition including water sports operators, fishermen, commercial boat trip operators, government biologists and local environmentalists (Ebanks and Bush 1990). Preceded by an extensive public information campaign and accompanied by strict enforcement provisions, the regulations led to the establishment of eight protected areas encompassing 8 000 ha of dry land, wetland and water. Several types of marine park were provided for, including Environmental Zones and Marine Park Zones, which respectively are equivalent to IUCN category I and II (this is highly protected) protected areas. The former prohibit the removal of marine life, anchor use, entry into the water and speeds above five knots, while the latter are intended mainly to protect coral reefs and control anchoring in heavily used locations off Seven Mile Beach. The largest Environmental Zone protects a portion of the Central Mangrove Wetland. The regulations also provided for the creation of Replenishment Zones (apparently IUCN category IV, or habitat protection parks) that protect the breeding grounds of selected marine species (CEP 1999). The largest such Zone encompasses the eastern half of the North Sound.

More recent examples of pro-environmental actions by government include a 1993 policy of restricting cruise ships to no more than three per day, or 5 500 passengers, which represented one of the first attempts to curtail the laissez-faire tourism growth policy. Concurrently, legislation was passed increasing the maximum fine to US$625,000 for any vessel convicted of polluting Caymanian waters, while the practice of monitoring cruise ships by air several times a day was introduced in the mid-1990s (Wilkinson 1997). Earlier actions initiated by the previously described anchor damage incident (see p. 46) was the construction of permanent moorings at more than 300 dive sites, and 1988 regulations that prevented vessels anywhere in Cayman waters from anchoring in a way that causes damage to coral (Ebanks and Bush 1990). Concerns over cruise ships arise from a variety of factors associated with this particular sector, including its less than impressive environmental track record in the Caribbean (see for example Allen 1992) and the fact that cruise ship excursionists account for three-quarters of all visitors but less than 10 per cent of all expenditures (The Tourism Company 2002). More than most other components of the tourism industry, the cruise ship sector is characterized by short-term periods of intensive congestion when passengers from increasingly large vessels arrive ashore and congregate in shopping areas or take transport to popular attractions. There is therefore a widely held attitude that the cruise ship sector has become too large and generates too many negative impacts relative to the economic benefits that it provides.

Certain actions were concerned with other elements of tourism or with tourism in general. These include the 1997 introduction of the Environmental Protection Fund, which levied a tax on all tourist arrivals to raise funds for the purchase of critical habitat at market rates (a measure intended to prevent the alienation of landowners) (Gore 2001). To address the ongoing problem with dredging (which was not covered in the 1986 Marine Conservation Regulations), a Coastal Works Advisory Committee was established in the late 1980s to advise government on dredging proposals (Ebanks and Bush 1990). More recently, the government has announced that no further dredging licenses will be issued for the North Sound (EIU 2002a). A critical event was a 2001 decision by the Planning Appeal Tribunal to uphold an appeal by the Cayman Islands National Trust against a proposal to remove and fill 1.5 million cubic yards of material from a mangrove area on the West Bay Peninsula. Significantly, the fact that the land reclamation was not accompanied by any specific development proposal was given as the main reason for opposing the proposal, this type of speculation being regarded as an unsustainable use of the land (Cayman Net News 2001). This indicated (a) a major challenge to the longstanding policy of permitting speculative land filling, and (b) a National Trust that was opposed to such speculative modification of the environment, but not necessarily to development per se.

On the social front, regulations were put in place in which new beachfront developments with 200 feet or more of frontage had to provide a six-foot wide public access path (Johnson 2001), while tourism officials promoted a policy of replacing expatriate workers with Cayman Islanders (George and Clark 1998).

Sustainable Development: Apparition of Consensus?

The longstanding macro-policy of accommodating both tourism growth and pro-environmental actions acquired vindication and definition in the late 1980s following the release of the so-called 'Brundtland Report', which popularized the concept of sustainable development, or development that meets the needs of the present without compromising the ability of future generations to meet their own needs (WCED 1987). It can be argued cynically that the widespread support subsequently expressed for sustainable development (as for example at the 1992 Rio Earth Summit where it formed the philosophical basis of the Agenda 21 plan for action) is a function of the concept's malleability, wherein environmentalists cite the 'sustainable' part of the term to support an environmentalist agenda, and industry cites the 'development' part to support a pro-growth status quo (Weaver and Lawton 1999). In many situations, the consensus of support at the conceptual level therefore evaporates when, in practice, the aspirations of the environmentalist lobby conflict with those of the pro-development lobby. The experience of tourism in the Cayman Islands thus far, however, appears to demonstrate the possibility that both agendas can be pursued concurrently and with reasonable harmony. Sustainable development is evident in Cayman Islands policy documents at least as early as the mid-1970s (if not earlier, as in the 1961 mandate of the Tourist Board – see p. 41). For example, the 1977 Development Plan expresses a desire to 'maintain and enhance' the environmental character of Grand Cayman Island, but also supports the continued expansion of tourism and offshore finance.

After 1990, the concept of sustainable development per se is explicitly or implicitly endorsed in Cayman policy documents and by stakeholder organizations as varied as the Cayman Islands National Trust and the Cayman Islands Tourism Association (CITA), the dependency's tourism industry umbrella organization (N. La Valette 2001, General Manager CITA, personal communication). More broadly, Strategy 10 of Vision 2008, which is an indication of the government's long-term objectives for the Cayman Islands, states: 'we will develop and implement a growth management plan to achieve and maintain a balance between the natural and built environment.' Moreover, the UK government's Partnership and Prosperity White Paper of the late 1990s, which seeks to modernize the relationship between the UK and its overseas territories, recommends the promotion of sustainable development as a priority policy directive (Foreign and Commonwealth Office 1999). As part of an Environment Charter between the UK Overseas Territories Conservation Forum and the governments of the UK and the Cayman Islands, the latter agrees as part of its Guiding Principles and Commitments to create a forum to 'promote sustainable patterns of production and consumption', implement obligations of the Multilateral Environmental Agreements that apply to the Cayman Islands, ensure polluter-pay policies, and abide by principles set out in the Rio Declaration on Environment and Development. The Charter, in addition, requires all signatories 'to aim for solutions which benefit both the environment and development' (UKOTCF 2001). Finally, the Draft Tourism Policy Framework of 2002 is required by government to be 'closely linked to sustainable development' and to follow 'principles of balanced growth' (The Tourism Company 2002, p. 3).

Aside from the facilitating factors discussed earlier (including the high standard of living, the widespread awareness of tourism's role in creating this wealth, and its relatively equitable distribution), the apparently successful implementation of sustainable tourism and OFC development in the Cayman Islands may be attributed to policies that formally or informally give priority in different locations to either development or the status quo natural/cultural environment. This idea of spatial compromise is evident in the use of flexible zoning parameters in the 1977 Development Plan to focus tourism development on the West Bay Peninsula and its near offshore. Subsequent planning has encouraged the concentration of tourism-related activity in this area, while leaving the rest of Grand Cayman Island as well as the sister islands of Cayman Brac and Little Cayman for small-scale up-market tourism and 'local' activities such as agriculture. According to Johnson (2001), the North Sound and its wetland fringe, as part of this compromise, was deliberately divided in half with the western portion being used for tourism activity (for example Stingray City, boating, housing development) and the eastern half for Replenishment and Environmental Zones. The 1994 Tourism Management Policy (Wilkinson 1997) and the Draft Tourism Policy Framework of 2002 introduces an additional but compatible element into this structure by advocating an emphasis on ecotourism in the eastern two-thirds of Grand Cayman Island and in the sister islands (The Tourism Company 2002), both of which also support a variety of endemic wildlife species (UNEP 1998). Supporting these spatial strategies and the concept of sustainable development more generally is the long-held perception among Cayman Islands stakeholders that the private sector should play the lead role in developing tourism, but that this should be carefully controlled by government planning and policy (Wilkinson 1997).

Limitations, Quotas and Challenges

Despite the appearance of unbridled success, the circumstances of the Cayman Islands tourism sector in the early 21st century are such that the trajectory of consensus-based and space-based sustainable development policy maintained during the previous thirty years may no longer be sustainable in its current form. This speculation arises because of the congestion and physical saturation that is affecting the West Bay Peninsula, and to the 'spillover' effect that is starting to affect other parts of Grand Cayman Island – areas, that is, which were previously exempt from intensive tourism-related development. The Draft Tourism Policy Framework of 2002 describes the growth of tourism throughout the 1980s and 1990s as 'unconstrained expansion', and calls for a move toward 'consolidation and sustainable growth' (The Tourism Company 2002, pp. 36–7). This is in response to perceptions that the growth of resident population and tourist arrivals is now having a detrimental impact on the market image of the Cayman Islands, with an increasing number of visitors reporting that the product is deteriorating due to congestion, excessive cruise ship traffic, high costs and the lack of a distinctive identity. These perceptions may in turn be partly responsible for recent stagnation in the stayover market and sluggish occupancy rates (The Tourism Company 2002). Earlier efforts to curtail this growth component of the sustainable development equation include the aforementioned 1993 quota on cruise ship arrivals (see p. 50) and a petition signed by 1 000 Cayman Islanders in the late 1980s calling for controlled growth, which led to the formation of a National Planning Committee in 1989 and its recommendation for a three-year moratorium on new hotel construction along Seven Mile Beach. Government accepted this, although condominiums, guesthouses and apartments were exempted along with extensions to existing hotels. The moratorium was lifted in 1993 due to pressure from the ailing construction industry (Wilkinson 1997).

The Draft Tourism Policy Framework of 2002 also recommends a cruise ship passenger cap of 9 200 per day (reflecting continuing concerns about this massive sector), and the limiting of planning permission for new hotels until a more desirable occupancy rate can be achieved. The authors of the Framework suggest in this latter context that the desire to control development among some influential tourism industry stakeholders may be due as much to concerns over low vacancy rates and stagnant stayover numbers as to concerns about the effects of congestion on the natural and socio-cultural wellbeing of the Cayman Islands. Accordingly, the potential for growing conflict between the tourism industry and the environmentalist lobby is high, since the latter supports quotas mainly because of concerns over the natural and socio-cultural environment, while the former is supportive mainly because of concerns about profitability arising from low occupancy rates and increasingly dissatisfied visitors. If stay-over numbers once again increase, then it is possible that the industry will not oppose the actual construction of approved and planned projects, while the environmentalist lobby will. The actual number and size of these potential new projects is not stated in the Framework, but their magnitude is indicated by the observation that the 1990s occupancy rates of 69 per cent and 52 per cent for hotels and apartments, respectively, could fall to an unsustainable 42 per cent and 36 per cent if all such units come to fruition without any significant increase in the current volume of stayover arrivals (The Tourism Company 2002). Each new project, therefore, could become a focus of conflict between the tourism industry and environmentalist lobbies if stayover arrivals start to increase once again. Other factors and developments that could lead to conflict include the continuing lack of a comprehensive protected area strategy that safeguards crucial habitat in the Central Mangrove Wetland and elsewhere, and the absence of an effective mechanism to compensate landowners for the loss of development rights (Burton 2001). Also contentious is an amendment in the building code at Seven Mile Beach that has increased the height limit of hotels and apartments from five to seven stories.

DISCUSSION AND CONCLUSIONS

The Cayman Islands provide a classic example of a situation where severe geographical disadvantages gave rise to the pursuit of economic innovations, in this case OFC activities and up-market international tourism, that have resulted in a high level of prosperity and economic development. Tourism emerged as a focus of the Cayman Islands economy in a policy environment characterized by a low level of conflict between parties that normally co-exist in a confrontational relationship, such as the environmentalist lobby on one hand, and the conventional tourism industry on the other. In large part, this resulted from common adherence – at first implicitly and later explicitly – to the concept of sustainable development, combined with common awareness of the pivotal role of tourism in creating and maintaining the dependency's exceptionally high standard of living. This arrangement was viable as long as the priorities of each group could be mutually accommodated through the formal and informal allocation of space (tourism concentrated mainly in the West Bay Peninsula), and the implementation of 'home turf' concessions where these were reasonable and/or in the interests of the groups dominant in that space. For example, the tourism industry was very amenable to, and often took the leadership role, in implementation of environmental measures (such as height restrictions, quotas on cruise ship passengers, regulations to protect coral reefs) that would improve the quality of the tourist experience in the West Bay Peninsula tourist strip. Similarly, there is no evidence that environmentalists were actively opposed to the establishment of low density, exclusive real estate development in other parts of Grand Cayman Island, or to tourist visits to attractions in these areas. Otherwise, the West Bay Peninsula was de facto the venue for pursuing the pro-growth impulse within sustainable development through an advocacy approach toward tourism, while the remaining parts of the dependency were reserved for the environmentalist, slow- or no-growth impulse.

Erosion of Consensus?

I argue that the Cayman Islands are now on the cusp of a situation where the spatial status quo outlined above will be increasingly violated, especially by tourism and real estate interests that are starting to expand beyond the congested West Bay Peninsula into the less developed portions of Grand Cayman Island. Confrontation and maneuvering by stakeholders grouped into ephemeral alliances is likely to increase in this kind of atmosphere, which exposes the contradictions inherent in the concept of sustainable development. Accordingly, the strategies described by Bryant and Bailey (1997) that are employed to exert control over the natural environment may become more evident. The first of these is to control the access of competing stakeholders to these natural resources, so that the benefits accrue mainly to the actor(s) exercising the control. This could involve lobbying by environmentalists to extend user quotas to all coral reefs as well as to sites such as Stingray City, and to restrict areas severely where dredging and infilling can occur. The second strategy is to control the sites at which environmental modifications are allowed to occur. The main option here for environmentalists is to push for the creation of high order protected areas in locations such as the Central Mangrove Wetland, so that they are not available for development or for certain types and intensities of tourist activity. A parallel initiative by groups such as the National Trust is to purchase sensitive habitat that can then be used to augment the main public protected area system. The third strategy is to seek control over the societal prioritization of environmental problems and projects. This could involve lobbying the government to place a higher priority on environmental protection than, for example, on improving the infrastructure to accommodate more tourists (which is what the tourism industry would probably support). Another means is to control government decisions through the political process, wherein it is possible that even more clearly 'pro-environment' and 'pro-business' political parties will emerge to contest future elections. Finally, environmental goals can be achieved through indirect 'discursive' means, or the attempted regulation of ideas by controlling the socially accepted version of events. Wherein it was previously possible for everyone to accept the idea of sustainable development (because of the reasons discussed above), we might expect increased conflict between each of the two dimensions of this concept. Environmentalists will cite issues of global warming and resource depletion to push for the public's support on the slow-growth approach, while the tourism industry and its allies will raise fears of unemployment and an eroding standard of living to gain popular support for measures to stimulate tourism.

The specter of a declining economy is an important ancillary factor in this purported new era of greater confrontation, since a government with extensive resources can simultaneously carry out measures that please a wide variety of stakeholders – for example, creating new protected areas as well as increasing marketing and infrastructure allocations for tourism. A cash-strapped government is more likely to favor one side or the other (depending on its own ideology), since reductions across the board may lead to disaffection across the board and the subsequent loss of a power base. While not to suggest that the prosperity of the Cayman Islands is in jeopardy, some indicators and factors merit attention. The GDP, for example, grew by just 2 per cent in 2001, down from 3.2 per cent in 2000, largely as a consequence of stagnation in the number of stayover arrivals. Concurrently, the overall deficit increased to US$74 million in 2001 while overall public debt increased by 33 per cent. In the late 1990s, the good image of the Cayman Islands as an OFC was shaken by accusations of money laundering, which caused the dependency to be placed on the OECD's Financial Action Task Force list of monitored jurisdictions (from which it has since been removed) (EIU 2002b). A more systemic problem is the realization that the hyper-mobility of capital operates in both directions, thereby making an OFC such as the Cayman Islands extremely vulnerable to the flight of capital, particularly as more jurisdictions in the Caribbean and elsewhere are pursuing the OFC option (Roberts 1995). The same issue of mobility applies even more ominously to the tourism sector, as demonstrated by the devastating impact of real or perceived terrorist threats, or more prosaically by the capricious nature of the tourist market and its sensitivity to issues such as perceived congestion, over-pricing, customer service, etc. In this latter sense, the frank comments about visitor perceptions contained in the Draft Tourism Policy Framework should be the cause of much concern.

A second factor that will affect this new environment is the influence of external forces. As described above, successive Cayman Islands governments have sought to increase their local decision-making autonomy while clinging tenaciously to their status as a UK Overseas Territory. Recent moves on the part of the British government, however, suggest the intention of the latter to intervene more actively in the internal affairs of its dependencies. In its Partnership for Progress White Paper, the Foreign and Commonwealth Office (1999) states that 'Britain has the right to expect the highest standards of probity, law and order, good government and observance of Britain's international commitments'. While this was largely motivated by perceptions of abuse within the growing number of territories pursuing the OFC option, many of these commitments are also related to the natural environment. These include the Convention on Biological Diversity, the Protocol concerning Specially Protected Areas and Wildlife (SPAW) in the Wider Caribbean Region, and the United Nations Conference on the Law of the Sea (UNCLOS), which includes a framework on protecting and conserving marine resources. The aforementioned Environment Charter (see p. 52) is an outcome of this White Paper that obligates Overseas Territory governments to develop 'appropriate, applicable and affordable environmental policies, legislation and standards'. The UK Overseas Territories Conservation Forum (UKOTCF) is a very active non-governmental organization that serves as a watchdog to ensure compliance with the Charter within Britain's dependencies. It remains to be seen whether this increased level of British involvement (or 'interference' to its critics) will increase the currently low level of support for independence.

In conclusion, it may well be argued that the Cayman Islands are anomalous as a case study because of their unique historical and geographical circumstances, and that little in the way of broader application can therefore be attempted. This may be true, but it is also the case that a growing number of small tropical island-entities in the contemporary era of globalization are attempting to emulate the Cayman Islands and the somewhat similar experience of Bermuda through the dual pursuit of international tourism and offshore finance. As these attempts progress, it will be interesting to explore the differences and similarities relative to the Cayman experience, particularly in entities more impacted by the plantation heritage (for example Antigua and Barbuda, St. Vincent and the Grenadines, and Seychelles). At the very least, the Cayman Islands case study contributes to the rich array of experiences that characterizes the political ecology of the world's tropical islands and their tourism industries.

REFERENCES

Allen, W. (1992), 'Increased dangers to Caribbean marine ecosystems: cruise ship anchors and intensified tourism threatens reefs', *BioScience*, **42**, 330–35.

Amit, V. (2001), 'A clash of vulnerabilities: citizenship, labor, and expatriacy in the Cayman Island', *American Ethnologist*, **28** (3), 574–94.

Anglo-American Commission (1945), *Caribbean Tourist Trade: A Regional Approach*, Washington DC: Anglo-American Commission.

Blume, H. (1974), *The Caribbean Islands*, London: Longman.

Bryant, R.L. and S. Bailey (1997), *Third World Political Ecology*, London: Routledge.

Burton, F. (2001), 'Raising awareness on wetlands of international importance in Cayman', in M. Pienkowski (ed.), *CALPE 2000: Linking the Fragments of Paradise: An International Conference on Environmental Conservation in Small Territories*, Gibraltar: UK Overseas Territories Conservation Forum, pp. 45–7.

Butler, R. (1980), 'The concept of a tourist area cycle of evolution: implications for management of resources', *Canadian Geographer*, **24**, 5–12.

Cayman Islands (1914), *Report for 1913–1914*.

Cayman Net News (2001), 'National Trust asserts itself as appeal withheld', *Cayman Net News, No. 97, 31 July–2 August*, available at: http://www.caymannetnews.com /Archive/Archivepercent20Articles/Augustpercent202001/Issuepercent2097/Natio nalpercent20Trust.html.

Caribbean Environment Programme (CEP) (1999), 'Status of Protected Areas in the Wider Caribbean Region', *CEP Technical Report, No. 36*, Kingston, Jamaica: UNEP – Caribbean Environment Programme.

Clark, S. (1952), *All the Best in the Caribbean*, New York: Dodd, Mead and Co.

Department of Tourism (2002), *International Tourism Arrivals, Air and Sea*, available at: http://www.caymanislands.ky/statistics/pop.asp?file=arrivals_inc/arri vals_current2.asp.

Ebanks, G. and P. Bush (1990), 'The Cayman Islands: A case study for the establishment of marine conservation legislation in small island countries', in M. Miller and J. Auyong (eds), *Proceedings of the 1990 Congress on Coastal and Marine Tourism*, Volume I, Newport, OR: National Coastal Resources Research and Development Institute, pp. 197–203.

Economist Intelligence Unit (EIU) (2002a), *Country Profile 2002: Barbados, British Virgin Islands, Cayman Islands, Netherlands Antilles, Aruba*, London: The Economist Intelligence Unit.

Economist Intelligence Unit (EIU) (2002b), *Country Report 2002: Barbados, British Virgin Islands, Cayman Islands, Netherlands Antilles, Aruba*, London: The Economist Intelligence Unit.

Foreign and Commonwealth Office (1999), *Partnership for Progress – Britain and the Overseas Territories, (Cm 4264)*, London: The Stationary Office.

George, S. and A. Clark (1998), 'Tourism educational and training policies in developing countries: a case study of the Cayman Islands (Caribbean)', *Journal of Third World Studies*, **15** (1), 205–20.

Gerrard, A. (1956), *The Cayman Islands: Information for Prospective Visitors*, George Town: The Commissioner's Office.

Gore, M. (2001), 'The use of environment protection funds in the Overseas Territories: the Cayman Environment Fund: original objectives', in M. Pienkowski (ed.), *CALPE 2000: Linking the Fragments of Paradise: An International Conference on Environmental Conservation in Small Territories*, Gibraltar: UK Overseas Territories Conservation Forum, pp. 118–9.

Jafari, J. (2001), 'The scientification of tourism', in V.L. Smith and M. Brent (eds), *Hosts and Guests Revisited: Tourism Issues of the 21st Century*, New York: Cognizant Communication Corporation, pp. 28–41.

Johnson, V. (2001), *As I See It: How Cayman Became a Leading Financial Centre*, Sussex, UK: The Book Guild.

Roberts, S. (1995), 'Small place, big money: the Cayman Islands and the international financial system', *Economic Geography*, **71** (3), 237–56.

Shackley, M. (1998), '"Stingray City" – managing the impact of underwater tourism in the Cayman Islands', *Journal of Sustainable Tourism*, **6** (4), 328–38.

Smith, S. (1988), 'Cruise ships: a serious threat to coral reefs and associated organisms', *Ocean and Shoreline Management*, **11**, 231–48.

The Tourism Company (2002), *Focus for the Future: A Draft Tourism Policy Framework for the Cayman Islands*, London: The Tourism Company.

Tratalos, J. and T. Austin (2001), 'Impacts of recreational SCUBA diving on coral communities of the Caribbean island of Grand Cayman', *Biological Conservation*, **102** (1), 67–75.

UK Overseas Territories Conservation Forum (UKOTCF) (2001), *Environment Charter: Cayman Islands*, available at: http://www.ukotcf.org/OTcharters/images/cayman.gif.

United Nations Environment Programme (UNEP) (1998), *Island Directory: Cayman Islands*, available at: http://www.unep.ch/islands/ISE.htm.

United Nations Educational, Scientific and Cultural Organization (UNESCO) (1998), *Grand Cayman, British West Indies. Environment and Development in Coastal Regions and in Small Islands*, available at: http://www.unesco.org/csi/pub/papers/bush.htm.

World Commission on Environment and Development (WCED) (1987), *Our Common Future*, Oxford: Oxford University Press.

Weaver, D. (1990), 'Grand Cayman Island and the resort cycle concept', *Journal of Travel Research*, **29** (2), 9–15.

Weaver, D. and L. Lawton (1999), 'Sustainable tourism: a critical analysis', *Research Report No. 1*, Gold Coast, Australia: CRC for Sustainable Tourism.

Wilkinson, P. (1997), *Tourism Policy & Planning: Case Studies from the Commonwealth Caribbean*, New York: Cognizant Communication Corporation.

3.   The Political Ecology of Tourism in the Commonwealth of Dominica

Trista Patterson and Luis Rodriguez

INTRODUCTION

It has long been recognized that small island developing states (SIDS) are confronted with a unique array of developmental challenges and opportunities. Their smaller scale often means that the many forms of everyday civic participation themselves constitute national level discourse. The selective identification and representation of environmental problems and crises is itself a political process (Blakie and Brookfield 1987; Bryant 1998). The complex and dynamic nature of island life means that problems embedded in political and economic structures are difficult to understand in cross-sectional, or discrete, analyses. The importance of understanding the community as a whole is often lost in polarizations that emphasize single issues and complexities that reinforce the status quo.

In response, the study of political ecology has sought to widen the range of acceptable scientific questions by testing for the frequency and disparity of asymmetrical costs and benefits following from development processes. The aim is to improve the lot of marginalized or socially disadvantaged groups by highlighting conflicts, disparities, and the political and human–environmental interactions that drive them, while challenging the path–dependent nature within each dynamic. Such consequences have been documented at various scales (Bryant 1992; Bryant 1998; Bryant and Bailey 1997); from local considerations such as threatened livelihoods (Bryant and Bailey 1997), indigenous knowledge bases (Bryant 1998), gender and household resource control (Rocheleau et al. 1996; Schroeder 1993), to broader economies, ecologies, and policies between national (Peluso 1992), and (to a lesser extent) internationally relevant institutions (see Bryant 1998). This chapter takes such a scale-based approach to the political ecology of tourism in the Caribbean Commonwealth of Dominica. It focuses on issues that routinely and forcefully engage the island population but which have escaped analytical discourse or examination to date, and whose persistence suggest they will widely influence the future allocation of tourism costs and benefits.

Dominica is a Caribbean, mountainous and volcanic island of 750 km^2, located in the Lesser Antilles (Figure 3.1). It is the largest, least populated isle (94.8 persons per km^2) of the Windward Island chain, with a population of 70 158 (2001 census). Unemployment estimates range from 15 to 25 per cent of the workforce and 27 per cent of island residents live in extreme poverty, unable to meet basic needs (PAHO 1999). Such conditions demand that policy makers pursue national strategies with the aim of invigorating the island economy, and tourism is seen as the principal way of doing this.

Non-market contributions to welfare on the island are great, in large part because of the successful human–social and human–environmental relationships that have been developed over long extents of time. Inevitably, as tourism brings about rapid changes, unintended consequences have arisen. Negative social and environmental impacts from the visits are evidencing themselves directly, from the development of tourism infrastructure/services and utilization of tourism attractions and amenities (DNBSAP 2002), and indirectly as impacts impinge upon ecosystem goods and services or slowly uproot culturally embedded forms of sharing and social cohesion. These threaten the knowledge, culture, and resource bases that make direct and substantial contributions to Dominican well-being and to the longer standing economic disposition of the island.

RESEARCH METHODS

This chapter presents information collected during a two-year study initiated for the University of Maryland/University of the West Indies atelier workshop 'Sustainable Tourism in Small Islands of the Caribbean: Lessons from Dominica'. Rapid assessment data–gathering techniques, interviews with governmental and private individuals, and development of a dynamic model (Patterson et al. 2003) preceded extensive on-site visits, stakeholder consultation meetings and expert panel discussions, which resulted in over 50 hours of tape-recorded interviews. Issues prominent in the interviews, consultations and national discourse, yet absent in the quantitative studies following from the workshop (Patterson et al. 2003; Rodriguez et al. 2003; Thurlow 2002), receive special consideration for the political ecology analysis at hand.

Our aim is to shed light on the relationships within and between economic, social and natural systems, and the dynamics determining the distribution of costs and benefits, including past and present class and ethnic conflicts, access to trade venues, and exercise of power in terms of authority, markets

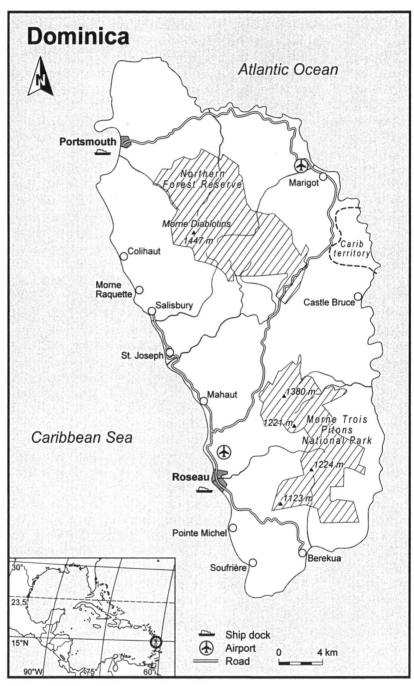

Figure 3.1   Dominica

and institutions. Analysis is realized at three scales; the domestic scale focuses on the appropriation of market and non-market values in the Carib Territory, and examines the role of social capital in tourism outcomes for gender, land tenure and micro-enterprise in Dominica. The trans–national scale explores three issues: formal and informal institutions with respect to foreign development, the effect of cruise lobbies and foreign ownership of infrastructure, as evidenced by increased imports to satisfy non-native consumptive habits; and finally, current foreign investment incentives, perception of environmental risk and local involvement in tourism development projects. The international scale focuses on the history of Dominica's voting position in the International Whaling Commission to illustrate the interrelatedness between tourism and politics at both national and international levels.

ISLAND OVERVIEW

With black volcanic beaches, waterfalls, and over 20 per cent of its surface allocated to national parks and protected areas (CEP 2000), Dominica distinguishes itself from nearby 'sand, sun and surf' islands with the title 'The Nature Island of the Caribbean'. The rainforest environment, scuba diving, whale watching, birding, extensive hiking trails and the opportunity to visit the only remaining Kalinago (Carib) Indian Territory in the Caribbean attract a particular set of tourists.

Nature-based assets contribute to tourism prospects and the lives of inhabitants alike. Large portions of islanders' welfare are due to a broad range of natural capital commodities not accounted for in Gross Domestic Product (GDP); those range from food and building materials to elements of cultural heritage and national identity. In addition, Dominica's social systems are characterized by the persistence of widespread, high quality social networks, which generate many positive externalities that promote well-being (Collier 1998; Narayan and Pritchett 1997). This provides a necessary complement to natural capital, especially benefiting the most vulnerable members of the population. Such positive effects are reflected in World Development Index (WDI) statistics: age expectancy is high (74 years) and infant mortality is low (8.75 per 1 000 live births) for the region, despite the island's average annual per capita income of only US$2,800 (World Bank 2000).

While the tourism sector has optimistic growth prospects, greater foreign investment is projected to increasingly expatriate profits and subject greater portions of the island economy tò volatile global economic dynamics (NDC 2001; Cater 1996). The particular vulnerability of the island's environment to anthropogenic impacts and environmental hazards suggests that any desirable economic change on the island would maintain the structure and function of the ecological and social systems that support the well-being of Dominican citizens.

GEOGRAPHY, ECONOMY AND TOURISM HISTORY

Dominica is politically divided in ten parishes. The capital Roseau (21 000 inhabitants) and the cities of Portsmouth in the north and Soufriere in the south are located along the more sheltered western coast. Sometimes called 'a patchwork of enclaves', the communities of the mountainous interior and the eastern coast were extremely isolated until roads improved communication and transport between the east and west coasts in 1956 (Honychurch 1995a; Trouillot 1988). There are currently 780 kilometers of road, half of which are unpaved; the limited road network has curbed the penetration of tourism into many village communities, especially those of the highlands.

The Dominican economy is characterized by high-energy costs, based on local hydroelectric (52.2 per cent) and imported diesel (47.8 per cent), though the potential for other energy sources (micro-hydro, geothermal and so on) is substantial (G. Flomenhoeft 2003, Gund Institute for Ecological Economics, personal communication; IMF 2000). Tourism (US$41.6 million), manufacturing (US$24.1 million), banana exports (US$14.4 million), and an offshore services sector ('economic citizenship', offshore banking and internet gaming) (US$3.6 million) are the largest contributions to GDP (Dominica budget report 1999). Inflation has averaged a moderate 2 per cent per year and the EC dollar conversion is pegged (US$1 = EC$2.7). Economic growth is low (0.9 per cent per year) and outstanding debts are high in relation to other island states in the Eastern Caribbean, representing 65 per cent of GDP, while debt servicing accounts for 17 per cent of the government's budget (Dominica budget report 1999). Dominica's economy is highly vulnerable to global market fluctuations, as well as to severe weather events such as hurricanes. The export economy is in turmoil due to World Trade Organization (WTO) rulings against the colonial preference system of the United Kingdom (Dominica's former colonial ruler). As a result, the trade balance has fallen from US$-52.7 million in 1995 to US$-68.7 million in 1999.

In contrast, the tourism sector has substantially increased in recent years. Increasing arrivals have been drawn by government initiatives, foreign aid lenders, the efforts of enterprising Dominican and foreign private investors, and multinational cruise conglomerates' foreign aid, which have sought to take advantage of increasing global tourism demand. In raw terms,

Dominica's cruise tourism visitors (202 000) have increased by almost 300 per cent in the past eight years, while stay-over visits (73 500) have increased by nearly 100 per cent over the same period; primarily from other Caribbean nations (60 per cent), the United States (20 per cent) and Europe (16 per cent) (CSO 1999). Average stay-over visits were a mean of 9 days, with a mode of 4–7 days (CSO 1999). The island had 867 rooms in 1999, 563 rooms in hotels, and the remainder in family-owned guesthouses and cottages. A relatively high (56 per cent) percentage of tourists stay in private residences. Sixty-nine per cent of Dominica's tourists arrive by air, the majority landing at Melville Hall (82 per cent) in the northeast, with smaller 'island-hopper' planes arriving at Canefield airport, just north of Roseau. Dominica relies on trans-Atlantic flights, as wind direction and mountainous approaches mean that neither airport is able to accept international jet arrivals. Several attempts have been made to finance an international jet airport, although this is seen as infeasible by international lending institutions (IMF 2000). The island has two cruise ship berths, one in Roseau (98 per cent of cruise arrivals) and another in Portsmouth. A small number of Caribbean resident tourists access the island via ferry from Guadeloupe, Martinique and Marie-Gallant.

Time constraints limit cruise ship visitations inland, as many tourists are unwilling to risk an untimely return to their ship. Most visits are thus concentrated at a small number of intensively used coast and waterfall sites. While independent vendors of souvenirs, crafts and refreshments have established themselves along 'tourism corridors' between these sites, vendors at the primary site parking lots (national parks etc.) are highly regulated by the National Development Corporation (NDC), a public organization responsible for tourism management. Meanwhile, the NDC has made attempts at 'community tourism', assigning the management of peripheral site kiosks to various village councils. These have been met with mixed success, as they are subject to the mercurial strengths and weaknesses of village politics (Thurlow 2002).

NATURAL HISTORY, VULNERABILITIES TO TOURISM

Dominica's rich flora includes 155 families, 672 genera and 1 226 species of vascular plants including 11 endemic species such *Sabinea carinalis*, the national flower – the island has the most diverse wildlife of all small Eastern Caribbean islands. All faunal groups are present, with bird and bat species particularly abundant. Two endemic parrot species, the imperial parrot or 'Sisserou' (*Amazona imperialis*) and the red-neck parrot 'Jaco' (*Amazona arausiaca*) are both considered threatened and are specially protected under Dominican law. Extensive plantations were never as pervasive on Dominica as other islands, nor has the island been targeted for large hotel or enclave resort construction; as a result, natural vegetation still dominates 65 per cent of the landmass. Biome classifications from the 1940s (elfin-montane, canopy rainforest, dry littoral forest, coastal shrub) have remained largely relevant, with rainforest still covering 42.5 per cent of the total surface (DNBSAP 2002; Hodge 1943). However, fragmentation and reduction of forest area still generate adverse effects on wildlife habitat, water quality and quantity, and soil retention. Biodiversity loss and environmental damage are most evident in areas with concentrated human activity, such as estuaries and near-shore areas. The invasion of the lemon grass *Cymbopogon citratus*, coupled with widespread burning, has halted succession over large areas, especially in the dry littoral and coastal forests, and where soils are disturbed by erosion or construction of housing, hotels and tourism facilities. Colonization thus presents an acute threat to island biodiversity for over 50 per cent of the land area (Patterson 2001).

The Lesser Antilles chain is distinguished ecologically and topographically by its volcanic origin, in contrast to the uplifted limestone karsts that form most Caribbean islands. Dominica has one of the highest concentrations of active volcanoes in the world (8 in only 750 km^2), with harm to island residents predicted within the next hundred years (Honychurch 2001; Shepherd et al. 2001). However, the most common and historically most significant natural hazards in Dominica have been tropical storms and hurricanes. As was well-documented following storms Hugo and Lenny, hurricanes can cause accelerated erosion to coastlines, and can damage physical features with high amenity values, such as beaches and reefs. The island's human population (Lugo et al. 1983), agricultural production (Grossman 1998), terrestrial biota (CCA 1991) and reefs (Hughes 1994; Wilkenson 2000) are seriously impacted approximately every 15 years. Some studies have shown that Dominica's forests are relatively resilient if structural composition is maintained, but as logging diminishes windbreak capacity, storms can spur changes in forest structure, species composition and increases in forest gap sizes (Lugo et al. 1983). Hurricane readiness and fear of increased susceptibility to severe storm damage (resulting from global warming) continues to be a broad public concern (B.M. John 2001, Dominica Environmental Coordinating Unit, personal communication), but until recently no disaster preparation planning had been developed (Honychurch 1995a; Ward 1980).

Tourism-driven development has had unintended consequences for Dominica. The island's volcanic origins attract tourists to the 'boiling' lake, mineral baths and 'champagne' scuba diving, while the rainforest is prized for bird watching and extensive hiking trails. Much of the island is categorized at high (37 per cent) and moderately high (20 per cent) erosion risk (DNBSAP

2002); more than US$117,000 annually is spent clearing landslides from roads (CCA 1991). Damage along tourism-dedicated trails is ongoing, and shoreline tourism infrastructure is particularly susceptible. Constructions of harbors, marinas, airports and hotels have had particularly severe environmental impacts for islands with narrow coastal shelves such as Dominica (Widfeldt 1996; Wilkenson 2000). While rapid coastal drop-offs make the island popular with dive tourists, corals and other sea life are limited to near-shore depths, and are thus more vulnerable to effluent discharges. With some areas of the island receiving 400 inches of rain annually, high discharge levels of eroded sediments, toxins and untreated sewage have caused visibly apparent damage (Christian 1992). One of the primary impacts to local marine biodiversity is quarrying for concrete sand (the majority going to tourism infrastructure); moreover, measures to protect that infrastructure (for example, modifications of river groins, retaining wall and sea wall structures) have caused severe erosion to beach and recreation areas such as Bell Hall and Douglas Bay (DNBSAP 2002). The anthropogenic effect of draining estuaries and wetlands for hotels (for example, Cabrits freshwater wetland) has changed the ecology of several areas by varying salinity and affecting nursery and refuge sites for several species.

ISLAND RACE, COLOR, CLASS AND ETHNO-CULTURAL ORIENTATIONS

The social and environmental processes occurring throughout the history of the area impel the degree to which those groups have had authority and hegemony, thus influencing the empowerment or disempowerment of stakeholders (Blakie and Brookfield 1987). Thus, distinct political, racial, and cultural groups have arisen over time in Dominica, controlling access to resources and the way they are used. A contemporary tendency is to view tourism as the great social equalizer, presenting win–win scenarios in which cultural differences are seen as positive attributes rather than sources of potential conflict. Such optimism obscures subtle, widespread and pervasive issues that influence tourism development trajectories (Duffy 2001). Failure to consider difficult historical realities (imperialism, slavery, ongoing racism, among others) in Dominica's collective experience risks misunderstanding current power relations, and preempts opportunities for more equitable future outcomes.

The Caribbean has been a site of human settlement for over 4 000 years. Between 3 000 BC to 400 BC the Ortoroid people controlled the area, followed by the Arawak tribes. From 1400 AD onward, the Kalinagos, or

Carib Indians controlled the area (Honychurch 1995a, pp. 15–18). Aided by the rugged island terrain and vegetation, Kalinagos held off colonizers from the island for 300 years after European 'discovery'. With the Treaty of Aix-la-Chapelle (1748) Britain and France agreed to leave the island to the Amerindians. Yet foreign aggressors continued to arrive, and by 1760 most Caribs had been driven to a portion of the northeast coast (Boromé 1972; Campbell 2002). Three more disputes between France and Britain between 1756 and 1783 volleyed possession of the island between the two colonial powers. The treaty of Versailles (1783) assigned Britain final possession, but language (English and French-Creole), bureaucratic formations and social customs evidence the island's mixed colonial history.

While much of Dominica's land area was deemed unsuitable for plantations due to topography or poor soil fertility, like other plantation-based colonial societies, the island's economy was formed around inexpensive African slave labor, a socio–economic system that only ended with emancipation in 1834. The period of British domination marked an explosion in the Caribbean slave trade, and in the five years following the Seven Years War alone, over 41 000 enslaved West Africans were brought to the island especially for sugar plantations (Rogozinski 1992, pp. 122–4). However, many escaped to the forested mountains and by 1785, thirteen self-sufficient subsistence communities of runaway slaves (called *maroons*) had formed in the highlands (Honychurch 1995b). This self-sufficient ethic, coupled with loyalty conflicts between *maroon-* and plantation communities, contributed to a tendency of some villages to remain isolated from the island's economy over time, and provides some explanation as to why so many today remain physically and economically removed from tourism as a marketplace.

When the slave trade ended in 1834 and over 14 000 slaves were freed, many took up legal smallholdings or squatted on Crown lands. Unlike other Caribbean islands, a portion of land (deemed less suitable for agriculture) was placed in land-trust for the Caribs in 1860, although the Carib Territory was not officially established until 1903. This territory includes 1 480 hectares on the eastern mountains, under authority of the Carib chief. The territory maintains a system of communal land tenure that has existed since pre-Columbian times and is probably the only substantial remnant of communal land in the region today (Caribbean Conservation Association 1991). In contrast, large estates outside Carib Territory have been divided and sold since independence in 1978; the increasing demand for land has resulted in government distribution of Crown lands to farmers. Nevertheless, forest encroachment is prevalent, though shifting cultivation was prohibited in 1946. Illicit land occupation is still a source of dispute for those maintaining subsistence gardens in the forest, but also for permission to occupy the 'queen's chain' (coastline currently held by the government), which is widely seen as a politicized issue (J. Tonge 2001, Planning Division, personal communication).

The use of force, the exercise of colonial status and social custom largely maintained social stratification in Dominica prior to 1823. Thereafter the balance of power shifted, and postcolonial power was transferred to non-ruling, non-economic elites to a greater degree than on other Caribbean islands (Green 1995). The co-existence of peasant-enclave (quasi or non-market), and plantation (market) modes of production in Dominica influenced the degree of cultural and racial integration. This is not suggesting that racial differentiation is absent in contemporary Dominica. Racial disparities in landholding persist into the present day (Trouillot 1988). Differentiation in village social structure contrasts the social stability of the longstanding 'peasant ridge villages' with the 'post-plantation valley villages', which suggests that historical patterns of race and class continue to influence contemporary economic development, including tourism (Honychurch 2001).

At the national level, debates about tourism development frequently polarize around class differences, especially the broad rift between Afro-Creole elites and the poor. The former actors advocate specialization, high standards, and licensing while the latter tend to lobby for increased basic employment and improvement of community level coordination to bring tourism enterprises to villages (Thurlow 2002). Caribbean societies exhibit disparities among islanders and foreigners, currently driving many racial or nationalist aspects of landholding and investment. Class and empowerment issues have also focused on race; prominent examples that affected tourism development are events associated with the Black Power Movement in the 1970s. Coupled with the conflict in Grenada, disputes promoted an international perception of political instability that limited tourism development in Dominica for more than a decade.

POLITICAL ECOLOGY ON THREE SCALES: DOMESTIC, TRANS-NATIONAL AND INTERNATIONAL DYNAMICS

The description of economic, ecological and social conditions outlined in the previous sections provide us with the background needed to examine the dynamics of political ecology of tourism in Dominica on three different scales: the domestic scale, which refers to interactions between Dominican actors within the borders of Dominica, the trans-national scale, which refers to dynamics among Dominican and foreign actors, and the international scale, which refers to issues at the interface between Dominican national, foreign and global policy. Within this section, a set of relevant examples is developed to explain the dynamics on each scale.

Domestic Scale Dynamics I: Appropriation of Value from the Carib Territory

The current tourism system of visits to the Carib territory illustrates a common paradox within tourism. Dominica's poorest community (de Albuquerque and McElroy 1999; PAHO 1999), is itself a tourist attraction, and contributes to the distinctive images promoted by the island. Meanwhile, potential Carib guides, vendors and others are dissociated from opportunities of equitable tourism earnings. The great majority of tourists to the territory are stay-over visitors who lodge outside the territory and arrange visits through hotel tour operators or with city taxis. Cruise ship visitors purchase guide and transport services from cruise ship franchises, or negotiate arrangements on the dock, paying around US$60 for a 6-hour tour. No entry fee to the territory is charged to tourists or tour companies; moreover, taxi drivers, tour guides and Carib vendors interviewed estimate the average visitor spends less than US$0.55 while visiting the territory.

Tourism actors appropriate economic value of indigenous heritage primarily through commodity, amenity and marketing values (Lal and Young 2000; Zeppel 2000). The primary commodity value is through souvenirs, mainly the sale of handicrafts such as baskets woven of the *larouma* reed or bags made of *heliconia* leaves. Traditional weaving is a cultural remnant of a social system which centered on fishing as the primary Carib economic production, when commodities were held in collective, and personal property and property rights were not culturally embedded in Carib society (Honychurch 1995b). When a designation in the 1860s relegated the Carib territory to an area of particularly dangerous sea-access, primary economic production shifted to increasingly individual pursuits: agriculture, forestry and (since the 1980s) tourism. As established patterns of economic production have altered over time, respondents report delayed, but concurrent changes in culturally embedded forms of social control (this is aspects of dispute resolution, division of labor, ritual practice, the centrality of elders in the community and overall wealth distribution) (Lipsanen 2001). Meanwhile, education, employment and logistics place territory residents at the bottom of the occupational hierarchies in each sector (de Albuquerque and McElroy 1999), suggesting limits on the advancement opportunities offered by economic transition of this form. Barring attention for these conditions, net social costs may outweigh net social benefits in future growth of the tourism industry.

With regard to amenity values associated with Carib territory tourism, such as hiking, fishing or access to specific sites on territory land, no fees are currently assessed. Some have questioned the practicality of instituting such fees, citing fear of discouraging tourism visitation. Meanwhile, tourist access to the territory brings costs to local residents that are more difficult to articulate in terms of dollar value (for example, photographing residents without permission). As one young respondent explained, he did not want to be compensated by money, but instead expressed the desired compensation using the word 'respect'.

Marketing values (such as the use of images to promote sales) are a third means of appropriating economic value from the territory. From web pages to tourism investment brochures, Carib images are more likely to be found promoting the entire island rather than the territory itself. Images of Caribs have been present since the first representations of tourism on the island, in 'decent dress' (1960s), shirtless, with drums and grass skirts (1970s), or in reproduction of the traditional dance costume (1980s). The rapid shifts in such portrayals illustrate a primary challenge to Caribs: their images are appropriated, made 'trendy' and promoted, yet their social status remains politically and socially disempowered and far removed from the active tourism marketplace.

There are many difficulties with articulating a distinctly Carib vision for the territory and integrating Carib knowledge in tourism development. Many Caribs perceive conservation and tourist efforts as uncoupled in current efforts, and programs initiated by non-Caribs all too frequently fail to adequately reflect a sense of 'Caribness' (G. Joseph 2001, Carib Chief, personal communication). This sentiment is reflected by comments regarding the Caribbean Development Bank funded 'Carib model village' constructed during the interview period: 'If this is a Carib place, why did they get men from Roseau to build it? . . . It is just political corruption, wasting money'. Another respondent referred to the fact that involvement in the Carib village was itself a politicized process, citing the exclusive involvement of certain individuals over others. The institution of 'standards' (limiting the market to select producers) was seen to conflict with communal ideals: 'This village won't be Carib, it is just a place for a few families . . . only some get to participate'. Concerns have been expressed with regard to the extent that non-Carib, or non-Dominican development can ever meet the full extent of the culturally relevant needs of the territory population.

Concomitant with changes in the market values already mentioned, discontinuities among economic, social and ecological cycles have also brought about declines in the stocks of non-marketed forms of capital in the Carib Territory. Natural capital such as ecosystem goods and services (Costanza et al. 1997) and cultural capital, understood as the set of attitudes, practices and beliefs that are fundamental to the functioning of a particular society's system of values and customs (Throsby 1999), are in decline. Combined, they support territory residents and continued tourism visitation alike, yet some losses can be directly traced to tourism developments.

The decline of the stock of natural capital in the territory is especially apparent in the prevalence of bare and compacted soil, and changes in the vegetation patterns in areas subjected to anthropogenic stress. Ecosystem services such as soil formation and retention, water supply and regulation, habitat and genetic resources, are particularly threatened due to intensive agriculture, forest burning and modifications of riparian areas in the territory. The most common explanation is that the Carib tribe members are not able to hold land title to what is considered collective land property. To be more explicit, the disruption of the traditional resource management systems and the breakdown of community-based institutions have altered group boundaries and organizations that regulate the use of the ecosystem goods and services. This has disrupted those social functions which previously served as monitoring activities, conflict resolution capabilities, and which reinforced both trust between the members, and the rules and norms that regulated resource uses. In the communal lands of the Carib Territory this most typically occurs when one land tenant leaves the land for a period and others immediately assume the use of it. Rapid tenure turnover eliminates most of the immediate incentives to following crop rotation calendars, corresponding fallow periods, or costly soil conservation measures. Communal lands cannot be used as collateral for loans, and as education and occupation levels are low with respect to other Dominicans (Pezeron 1993), this compounds the difficulty of securing capital for land improvements or other investments.

Changes associated with tourism development may prove to have devastating effects on natural capital stocks, setting the ecosystem on an irreversible trajectory, especially when fire is employed for forest clearance, and when land use includes soil and vegetation disturbance. Roads are frequent vectors for such changes, and the first asphalted road to be cut through the territory (1970) was no exception. Occurring simultaneously with forest and riparian area removal, the soil that formed the base of the paved area was brought from other areas of the island. According to territory residents, this soil brought with it seeds for two particularly persistent grasses that were not present in the reserve before the road was built. When burning (a traditional means of controlling small areas of bush) was regularly applied to the grasses, winds frequently spread the fires out of control, while the roots of the grasses persisted.

Large physical infrastructure projects designed to assist tourism access are often not accompanied by ecological or social contingency plans to deal with externalities. Respondents to a National Biodiversity Strategy and Planning (NBSP) consultation reported widespread losses of species abundance and diversity in territory gardens and in the wild. The loss of trees and riparian vegetation has precipitated a loss of streams, especially in the last 50 years, while discontinuation of government–supported soil–conservation programs has greatly increased sediment runoffs to streams and coastal areas that support Carib fisheries. The changes noted in the NBSP consultations can be seen as evidence that Carib social institutions are failing and the current configuration of the Carib Territory representation in the Government of Dominica is inadequate to preserve their natural and cultural patrimony.

Moreover, research conducted by the Environmental Coordinating Unit suggests that traditional knowledge bases are declining, especially among Carib youth. Parents report interest in cultural traditions such as Carib dance, language or craft making is atypical among their children. Many young people express enthusiasm towards tour guiding careers, although most who do so will need to leave the territory to pursue their goals in Roseau or Portsmouth. When individuals leave the territory to seek work elsewhere, human capital losses are joined with a loss of cultural capital. Such cumulative effects jeopardize traditional knowledge and environmental literacy of the Carib population, further endangering the territory's ecosystem goods and services. Environmental literacy is still higher among Caribs than their Afro-Creole counterparts (Honychurch 2001), generating differences in the perception and valuation of ecosystem goods and services between the two groups (Rodriguez et al. 2003). Unfortunately, despite high awareness of disappearing species and changes to landscape and ecology, formal education rates are lower for Caribs than any other group in Dominica (de Albuquerque and McElroy 1999) and this underscores the concurrent need to control human capital losses and disparities, among ecological and cultural concerns.

The current structure of power in the Carib Territory and the configuration of indigenous and governmental institutions are insufficient to deal with the profound and difficult problems facing the territory. A Carib chief, a parliamentary representative and the Carib council serve the primary governing bodies of the territory although the Government of Dominica is responsible for the overall planning and development of the Carib reserve. Unfortunately, with the exception of occasional visits from agriculture extension officers, national assistance in resource management is not provided from outside the reserve. The Carib territory is considered to be outside the jurisdiction of the Forest Service, and exceptionally few environmental or enforcement officers visit the territory.

The process by which economic, public and indigenous institutions collectively deal with tensions between individual and communal needs will eventually also influence the environmental impact of tourism on the territory. The lack of environmental, forestry, silviculture and waste collection/treatment services, is a large barrier to controlling the impacts of an expanded tourist visitation to the territory, and is a barrier to increasing tourism returns to one of the poorest areas of the country that also has real economic potential. Solid waste collection for toxics and non-degradable waste is inadequate to non-existent. When profits accrue, they do so to non-Caribs, while the territory is left to bear the impact costs to natural and cultural capital without the support of government services. An effective tourism policy for the Commonwealth of Dominica depends on its ability to include effective investment in the Carib territory as an asset, and to adapt policies for the needs of a communal and culturally sovereign part of the country. Effective institutions operating in a culturally relevant way for the Caribs will preserve the Carib culture as a cultural heritage asset for future generations of residents and visitors.

Domestic Scale Dynamics II: Gender, Social Networks and Land Tenure

It has been estimated that less than 240 km^2 (32 per cent) of Dominica's terrestrial area is under cultivation or inhabited (Trouillot 1988), most of which is not considered suitable for enclave tourism development. The island exhibits a combination of private and commonly held tenures, which contributes to asymmetrical political ecology outcomes. The costs and benefits of tourism impacts on shared or public lands are not effectively accounted for, in part because of the tendency for profits to accrue to individuals and costs to accrue to communities. Further, as tourism presents opportunities of immediate profits coupled with delayed or latent costs, this predisposes areas with high land tenure turnover to problems of intergenerational distribution. In this way, socio-political hierarchies are sustained that promote inequity in the distribution of resources and power, and alter existing social systems, including smallholders' associations and gender-based institutions. In this section we briefly explore the role of social capital, defined as the norms and networks that facilitate collective action (Woolcock 1998), as it relates to land tenure, smallholder involvements in new tourism enterprises and gender divisions of the tourism labor pool.

Social capital is a broad concept that is still in process of development and formalization. Current considerations of social capital indicators exhibit site-dependency, and thus allow for a collection of variables, which describe rates of social capital (Grootaert and van Bastelear 2002). Some proxy variables for social capital refer to the existence of associations in the community, the participation rate of group members and the occurrence of leadership. The pervasive women's networks can be seen as evidencing strong social capital in Dominica. They promote positive externalities (Collier 2002) as a consequence of social interactions: information sharing about the behavior of others, about the environment and resources, and mainly the promotion of collective action. Nevertheless, debates (as to whether or not those forms of association effectively guide the creation of social capital) are still open as membership and participation can take different forms.

Social capital contributes to wealth distribution and effective management of both land and sea resources on Dominica. The treatment of common property as it relates to daily life is not limited to the past, nor is it exclusive to the Carib population. It is pervasive in contemporary life across the island, and contributes to social cohesion and equitable distribution of resources. For example, daily fish harvests in Soufriere are announced by a call blown on a conch shell. All who assist with bringing in the bay net bring home fish, in an array of non-written norms where group boundaries and quotas are well defined. Social networks and norms also play a part in smallholdings, which are prevalent as national land redistribution efforts broke up most large estates, and a French historical precedent divides land equally among all heirs of a deceased person. Thus today, Dominica's land tenure scenario is dominated by a large number of smallholders, especially banana farmers, who have demonstrated a clear disposition to work among well-organized collectives. Agriculture networks have improved information sharing, income distribution, informal lending opportunities and cooperative labor in rural areas (Grossman 1998). These factors have strengthened the tendency of smallholders to enter new marketplaces, including that of tourism, and underscore the importance of social networks in Dominica.

The island's West-African roots of the Afro-Creole culture are apparent in the strength of Dominica's matriarchy. Women's networks have been particularly active in the power and mobilization of the agriculture hucksters union, and many small businesses and cooperatives are owned and managed by women (Grossman 2000). The success or failure of many smallholder ventures on the island has been determined by the strength of the women's network behind it. Large-scale foreign financiers and aid organizations, in contrast, typify most tourism development on the island. These tend to operate among networks that are institutionalized, established and apparent, and thus they are more likely to cooperate with outwardly visible groups of entrepreneurs or lobbyists. In Dominica, these are considered exclusive cohorts, presenting a challenge for the inclusion of women, communities and smallholders in tourism development.

Gender and social position regularly influence the range of attainable employment, as well as salary levels and management responsibility (Davidson et al. 2002). Tourism is not exceptional in this sense – women typically fill the lowest paying service jobs such as housekeepers, cooks, receptionists, etc. Such jobs are unlikely to be unionized in Dominica; even organizations such as the Taxi Drivers Association or the Hotel Owners Association are unable (or perhaps unwilling) to support reform or improvement of working conditions. While tourism opportunities increase formal employment opportunities for some, domestic and social obligations for working women do not decline (Davidson et al. 2002). In 1991, women headed 36.6 per cent of all Dominican households, the vast majority of which are single-parent homes (PAHO 2001). While reliable statistics are not available, respondents suggest that these women routinely work double shifts while also caring for their families. Thus, the combined burden for those who maintain households (or at least childcare) in addition to as many as three jobs may reduce well-being, rather than improve it (Davidson et al. 2002; Moser 1993). This has strong implications for the effects that growing tourism might have on the social structure and domestic life of Dominicans, and clearly demonstrates that women have borne (and will continue to do so, barring reforms) a disproportionate share of resulting social costs.

Trans-national Scale Dynamics I: Formal Policies and Informal Networks

Dominicans have a great deal of pride in their island culture, and a reverence for the natural forces and beauty of the island that borders on spirituality (Honychurch 1988). Self-sufficiency, well-being and cultural identity are characteristics particularly strong in Dominican culture (R. Lawrence 2001, Chief Cultural Officer, personal communication). Social interactions related to these characteristics have reinforced the abilities of small, unaffiliated entrepreneurs to enter the tourism market, and have also upheld the ability of the island as a community to resist prospectively deleterious foreign-driven developments. One example is the (narrowly-avoided) Canadian BHP copper mine which would have affected 10 per cent of the island, and most all of the Carib territory, in return for 5 per cent of net profits (A. Martin 2001, Caribbean Conservation Association, personal communication). In other words, Dominica's strong social capital networks have promoted collective actions, allowing weaker actors to withstand such external forces with regards to broad scale, environmentally destructive development. The successes of grass-roots initiatives highlight the importance of maintaining the networks and social cohesion in the future. Further, this point also applies to future orientations of foreign aid and foreign tourism investments. A critical degree of consonance with Dominican social networks and domestic life is necessary for projects to avoid high transaction costs and the insufficient social embedding that promotes project failure.

Environmental ethics have played a quiet, but nevertheless present aspect of national policy. Dominica's current major political associations are the United Workers Party (UWP), the Freedom Party (DFP) and the Labor Party (DLP). A coalition between the DFP and DLP helped to elect Pierre Charles (DLP) as Prime Minister in 2001. Some of this cooperation has been attributed to shared environmental priorities, employment promotion plans and economic development issues common to both parties' agendas, and central to many current government policies. Evidence that social institutions on the island are more effective than others in the Caribbean is most clearly reflected in the high proportion of the island still under forest cover and efforts on the part of the government to raise island awareness for global issues such as climate change. Some proponents of ecotourism enterprises argue that public policy should not deviate from a national policy of conservation and environmental controls, highlighting the importance of non-market ecosystem services, such as clean air and water. Still, a majority of Dominican citizens might believe that clean water is not enough. Such divisive issues leave the island's polity fragmented, limiting efforts to articulate a shared vision.

Trans-national Scale Dynamics II: Tourism Multipliers and Foreign Ownership

Tourism development is often promoted by foreign investments based on vigorous publicity, infrastructure development and tax cuts (Apostolopoulos and Gayle 2002). The Caribbean as a whole has been cited as the most tourism-dependent area in the world (Gayle and Goodrich 1993). Tourism visits to Dominica remain relatively low, and the challenges to maintaining a diversified economy are significant.

Dominica (as other small island states) is under great pressure from an increasingly globalized economy. Historically, the country has made few efforts towards developing a self-supported economy (Mandle 1996); imports currently compensate for the limited ability of the island economy to accommodate diverse demands. Localization policies (minimizing transport and encouraging economic diversification) have been suggested (Norberg-Hodge 1996). Nevertheless, a narrow resource base and physical isolation limits Dominica's ability to exclusively supply the developing tourism sector. This is not uncommon among island nations; even when they possess great natural wealth, they must promote themselves to the world, often competing with other destinations that provide similar experiences at lower prices. Moreover, they must be able to provide the high level of amenities to which tourists from the industrialized countries have become habituated.

The cruise tourism industry highlights an example of excessive foreign ownership and vertical integration of multinational corporations. Apart from potable water, which the ships load from Dominica, cruise tourism purchases few local products. Many challenges exist to link tourism to local agricultural production (Belisle 1984), not the least of which are agreements that bind the cruise ships to buy products before departure in Florida (G. Thomas 2001,

General Manager Dominica Export Import Agency, personal communication). Thus, a banana consumed by a cruise ship tourist while whale watching in Dominica is likely to have been grown in South America, transported to Florida, and brought into Dominican waters for consumption. Another related issue is that cruise lines must negotiate permission to dump waste and wastewater on Caribbean islands, as part of the annual visitation contracts. Because individual islands rely on cruise tourism to generate foreign exchange and rectify trade imbalances, island negotiation positions are weakened. This is especially the case when it is publicly perceived that cruise companies are threatening reduced visitation in response. Efforts by island destinations to bargain collectively in order to negotiate more favorable trade agreements, or controls or compensation on tourism impacts have been unsuccessful, and small island nations remain divided.

Partly because of their smaller size and relative isolation, small island states tend to have more open economies than their larger continental counterparts. Increased tourism volumes may generate trade imbalances, as they attempt to satisfy the demands of a tourist population with foreign consumptive habits, importing products from food to modern electronic devices, developing costly infrastructure improvements and accepting profit repatriation in exchange for foreign investment (Widfeldt 1996). Therefore, although tourist volumes may grow, financial benefits to host countries may decline. The tourist multiplier effect – the extent to which funds spent by foreign visitors continue to be re-spent within local economies – is well documented in the literature (Bull 1991; Lundberg et al. 1995; Saleem 1994). Tourists in Dominica spend less than their counterparts on more developed islands and consume fewer imports (Weaver 1991). This means that for each tourist dollar spent locally, a relatively smaller proportion leaves the country to buy foreign goods, thereby contributing more to the local economy. This effect has been enhanced by the high degree of domestic ownership in the tourism industry. As late as 1991, Dominican investors directly controlled 62 per cent of local hotel assets and shared management of an additional 19 per cent (Weaver 1991). However, evidence suggests this situation has changed substantially since 1995, with a larger share of new tourism profits being expatriated by either foreign owners or locals investing abroad (Cater 1996; Patterson et al. 2003).

Trans-national Scale Dynamics III: Incentives, Risk and Local Communities

Dominica is characterized by very steep and rugged terrain, covered by natural forest. The extreme topography is a major constraint to development, because approximately 70 per cent of the island surface is unsuitable for human settlements and agriculture due to erosion risks, water logging or poor soil quality. Historically, the bulk of Dominican settlements have been limited to a narrow coastal belt with generally flatter land. However, much of the current development (especially of tourism facilities) is taking place in coastal areas vulnerable to storms and erosion, or in relatively flat but ecologically fragile riparian areas. Increased urbanization has changed the composition and volume of solid and liquid wastes, with subsequent negative environmental impacts. Modern waste collection, treatment and disposal systems are being established, but these have yet to mitigate the impacts of human waste on coastal areas significantly (Christian 1992).

Vulnerabilities to hurricanes, flooding or bank instability are among a set of risk factors which frequently escape thorough evaluation in the development feasibility studies performed by foreign professionals. In contrast Caribbean residents, who have witnessed the impacts of severe natural disturbance events over the past decades, are risk averse and tend to view ambitious tourism developments as foolhardy, or motivated merely by short-term profit. One respondent pointed out that many foreign-spurred developments benefit from tax holidays and foreign-aid dollars: 'only a fool would build there, they just want the profit for the first years and the insurance money when it falls'.

Many infrastructure ventures are developed within agreements to cede ownership from foreign investors to the Dominican government after 5 years. Not surprisingly, many structures begin to exhibit a high level of deterioration and incur high maintenance costs thereafter. For hotels over five bedrooms, profits for the first 20 years are tax-free in Dominica, and a broad range of additional tax exemptions cover building materials, furniture and equipment. Foreign investors are allowed to repatriate 100 per cent of profits and receive special treatment in land acquisition, such as exemptions from licensing fees and government assistance in expediting the land sales (NDC 1999). The 'economic citizenship' program offers benefits of overseas tax shelters and income tax exemptions. While all these benefits are justified in order to promote employment opportunities for Dominicans, foreign ventures usually use resident work permit grants to fill higher paying mid- and upper-level management positions with foreign labor.

When it comes to interaction with foreign counterparts, many community, government and local non-governmental representatives have extensive experience. Yet all too frequently, this amounts to personally witnessing discrepancies between what is planned and promised by foreign actors, and what results. Once initiated, development projects may encounter skepticism from local actors who, despite incentives or intentions to include local enterprise, thus resist vesting themselves personally in broad-scale foreign initiated development. Similar difficulty can be encountered while attempting to include local participation in foreign initiated studies, conservation or research efforts. Local community members may view efforts as quixotic, while their reactions register with foreign planners as apathetic host community response. This poses a genuine challenge to numerous initiatives targeting 'local community involvement' in tourism enterprise, research or conservation efforts (Young and Eristheé 2002).

International Scale Dynamics I: Dominica in International Policy Arenas

Coincident with forces on domestic, and trans-national scales, international events affect tourism dynamics on the island. In the international policy arena, Dominica is vulnerable to many pressures and conflicts. The case of Dominica's voting position on the International Whaling Commission (IWC) illustrates the interrelatedness between national and international politics and the tourism industry.

The IWC includes 35 countries, including six nations that are members of the Organization of Eastern Caribbean States (OECS). World attention has focused on the IWC annual meetings since OECS nations unexpectedly proposed in 1998 a resolution to resume coastal whaling of species not present in Caribbean waters. International media concurrently reported Japanese donations of extensive fisheries complexes. Internationally, a portion of public perception registered that Dominica and other poor island nations had been 'bought off' by wealthy whaling nations, while others argued that Dominica's efforts to maintain a diversified economy logically required investment and economic assistance from foreign sources. Locally, each year the IWC votes, the island is effectively polarized along economical and ethical lines, with government making the final call. Thus, one portion of the population, witnessing decline of island coastal fisheries, cites the need for economic assistance from whatever sources are offered. Others, noting increasing receipts from the whale-watching industry, and the growing perception of Dominica as 'the nature island of the Caribbean', express fears of boycott, tourism cancellations and layoffs. These are not unfounded concerns, as leading up to the 2001 vote (when Dominica voted to lift a whaling ban), international environmental organizations appealed to sentiments of tourism markets in Europe and the United States, calling for an island-wide boycott. A minor impact on island visitation resulted (C. Armour 2003, Anchorage Hotel, personal communication).

The official government position considers whaling to be an issue of sovereignty and political expediency. As one policy maker expressed, 'Dominica as a country, does not vote with or for anybody. Evidence is presented, and decisions made'. From this point of view, attempts to sway national governing strategy through fisheries aid or tourism boycotts are akin to denying the government the right to pursue its best national interest, as well as the right to use the best scientific evidence to make decisions. Nevertheless, some have expressed reservations that the island was prepared to deal with the scientific uncertainty surrounding sustainability questions; they also voiced discomfort at the idea that small island states would effectively decide such issues for the rest of the world. Meanwhile, other Dominicans consider that the right of international influence should be defended, arguing that environmental choices taken by other countries affect small island nations disproportionately (for example, global warming).

The way in which small island states comport themselves in international policy deliberations reflects the strength of various economic lobbies, social groups and the effectiveness of civil democracy. However, in Dominica a referendum on a topic such as the IWC vote is unlikely to occur, due to perceived education and knowledge gaps between elites and 'banana farmers'. This points out the difficulty in developing truly representative and responsive public policy as many Dominican residents feel that decisions reached at the international level should reflect a shared national vision with respect to environment, society and tourism development strategy.

CONCLUSIONS

Development has been slower and less dramatic on Dominica than other Caribbean islands. The importance of non-market assets and social cooperation remains central to the daily life of many residents. Long-standing cultural beliefs, social mechanisms and institutions have supported environmental quality and a strong sense of community. Human well-being is derived from a range of market and non-market goods and services, produced and protected by individual and collective actors. Certain components of a human-ecosystem support short-term production of assets, opportunities and relationships, while others support their long-term nature. Faced with such changes, any factors contributing to insular prosperity will depend on social and economic flexibility (Apostolopoulos and Gayle 2002). However, there is danger in structuring economies, societies or ecosystems around short-term goals such as reorganization and throughput, while sacrificing or ignoring factors that contribute to longer-term sustainability.

Such aspects of this arrangement are apparent in tourism development in its present form. In a capitalist market-driven economy, transactions favor values realized by the market or through individual actors (for example, labor, property or amenity values) over those represented by non-market, or socially collective attributes (for example, ecosystem services or domestic production), and profits which can be realized immediately take priority over assets which could support future generations (for example, topsoil loss and fishery exploitation). Government, particularly eager to stimulate employment opportunities, foreign exchange, aid and investment, may make additional offerings which due to inadequate planning, implementation or monitoring, prove to have unintended consequences for such societal-collective or non-market goods and services.

Another source of threat is associated with the degree to which Dominica and other Caribbean islands are sensitive to system-wide disturbances, and the manner in which risk and reward are understood and distributed. Broad-scale external disturbances test human-ecosystem resilience and their capacity to reorganize, while contributing to the demands that influence governmental decisions. These may be of natural (hurricanes, ENSO, climate change), or anthropogenic (shifting trade preferences, international laws, trends in tourism visitation, global recession) origins or a combination of both. Disorder and reorganization can be brought about by forces that are severe and punctuated (as above), or persistent and pervasive (for example, tourism). While local-level costs are disproportionately borne by those least able to avoid them, Dominica is itself victim to repeated instances of 'capital flight', following international investor decisions. The country is thus faced with the challenge that seeking larger-scale solutions inevitably requires subjecting a larger proportion of the economy and society to global forces and instabilities.

A third source of threat emerges from interactions between the structure and function of formal (for example, laws, governmental units, enforcement) and informal (for example, cultural rules and norms, civic networks) social institutions. This chapter has cited several cases in which market mechanisms inherent in tourism development are at odds with social institutions that sustain non-market, collective values. Value is routinely appropriated from socially disenfranchised or marginal actors by more powerful actors, following historical patterns of wealth, political lobbies, and the contemporary and growing scale of globalized/foreign interest. These impacts can be direct – as more powerful actors directly appropriate land, labor, capital, or indirect – as tourism affects an ecosystem or community's ability to provide self-sufficient and sustainable levels of goods, services and organization. This chapter has attempted to illustrate local Dominican perceptions of such exchanges and outlined some of the barriers to overcoming them.

It bears repeating that the issues covered in this chapter are viewed as latent to many forms of analysis, and thus have received little prior attention. Issues which are viewed as 'too complex' are sometimes so because they are embedded in economic and social structures which uphold elite interests, are manifesting in areas or populations viewed as marginal, or because drawing attention to them involves challenging existing cultural, political and economic arrangements. Accordingly, a political ecology perspective of tourism development in Dominica argues for the continued exposure and exploration of such examples. Thus acquired learning will better ensure the conservation of institutions and social mechanisms that take special account of aspects of natural, cultural and economic patrimony that might otherwise be lost in efforts to develop the country's tourist industry.

ACKNOWLEDGMENTS

The authors would like to thank the participants of the Atelier Workshop 'Sustainable Tourism in Small Islands of the Caribbean; Lessons from Dominica', and those who assisted with associated data, interviews, logistics and information. We extend a hearty thanks to Ken Cousins, Robert Richardson and Rosimery Portela who made extensive and constructive comments on the draft, and along with Stefan Gössling, Timothy Gulden, B. Mark John and Larry Love contributed to particularly fruitful discussion.

REFERENCES

Apostolopoulos, Y. and D.J. Gayle (2002), *Island Tourism and Sustainable Development. Caribbean, Pacific, and Mediterranean Experiences*, Westport, Connecticut: Praeger.

Belisle, F.J. (1984), 'Food production and tourism in Jamaica: obstacles to increasing local food supplies to hotels', *The Journal of Developing Areas*, **19** (1), 1–20.

Blakie, P. and H. Brookfield (1987), *Land Degradation and Society*, London: Methuen.

Boromé, J. (1972), *Aspects of Dominican History. The French and Dominica, 1699–1763*, Roseau, Dominica: Government of Dominica.

Bryant, R. (1992), 'Political ecology: an emerging research agenda in third-world studies', *Political Geography*, **11** (l),12–36.

Bryant, R. (1998), 'Power, knowledge and political ecology in the Third World: a review', *Progress in Physical Geography*, **22** (1), 79–94.

Bryant, R. and S. Bailey (1997), *Third World Political Ecology*, London and New York: Routledge.

Bull, A. (1991), *The Economics of Travel and Tourism*, Melbourne: Pitman Publishing.

Campbell, S. (2001), 'Defending aboriginal sovereignty: the 1930 Carib War in Waitukubuli (Dominica)', *Proceedings of the University of West Indies Dominica Country Conference, January 2001*, available at: http://www.uwichill.edu.bb/bnccde/dominica/ conference/papers/filename.html.

Caribbean Conservation Association (CCA) (1991), *Dominica Environmental Profile*, St. Michael, Barbados: USAID.

Caribbean Environment Program (CEP) (2000), *Status of Protected Area Systems in the Wider Caribbean Region: Dominica*, available at: www.cep.unep.org/pubs/ techreports/tr36en/countries/dominica.html.

Cater, E. (1996), 'Ecotourism in the Caribbean: a sustainable option for Belize and Dominica?', in L. Briguglio, R. Butler, D. Harrison and W.L. Filho (eds), *Sustainable Tourism in Islands and Small States: Case Studies*, London and New York: Pinter, pp. 122–46.

Central Statistical Office (CSO) (1999), *Dominica Travel Report*, Roseau, Dominica: Government Printery.

Christian, G.J. (1992), 'Nature island fading? The struggle to preserve Dominica's natural environment', in I.W. Andre and G.J. Christian (eds), *In Search of Eden. Dominica, the Travails of a Caribbean Mini-State*, Upper Marlboro, Maryland: Pond Casse Press, pp. 170-91.

Collier, P. (1998), *Social Capital and Poverty*, Washington DC: World Bank.

Collier, P. (2002), 'The Macroeconomic Repercussions of Agricultural Shocks and their Implications for Insurance', Discussion Paper No. 2002/46, Helsinki, Finland: The United Nations University, World Institute for Development Economics Research.

Costanza, R., R. d'Arge, R. de Groot, S. Farber, M. Grasso, B. Hannon, S. Naeem, K. Limburg, J. Paruelo, R.V. O'Neill, R. Raskin, P. Sutton and M. van den Belt (1997), 'The value of the world's ecosystem services and natural capital', *Nature*, **387**, 253–60.

Davidson, P., T. Jones and M. Schellhorn (2002), 'Women as producers and consumers of island tourism: towards an analysis of gender contexts', in Y. Apostolopoulos and D. Gayle (eds), *Tourism, Sustainable Development and Natural Resource Management. Experiences of Caribbean, Pacific and Mediterranean Islands*, Westport, Connecticut: Praeger, pp. 199–221.

De Albuquerque, K. and J. McElroy (1999), 'Race, ethnicity, and social stratification in three majority Afro-Caribbean societies', *Caribbean Studies*, **24** (4), 1–29.

Dominica Budget Report (1999), *Review of the Economy*, Roseau, Dominica: Government Printery.

Dominican Government Environmental Coordinating Unit (DNBSAP) (2002), *Dominica National Biodiversity Strategy and Action Plan*, Roseau, Dominica: Government Printery.

Duffy, R. (2001), *A Trip Too Far: Ecotourism, Politics and Exploitation*, London: Earthscan.

Gayle, D.J. and J.N. Goodrich (1993), 'Caribbean tourism marketing, management and development strategies', in D.J. Gayle and J.N. Goodrich (eds), *Tourism Marketing & Management in the Caribbean*, London and New York: Routledge, pp. 1–19.

Green, C. (1995), 'Gender, race and class in the social economy of English-speaking Caribbean', *Social and Economic Studies*, **44** (2–3), 65–102.

Grootaert, C. and T. van Bastelear (2002), *Understanding and Measuring Social Capital: A Multidisciplinary Tool for Practitioners*, Washington DC: World Bank.

Grossman, L. (1998), *The Political Ecology of Bananas: Contract Farming, Peasants and Agrarian Change in the Eastern Caribbean*, Chapel Hill: University of North Carolina Press.

Grossman, L. (2000), 'Women and export agriculture: the case of banana production on St. Vincent and the Eastern Caribbean', in A. Spring (ed.), *Women Farmers and Commercial Ventures: Increasing Food Security in Developing Countries*, Boulder, Colorado: Lynne Reinner Publishers, pp. 295–316.

Hodge, W.H. (1943), 'The vegetation of Dominica', *The Geographical Review*, **33** (3), 349–75.

Honychurch, L. (1988), *Our Island Culture*, Barbados: Letchworth Press.

Honychurch, L. (1995a), *The Dominica Story: A History of the Island*, London: Macmillan.

Honychurch, L. (1995b), 'Caribs, Creoles and concepts of territory: the boundary between France and Dominica', *Caribbean Geography*, **6** (1), 61–70.

Honychurch, L. (2001), 'Slave valleys, peasant ridges: topography, colour and land settlement on Dominica', *Proceedings of the University of West Indies Dominica Country Conference, January 2001*, available at: http://www.uwichill.edu.bb/bnccde/dominica/conference/papers/filename.html.

Hughes, T.P. (1994), 'Catastrophes, phase shifts, and large-scale degradation of a Caribbean coral reef', *Science*, **265**, 1547–51.

International Monetary Fund (IMF) (2000), *International Monetary Fund Dominica: Staff Report for the 1999 Article IV Consultation*, IMF Staff Country Report No 01/16, Washington DC: International Monetary Fund.

Lal, P. and E. Young (2000), 'Role and relevance of indigenous notion of cultural capital in environment management in Australia and the Pacific', Proceedings of *the Heritage Economics Challenges for Heritage Conservation and Sustainable development in the 21st century*, 4 July 2000, Canberra: Australian National University, Australian Heritage Commission.

Lipsanen, N. (2001), *Naturalistic and Existential Realms of Place in Roseau, Dominica*, M.Sc. Thesis, Helsinki: Department of Geography, Helsinki University.

Lugo, A., M. Applefield, D. Pool and R. McDonald (1983), 'The impact of Hurricane David on the forests of Dominica', *Canadian Journal of Forest Research*, **1** (13), 201–11.

Lundberg, D.E., M. Krishnamoorthy and M.H. Stavenga (1995), *Tourism Economics*, New York: John Wiley & Sons.

Mandle, J.R. (1996), *Persistent Underdevelopment: Change and Economic Modernization in the West Indies*, Amsterdam: Gordon and Breach.

Moser, C.O.N. (1993), *Gender, Planning and Development*, London and New York: Routledge.

Narayan, D. and L. Pritchett (1997), *Cents and Sociability: Household Income and Social Capital in Rural Tanzania*, Social Development and Development Research Group, Policy Research Paper No. 1796, Washington DC: World Bank.

National Development Corporation (NDC) (1999), *National Development Corporation Development Checklist*, Roseau, Dominica: Government Printery.

National Development Corporation (NDC) (2001), *National Development Corporation, Projected Investments Report for 2001–2003*, Roseau, Dominica: Government Printery.

Norberg-Hodge H. (1996), *The Case Against the Global Economy*, San Francisco: Sierra Club Books.

Pan American Health Organization (PAHO) (1999), 'Health situation in the Americas. Basic indicators 1999: selected basic indicators', *Epidemiological Bulletin*, **20** (3), 1-17.

Pan American Health Organization (PAHO) (2001), *Basic Country Health Profiles 2001*, available at: http://www.paho.org/English/SHA/prfldom.htm.

Patterson, T. (2001), *Landscape Dynamics of the Spread of the Lemongrass* 'Cymbopogon citratus', Paper presented at the 2001 University of Maryland Conference: 'Sustainable Tourism in Small Islands of The Caribbean, Lessons from Dominica', College Park, Maryland: University of Maryland.

Patterson T., T. Gulden, K. Cousins and E. Kraev (2003), 'Integrating environmental, social and economic systems: a dynamic model of tourism in Dominica', *Ecological Modeling*, in press.

Peluso, N. L. (1992), *Rich Forests, Poor People: Resource Control and Resistance in Java*, Berkeley, California: University of California Press.

Pezeron, S. (1993), *The Carib Indians of Dominica Island in the West Indies*, New York: Vantage Press.

Rocheleau, D., B. Thomas-Slayter and E. Wangari (eds) (1996), *Feminist Political Ecology: Global Issues and Local Experiences*, London and New York: Routledge.

Rodriguez, L.C., R. Portela, R. Boumans and C. Miller (2003), *Land Use Change Simulations Under Alternative Valuation Scenarios for Ecosystem Goods and Services: the Kalinago and Afro-Creole Populations of the Commonwealth of Dominica Western Indies*, unpublished paper, Burlington, Vermont: Gund Institute for Ecological Economics.

Rogozinski, J. (1992), *A Brief History of the Caribbean: From the Arawak and the Carib to the Present*, Oxford: Facts On File.

Saleem, N. (1994), 'The destination capacity index: a measure to determine the tourism carrying capacity', in A. Seaton (ed.), *Tourism: the State of the Art*, Chichester: John Wiley & Sons, pp. 144–51.

Schroeder, R. (1993), 'Shady practice: gender and the political ecology of resource stabilization in Gambian garden/orchards', *Economic Geography*, **69**, 439–65.

Shepherd, J., J. Lindsay and M. Stasiuk (2001), 'Volcanic hazards in Dominica', in *Proceedings of the University of West Indies Dominica Country Conference*, January 2001, available at: http://www.uwichill.edu.bb/bnccde/dominica/conference/papers/filename.html.

Throsby, D. (1999), 'Cultural capital', *Journal of Cultural Economics*, **23** (1–2), 3–12.

Thurlow, K. (2002), *Community Tourism in Dominica*, M.Sc. Thesis, New Haven, Connecticut: Yale University, Yale School of Forestry.

Trouillot, M.R. (1988), *Peasants and Capital: Dominica in the World Economy*, Baltimore: Johns Hopkins University Press.

Ward, F. (1980), 'Dominica', *National Geographic*, **158** (3), 354–8.

Weaver, D.B (1991), 'Alternative to mass tourism in Dominica', *Annals of Tourism Research*, **18** (2), 414–32.

Widfeldt, A. (1996), 'Alternative development strategies and tourism in the Caribbean', in L. Briguglio, R. Butler, D. Harrison and W. Leal Filho (eds), *Sustainable Tourism in Islands & Small States, Case Studies*, London and New York: Pinter, pp. 147–61.

Wilkenson, C. (2000), 'Status of coral reefs of the world: 2000', *Global Coral Reef Monitoring Network*, available at: http://coral.aoml.noaa.gov/gcrmn/status_2000.pdf.

Woolcock, M. (1998), 'Social capital and economic development: toward a theoretical synthesis and policy framework', *Theory and Society*, **27** (2), 151–208.

World Bank (2000), *World Development Indicators 2000*, CD-ROM, Washington DC: World Bank.

Young, S. and N. Eristheé (2002), *Toward A New Paradigm for Environmental Research in the Caribbean*, presented at ISLANDS VII, Islands of the World Conference, 26-30 June 2002, Charlottetown, Prince Edward Island: University of Prince Edward Island.

Zeppel, H. (2000), 'Indigenous heritage tourism and its economic value in Australia', Proceedings of *the Heritage Economics Challenges for Heritage Conservation and Sustainable development in the 21st century*, 4 July 2000, Canberra: Australian National University, Australian Heritage Commission.

4.   Tourism Policy and Planning in St. Lucia[1]

Paul F. Wilkinson

INTRODUCTION

This chapter analyses the political ecology of the development of tourism in St. Lucia, a Caribbean island state whose economy has been greatly influenced – and, indeed, even currently dominated – by tourism. The history of tourism is examined in order to examine the changing role of the tourism sector in national development, thus setting the stage for recent policy and planning activities.

Located in a central position in the Windward Islands, St. Lucia has an area of 616 km^2 and maximum dimensions of 42×22 km (CCA 1991) (Figure 4.1). With a maximum elevation of 950 m above sea level at Mt. Gimie, it is a mountainous island of volcanic origin. There is little flat land: only about 10 per cent of the island has slopes of less than 5 per cent, and only about 5 per cent of the land is suitable for agriculture. The climate is tropical marine, with vegetation ranging from Mediterranean to rainforest, depending on orientation, topography and the steep precipitation gradient (between 1 500– 3 500 mm). Deforestation, caused by cutting for firewood and charcoal and by expansion of agricultural land, is a serious problem. The only known mineral resource is a vast untapped source of talc.

St. Lucia was first occupied by the Ciboney in approximately 500 BC, followed by the Arawaks who had become firmly established on the island by about 200 AD. They in turn were invaded by Caribs around 1000 AD; within 200 years, the Arawaks had been totally taken over by the Caribs (CCA 1991; Devaux 1992; Devaux 1984; Devaux 1975). The Carib name for the island was *Iouanalao* (thought to mean 'there where the iguana is found'); the pronunciation eventually evolved into *Hewanorra* (the present name of St. Lucia's international airport). The first European explorer to see St. Lucia may have been Juan de la Cosa, Columbus's map-maker, who sailed through the southeastern Caribbean in 1499 and included an island called 'The

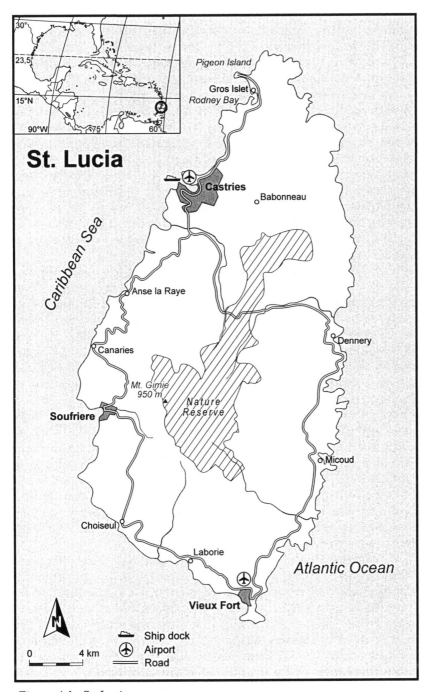

Figure 4.1   St. Lucia

Falcon' on a map a year later; or Columbus's lookout may have seen the island in June 1502 when the Admiral's fleet put into nearby Martinique. It is not known which Spaniard gave the island the name of Santa Lucia; the name was later changed to Ste Lucie by the French and to St. Lucia by the English.

The first attempt at European settlement occurred in 1605 when 67 Englishmen bound for Guiana put into the Vieux Fort area because of a food shortage on board; most were killed by the Caribs. A similar fate awaited a formal attempt at settlement in 1639 by an English planter from St. Kitts. Later English attempts were more successful, with the Caribs eventually being defeated in 1663. Meanwhile, the French also laid claim to the island, through a grant of territory to the newly-formed French Company of the Isles of the Americas. The result was 150 years of turbulent history, with the island changing hands between France and England 14 times prior to 1803, when England retained eventual control; St. Lucia was formally ceded to Britain with the 1814 Treaty of Paris.

In addition to being an important naval base, the island had a plantation industry focused on indigo, coffee, tobacco and cassava, using slaves originating in Africa. Because of the continuing warfare, sugar cane did not emerge as the primary cash crop until the beginning of the 19th century when it soon came to dominate the economy. With Britain abolishing slavery in 1834 and emancipation being secured in 1838, approximately 13 300 former slaves were freed. Attempts were made to find new cash crops; for example, coconut plantations were first established in the 1870s. A major form of economic diversification came with the construction of new shipping wharves in the fine natural harbor of Castries, which resulted in it becoming a major coaling station for the region. Between 1880 and 1930 (when oil replaced coal as a fuel for ships), more than a thousand steamships per year called at the coal-bunkering station. Triggered by a strike of coal carriers in 1907, the early part of the century was characterized by labor unrest, as was the Depression when a strike of sugar workers in 1937 led to reformist labor legislation. The first half of the century saw some further agricultural diversification, including sea-island cotton, bananas and limes, but sugar remained dominant until 1956.

While English is the official language, the population is mainly Black and Roman Catholic, with a French-based patois (*Kwéyol*) as an important language (unwritten, until recently) and a land tenure system based on the *Code Napoléon* – a result of the fact that the island was primarily occupied by the French prior to 1803, with English occupation being limited to five short interludes totaling less than 12 years. A strong sense of local tradition and culture exists. A British possession until 1967 when it was granted associated statehood, St. Lucia achieved complete independence in 1979. It is governed by a Governor-General appointed by the British Crown, an elected legislative assembly and an appointed Senate, with a legal and legislative system based on that of Britain.

With a population in 2001 of 158 000 (GOSL 2003), St. Lucia is extremely densely settled: 256 persons per km^2. The population is almost equally divided between urban and rural areas, with the pattern of distribution being characterized by a drift towards the capital city, Castries (with a population of approximately 45 000) and its environs.

THE ECONOMY

Venner (1989, p. 80) notes that the economic history of St. Lucia is marked by dependence on a series of singular activities, particularly cane sugar, military outpost, the Port of Castries as a coaling station, United States military base in World War II and bananas: 'it is only in very recent times that more than one economic sector has played a significant role in the economy at the same time'. Currently, compared to many Windward and Leeward Islands, St. Lucia has a relatively diversified economy: export agriculture (mainly bananas), tourism and manufacturing for the regional market. Nevertheless, while the GDP per capita (US$2,800 in 2000; CTO 2002, p. 11) is higher than many other developing countries, it is one of the lowest in the Caribbean region.

This diverse economy, and its ongoing strengths and weaknesses, can be related to the argument that St. Lucia has seen four major economic revolutions since World War II. First, the wartime British/American Lend–Lease Program saw the construction of a sea-plane base north of Castries and a major air base at what is now Hewanorra Airport near Vieux Fort, the second largest town. The result was new-found – if temporary – prosperity resulting from employment in construction and service industries. There also was significant cultural change because the war-related decline in sugar exports led to a decrease in the agricultural workforce and a shift to the towns. The expanding urban population and the growing cash economy resulted in modest beginnings for locally-based manufacturing, particularly for consumer goods. The existence of an airport capable of being relatively easily upgraded to international standards just as jet charters became a factor also provided the opportunity for a very fast entry into the mass tourism market.

Second, the island was just emerging from a post-war economic depression when the world sugar-cane market collapsed in 1956. Within one year, St. Lucia's sugar cane was almost totally replaced by bananas – one export monocrop succeeding another. By 1964, bananas accounted for 85 per cent of the value of St. Lucia's exports (Persaud 1966). The recovery was significant, particularly as British-based Geest Industries developed a virtual monopoly over banana exports in the British Windward Islands and guaranteed entry to a single market, Great Britain. In the long run, however, this left the industry vulnerable to changes in European Community (EC) tariff policies after 1993; it is now in serious decline, with agriculture (mainly bananas) accounting for only 6 per cent of GDP in 2001 (Anthony 2002), a figure which is likely to continue to decline. Also, the altered nature of agricultural production resulted in the need for fewer agricultural workers (although workers had greater access to cash payments for their crops) and increased rural–urban migration.

The third revolution was the tourist 'boom' which began in the mid-1960s, a change which was to affect all sectors of St. Lucian society. Just as tourism was becoming a central feature in the economy, the fourth revolution was initiated by the 'energy crisis' in 1973 which resulted in disruption of all sectors of the economy, rapid inflation and a growing balance of payments problem. Up to that point, largely because of the growth of tourism and the strength of the banana industry, the economy had enjoyed rapid expansion during the 1960s and early 1970s when GDP growth averaged over 7 per cent per year and inflation was relatively low. Despite the world economic recession that began in the mid-1970s and concomitant declines in national agricultural production, the economy soon began to experience satisfactory growth, in part because of the rebounding of the tourism sector.

In 1979, however, growth was again curtailed by world recession, rapid inflation, rising energy costs and the closing of several industries. Unemployment was officially 20 per cent by 1980 (Dann 1992), but unofficially much higher. The problem was exacerbated by Hurricane Allen in August 1980 which severely damaged several hotels, some of which were not fully operational for over a year. It also destroyed the banana crop, resulting in no banana exports until February 1981. Despite the serious curtailment of foreign income for nearly a year, the energy import bill continued to rise. There were delays in shipments of gasoline, diesel fuel and propane, causing gasoline shortages, electricity outages and cold water in hotels – and increased deforestation resulting from increased local demand for wood and charcoal, as petroleum-based energy prices rose (Wilkinson 1984). After several years, banana production began to increase because of relatively high world prices, with receipts of US$65.6 million in 1988 on a production of 136 000 tons (an increase of 47 per cent over 1987). (As a measure of the current decline in the agricultural sector, banana production in 2001 was only about 50 000 tons (Anthony 2002).)

It is not surprising, particularly given the expansion of tourism, that construction is a growing activity in St. Lucia, with major projects for hotels, commercial projects, housing, capital works and industrial estates.

Government and private sector attempts to attract more manufacturing have, however, met with little success. Despite some improvement through intra-regional trade, growth in manufacturing has been hindered by the relatively high costs of production, limited access to regional and international markets, limited pools of managerial and entrepreneurial skills, difficulties in gaining access to domestic credit, small size of domestic market, high cost of imported inputs and relatively high wage levels.

Venner (1989, p. 81) argues that:

> ... [W]hile there has been growth and modernization, the all round development of the economy has lagged as it is still structurally unbalanced and not capable of self sustaining growth. To put it in the jargon of the economist it is open, vulnerable and dependent.

One of the most serious indicators of these characteristics is the ongoing estimated annual balance of payments deficit on visible trade (US$83 million in 1999; GOSL 2003). When all trade (including the 'invisible' exports related to tourism) is included, the current account balance of payments situation is much more positive; indeed, in this sense, St. Lucia is among the better managed economies in the region.

Since the late 1980s, the national economy has had a wildly fluctuating rate of real growth; for example, the rate was 3.6 per cent in 1999, 0.2 per cent in 2000, and -5.4 per cent in 2001, the last figure reflecting slumps in both tourism and bananas (GOSL 2003). A growth of 7 per cent, however, is needed to absorb increases in the labor force of 2 000 per year and to deal with unemployment which officially was 18.9 per cent in 2002 (GOSL 2003). This level of unemployment is a result of the high rate of population growth (2 per cent per year; Renard 2001, p. 1), low rate of job creation and fast turnover of school-leavers. The majority of unemployed are unskilled workers and women whose labor force participation has increased in recent years. Moreover, the unemployment problem could accelerate if agricultural workers are eventually displaced by EC policy changes.

Other infrastructure problems exist, largely related to the government's financial problems, that negatively affect the economy. For example, despite a major British aid program in the early 1990s, the road system (which once could be described as one of the best among the smaller Caribbean islands; Peters 1980, p. 18) is in a serious state of disrepair, as a result of the lack of continuing foreign aid support for road maintenance; indeed, Dann's (1992) comment that road transportation was the main handicap to St. Lucia's tourism development remains true. In recognition of this fact, the government recently announced a major road improvement program (Anthony 2002). The high proportion of food that is imported is also a serious economic concern.

THE TOURISM SECTOR

The government has had a long-standing interest in promoting tourism as a means of diversifying St. Lucia's economy beyond its agricultural (and, to a much lesser extent, industrial) base. With some exceptions, its attitude has been a 'hands-off' approach which has welcomed increased foreign investment in the tourism sector, resulting in its steady growth. As a result, St. Lucia's tourism sector is characterized by rapid change, foreign investment and control, large-scale hotels (particularly all-inclusives), tax incentives and significant cruise ship activity.

The Beginnings

St. Lucia offers an attractive tourism product: 'good climate and beaches, lush tropical landscape and arresting mountain and sea views, outstanding yacht cruising, inexpensive arts and crafts, and warm, welcoming people' (Spinrad 1982, pp. 70–1). Interest in tourism surfaced immediately after World War II, as indicated by the formation of the St. Lucia Tourist Board (SLTB) (now a statutory arm of the Ministry of Commerce, Tourism, Investment and Consumer Affairs) in 1946. While tourism emerged as 'the lead sector in the post-war restructuring of the St. Lucian economy' (CCA 1991, p. 211), the tourism sector did not really take off until the mid-1960s with the advent of jet charter tours from the United States, Great Britain, Western Europe and Canada. These remain the major sources of tourists, although the number of tourists from within the Caribbean region is growing, representing 20.2 per cent of stay-over arrivals in 2000 (CTO 2002, p. 216). St. Lucia was well-poised to enter into this tourism explosion because the former American Air Force base at Vieux Fort was easily transformed into an international airport. The presence of the airport also allowed St. Lucia to become one of the first Eastern Caribbean tourism destinations to tap successfully the European market (Spinrad 1982).

Related to both tourism and broader national economic development, international aid programs resulted in significant investment in housing and roads (Great Britain), the airport (Canada) and health services (United States). Encouraged by government policy on favorable tax concessions for foreign investors, major investments in hotels were made by multinational corporations (MNCs), notably Cunard Lines, Court Lines (both British), Holiday Inns International (Canadian) and Steigenberger AG (West German). In cooperation with major international tour operators (such as Kuoni, Thomson, Skylark, Paramount), several airlines began to operate regular (such as Eastern, British West Indies Airlines, British Airways, Air Canada) and charter (for example Wardair) flights into Hewanorra Airport. Leeward

Islands Air Transport (LIAT) and several minor regional airlines use the smaller Vigie Airport in Castries.

Stay-over Tourist Arrivals

There were only 5 000 tourists in 1959 (CTA 1960), a figure which rose to about 30 000 in 1970 (Gilles 1980); this dramatic growth saw annual increases exceeding 20 per cent between 1961 and 1968 (Bryden 1973). The number of tourists more than doubled between 1969 and 1974 to a peak figure of 51 816, but, because of the 'energy crisis' of 1973, the number of visitors dropped dramatically in 1975. This was caused mainly by the bankruptcy of Court Lines (then Britain's largest tour operator) in 1974 as a result of several factors, including rising energy costs, and the temporary closing of four hotels in St. Lucia affecting more than one-quarter of the island's hotel rooms (Britton 1978, p. 180). These hotels, plus a Holiday Inn, were soon taken over by various combinations of foreign and government support. Nevertheless, St. Lucia's performance in the 1970s ranked among the top third of 20 comparable destinations in the Eastern Caribbean (McElroy and de Albuquerque 1989), as the number of tourists rose steadily to 105 500 in 1978 with improvements in marketing and infrastructure.

Tourism growth was again halted when several airlines and tour operators cut back flights as a result of increased fuel costs in 1979 and when several hotels were severely damaged by Hurricane Allen in 1980. With stay-over tourist arrivals in 1980 dropping to 79 694 (CTRC 1986, p. 92), the government was forced to take over the Halcyon Days Hotel near Vieux Fort, the largest (256-room) hotel on the island, and to keep it open with foreign management. In the next few years, there were also cutbacks in the construction of new hotels, with several small (locally-owned) hotels not proceeding with planned expansions and one major complex completely halting. Steigenberger AG's proposed 1 500-bed complex – which would have increased energy demand on the island by 30 per cent – was canceled, thus postponing the government's need to make a decision to overhaul the electricity system.

At about the same time, a (confidential) report by the Organization of American States suggested a vast increase in the island's tourism infrastructure, including several large new first-class hotels, an aquarium complex and various improvements in existing tourist attractions (for example the national park and museum). No action, however, was taken on this report because of the softening of the tourist market, its energy implications and the government's mounting balance of payments problem. This report seems to have suffered from the problem noted by Peters (1980, p. 16): 'too often in the past, so-called tourism master plans, funded by donor nations, have been drawn up with grandiose disregard for absorptive capacity and for market potential. These studies neglected implementation – which is of crucial importance to development'.

Despite some instability among tour operators (for example the collapse of Sunflight and Skylark in Canada), a modest recovery began in 1982, with tourist arrivals slowly rising to 1979 levels by 1984. Since then, there has been an almost steady rise, to 269 850 tourist arrivals in 2000 (CTO 2002, p. 216), a 228.6 per cent increase since 1980; however, 2001 saw a decline of 7.6 per cent to 249 251 largely because of the events of 11 September (CTO 2002, p. 15) (Table 4.1).

Table 4.1 St. Lucia tourism statistics

Year	Stay-over tourists		Cruise passengers		Excursionists		Total visitors	
	Number	Annual Change	Number	Annual Change	Number	Annual Change	Number	Annual Change
	('000s)	%	('000s)	%	('000s)	%	('000s)	%
1980	79.7	-9.3	59.0	n.a.	2.1	0.0	140.8	n.a.
1981	68.6	-13.9	18.9	-68.0	2.1	0.0	89.6	-36.4
1982	71.5	4.2	33.8	78.8	2.1	0.0	107.4	19.9
1983	77.4	8.3	33.3	-1.5	1.9	9.5	112.6	4.8
1984	87.3	12.8	37.2	11.7	2.6	36.8	127.1	12.9
1985	94.5	8.2	55.0	65.2	2.1	19.3	151.6	19.3
1986	111.7	18.2	58.8	6.9	3.8	81.0	174.3	15.0
1987	117.6	5.3	83.8	42.5	7.8	105.3	209.2	20.0
1988	133.0	13.1	79.5	-5.1	9.5	21.8	222.0	6.1
1989	132.8	-0.2	104.3	31.2	5.6	41.1	242.7	9.3
1990	138.4	4.2	101.9	-2.3	7.7	37.5	248.0	2.2
1991	159.0	14.9	152.8	50.0	7.0	-9.1	318.8	28.5
1992	177.5	11.6	164.9	7.9	6.5	-7.1	348.9	9.4
1993	194.1	9.4	154.4	-6.4	6.5	0.0	355.1	1.8
1994	218.6	12.6	171.5	11.1	5.9	-9.2	396.0	1.5
1995	232.3	6.3	175.9	2.6	5.6	-5.1	413.8	4.5
1996	2357	1.5	182.2	3.6	5.5	-1.8	423.3	2.3
1997	248.4	5.4	310.3	70.3	5.0	-9.1	563.6	33.1
1998	252.2	1.5	372.1	19.9	5.3	6.0	629.6	11.7
1999	260.6	3.3	351.2	-5.6	6.0	13.2	617.8	-1.9
2000	269.9	3.5	443.6	26.3	12.9	115.0	726.3	17.6

Notes: new accounting method
          n.a.: not available

Source: CTO (2002); Wilkinson (1997)

This overall growth in tourist arrivals, however, represents only the 16th highest rate of increase of 30 countries in the Caribbean region throughout the period; as a result, St. Lucia's position as the 17th most visited destination (CTO 2002) in the region remained constant. The question arises as to whether this pattern is related to the fact that the SLTB's marketing expenditure per stay-over visitor remains among the lowest in the region. Perhaps spurred by the events of 11 September 2001, the government has announced increased funds for marketing, with a focus on its traditional markets of the United States (37 per cent in 2000), Great Britain (27 per cent) and Canada (6 per cent), rather than its previously announced plans to diversify its focus to include Sweden and Germany (Anthony 2002; CTO 2002). Increased emphasis is also being placed on fostering the Caribbean regional market (GOSL 2002b).

It should be noted that, each year, there is also a small number of excursionists, such as single-day visitors who arrive by yacht or air, but who have very little overall economic impact.

Accommodation

The growth in the number of tourists is clearly correlated with the expansion of the hotel industry: in 1964, there were only two hotels with a total of 20 rooms; a decade later, there were over 1 000 rooms (World Bank 1985). The 1974 bankruptcy of Court Lines, however, forced the temporary closure of over one-quarter of St. Lucia's hotel beds (Britton 1978). The fact that one MNC can represent such a major force reinforces the fragility of tourism in such a small nation. Expansion soon began again, however, and, by 1980, there were 1 245 rooms. Spinrad (1982) describes St. Lucia at that time as having 'a rapidly growing tourist industry' characterized by 'explosive growth'. Only a few years later, it appeared that the explosion had ended and that, at best, tourism had reached a plateau.

A major problem in the early 1980s was the continuing financial instability of Halcyon Days, which was finally closed by the government in 1984. The impact on tourist arrivals was minimal because the deteriorating condition of the hotel had resulted in lack of interest by tour operators, but the impact on local employment was extremely serious. At least one MNC expressed an interest in the property, but only if it were granted a gambling concession. A vigorous national debate ensued, in which religious interests and other groups concerned with maintaining traditional island culture were strongly involved; eventually, the government decided against gambling. The current government maintains that policy, but there have been frequent debates on the subject, with the religious and cultural opposition remaining strong. Finally, an arrangement was made with Club Méditerranée, which re-opened the hotel in 1986. (As a result of the company's financial difficulties worldwide following 11 September 2001, Club Méditerranée closed the hotel; the resulting unemployment of several hundred workers has again created serious social and economic problems in the Vieux Fort area). The effect of increased employment was generally considered to be more important than any suspicion about the results of what was recognized to be increased 'enclave' tourism merely one kilometer from the international airport.

By 1987, it was clear that the supply of visitor accommodation was constraining tourism development. Although there had been selective extensions to existing hotels, no new hotels had been constructed in the previous ten years. The fact that 1988 saw a record average annual occupancy rate of 74.5 per cent spurred construction of hotels and villas (CTO 1990; World Bank 1990, p. 64), such as the Royal St. Lucian Hotel and the villas of Windjammer Landing Resort. By 1993, considerable expansion resulted in a total of 2 919 rooms (CTO 1994).

A growing trend in St. Lucian tourism is all-inclusive resorts. By 1990, 41.2 per cent of all hotel rooms were in all-inclusive resorts (for example Club Méditerranée, Couples) (GOSL 1990). The trend continues: Renard (2001, p. 1) provides a figure of 60 per cent of rooms in all-inclusives by 2000. The Jamaican-owned Sandals chain opened another all-inclusive property, the Sandals Grande St. Lucian (formerly a Hyatt resort), in June 2002 in the Gros Islet area in addition to its two other properties near Castries. There has also been an increase in up-market MNC hotels that are not all-inclusives. By 2000, the total number of rooms had risen to 4 525, with more than 70 per cent of them being in hotels of 100+ rooms (CTO 2002).

While Poon (1988) argues that all-inclusives are an innovation that provides a competitive edge to the Caribbean in terms of tapping a growing market segment, concern has been expressed in St. Lucia that there could be an over-supply of this type of vacation product which would militate against a prudent diversification of the sector. Furthermore, because most of the all-inclusive tourists' expenditure takes place (pre-paid in the origin country) within an individual resort, the effective diffusion of such expenditure throughout the economy is severely restricted (World Bank 1990). Mather and Todd (1993) provide the arguments for and against all-inclusives in the context of St. Lucia: high environmental standards, longer average length of stay, a more consistent pattern of demand, higher annual occupancy rates, higher profits, linkages with airlines and considerable marketing clout. They caution, however, that enthusiasm is usually limited to just two or three all-inclusives on a small island, a figure that St. Lucia currently exceeds. Moreover, with foreign ownership and large quantities of imported foodstuffs, much of the profits is not retained on the island; the segregated environment creates resentment towards visitors among the local population; and very little money filters out into the local community in terms of use of services, restaurants, etc. On the other hand, with occupancy rates being high all year long, employment levels are high and stable; for example, one all-inclusive resort with an annual occupancy rate of 90 per cent reports an employee : room ratio of about 2 : 1, rather than a more common 1.5 : 1 for a high-end hotel, with a very low employee turnover rate of less than 5 per cent (M. James 2003, former resident manager, Wyndham Morgan Bay Resort, personal communication). This is contrary to Wilson's (1996, p. 82) finding that many St. Lucians feel that all-inclusives 'employ fewer people as no staff were needed to take money, sort out bills or process accounts'.

This proliferation of all-inclusives is contrary to the government's policy (see below) to encourage small-scale local hotels; nevertheless, it is understandable why the government permits all-inclusives when faced, for example, with possible closure of otherwise unprofitable large hotels as was the possibility with the Cunard La Toc Hotel near Castries, which became a Sandals all-inclusive resort.

Cruise Passengers

As a result of the Caribbean cruise industry's use of larger, more fuel-efficient carriers (formerly not easily accommodated in St. Lucia) and the demand for shorter trips from the main gateway port in Miami, the number of cruise passengers arriving in St. Lucia declined from a peak of 69 084 in 1976 to 18 934 in 1981 with rising energy prices and the worldwide recession (CCA 1991; CTRC 1988). Despite this serious downturn in the early 1980s, St. Lucia has been able to attract a rapidly growing number of cruise passengers in recent years, with a total of 443 600 passengers in 2000, improving its ranking as a cruise destination, rising from 16th to 11th in 2000 of 24 countries in the Caribbean region (CTO 2002). On average, there is slightly more than one cruise ship in harbor every day. The numbers have increased in part because of the Pointe Seraphine pier and shopping facilities in Castries harbor, which were built in the early 1990s and further upgraded in the late 1990s, allowing for better and easier docking and for access by newer, larger ships. The new pier, however, has caused serious erosion problems in the harbor because of changes in wave patterns.

Tourist Expenditures

Rising slightly from 19th to 16th highest in the region between 1980–2000, estimated visitor expenditures were US$276.7 million in 2000, representing as much as 63.8 per cent of GDP in 2000 (CTO 2002).

Cruise passengers are much less important than stay-over visitors in economic terms, although estimates of their proportion of total visitor expenditures in St. Lucia have risen with the increasing numbers of cruise passengers. In the early 1990s, estimates of the contribution of cruise passenger expenditures to total visitor expenditures ranged from 2.5 per cent (GOSL 1990) to 5 per cent (CCA 1991), in contrast to the figure for 2000 of US$23 million or 8.3 per cent of the total of US$276.7 million (CTO 2002). It has been estimated that a cruise passenger spends only about US$52 during a short stay of a few hours in St. Lucia, as compared to a stay-over tourist who spends US$940 over an entire stay (CTO 2002).

It is hard, however, to estimate what the net total tourist expenditure is after leakages are taken into account. Leakages are important measures because gross expenditure figures mask net local economic impact, that is, a large proportion of expenditure does not remain in the local economy. For example, 62 per cent of the tourists surveyed by Dann (1992) were traveling on pre-paid package tours, resulting in much of their expenditure on accommodation being retained by travel agents in their countries of origin and in the accounts of hotel MNCs; even with direct expenditures on food and drink (to say nothing of package or all-inclusive food and drink arrangements), much leaks out as tourists consume, among other things, steaks from the United States and whisky from Scotland.

There has been no recent or definitive study of the leakage rate in St. Lucia, but an estimate of 50 per cent is suggested as not being unreasonable given earlier estimates. For example, Smith and Jenner (1992) state that the leakage rate for St. Lucia was 44.8 per cent in 1978, which is very similar to Spinrad's (1982) estimate of 45 per cent in same year, while Laventhal and Horwath (1986) estimate 60.7 per cent for 1986. While they do not give an exact figure, Poon et al. (1990) state that direct imports for the tourism sector amounted to US$37.42 million, 28 per cent of the US$134.2 million in total imports in 1989; they argue that the total leakage was considerably higher when all second and subsequent round expenditure is taken into account.

Employment generated by tourism is another measure of the economic impact of tourism; however, there have been many estimates of tourism-related employment, with very little agreement, let alone the provision of data collection methods to allow for a comparative analysis. It seems reasonable to estimate, however, that tourism provides approximately 5 200 direct jobs (CTO 2002) and probably an equal number of indirect jobs. Renard (2001) provides a similar estimate of 10 000 direct and indirect jobs. For many people employed directly in tourism, their jobs provide a personal income that is undoubtedly higher than that of the average St. Lucian worker, although that latter figure is not available. For example, Dann's (1992) survey of 70 (non-managerial) hotel employees indicates an average total annual income (salary plus tips) of over US$4,000.

It is also important to note that the vast majority of tourism-related jobs are concentrated in the Castries-Rodney Bay area; with the closing of the Club Méditerranée near Vieux Fort, Soufriere remains the only other node, albeit a minor one, of tourism employment. In addition, with this concentration has come a rapid expansion of construction activity in the area relating to not only housing, but also retail and commercial development, including, for example, the opening of several new shopping malls. Some negative environmental impacts in the area are obvious (such as greatly increased traffic on the single highway), while others are anecdotal (such as water shortages, increased pollution of the sea from over-taxed sewage facilities, illegal sand mining, fears of electricity shortages). An obvious, but un-answered, question is whether all of these changes have had negative social and cultural impacts. As someone who has visited St. Lucia numerous times in the past 20 years, this writer has a subjective feeling that, for some proportion of the St. Lucian people, life has changed dramatically, becoming more like mainstream Western life and less 'Caribbean', but the question, again unanswered, arises as to how much of this change is a result of tourism as opposed to other forces of change, such as communications media and higher levels of education.

TOURISM AND POLICY PLANNING

Given the growing importance of tourism in St. Lucia's economy and the government's stated intention to use tourism to increase employment, a policy and planning framework has evolved to carry out this goal of increased dependence on tourism.

Responsibility for tourism policy appears to be formally vested in the (now) Ministry of Commerce, Tourism, Investment and Consumer Affairs, but is actually controlled at the Cabinet level. Urban and land use planning became a formal part of the administrative fabric of government in 1946, with the passage of the Town and Country Planning Ordinance; while focused on human settlements and public health concerns, the law established the basis for planning through the preparation of 'regional schemes' and the regulation of building construction and general development control. Clearly, tourism has been only one concern within the planning process, but it has received considerable attention over the years.

The Beginnings

As the post-war world-wide tourism boom began to affect the Caribbean, the government recognized the need to encourage expansion of the very small accommodation sector. Under the Hotel Aids Ordinance of 1959, hotels and other guest accommodations could obtain an income-tax holiday for seven years and import duty-free the materials and equipment required for construction. The ordinance had little immediate effect, but clearly provided incentives to hotel developers (particularly MNCs, such as Cunard, Holiday Inns) beginning in the mid-1960s when the jet charter boom began.

Private sector investment, however, did not increase as fast as the government had hoped, forcing it to become an active player. Its first major direct involvement occurred in 1970 with the formation of Rodney Bay Ltd., 90 per cent of the equity being held jointly by the government and Britain's Commonwealth Development Corporation (Towle 1985). The company was formed to develop the tourist potential of Rodney Bay in the north of the island, following major infrastructure works to create marina lagoons and over 160 ha of development land, including one km of new beach, reclaimed in the creation of an isthmus between the mainland and Pigeon Island (GOSL 1977). The peak construction boom in 1970-1973 resulted in several MNC-owned major hotels on the bay, followed by a slow process of further hotel and marina construction that goes on to the present; although it did not develop as originally envisioned, several new up-market hotels have been built on the isthmus in recent years.

The creation of the isthmus, however, has had serious negative environmental impacts. Because the isthmus cut off southern-flowing currents, serious erosion problems have occurred along the shoreline due to disruption of sand deposition processes; in fact, the beach in front of one hotel eroded so seriously that major shoreline armoring had to be put in place to avoid structural damage to one wing of the hotel. With no central sewage system, many of the hotels dump their wastewater directly into the sea, thus raising concerns about water quality. The isthmus also had serious social and economic impacts on the local people. The village of Gros Islet was cut off from the north–south coastal road leading to the major cluster of hotels by creation of the channel into Rodney Bay, although it was connected with a new highway that went around the bay. There was much resentment and a feeling of being excluded from tourism jobs, until a Friday-night street party or 'jump-up' developed into a long-term tourist attraction, with bus-loads of tourists spending freely on food and drink and being entertained by local musicians and dancers. While the Friday party continues to attract large numbers of tourists, local people have turned their resentment on non-local St. Lucians who have come to dominate the event because they had sufficient capital to purchase property and invest in bar, restaurant and entertainment facilities (D. Coathup 1998, ecotourism consultant, personal communication).

After a virtual halt in the expansion of the accommodation stock for several years in the early 1980s because of the world-wide recession, St. Lucia continues to attract major hotel investments, largely because of the favorable taxation and incentives climate initiated with the 1959 Ordinance that continued with three further acts. A 1991 Tourism Incentives Act dealt with a wide range of tourism projects: construction of new or renovation of existing hotels (of at least six rooms), furnishing and equipment of hotels, recreation facilities, historic attractions, restaurants, information and interpretation centers and museums. Projects approved by government were eligible for certain tax benefits: income tax holidays for up to 15 years (including changes in ownership) for new construction and ten years for renovations, exemption from customs and excise duties on building materials and equipment. Tourism investment subsidies available in St. Lucia included: assistance with project financing, tax holidays, investment and other tax credits, accelerated depreciation, double tax relief, leasing of property, marketing support and training support (Arthur Young 1988).

A subsequent 1996 Tourism Incentives Act contains income tax benefits and customs duty exemptions to any approved tourism project. While MNC-owned hotels have undoubtedly benefited from these incentives, there also appears to have been an impact in terms of the construction of several new, small, locally-owned hotels. The 1996 Act was in turn replaced by the 2002 Tourism Hospitality and Development Act which widens the definition of 'an approved tourism project' to include not only hotels, but also restaurants, villas, time-share properties, recreational facilities and leisure craft (Anthony 2002).

Plans and Planning – Formulated but Not Approved

As infrastructure expansion and suburbanization grew in the late 1960s and early 1970s in the Castries area caused by economic growth related to tourism development and construction, there were increasing demands for improved management of urban areas and for long-term planning. In 1971, the Land Development (Interim Control) Act (amended in 1984) was implemented; its purpose was to extend planning control to the entire island without the requirement of a physical plan. It was to be an interim measure while full planning legislation was considered; however, a Land Planning and Development Act, although circulating in draft for several years, was not approved.

In 1977, as a result of administrative problems associated with the dispersal of 'planning and development' functions throughout the government, coupled with external donor pressure for improved project management, a Central Planning Unit (CPU) was formed as the core of the (then) Ministry of Planning, Personnel, Establishment and Training. The CPU developed a St. Lucia National Plan (GOSL 1977); it was never formally adopted by government, but its Physical Development Strategy and Technical Supplement remains the most comprehensive attempt at national physical planning in St. Lucia. The Plan noted that, as tourism began to take off, several problems had become apparent: socio-economic imbalances, seasonality, boom and recession cycles, and limited air access (GOSL 1977). Nevertheless, the government decided to make tourism a key focus of the Plan:

> Government is committed to promoting the growth of tourism to fully utilize the natural resources of climate and scenic beauty with which the island is richly endowed. These qualities, coupled with the warmth and traditional friendliness of the people, offer every prospect for St. Lucia to keep ahead of its competitors in this field (GOSL 1977, p. 33).

Eight specific objectives are stated to guide policy decisions over the following decade: effective marketing and improved airline services; controlled and balanced growth of the tourist sector; full and stable employment in the hotel industry; establishment of links with the agricultural and manufacturing sectors; concentration of tourist activity in selected areas; identification, development and protection of environmental attractions; the development of local support services; and harmonization of the growth of tourism with regional development thrusts (GOSL 1977, p. 34).

Despite later approvals of major proposals, the government seems, however, to have been somewhat wary of large-scale development:

> Government will not generally encourage the development of luxury hotels until there is evidence of substantially improved occupancy and minimal seasonal fluctuations in the existing units. Government has already found it necessary to legislate to protect jobs through financial and other direct intervention in the hotel industry in the wake of the problems created by the [1973] energy crisis (GOSL 1977, p. 34).

The Plan goes on to state that the policy would be to promote the development of smaller hotels and guesthouses with development concentrated in the Rodney Bay area where efforts were to be made to attract investment to develop a 'series of flexible-unit low rise holiday villages' (GOSL 1977, p. 35), which, however, did not occur.

With an ambitious target by the year 2000 of 6 000 new beds being added to the existing 2 000 tourist beds, the Plan calls for tourism development to be focused on the northwest coast (4 000 beds), including the Rodney Bay area, with secondary concentrations around Vieux-Fort (1 500 beds) and Soufriere (500 beds). This ceiling of 8 000 beds reflects the view that further expansion could result in the over-weighting of tourism in the socio-economic structure because tourism, by creating 2 500–3 000 new direct jobs, would then directly and indirectly employ approximately one-third of the labor force. While the targets were not be reached by the year 2000, development has largely maintained the spatial pattern set out in this (unapproved) Plan.

The government recognized that a major problem in international tourism was seasonality (a problem which eventually was overcome, largely due to the popularity of all-inclusive resorts); therefore, one of the aims of the Plan is to develop facilities (most of which were never built) which would attract Caribbean tourists to St. Lucia to help bridge the gap created by the off-peak season of the traditional tourist sector. Similarly, programs for the conservation and enhancement of the island's natural and human-made attractions were to be instigated; some development took place at Pigeon Island and Soufriere, but lack of capital and operating funds were constant problems. Also, there was to be regional cooperation on inter-island air transport; despite the fact that the government is a minor shareholder in LIAT, this remains a problem area. Similarly, other overall elements of the plan did not materialize. The creation of horizontal links with the agricultural sector by gearing production and marketing to the hotels of local produce as a substitute for imported food-stuffs, while laudable, was not realized: only 10–15 per cent of food consumed in hotels is locally-produced (mainly fruit) for a variety of reasons, including volume, tradition, quality control and tourist preferences. A cooperative craft market, established with government support, did eventually develop.

Finally, one overall goal that was at least partially achieved was the development of training programs for hotel management and catering skills. A Hotel Trades School (now part of the Sir Arthur Lewis Community College) was instituted, but there have been many calls for the expansion of its program and/or more private sector initiatives to meet the demand for skilled labor.

The tourism section of the Plan ends on a positive note: 'if, as many expect, the growth of tourism experiences another boom matching that of the early seventies, government aims to be in a position to respond swiftly in rapidly changing circumstances' (GOSL 1977, p. 35).

As a follow-up to the 1977 Plan, a consulting firm (Economic Consultants 1979) was hired to identify and assess the market potential of tourism to St. Lucia, to identify current deficiencies in the tourism sector and to propose appropriate remedial actions. The resulting Tourism Development Study, however, has some suspect figures. For example, the number of stay-over tourists in 1978 is presented as 69 000 (Economic Consultants 1979), whereas the actual figure appears to be less than 33 000 (CTO 1990). The report does predict relatively accurately a total of 129 000 stay-over visitors by 1990 (the actual figure being 138 400), but the validity of this figure is spurious given that the base was incorrect and the result was a function of selecting a modest growth rate of 4 per cent. Moreover, it predicts that this number of visitors would require about 2 900 rooms (Economic Consultants 1979), far above the 2 370 rooms that in 1990 well-served a similar number of tourists at an annual occupancy rate of only 70.4 per cent. The report is slightly more accurate – probably by luck rather than skill – in predicting the number of cruise passengers, suggesting an increase from about 76 000 in 1978 to a (very broad) range of 109 000–150 000 in 1990 (Economic Consultants 1979).

Despite the growing economic importance of tourism in the 1980s, the government devoted little formal attention to either tourism policy or planning. Tourism, however, was not alone, as the only official development policy activity occurred in the early 1980s, when the CPU produced an unpublished series of issue papers on 13 major physical development topics. The result was a new (draft) Physical Development Strategy for the years 1986–1991; however, this document was neither officially endorsed nor released by government. Even if it had been accepted, the impact on tourism would have been minimal as very little of the document was devoted to tourism.

The Greening of Tourism

It could be argued, however, that the government did indeed have a tourism policy because the SLTB, a government-funded statutory agency, developed a marketing plan which positioned the country as an up-market destination because of several factors: high air travel costs from the major markets; a focus on high-income tourists in order to maximize economic benefits and to minimize environmental impacts; and the high demand for the island's natural beauty, making price less important in the buyer's decision-making process (Francis 1993). As a result, the SLTB worked with the government's Development Control Authority to promote new accommodation and facilities that would be acceptable to an up-market clientele. The feeling was that the economic impact of mass tourists, although positive, is limited, while the socio-cultural and environmental impacts are mainly negative (Francis 1993).

As a result, in 1990, the SLTB developed a new 'Green Tourism' marketing theme, as proposed several times previously (cf. Canford Associates 1990). A 'green' market positioning – defined in terms of ecotourism – was agreed on, with the target market being environmentally-conscious tourists. The goal was not to constrain the existing market, but to augment the volume of tourist traffic, while at the same time having minimum negative impacts on the environment.

The SLTB's green theme was being developed at approximately the same time as a Ministry of Tourism's national tourism policy (GOSL 1989) – which was never formally published or adopted by the government – which includes a similar approach, so it appeared that this would be a major marketing strategy for St. Lucia in the future. The development context is described in a series of national development goals and objectives: sustainable economic growth, expansion of employment opportunities and reduction in unemployment, a diversified production base and a continuous expansion of production and exports, and improved general welfare of the population (GOSL 1989, pp. 1–2). Arguing that the economic, physical and social infrastructure has greatly improved in recent years, the Policy calls for this foundation to be more firmly established by broadening its base through economic diversification – one route to which is tourism. Specifically, tourism is seen as having the potential for providing:

- Increased national income, employment, foreign exchange earnings, and linkages with agriculture, manufacturing and services (thus decreasing leakages);
- Increased social and economic benefits;
- Financial justification for the preservation of historical attractions and for the expansion of artistic expression.

Conversely, it is recognized that the effects of an improperly-managed tourism sector on the physical, cultural and social environment can be catastrophic (GOSL 1989). Because of the important role that tourism plays in the economic development of the country, the Policy states that the sector cannot be permitted to develop in an ad hoc manner; rather, a policy framework is required which establishes the parameters within which the development and expansion of the sector will be encouraged. Fundamental for the orderly growth of the sector are the following principles:

- Tourism can and must play a vital role in economic development;
- While a continuing need exists for attracting foreign investment and technology transfer, the sector must be open to full participation by all segments of St. Lucian society and its benefits as widely distributed as possible;
- Over time, the sector must be characterized by increasing levels of local ownership and management;
- Linkages with agriculture, manufacturing and services must be exploited
- The people's right to enjoyment of scenic and other natural resources should be safeguarded in the development of the sector;
- Protection of the physical and social environment must be of paramount concern in the planning and development of tourism;
- These principles inform the following policy measures which constitute a 'tourism development strategy': encouragement of investment, including provision of incentives;

- Increased local participation in accommodation development and in support services;
- Increased public support for tourism through education;
- Consultation among public and private sector agencies to protect the physical environment, including strengthening existing legislation;
- Monitoring market segmentation and all-inclusive packages to avoid over-concentration in any one area;
- Diversification of the tourism plant and of markets, by directly seeking to develop new markets and working with other Caribbean countries in the development of multi-destination arrangements;
- Promotion of St. Lucia's competitiveness and uniqueness;
- Development and maintenance of a reputation for good quality and value;
- Establishment of a Consultative Group on Tourism Development with membership from a wide cross-section of the community (GOSL 1989, pp. 6–10).

In essence, the Policy calls for a 'hands off' attitude towards public sector entrepreneurship and ownership of tourism-related business and, instead, 'an active and leading role in the provision of the infrastructure, fiscal and other incentives together with promotional support for tourism' (McHale 1989, p. 35). This Policy responds directly to concerns expressed by external agencies about the direction of tourism development in St. Lucia. The World Bank (1988; 1986; 1985), for example, emphasizes the need to increase local involvement in tourism in order to increase employment opportunities and point out particular areas of concern: promotion, facilities, foreign exchange leakage, seasonality, occupancy rates, training, costs, marketing, and weak linkages between agriculture and tourism. It (1988, p. iii) also warns about a likely softness in demand in the future due to slower growth projected in the main tourist markets, a relatively slow growth in Caribbean tourism and the emergence of cheaper destinations (such as Mexico, Venezuela, Dominican Republic).

Nevertheless, the government continues to the present time to encourage the expansion of hotel facilities in general and of large, international-scale hotels in particular. Such developments seem to contradict the government's stated policy of encouraging small-scale local hotels. The creation of immediate jobs appears to be taking precedence over the creation of a sector geared to maximizing local participation; moreover, the lack of policy and action regarding training on a national level for the tourism sector appears to be symptomatic of emphasis being placed upon the development of the physical plant without the development of human resources to service the plant.

With respect to market diversification, while the Policy does not specify which non-traditional markets are of interest, there are at least three obvious ones which are well-suited to St. Lucia and which have already received some degree of study and interest (including the SLTB's 'green' theme described above): ecotourism or nature tourism, scuba diving tourism and historical tourism.

Towards the Future

In 1992, the government accorded the tourism portfolio a higher national priority by transferring it from the Ministry of Trade, Industry and Tourism, where it was not a major focus, to the (then) Ministry of Tourism, Public Utilities, Civil Aviation and National Mobilization, in which tourism would be the main area of responsibility. This was a result of both a strong lobby from the private sector and the then Prime Minister's view of the importance of the sector (Mather and Todd 1993). Claiming a commitment to environmentally-sound tourism, the government placed a temporary moratorium on new hotel development until a full-scale economic impact study of the tourism sector had been carried out. The study, however, was not conducted and the moratorium was soon quietly dropped. Importance was also accorded to establishing linkages with other sectors such as agriculture and manufacturing, increasing tourism awareness, and greater participation by the local population in, for example, the running of guesthouses or small-scale businesses supplying the tourism sector. Mather and Todd (1993, p. 105) suggest that:

> With the creation of a new ministry and the increased tourism budget, tourism has been placed at the forefront in St Lucia. In this the government appears to be recognizing that tourism is going to be the main engine of growth for the country's economy and dynamism that is clearly apparent in the new team reflects this commitment.

There was also an expansion of the SLTB's role, previously concerned mainly with the promotion of St. Lucia, to include a technical advisory capacity focused on the future direction of the sector and the task of making recommendations to the Minister to take to cabinet. The SLTB was reorganized so that the sales and the administrative functions are separated and staff additions included the areas of product development (including public awareness), marketing, finance and education. More cooperative work with the private sector was planned, partly through a plan for a tourism fund, with hoteliers contributing US$1 per occupied room and businesses 3 per cent of gross profits, which would be utilized for marketing, but also for other aspects such as an education awareness program; a marketing development committee (with hotel industry, Chamber of Commerce and government members) would manage the fund. The goal was to focus on up-market and green images, previously described as being concerns of the Board.

With a change of government in 1997, a Tourism Advisory Council was set up to advise the Minister of Tourism (GOSL 1997), but it does not appear to have been very effective. The government realized that regional co-operation in tourism issues, rather than competition, was appropriate given the small scale of the island's tourism sector in competition with such larger players as the Dominican Republic. It worked with the Organization of Eastern Caribbean States (OECS) to develop a regional Sustainable Tourism Strategy, the objectives of which included the development of tourism that would be sustainable, internationally competitive and domestically viable, and would aim for economically-sustainable growth, environmental protection and cultural integrity (GOSL 1998). As part of the Caribbean Tourism Conference, the government also began to participate in Caribbean-wide joint marketing strategy (GOSL 1999).

Faced with increasing weakness in the banana market, there was growing concern about rising unemployment and poverty. The government recognized that tourism had come to dominate the national economy, but few of its benefits trickled down to the poor. As a result, it initiated the St. Lucia Heritage Tourism Programme in 1998 with the following mission:

> . . . [T]o establish heritage tourism as a viable and sustainable component of St. Lucia's tourism product by facilitating a process of education, capacity building, product development, marketing, credit access and the promotion of environmental and cultural protection for the benefit of host communities and St. Lucians (Renard 2001, p. 2).

The Programme's goal is not to replace mass tourism, but to place more emphasis on the heritage tourism niche. Its objectives are as follows:

- To develop the island's tourism product, thus enriching the visitor experience through the provision of unique, authentic and natural/cultural visitor activities;
- To enhance St. Lucia's image in the market place as a 'green' destination, with a unique blend of attractions, and types of accommodation;
- To diversify and decentralize the tourist product and benefits, resulting in integration of rural communities island-wide into the tourism industry, providing jobs, and a sense of participation in and ownership of the industry;
- To contribute to the sustainable management of the island's natural and cultural resources (Renard 2001, p. 2).

The Programme is involved in a variety of activities, including product development and management, marketing, capacity building, awareness and communication, and policy and programming. Renard (2001) provides a detailed analysis of the first phase of the Programme, including case studies concerning participatory planning in a village; creation of a marketing brand, 'Heritage Tours, Explore St. Lucia', and authorization for its use by ten sites or tours around the country; locally-based tourism in a village; and development of a heritage tourism Internet site.

The Programme appears to have been successful and its second phase began in late 2002 (SLHTP 2003), with a loan of US$3.36 million from the Caribbean Development Bank (CDB). The newly-stated aims are to make 'St. Lucia the most diversified and sustainable [tourism] destination in the Caribbean' and 'to ensure that the benefits derived from tourism are distributed more evenly throughout the island and especially to rural communities' (SEDU 2003). While the Programme is partly based on the premise of encouraging mass-market tourists to spend more time and money in parts of the island other than the Castries-Rodney Bay corridor, it appears that niche marketing is the major purpose, with its primary goal being the 'development of a complementary marketing strategy in collaboration with the St. Lucia Tourist Board, for the nature/heritage tourism niche market' (SEDU 2003). The list of community activities that enhance heritage tourism products and services which may be eligible for technical assistance, training, loans and grant funding is extensive: nature trails; community enhancement; renovation of heritage sites/structures; gardens, walkways, recreational parks; interpretation and visitors' centers, signs and murals; waste management systems; pre-feasibility studies, site design and planning; sponsored training, capacity building; arts and crafts; preparation and sale of indigenous foods and beverages; cultural attractions and activities; accommodation such as eco-lodges and tented sites; and marketing (SEDU 2003). To be eligible for assistance, projects are required to be environmentally-friendly and community-based in scope, able to contribute to economic linkages within the community, assured of economic viability, contribute to the enhancement of the tourism product and able to guarantee benefits to the community (SEDU 2003). Such major financial support from the CDB suggests that much faith is being placed in the Programme and that it has the potential to meet its goal.

Reflective of another policy shift, the government, in its report to the 2001 World Summit on Sustainable Development (GOSL 2001), seems to be signaling its commitment to spread the benefits of development, including tourism, throughout the country and not limiting it to a small proportion of St. Lucians and a relatively limited geographical area. It bluntly notes that past governments have left St. Lucia in a position where there is an absence of clearly articulated national development policies or goals in which to situate sector policies or plans. As a result, it established the Development Cooperation and Programme Planning Division within the Ministry of Planning, Development, Environment and Housing with a mission to 'foster sustainable improvement in the quality of life of all St. Lucians, through effective integrated planning, coordination, implementation and monitoring of physical/spatial, technological, economic, environmental and social development activities' (GOSL 2001, p. 2). One of its tasks will be the development of a national land policy (no such policy has ever been adopted in St. Lucia, although the proposed 1977 policy has been tacitly used since then), overseen by a National Land Policy Committee (NLPC). One of the NLPC's sub-committees will focus on tourism.

An effort is also underway to develop a new national tourism policy. A National Tourism Policy Forum, held in March 2002, began a process to formulate both a policy and an implementation plan (GOSL 2002a). Despite the stated intention to have the policy in place within six months, there are no results to date.

The Limits to Growth

Despite this apparent increase in government interest in tourism policy and planning, the future of St. Lucia's tourist sector remains unclear. Given the positive economic climate backed by strong public support for tourism, particularly because of foreign exchange and employment benefits, expansion of the hotel plant in the form of international-class hotels (including one with a convention center and potential facilities for a large-scale casino) and several all-inclusive resorts was permitted. Volatility in the world airline industry after the events of 11 September 2001, however, leaves growth plans with a question mark. In general, increased tourist arrivals will depend on increased stability in the airline and tour operator industries and on improved marketing.

There are clear indications, however, that St. Lucia has long faced environmental stresses related to tourism; while no substantive environmental research has been published more recently, the arguments made then appear to remain valid to the present time. For example, Williams (1983, p. 112) long ago notes that the St. Lucian tourist sector did not demonstrate much interest in environmental quality; he describes alteration of coastal configurations and beach profiles, discharge of untreated sewage wastes, removal of beach sand for construction or other purposes, destruction of wetlands and mangroves, construction of large hotels in areas of high scenic value, and restrictions placed on the island citizens' freedom of access to beaches. These negative impacts have a direct relationship to the choice of the type of tourism development:

> Such amenity losses threaten the comparative advantage provided by the tropical island environment and mark the transition away from natural attractions toward high-volume, man-made attractions such as duty-free shopping and gambling.

The policy dilemma now facing St. Lucia is whether to devise strategies to compete more fully in the riskier, high-density, mass tourism market or to resist that transition in favor of the low-density tourism style that has succeeded in the past. While this is a policy issue open to debate, the latter approach has demonstrated comparative advantages elsewhere, including improvement of the rate of domestic return, diminishment of import leakages, and enhancement of the long-term viability of cultural and environmental amenities (CCA 1991, pp. 222–3).

Four factors argue for taking the low-density option: the fastest-growing, most lucrative Caribbean tourism markets reflect this style; it is less vulnerable to political pressures and more socially acceptable; it is less stressful to both human and natural environments; and it tends to require resource management policies which preserve options for future development.

In the only comprehensive overview of the St. Lucian environment, the CCA (1991, pp. 223–4) argues that if St. Lucia is to preserve and enhance its distinctive tourism style, specific environmental, economic and infrastructural needs have to be addressed:

- *environmental*: a coastal zone management policy and related legislation;
- *economic*: long-term tourism planning that emphasizes increasing the tourism multiplier, rather than more short-term policies which are usually directed at raising the volume of visitors;
- *infrastructural*: review of large-scale projects because of their potential to alter the country's low-density tourism style and to place stress on the natural environment and overload available infrastructure; and consideration of requirements for energy and potable water self-sufficiency, self-contained sewage treatment plants, tippage fees for solid waste, yardage fees for construction sand, and maintenance of a dispersed pattern of distribution of infrastructure and large-scale facilities.

The CCA (1991, p. 224) concludes that ongoing expansion of tourism facility construction and increasing international recognition of the island as a prime Caribbean destination suggest that:

> . . . [M]arket momentum may be carrying St. Lucia forward along the continuum from low-density to high-density tourism. If this movement is sustained over the near-term, it will alter the country's present tourism style and leave open to question the long-term economic viability and environmental sustainability of this key economic sector.

There are many government and quasi-government agencies in St. Lucia with potential, but untapped, linkages to tourism planning. The CCA (1991) concludes that St. Lucia's sector-specific approach to resource management has prevented serious attempts at integrated resource management or protection strategies. On the other hand, the technical expertise of personnel in several of the government's resource management units is highly regarded both in the country and in the Eastern Caribbean. The lack of strong cross-sectoral coordination between agencies weakens the ability of any single unit to share information and mitigates against country-level assessments of cumulative environmental impacts.

While the CCA's (1991) concerns cover environmental issues in general, it does make seven recommendations which remain directly relevant to tourism planning. These procedural changes, some requiring legislative action, would allow the government to integrate environmental considerations into the decision-making process and to facilitate the resource management responsibilities of government:

- Provide legislation for and require standardization of environmental impact assessments for development projects;
- Prepare and approve a national land use plan, augmented by local development and land use plans where appropriate;
- Formalize procedures for environmental input at all phases of project planning, implementation and assessment;
- Harmonize and rationalize environmental laws and avoidance of overlaps in institutional responsibilities;
- Provide public consultation and participation in national and local planning;
- Create a public information and documentation center;
- Establish monitoring programs as an integral part of resource management activities.

The CCA (1991, p. 291) concludes that effective implementation of resource management programs in St. Lucia will require public sector consensus on general resource management objectives, sufficient political will to support those objectives, and sharing of program goals and development objectives between central government agencies, interest groups and local communities. This conclusion echoes a long-standing complaint both about small countries in general and St. Lucia in particular:

Most small countries adopt no explicit natural resource conservation policies. In the medium- to long term, however, such inaction may jeopardize their development prospects. Among the reasons for this absence of resource conservation activities from current government planning are the perception of

conservation activities as a burden, the paucity of accurate quantitative data, institutional weaknesses, and the myopic nature of the development process itself
. . . .
To break the vicious circle caused by inadequate information and weak institutions, strong political commitment from involved governments is required (Rojas et al. 1988, p. 282).

The problem is compounded by a planning philosophy which tends to deal with each new development proposal in an isolated, non-integrated manner. While referring specifically to coastal zone management, the CCA (1991, pp. 143–4) describes the state of planning as a whole in St. Lucia as focusing on each new project as an isolated activity. Such 'compartmentalized' development suggests that a conceptual, structural planning problem exists, thus increasing the risk of user conflicts and adverse impacts, and that a more comprehensive approach to coastal resource planning and management is required, including the adoption of formal environmental impact assessment procedures as a requirement for all coastal and marine development projects.

CONCLUSION

The tourist industry will be one of the major foundations of the St Lucian economy in the 21st Century (Venner 1989, p. 92).

With five important exceptions, the history of tourism policy and planning in St. Lucia has been characterized by a 'hands-off' philosophy in which the government has focused on dealing with specific private-sector (usually foreign) development proposals on a project-by-project incremental basis. In effect, the approach has basically been characterized by site-specific land-use planning. The results have been mixed. On the one hand, the number of tourists and the level of expenditures have slowly but continuously risen over the past decade and new developments and development proposals have steadily come on line. The consequence is what the CCA (1991) describes as an intermediate position between low- and high-density tourism. High-density tourism refers to extensive zones of tourism development as occurs, for example, in Cancun; the Rodney Bay area is the only example of such development in St. Lucia. On the other hand, a transition to high-density tourism – which potentially could cause severe environmental stress – seems almost inevitable unless the government takes a more pro-active role in tourism policy and planning. Such an emphasis on high-density tourism could cause local dissatisfaction, because there is strong evidence that the St. Lucian people want more local involvement in the sector; for example, Dann (1992) finds that three-quarters of his sample of residents want local people to have more say in tourism decision-making.

The five exceptions indicate the willingness of successive governments to consider alternative forms of involvement in the tourism sector. The first two exceptions concerned direct government participation in tourism development and operation. In the Rodney Bay Development, the government was an active partner in a scheme to develop a major tourism zone (which was only partially completed). The second instance was reactive, in which the government became involved in the operation of several financially-troubled hotels in the mid-1970s. Most notably, it took over the bankrupt Halcyon Days Hotel and ran it while searching for an international hotel chain to take it over. The ensuing debate on gambling led to a major policy stance based on strong cultural convictions of the public – which may be reversed in the future on pragmatic grounds related to major employment opportunities represented by casino development. Given the fiscal position of the government, however, future direct participation in the tourism sector seems unlikely, a policy position stated in the 1991 National Tourism Policy.

The third exception was the 1977 National Development Plan, which was never adopted officially, but which set the framework for tourism zoning that remains today.

Fourth, the unpublished and un-adopted 1989 National Tourism Policy seems to provide a strong direction to guide the future style, form and location of tourism development. The question remains, however, as to how and whether such a policy could be integrated with a land-use planning process which is focused on particular development proposals, rather than the overall structure of the tourism sector. For example, while the Policy calls for an emphasis on small hotels with a high degree of local participation, there seem to be few resources available to foster such development and, indeed, innovation in general in the tourism sector. Conversely, the government continues to approve large-scale hotels owned by MNCs.

Finally, the government's support of the St. Lucia Heritage Tourism Programme suggests that there is an increasing awareness that the concentration of tourism development in the Castries–Rodney Bay area does not promote the dispersal of the benefits of tourism to the entire country, particularly to rural communities hard hit by the downturn in banana exports.

Unless there is a shift in the mix of types of tourism development towards such alternative forms of tourism, the danger is clear: domination by mass tourism characterized by large numbers of tourists, but tourist expenditures with high leakage rates and low multipliers – and increased environmental stress in terms of water supply, air and water pollution, traffic and beach erosion. Clearly, a reconciliation of policy and practice is in order; otherwise, serious environmental degradation is likely. The question remains as to whether the current government's intentions concerning a national land use plan and a tourism policy will deal with these crucial issues.

Who are the winners and who are the losers in the history of St. Lucia's tourism sector? The clearest winners are MNCs, particularly those controlling all-inclusive resorts with their year-long high occupancy rates (even post-11 September 2001). Some local entrepreneurs have also been winners, including the local owners of one all-inclusive resort, but also others in the construction, retail and commercial sectors who have benefited directly and indirectly from the growth in tourism. Then there are the 10 000 people employed directly and indirectly in tourism; while in many cases their wages are not high, the prospects for alternative employment are few, particularly in the shrinking agricultural sector. Finally, the government is a winner; while tourism is not without its problems, it is the backbone of the economy and government finances.

It is less clear who are the losers. On the one hand, it could be argued that communities not involved in tourism, particularly those in rural areas hard hit by the decline in banana exports, have been hurt by the government's focus both on tourism per se and development in the Castries–Rodney Bay area in particular, resulting in a lack of serious efforts to improve their quality of life. On the other hand, without tourism, the St. Lucian economy would be in a shambles, resulting in even further hardships for these communities. The one ray of hope for them is the St. Lucia Heritage Tourism Programme which has the potential to bring them some of the benefits of tourism, in the form of tourism that is appropriate to 'the promotion of environmental and cultural protection for the benefit of host communities and St. Lucians' (Renard 2001, p. 2).

This latter point raises the question as to whether the biophysical environment of St. Lucia has been a loser. The answer is an equivocal maybe. Tourism development has clearly had negative impacts in the Castries–Rodney Bay area, but the great majority of St. Lucia's land and sea area have not been affected directly by tourism. It is suggested that banana-based agriculture, with its heavy inputs of chemicals, and deforestation, related to high energy costs, have been much more negative for the environment. The potential future danger, however, is that large-scale, environmentally un-friendly, mass tourism will expand to other parts of the island.

NOTES

1. An earlier version of this case study can be found in Wilkinson (1997).

REFERENCES

Anthony, K. (2002), 'Enhancing investment, revitalizing agriculture and stimulating recovery', *2002-2003 Budget Address of the Prime Minister of St. Lucia*, available at: www.stlucia.gov.lc/ primeminister/budgetaddresses/2002_-_2003_budget_addr ess.htm.

Arthur Young Ltd. (1988), *A Study of the Impact of Tourism Investment Incentives in the Caribbean Region*, report for the Caribbean Development Bank.

Britton, R.A. (1978), *International Tourism and Indigenous Development Objectives: a Study with Special Reference to the West Indies*, Ann Arbor, Michigan: University Microfilms.

Bryden, J.M. (1973), *Tourism and Development: A Case Study of the Commonwealth Caribbean*, London: Cambridge University Press.

Canford Associates Ltd. (1990), *St. Lucia: a Market Position for the 1990's and Beyond Accompanied by Executional Considerations for a Competitive Identity and Promotion*, report for the St. Lucia Tourist Board.

Caribbean Conservation Association (CCA) (1991), *St. Lucia: Country Environmental Profile*, St. Michael, Barbados: Caribbean Conservation Association.

Caribbean Tourism Association (CTA) (1960), *Review of Members*, New York: Caribbean Tourism Association.

Caribbean Tourism Organization (CTO) (1990), *Caribbean Tourism Statistical Report 1989*, Christ Church, Barbados: Caribbean Tourism Organization.

Caribbean Tourism Organization (CTO) (1994), *Caribbean Tourism Statistical Report 1993*, St. Michael, Barbados: Caribbean Tourism Organization.

Caribbean Tourism Organization (CTO) (2002), *Caribbean Tourism Statistical Report: 2000–2001 Edition*, St. Michael, Barbados: Caribbean Tourism Organization.

Caribbean Tourism Research and Development Centre (CTRC) (1986), *Caribbean Statistical Report 1985*, Christ Church, Barbados: Caribbean Tourism Research and Development Centre.

Caribbean Tourism Research and Development Centre (CTRC) (1988), *Caribbean Tourism Statistical Report 1987*, Christ Church, Barbados: Caribbean Tourism Research and Development Centre.

Dann, G. (1992), 'Socio-cultural impacts of tourism in Saint Lucia', *Studies in Tourism*, **3** (draft), Port-of-Spain, Trinidad: United Nations Economic Commission for Latin America and the Caribbean.

Devaux, R. J. (1975), *St. Lucia Historic Sites*, Castries: St. Lucia National Trust.

Devaux, R.J. (1984), 'Who discovered St. Lucia?', *The Voice of St. Lucia*, 6 December 1984.

Devaux, R.J. (1992), 'Why Qualibou?', *Qualibou (Newsletter of the Soufriere Regional Development Foundation)*, **1**, 1–2.

Economic Consultants Ltd. (1979), *Saint Lucia: a Tourism Development Study – Summary Report*, report for the Government of St. Lucia and Commonwealth Fund for Technical Cooperation.

Francis, A. (1993), 'Tourism product development and marketing in St. Lucia', in D.J. Gayle and J.N. Goodrich (eds), *Tourism Marketing and Management in the Caribbean*, London: Routledge, pp. 69–77.

Gilles, E. (ed.) (1980), *The Big Picture: World Travel Trends and Markets*, New York: ASTA News.

Government of St. Lucia (GOSL) (1977), *St. Lucia National Plan – Development Strategy*, Castries: Government of St. Lucia.

Government of St. Lucia (GOSL) (1989), *National Tourism Policy*, unpublished draft, Castries: Ministry of Industry, Trade and Tourism.

Government of St. Lucia (GOSL) (1990), *Economic and Social Review 1989*, Castries: Ministry of Finance, Statistics and Negotiating.

Government of St. Lucia (GOSL) (1997), *New Think Tank for Tourism*, press release, available at: www.stlucia.gov.lc/pr1997.

Government of St. Lucia (GOSL) (1998), *OECS Sustainable Tourism Strategy*, press release, available at: www.stlucia.gov.lc/pr1998.

Government of St. Lucia (GOSL) (1999), *Caribbean to Embark on a Joint Marketing Strategy*, press release, available at: www.stlucia.gov.lc/pr1999.

Government of St. Lucia (GOSL) (2001), *St. Lucia National Report to the World Summit on Sustainable Development*, Castries, St. Lucia: Ministry of Planning, Development, Environment and Housing.

Government of St. Lucia (GOSL) (2002a), *More Consultation Towards a New National Tourism Policy*, press release, available at: www.stlucia.gov.lc/pr2002.

Government of St. Lucia (GOSL) (2002b), *Tourist Board to Hold First Regional Marketing Meeting*, press release, available at: www.stlucia.gov.lc/pr2002.

Government of St. Lucia (GOSL) (2003), *St. Lucian Statistics: The Official Web Site of the Government Statistics Department*, available at: www.stats.gov.lc.

Laventhal & Horwath Ltd. (1986), *Leeward and Windward Islands Tourism Sector Study*, Volume I, Report for Canadian International Development Agency.

Mather, S. and G. Todd (1993), *Tourism in the Caribbean*, Special Report No. 455, London: Economist Intelligence Unit.

McElroy, J. and K. de Albuquerque (1989), *Tourism Styles and Policy Response in the Open Economy–Closed Environment Context*, Conference on Economics and the Environment, Caribbean Conservation Association, Bridgetown, Barbados, 6–8 November 1989.

McHale, A.H. (1989), 'Tourism is our business', *Saint Lucia: 10th Independence Anniversary Souvenir Magazine*, 35–6.

Persaud, B. (1966), *An Abstract of West Indian Banana Statistics (With Special Reference to the Windward Islands)*, Cave Hill, Barbados: Institute of Economic and Social Research, University of the West Indies.

Peters, M. (1980), 'The potential of the less-developed Caribbean countries', *Tourism Management*, **1** (1), 13–21.

Poon, A. (1988), 'Innovation and the future of Caribbean tourism', *Tourism Management*, **9** (3), 213–20.

Poon, A., A. Sobers, S. Williams and W. Mitchell (1990), *The Economic Impact of Tourism in St. Lucia*, Christ Church, Barbados: Caribbean Tourism Organization.

Renard, Y. (2001), 'Practical strategies for pro-poor tourism: a case study of the St. Lucia Heritage Tourism Programme', *PPT Working Paper No. 7*, London: Pro-Poor Tourism Project, Greenwich: Overseas Development Institute, International Institute for Environment and Development, and Centre for Responsible Tourism at the University of Greenwich.

Rojas, E., R.M. Wirtshafter, J. Radke and R. Hosier (1988), 'Land conservation in small developing countries: computer assisted studies in St. Lucia', *Ambio*, **XVII** (4), 282–8.

St. Lucia Heritage Tourism Programme (SLHTP) (2003), *The St. Lucia Heritage Tourism Programme*, available at: www.stluciaheritage.com.

Small Enterprise Development Unit (SEDU), Ministry of Commerce, Tourism, Investment and Consumer Affairs, Government of St. Lucia (2003), *The St. Lucia Heritage Tourism Programme*, available at: www.sedustlucia.com/projects/slhtp.htm.

Smith, C. and P. Jenner (1992), *Travel & Tourism Analyst*, Report No. 3, London: Economist Intelligence Unit.

Spinrad, B.K. (1982), 'St. Lucia', in S.B. Seward and B.K. Spinrad (eds), *Tourism in the Caribbean: The Economic Impact*, Ottawa: International Development Research Centre, pp. 67–92.

Towle, E. (1985), 'St. Lucia – Rodney Bay/Gros Islet', in T. Geoghagan (ed.), *Proceedings of the Caribbean Seminar on Environmental Impact Assessment*, St. Michael, Barbados: Caribbean Conservation Association and Institute for Resource and Environmental Studies, Dalhousie University, Halifax, pp. 228–43.

Venner, K.D. (1989), 'The Saint Lucian economy in the 21st Century', *Saint Lucia: 10th Independence Anniversary Souvenir Magazine*, pp. 79–95.

Wilkinson, P.F. (1984), 'Energy resources in a Third World microstate: St. Lucia household energy survey', *Resources and Energy*, **VI** (3), 305–28.

Wilkinson, P.F. (1997), *Tourism Policy and Planning: Case Studies from the Commonwealth Caribbean*, New York: Cognizant Communication Corporation.

Williams, M.C. (1983), 'Country summary for St. Lucia', in J. Wood (ed.), *Proceedings of the Workshop on Biosphere Reserves and Other Protected Areas for Sustainable Development on Small Caribbean Islands*, Virgin Islands National Park, St. John, USVI, and United States Department of the Interior National Parks Service, Southeast Regional Office, Atlanta, May 10–12, pp. 110–8.

Wilson, D. (1996), 'Glimpses of Caribbean tourism and the question of sustainability in Barbados and St. Lucia', in L. Briguglio, R. Butler, D. Harrison and W. Leal Filho (eds), *Sustainable Tourism in Islands and Small States: Case Studies*, London: Pinter, pp. 75–102.

World Bank (1985), *St. Lucia: Economic Performance and Prospects*, Washington DC: World Bank.

World Bank (1986), 'St. Lucia economic memorandum', *Report No. 6385-SLU*, Washington DC: World Bank.

World Bank (1988), *Caribbean Countries: Economic Situation, Regional Issues, and Capital Flows*, Washington DC: World Bank.

World Bank (1990), 'Long-term economic prospects of the OECS countries', *Report No. 8058-CRG*, Washington DC: World Bank.

5. The Political Ecology of Marine Protected Areas: The Case of the Bay Islands

Susan C. Stonich

INTRODUCTION

Traditional measures to regulate and protect marine areas from fishing and other human activities are centuries old among island peoples of Asia, Oceania and elsewhere. However, over the last few decades, a variety of new forms of marine protected areas (MPAs) have emerged as important environmental management tools and as strategies to protect marine biodiversity. Currently, MPAs are being promoted by major multilateral public donors, bilateral funders, international environmental organizations, non-governmental organizations (NGOs), and national governments as well as by private/corporate investors. Despite significant environmental and ecological differences conceptually and in terms of application (Carr et al. 2003), MPAs share a great deal with their predecessors, terrestrial protected areas (TPAs). In addition, the designation of MPAs raises similar ecological and social issues and uncertainties as those raised with the designation of TPAs (Western et al. 1994). Like their terrestrial counterparts, especially in developing countries, most MPAs include tourism as an important component or justification; most attempt to integrate so-called public participation and community-based management and conservation into their design and implementation; and most involve the cross-scale interaction of a variety of contending interest groups at various scales, from the local through the national and international/global. Unfortunately, like their terrestrial counterparts, MPAs also have generated serious, ongoing, and often unresolved social conflict in the locales in which they have been proposed or implemented. It is clear that the creation of MPAs may produce significant social impacts related to essentially coercive conservation measures and other conflicts over resources. The most serious conflicts are likely based on diverse consequences regarding who benefits and who pays the price related to the creation and implementation of MPAs – suggesting the relevance of political ecological analysis to this situation.

This chapter uses a political ecological approach to analyzing and evaluating the creation of MPAs in the Bay Islands, Honduras – as a case study of the consequences of establishing MPAs in tropical islands that are economically dependent on tourism. The analysis expands previous work by the author that used a political ecology framework to analyze various costs and benefits of tourism development and conservation strategies on the economic livelihood strategies, human nutrition and food security, human environmental health, and environment and ecology of the Bay Islands (Stonich 2000). While discussion of the several terrestrial and marine conservation initiatives implemented on the Bay Islands were part of that comprehensive analysis, that work did not focus specifically on the establishment of MPAs. In general, however, environmental conservation strategies, both terrestrial and marine, had multiple and often contending objectives, including maintaining biodiversity, improving environmental management, and most importantly preserving the Islands' desirable tourist attractions, especially coral reefs.

GLOBALIZING MARINE PROTECTED AREAS

Although the potential conservation and management benefits of various forms of marine protected areas have been touted by conservationists and scientists for the past 30 years, only in the last decade have protected areas been extensively established. According to the International Union for the Conservation of Nature (IUCN), in 1970, 118 MPAs had been established in 27 nations with 100 others in the proposal stage (NRC 2001). By 1985, 430 MPAs existed in 69 countries with an additional 298 proposed (Silva and De Silvestre 1986). By 1994 the IUCN had identified 1 306 MPAs with hundreds of other proposed sites (Kelleher et al. 1995). Today several thousand MPAs have been established globally with several thousand more proposed throughout the world.

Heightened interest in MPAs came about in light of growing concern over declining yields in many fisheries and degradation of many marine habitats (especially coral reefs), which pointed out the inadequacies of conventional approaches to marine management (NRC 2001). Currently, MPAs are widely seen as promising components of a comprehensive, ecosystem approach for conserving marine and coastal environments (NRC 2001). Although MPAs vary considerably in scale, form and function, the most important categories include Marine Protected Areas (MPAs), the most general, inclusive category, defined as a geographic area with discrete boundaries that has been designated to enhance the conservation of marine resources; Marine Reserves (MRs), 'closed' or 'no take zones' a stipulated area in which some or all of the biological resources are protected from removal, disturbance and other human activities; and Multiple-use MPAs, an approach often employed over large (eco)regions that allows for integrated management of complete marine ecosystems usually through a zoning process (NRC 2001).

MPAs also vary in terms of goals and objectives, contributing to their versatility as well as presenting challenges to their design and implementation. According to a recent panel of the US National Academy of Sciences/National Research Council the multiple goals of MPAs in order of importance include:

1. Conservation of marine biodiversity and habitats;
2. Improvement of fisheries management;
3. Increased scientific knowledge;
4. Expanded educational opportunities;
5. Enhanced tourism and recreational activities; and
6. Protection of cultural heritage (NRC 2001).

A 1994 review of the objectives of MPAs as presented in peer-reviewed journals concludes that conservation and scientific goals are paramount and to a great extent the objectives and goals of MPAs are set by the conservation and scientific communities and by governments (Jones 1994). Especially in developing countries, MPAs are linked to tourism development as a way to integrate conservation and economic development. While the promotion and control of tourism at the more macro-economic level (this is, enhancing foreign exchange earnings) are mentioned as important goals in most articles, glaringly absent in most cases are goals at the community and household level – including sustaining communities, lives and livelihoods through MPAs. Yet there is increased recognition that community participation and sustaining human lives and livelihoods are essential components to effective MPAs (Agardy 2000).

Designing and Evaluating MPAs: The Missing Dimension

The neglect of the human dimensions of MPAs (both in terms of human activities as driving forces and the impacts of MPAs on human systems) is the missing dimension in recent attempts to design and to evaluate MPAs (Suman et al. 1999). The proliferation of MPAs in the last decade has led to a related explosion of research aimed at evaluating MPAs and at improving their design and implementation. Two of the most important syntheses of these efforts are 'Marine Protected Areas: Tools for Sustaining Ocean Ecosystems', published by the United State's National Research Council (NRC), Committee on the Evaluation, Design, and Monitoring of Marine Reserves and Protected Areas in the United States, Ocean Studies Board, and the Commission on Geosciences, Environment, and Resources (2001), and the Supplement to Volume 13, Number 1, Ecological Applications entitled 'The Science of Marine Reserves' (February 2003). The NRC study concludes that 'a growing body of literature documents the effectiveness of marine reserves for conserving habitats, fostering the recovery of overexploited species, and maintaining marine communities' (NRC 2001, p. 175). Among the other major conclusions and recommendations of the NRC study report is that 'effective implementation of marine reserves and protected areas depends on participation by the community of stateholders' (NRC 2001, p. 4). Throughout the report the NRC emphasizes the importance of integrating social, economic and cultural factors (the human dimension) into the analyses, design, implementation, management, monitoring and evaluation of MPAs. However, these recommendations are largely rhetorical and do not reflect the current imbalance in research on, and evaluation of, MPAs. For example, in the introduction to the special supplement of Ecological Applications, Lubchenco et al. admit that the efforts of the workshops on which articles in the special edition were based, 'only began to address the crucial interaction between the broad range of human stakeholders and reserve success, or the best methodologies for engaging different interest groups in the process of marine reserve research and design' (Lubchenco et al. 2003, p. 5–6). They go on to conclude that the various 'socioeconomic disciplines have much to offer to the topic of marine reserves' (Lubchenco et al. 2003, p. 6). Yet in the concluding article to that same edition, Roberts et al. maintain that biological and biodiversity criteria are paramount and should take precedence over, and inform, social and economic concerns (Roberts et al. 2003). The remainder of this chapter attempts to answer the following questions: how would MPAs be different if human (social, economic, cultural) objectives were included as primary goals? Is it possible to integrate potentially conflicting objectives into MPAs that simultaneously sustain human communities, lives, and livelihoods, conserve natural resources and promote tourism/ecotourism development? These questions are addressed using the lessons learned from the attempts to create locally based MPAs (such as the Sandy Bay–West End Marine Reserve) and nationally based MPAs (such as the Bay Islands National Marine Park) in the Bay Islands.

THE CASE OF THE BAY ISLANDS

It is beyond the scope of this chapter to review in detail the significant growth of tourism in Central America over the last two decades which has been discussed elsewhere (Stonich 1998; Stonich 2000). Since 1990 both the number of tourist arrivals and the amount of tourist receipts to Central America increased significantly: from 1.75 million tourists to 4.27 million tourists annually and from US$869 million to almost US$3 billion. Tourist arrivals to the region have continued to increase after 11 September 2001 suggesting that Central America may be an acceptable, alternative tourist destination during politically troubled times. International tourist receipts to Central American nations constitute an increasingly large percentage of total export earnings: accounting for a low of 7 per cent of export earnings in El Salvador to a high of 58 per cent in Belize in 2000 (calculated from data in IMF 2001). Tourist arrivals and receipts to Honduras also increased significantly during the same period, with the number of arrivals increasing from 290 000 to 408 000, and receipts growing from US$29 million to US$240 million between 1990 and 2000 (WTO 1993, 2002). Remarkably this growth continued after Hurricane Mitch in October 1998, which virtually destroyed the nation's infrastructure in addition to causing more than 8 000 deaths and widespread environmental destruction. Tourism continues to make an increasingly important contribution to the Honduran economy, moving from fifth to first-ranked activity in terms of generating foreign exchange earnings between 1995 and 2001 (IDB 2002). Preliminary estimates for 2002 suggest that more than 600 000 tourists visited the country, contributing about US$328 million to the nation's economy. The Bay Islands constitutes the most popular tourist destination in Honduras with more than 100 000 international and domestic tourists visiting the Islands annually.

Introduction to the Bay Islands

The Bay Islands are located about 50 km off the coast of northern Honduras and now are easily accessible from the mainland by plane, boat and ferry as well as by direct international flights from the United States, El Salvador and Belize. They are made up of three main islands and over 60 smaller cays having a total land area of approximately 260 km². The largest of the islands is Roatan, which covers 127 km² and until recently was the site of most tourism development. A mountainous ridge bisects the length of the island from northeast to southwest and steep hillsides end abruptly at the coastline. While Roatan boasts only a few palm-fringed, white sand beaches (most notably West Bay Beach, Alligator Nose Beach and Camp Bay), they are spectacularly beautiful and provide ideal sites for swimming, snorkeling and sunbathing – the major pastimes of domestic tourists and important as well to many international tourists. The islands' main international tourist attraction, however, is the fringing coral reef which is part of the Mesoamerican Barrier Reef System and which scuba devotees regard in the same class as the Great Barrier Reef of Australia. The reef performs important ecological functions, such as providing critical habitats for numerous marine species and shielding the shorelines from inundation. Although rainfall averages at least 2 000 mm per year on all of the Bay Islands, most precipitation occurs during the short rainy season – especially during October and November. The primary tourist season is during the dry season from January through June during which less than 100 mm of precipitation falls (Stonich 2000).

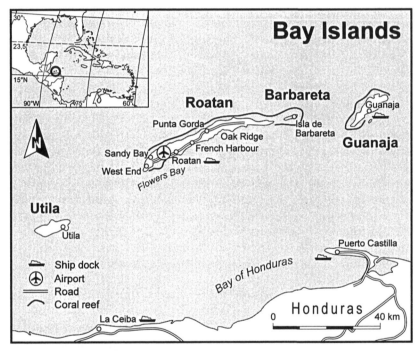

Figure 5.1   Bay Islands, Honduras

In addition to enchanting tropical beaches and spectacular coral reefs, reminders of the islands' colorful history are evident in remnants of prehistoric archeological sites, pirate strongholds, English fortresses, underwater ship wrecks and an ethnically diverse population (English/Creole speaking Afro-Caribbeans, Anglo-Caribbeans and North Americans; Garifuna [Black Caribs]; and *ladinos*). Together these attractions make the Bay Islands suitable for the principal types of Central American tourism development –

sun, sea and sand tourism; adventure and ecotourism; and cultural heritage tourism. Their important potential for tourism development has made the Bay Islands a focal point of federal legislation since they were declared a Tourism Zone in 1982 (Acuerdo Número 87). Particularly significant are the 1991 Acuerdo Ministerial Número Dos which established the minimum standards for any Bay Islands' development, including restrictions on coastal building and protective measures for mangroves and offshore coral and marine life, and the 1993 Decreto 83–93 which created a Bay Islands Commission to promote development, review all development plans and preserve the Islands' environment.

The recent efforts of the government of Honduras (GOH) to promote tourism in the Bay Islands required that it face several hundred years of Anglo-Hispanic conflict during which time control of the islands alternated between British and Spanish/Honduran political powers. Even after Honduras eventually gained sovereignty over the islands through the Wykes–Cruz Treaty of 1859, the islands' overwhelmingly dominant Anglo-Caribbean and Afro-Caribbean population successfully isolated itself from Honduran control. To a great extent, islanders retained their ethnic, cultural, linguistic (English/Creole) and religious (Protestant) heritage; maintained their social, cultural and economic ties to the other English-speaking enclaves in the Caribbean – especially to Belize and to the Cayman Islands – and intensified their links with the United States. Today, many islanders refer to themselves as 'British' rather than 'Honduran' and convey sentiments of political independence from Honduras and allegiance to the United States. The recent boom in tourism is linking the Bay Islands into the mainland polity, economy, society and culture as never before. Not surprisingly, enhanced integration has been accompanied by heightened friction between longtime resident Anglo-Caribbean, Afro-Caribbean islanders and recently arrived Spanish speaking *ladinos* from the mainland (this is, government agents/officials, the army/police, national elites and poor immigrants).

Until the late 1980s, the Bay Islands remained relatively isolated, had poor telecommunications capacity, lacked infrastructure, had minimal tourist facilities and a relatively low human population density. These characteristics protected the Bay Islands from many of the adverse social and environmental costs of tourism that characterize much of the eastern Caribbean. Beginning in the 1960s, a small tourist industry made up mostly of divers and recreational sailors began to enjoy the splendid reef, clear waters, secluded harbors and tranquil beaches. At the same time, according to most social, economic, education and health measures, the Bay Islanders managed to maintain a quality of life that significantly surpassed that of Honduran *ladinos* on the mainland. Unfortunately, these conditions began changing radically in the 1980s, in the context of the largely unregulated and uncontrolled growth of the tourism industry. In 1990 an estimated 15 000 visitors visited the Bay Islands making the islands the most popular tourist destination in Honduras. By 2000, more than 100 000 tourists visited the islands annually – significantly exceeding the projected estimates that had been made just a few years earlier. Expansion of the industry stimulated the migration of thousands of desperately poor *ladinos* from the mainland seeking a better life through employment in the tourism sector. According to the most recent national census of population conducted in 2000, the current resident population of the islands is almost 50 000 people, the majority, Spanish speaking *ladinos* from the mainland (IDB 2002). In addition to tourists and *ladino* mainlanders, the islands' population currently is being augmented by a growing number of foreigners. Until recently, Bay Island and other Honduran interests dominated the tourist industry on the islands. More recently, however, these initial promoters have been joined by a number of foreign real estate developers and other well capitalized investors whose aims include converting previously undeveloped portions of coastal and upland areas into large-scale resorts and up-scale housing subdivisions. Their efforts have provoked widespread land speculation, an upward spiral in land prices and intensified social conflicts – not only over land but also over access and use of the islands' limited freshwater and marine resources. Although a small number of expatriates and retirees from the United States, Great Britain and elsewhere have started businesses and/or made the islands their permanent or vacation home for several decades, the recent arrival of large-scale foreign developers has exacerbated conflicts markedly.

The Political Ecology of Tourism in the Bay Islands

The research reported here is based on a collaborative project in which a political ecology framework was used to measure the heterogeneous human and biophysical consequences of tourism development. Research focused on three communities on Roatan (Sandy Bay, West End and Flowers Bay) which were 'hot spots' in terms of the pace of tourism growth. The methodology and results of this research have been reported in depth elsewhere (Stonich 2000). In summary, the consequences of tourism have included increased social differentiation and a growing gap between rich and poor; the assignment of the majority of *ladinos* and islanders to low-status, low-paid, temporary jobs; reduced access for local people to the natural resources on which they depend for their livelihoods; escalating prices for food, manufactured goods and housing; land speculation and spiraling land costs; increased outside ownership of local resources; and deterioration of the biophysical environment. According to measures of economic production, income, wealth, consumption and nutrition, Afro-Caribbean islanders range in wealth from very rich to very poor while *ladinos* on average tend to be significantly poorer and at higher nutritional risk than islanders. The most telling result of the anthropometric studies of children less than 60 months of age, was that undernourishment was found only among *ladino* children – albeit at rates lower than on the mainland (Stonich 2000). Many recent *ladino* immigrants express disappointment about their lives on the islands as did this 31-year-old mother of four who said, 'We came here because we had no land and there was no work in Belfate [on the mainland] . . . but there's not enough work here either . . . no good work . . . we make [earn] more here when we find work but things cost twice as much'. For poor *ladino* and islander families, inadequate benefits from employment in the tourism sector have combined with reduced access to what had been publicly available fishing, hunting and gathering resources: for example, through the establishment of the Sandy Bay Marine Reserve. In the words of a 35-year-old ladino immigrant,

> I do plantation work (such as yard work), my wife works as a maid at Palm View Cabins, and my kids sell fish when they can catch them. It's hard and sometimes only the little ones eat. Sometimes at night I go out and fish on the reef or hunt iguana in the hills. They tell us not to [take fish and shellfish from the reef or hunt iguana] but my kids have to eat.

Many poorer island residents (islanders and *ladinos*) are indignant about being urged to end or reduce their fishing and hunting activities by wealthier inhabitants. Less powerful residents are well aware that it is these more powerful stakeholders who are the owners of commercial fishing fleets, hotels, resorts and other businesses, who are responsible for over-fishing shrimp and lobster and who are engaged in a real estate and hotel building spree (despite the existing shortage of fresh water and the absence of sewerage and other solid waste disposal systems), unsound road building, mangrove destruction, extensive dredging of the reef and other environmentally destructive activities. Many poor local people feel that their own temperance will be of no benefit unless everyone can be made to restrict his or her fishing effort or other environmentally destructive activity. 'I'll stop hunting iguanas when they [island elite and foreign investors] stop dredging for new marinas and hotels and over-fishing', said a 72-year-old Afro-Caribbean islander whose family had lived on the Islands for several generations. The gap in wealth between resort owners, whose guests make the most use of the reef, and local subsistence users, only strengthens the stance of poorer residents who feel they should not bear the burden of environmental conservation. It is not surprising that the one marine reserve (the Sandy Bay–West End Marine Reserve) established in Sandy Bay 1989 and expanded to include West End and the West Beach area in 1993 is having difficulty restricting use despite the fact that it is part of the official Honduran protected area system.

Less powerful stakeholders, including most poor and middle class islander and *ladino* residents, also feel estranged from the goals and activities of the best known environmental conservation organization on the islands – the Bay Islands Conservation Association (BICA). Although BICA works closely with several international development donors and environmental organizations, BICA's emphasis on mainstream conservation efforts (for example, turtle conservation projects, cosmetic beach clean-ups and environmental education) has not addressed the environmental, social, cultural or health concerns of most island residents. The fact that the families of the two highest officers of BICA are major stakeholders in the tourism industry and significantly benefit financially from the expansion of tourism adds to the skepticism of local people about the motives of the organization.

MARINE PROTECTED AREAS IN THE BAY ISLANDS

The Bay Islands are characterized by unusually high biological diversity including an abundance of corals and reef fishes. The islands also support regionally significant mangroves, wetlands and endemic pine forest, and other island ecosystems representative of the Caribbean. As such, the Bay Islands have been recognized as a national priority for conservation. The 1997 Honduran Presidential Executive Order (Acuerdo Ejecutivo Número 005-97) created the Bay Islands National Marine Park and integrated the park into the National System of Protected Areas of Honduras. The order was justified on the basis of several legal, regulatory and environmental considerations (GOH 1997). According to Articles 172 and 340 of the Honduran Constitution and Article 35 of the General Environmental Law, the Honduran State is responsible for conserving the country's biological, hydrological, historical and cultural resources, and for contributing to sustainable development in surrounding communities. Article 41 of the General Environmental Law specifically stipulates that the GOH is responsible for the protection of the coastal and marine ecosystems of the Bay Islands. The presidential decree recognizes that the islands' terrestrial and marine ecosystems currently are at risk, and identifies a number of particular environmental problems currently plaguing the islands including: deforestation, erosion, related increases in sedimentation, and the associated degradation of coastal and marine ecosystems. It highlights the loss of approximately 249 hectares of mangroves since 1989, primarily attributed to urban growth, inappropriate land use (especially the conversion of upland forest to pastures), and the construction of tourist-related infrastructure and facilities. Also noted is the absence of public drinking water, sewerage and solid-waste disposal systems. The order points out that due to these deficiencies most human generated waste is directly deposited into the sea and causes serious environmental decline in coastal and marine areas. The order also indicates that overexploitation by the islands' extensive fishing fleet has significantly reduced fishing yields – thereby negatively affecting one of the principal economic activities of the Bay Islands. Significantly missing from the GOH decree is any mention of the repercussions of increasing human populations on the islands' environment and natural resources.

According to the presidential order, the recently created marine park has several objectives (GOH 1997). The most important is 'to promote economic development through the rational exploitation of renewable and nonrenewable resources, especially through the least destructive means, tourism and recreation' (GOH 1997). Another stated goal is to maintain an 'ecological equilibrium' that protects the genetic resources and biological diversity of the islands, while a third objective is to establish a system of protected areas aimed at conserving the islands' marine and coastal resources. The order proposes to manage human activities within the park through the passage and enforcement of environmental legislation, the installation of control buoys, the implementation of use restrictions and the monitoring of environmental conditions. Zonation is also proposed as a means of delimiting various use and protected areas. These include multiple use zones, economic development zones, zones in which fishing is restricted, and protected zones in which no economic activities are allowed. To facilitate these goals, broader public support is to be promoted through the involvement of community users in the planning, implementation and management processes. The park will be administered through a Unidad Administrativa (United Administration) that includes representatives of the island municipalities and members from the Department of Protected Areas and Wildlife of the Honduran Forestry Development Corporation (Dirección de Areas Protegidas y Vida Silvestre de la Corporación Hondurena de Desarrollo Forestal [DAPVS/AFE-COHDEFOR]), the Commission for Integrated Coastal Zone Managment (Comisión de Manejo Integral Costero [COMICO]) and the Ministry of Natural Resources and Environment (Secretaría de Recursos Naturales y Ambiente [SERNA]). Finally, sustainable financing of the park is to come from the implementation of a cost recuperation system that generates income: for example through admission and use fees.

The problems and prescriptions presented in the ambitious presidential decree are not unique but reflect perceptions of environmental problems and potential solutions that have been proposed for almost two decades by various international donors as well as by the GOH itself (Stonich 2000). Major regulatory authority for conserving the environment of the Bay Islands was first conferred on the Honduran Ministry of Culture and Tourism (SECTUR) in 1982 when the GOH declared the Bay Islands a tourist zone. A second important ministerial decree for environmental regulations on the Bay Islands was Agreement Two (Acuerdo Dos) which adopted the master plan contained in an environmental study of Roatán completed in 1983 (Halcrow and Partners 1983). This decree, issued by the Ministry of Government and Justice in February 1991, established general norms for development on the islands, including specific regulations governing authorizations for development projects, zoning and protection of natural resources. It requires the following: approval of all applications to undertake development projects, with approval first required from the municipality and then by the Honduran Institute of Tourism (IHT); establishment of a specific zoning plan to govern development of any structures within 140 m of the beach; a grace period of 1.5 years from declaration of the law for industrial factories to begin treating their waste products; and protection of the reef and its ecological communities from the discharges of wastes from ships on the open sea and from dredging and construction projects. In addition, Agreement Two specifically prohibits the collection of black coral, the use of harpoons, the use of toxic substances in the reef, the felling of mangroves, the exploitation of the reef for minerals, and water lots (the construction of buildings in shallow water).

A subsequent presidential decree established the Commission for Development of the Bay Islands (the Commission) in May 1993 whose purpose was to encourage development programs and projects for the Bay Islands that maintain the integrity of the environment. This non-profit foundation has legal status, its own financial resources and is composed of individuals from both the government and private sectors. Members of the Executive Council include the President of Honduras who also is the President of the Commission; the Minister of Government and Justice; the Director of Tourism; the Governor of the Bay Islands; and the mayors from the four island municipalities. One of the first tasks of the Executive Board was to choose eight representatives (and eight alternatives) from the private sector. These included the owners of the largest resorts and other prominent business people as well as one member each from the islands' two major non-governmental organizations, the now defunct Bay Islands Conservation Association (BICA) and the Bay Islands Development Promotion Association (APRODIB). Of these members, half plus one must be Hondurans with five or more years of residency in the Bay Islands. Like the 1997 presidential decree that established the Bay Islands National Marine Park these regulatory means attempt to reconcile economic development with environmental conservation. Particularly noticeable in the structure of the Commission is that regulatory power remains in the control of government officials and island elite. Not surprising most evaluations of the Development Commission regard it as a failed attempt at creating institutional alliances for environmental management in the Bay Islands due to problems of representation (this is, its domination by elites) and lack of funding.

As a means of addressing possible environmental costs stemming from its various economic and fiscal incentives, the GOH passed the General Environmental Law in June 1993 which founded the Ministry of the Environment (Secretaría de Estado en el Despacho de Ambiente [SEDA]) and established the legal process for obtaining an Environmental License. Under this legislation, all projects and/or economic activities likely to degrade or contaminate the environment must present an environmental impact study approved by SEDA prior to receiving any concession or project permit from a government agency. Moreover, the execution of any project without first obtaining an Environmental License constitutes an environmental crime. In the Bay Islands, as in the rest of Honduras, SEDA as a ministry level office was given significant power to oversee the environmental feasibility of tourism-related projects. One of SEDA's important roles in the Islands was to execute the US$23.9 million Bay Islands Environmental Management Project funded by the IDB that is discussed below.

Over the years, concern over achieving a balance between economic growth and environmental integrity on the islands led to the development of several plans to address simultaneously initiatives to expand tourism and conserve the environment. Some of these studies focused primarily on marine ecosystems while others were more concerned with watershed management and forest protection. Until the early 1990s, the most thorough environmental study was the Environmental Control Plan for Roatán (Halcrow and Partners 1983), which provided the basis for Acuerdo Dos.

Major Conservation Efforts
Major environmental conservation efforts on the Bay Islands, both terrestrial and marine, are integrated in a large network of international and national institutions, organizations, programs and projects. The most important of these are the Mesoamerican Biological Corridor, the Mesoamerican Barrier Reef System Project and the Bay Islands Environmental Management Project (Stages I and II).

Mesoamerican Biological Corridor
In addition to the Bay Islands National Marine Park, certain areas or all of the Bay Islands are part of several other international, national and municipal conservation initiatives. These include the Mesoamerican Biological Corridor, the most recent reincarnation of the Path of the Panther (Paseo

Pantera) project sponsored by the Wildlife Conservation Society (WCS) with significant funding from the United States Agency for International Development (USAID). This remarkably ambitious endeavor is based on the recognition that Central America is not composed of seven separate tropical ecosystems belonging to seven sovereign republics. Rather, it's a single ecological system whose germplasm, mammals and migratory birds do not recognize political boundaries. In 1994 at the Presidential Summit of the Americas in Miami, all seven Central American countries agreed in principle to create a single Mesoamerican Biological Corridor composed of a network of national and trans-border nature reserves and protected areas combined with environmentally benign forest plantations. The Mesoamerican Biological Corridor has been gaining fame, not as a 2 000-mile-long nature preserve, but as an integrating concept into which a variety of environmental projects can fit. The United States and European governments, private foundations and international development banks have committed some US$600 million. The World Bank is the single largest donor with US$160 million. The projects range from managing forests, to preserving indigenous land rights, to strengthening national environmental laws. In the Bay Islands WCS efforts have focused on developing a management plan for the Sandy Bay–West End Marine Reserve which will be discussed later in this chapter.

Mesoamerican Barrier Reef System Project
Another regional agreement aimed specifically at protecting the Mesoamerican Barrier Reef System, the largest coral reef system in the Atlantic, was first signed in July 1998 by the presidents of Belize, Guatemala, Mexico and Honduras. On 20 June 2001, a more comprehensive project, The Project for the Conservation and Sustainable use of the Mesoamerican Barrier Reef System (MBRS) was launched on Ambergris Caye in Belize (MBRS 2002). Present were the Prime Ministers of the Environment from the four Mesoamerican nations – Mexico, Honduras, Belize and Guatemala. Also present were members from the Central American Commission on Environment and Development (CCAD), the World Bank, the Global Environmental Facility (GEF), the United Nations Development Programme (UNDP), IDB and various dignitaries. The US$17.8 million joint World Bank and GEF MBRS project was declared 'effective' by the World Bank on 30 November 2001. Supported, in part, by the World Wide Fund for Nature, the MBRS creates an 'action plan' that sets forth a series of local, national and regional initiatives to preserve the region's extensive reef system that stretches from the coast of Cancun, Mexico to the Bay Islands, including a number of multi-use MPAs and Marine Reserves. The Mesoamerican Barrier Reef has been designated as a World Heritage Site by the United Nations Educational, Scientific, and Cultural Organization (UNESCO) and

recognized as one of the 'Global 200' sites of critical importance to biodiversity. To date, only one existing protected area in Honduras, Turtle Harbor on Utila has been identified for support through the MBRS MPA component. The ambitious GEF MBRS Project also includes tourism and policy components. Co-financing for this aspect of the project in Honduras is provided through a credit from the World Bank's concessional lending agency, International Development Assistance (IDA), to the Government of Honduras to promote a national strategy for Sustainable Coastal Tourism along the north coast and the Bay Islands of Honduras. A parallel US$17 million project of the IDB, the Bay Islands Environmental Management Program (Stage II) is aimed at collaborating closely with the GEF MBRS project.

Bay Islands Environmental Management Program (PMAIB Stage I, II)
The Bay Islands' most comprehensive, ambitious and well-funded environmental conservation efforts to date are in the process of being implemented – a two stage environmental management plan to guide development and conserve the islands' natural resources financed by the IDB. In late 1994, after several years of conducting feasibility studies through the United Nations Development Program, the IDB approved financing for the Bay Islands Environmental Management Project (PMAIB Stage I) with a loan of US$19.1 million from the IDB supplement with US$4.8 million from Honduras. The project was fully funded and operational as of April 1996. According to project documents, the IDB is to work with SEDA and Island NGOs, including APRODIB and BICA. The general objective of the ambitious project is 'to maintain and improve the quality of the environment on the Bay Islands as a basis for sustainable economic development based on tourism' (IDB 1994, Part II, p. 1) and 'must benefit the 24 000 people who live on the Islands', according to the project's former executive director. Among the stated objectives are protecting coastal and marine ecosystems through a system of integrated management; strengthening local capacity for planning, management and administration; and improving the standard of living of the inhabitants through improvements in water supply and construction of basic sanitation. Similarly to the 1997 presidential degree, the IDB project did not address directly the social or environmental problems emanating from escalating human populations. Despite the participatory rhetoric written into the project summary, interviews with local people in the communities of Sandy Bay, West End and Flowers Bay during the summer of 1995 revealed that few residents (apart from a small group of wealthier business owners) were well informed about the project or had been consulted in any way. Some residents were badly misinformed believing that the US$23.9 million would be distributed among island residents.

In 1996, the executive director of the IDB project resigned over major differences of opinion with the leadership of SEDA and the GOH over how the project should be managed. Especially contentious was the 'decentralized' approach that had originally been agreed upon and the growing reluctance of the GOH to transfer the needed administrative autonomy to the Roatán project unit – an aversion that persists until today. Not long after, the two members of the Roatán project unit were fired by the GOH – thereby dissolving the unit. The IDB traditionally takes an 'at arm's length' approach to supervision and monitoring once a project has been approved. The bulk of the responsibility for project execution rests with the government, at least in principle. Responsibility within the IDB to monitor project execution lies with the local offices, in the Bay Islands case the IDB office in the Honduran capital of Tegucigalpa. The loss of the IDB project's executive director in Tegucigalpa and the field staff on Roatán seriously impeded the implementation of the project (Senior IDB staff member 1997, personal communication).

The decision by the GOH in December 1996 to 'restructure' its ministries, ostensibly as part of efforts to cut government expenditures, added to anxiety over the ultimate implementation and fruition of the IDB project in the Bay Islands. As part of this restructuring, SEDA was 'reorganized' and downgraded from its ministry level. Although it is not clear what the implications of this reorganization will be for the eventual success of the IDB project, in 1997 a senior staff officer of the Regional Water and Sanitation Network of Central America characterized the project as 'dragging its collective heels' (Senior IDB staff member 1997, personal communication). Serious reservations were expressed by staff of a major bilateral development assistance agency who are concerned that the sanitation investments may rely on inappropriate technology and levels of discharge that will be potentially damaging to reefs. An informal evaluation of the project in late 1997 by a senior IDB staff member is telling:

> I tend to agree . . . of having to confront political and economic realities in the Islands. And it may take a more direct approach from the international community including ourselves. My concern is that the upper reaches of the Bank may be under the impression that all is well since, after all, the loan was approved. In reality, Honduras has started paying commission fees on a loan with diminishing prospects of ever seeing any environmental and social benefits. This weighs heavily on the minds of those of us who made a case for the project two years ago (Senior IDB staff member 1997, personal communication).

In 1998 the IDB transferred the program to the Tourism Secretariat which established a new Project Coordination Unit (PCU) in Roatán which seems to have facilitated execution of the project (IDB 2002). According to project documents, PMAIB I resulted in several notable achievements including: the creation of a comprehensive geographic information system for environmental management; completion of a cadastre for the entire archipelago; improvements in water supply and wastewater collection systems for an estimated 11 000 residents of the island's largest towns (Coxen Hole, French Harbour and Oak Ridge) (IDB 2002). Project documents also point to a number of main issues still to be resolved. These include: the extraordinarily high rate of population growth due both to immigrants to the islands and to the increasing number of tourists; uncontrolled tourism development exacerbating problems of coastal water quality; limitations in existing institutional arrangements that are not conducive to environmental management of land and coastal areas in an integrated way. Key factors identified during PMAIB I as obstacles to successful environmental management were: lack of representativeness and accountability of local stakeholders; insufficient local capacity in environmental management; insufficient institutional arrangements and financial mechanisms to carry out project activities (IDB 2002).

In light of these and other critiques, the IDB concluded that an effective foundation had been set for a second stage of the program (PMAIB II) aimed at addressing the above issues and at achieving a self-sustaining program that 'can maintain environmental quality while supporting growth and competitiveness in tourism' (IDB 2002, p. 13) – the same overarching goal that the IDB identified for their earlier project (PMAIB I) in 1994. This objective is part of the IDB's current strategy for Honduras which aims at promoting sustainable economic growth within a framework of enhanced social equity. The IDB project profile specifically mentions the opportunity of the PMAIB II to strengthen the representation and meaningful participation of Afro-Caribbean communities as well as to strengthen the capacity for managing a significant portion of the Mesoamerican Barrier Reef System (IDB 2002).

MARINE PROTECTED AREAS: LOCAL PERSPECTIVES

For two centuries, Bay Islanders have been free to overharvest fish, jettison trash, even dredge and fill bays and inlets to build more commodious beachfront homes . . . As a public official and resort owner, [the owner of Cooper's Key Resort] was in a prime position to see that the economy of his island and the health of the reefs were intertwined . . . A man of action, he bought a fiberglass skiff, recruited his own marine patrol, and set out to protect the dive site sites within reach of his resort. And he gave his new 'reef police' a strict mandate to hit poachers hard, with stiff sentences, including jail terms for repeat offenders. Fortunately, no one challenged the resort owner's authority to make his earliest arrests – statutory authority over the sanctuary now known as Sandy Bay Marine Reserve was only obtained this year (Gordon 1993).

For my patrol, I picked the guys who were out there spearing the fish, who were out there polishing the coral and selling it to the tourists . . . I'm the beneficiary of the reef . . . The reef's beauty is what I sell, and I should be the person who pays for its upkeep (Owner of Cooper's Key Resort, quoted in Gordon 1993)

The above quotations are from an article entitled, 'An octopus' garden: a guide to marine parks and reserves', that appeared in the December 1993 issue of *Hemispheres*, the onboard magazine of United Airlines. In it, the author points to the Sandy Bay Marine Reserve as a positive example of marine conservation. The first quotation is by the freelance reporter who investigated and wrote the article, based in part on interviews with BICA leaders and the owner of Cooper's Key Resort (a pseudonym) in Sandy Bay. The second statement is by the owner of Cooper's Key Resort. Together they disclose a great deal about the political ecology of tourism and MPAs in the Bay Islands, as well as about media coverage and public perceptions of environmental problems and conservation initiatives. The reporter ascribes blame for the serious decline in the health of the islands' reefs to hundreds of years of overexploitation by Bay Islanders in general, who, according to him, have been free to engage in all sorts of environmentally destructive behaviors including over-fishing, dredging and construction of luxurious residences. He then attributes salvation of the reef to the efforts of a 'man of action' who took it upon himself to save the reef by hiring his own 'reef police' to guard the reserve and enforce its rules. The author asserts that it is fortunate that no one questioned this resort owner's authority since the 'reserve' had not yet been designated as such by any local or national government authority. In his remark, the owner of Cooper's Key Resort, a member of the Island elite, acknowledges that he benefits economically from a healthy reef and so is willing to pay to maintain its integrity. He also attests that he hired patrol guards from among those who exploited the reef for their own economic advantage.

The views presented in this article both reinforce and conflict with the analyses and concerns raised in this chapter. First, environmental degradation at its present level has not been going on for the last several hundred years – although the consequences of hundreds of years of human activities are detectable in the present landscape. The most severe environmental problems are the result of human activities that have occurred over the last few decades – the result of commercial fishing, migration from the mainland and the unregulated growth of the tourism industry. Second, it is not all Bay Islanders who are responsible for the most egregious environmental problems – but predominantly the island elite and foreign developers (including the owner of Cooper's Key Resort). Third, the reporter is correct in saying that the resort owner was on shaky ground – fining and arresting 'poachers' – because his attempt to privatize a national/public/communal resource was both illegal and unconstitutional. The reporter's remarks expose the coercive nature of the marine reserve and its oligarchic control by the powerful resort owner. It recalls the observation made by Jane Houlson, who visited the islands in 1934, that the white island elite, 'rules with a feudal right unquestioned' (Houlson 1934, p. 68). The comments by the owner of Cooper's Key Resort reinforce this. To him, the 'reef police' are 'my patrol'. Through his remarks, the owner appears to claim 'ownership' of the reserve and its resources even though shoreline and inshore areas cannot be privatized according to Honduran law. He also seemingly takes credit for establishing the reserve although the notion of the reserve initially came from environmentally concerned community members. While it is true that the resort owner provided the majority of funding for the reserve for several years, as he said, he was a major beneficiary of the reserve. Moreover, his financing stopped when management of the reserve expanded to include other business owners and community members who questioned his authority and behavior.

The article also reveals the power of this individual to frame the understanding of the islands' environmental problems as well as their potential solutions for the international media – who in turn communicate this framework to the public. To diving enthusiasts, Cooper's Key Resort is one of the best known diving resorts in the Caribbean and is widely respected as environmentally concerned and involved. Professionals, as well as the public, have constructed their perceptions of the islands predominantly on the basis of the images, views and perspectives of island elites, government officials, or travel writers with very short-term experience. For example, the team of consultants who authored the conservation strategy for the Bay Islands prepared for USAID and Paseo Pantera that is cited elsewhere in this chapter, acknowledge the assistance of BICA and the owner of Cooper's Key Resort with 'logistics and advice on how to approach the relevant conservation and development issues in the islands' (Vega et al. 1993, p. 7). In addition, a growing number of conservation organizations, environmental scholars and their students, many associated with prestigious universities, have used the research facilities available at the resort's for-profit marine science center. Members of the media, consultants, researchers and students, like thousands of tourist divers, apparently are unaware of the environmental and social controversies that have surrounded the resort and its owners or of the larger political ecological context in which tourism and conservation on the islands are situated.

Honduras has established a system of protected areas based on the model of the system used by the International Union for the Conservation of Nature (IUCN). In addition, populations of local flora and fauna have been granted special protected status. In the Bay Islands seven marine and terrestrial protected areas or reserves have been established by municipal ordinance since 1961. Vega et al. (1993, pp. 81–4) recommended that 12 areas be designated in order to preserve the Bay Islands' biodiversity and fresh water supply as well as to benefit the tourism industry. Five areas on Roatán were suggested including the Sandy Bay Marine Reserve (which subsequently was expanded to become the Sandy Bay–West End Marine reserve) and the West End forest. On Utila, four areas were designated and on Guanaja two areas. The study also recommended that the entire area around the Bay Islands be declared a marine area. This recommendation differed to some degree with the proposal prepared by the GOH and UNDP advisors. While the former recommended that the entire area be a marine protected area encompassing smaller marine parks, the latter advocated that the entire area around the Bay Islands be considered a national marine park with small, internal zones of special management. The latter recommendation is in line with the presidential decree that established the Bay Islands National Marine Park in 1997.

The 1992 USAID/WCS study concluded with a series of nine principal recommendations that remain relevant today:

1. The maximization of agricultural lands through the cultivation of appropriate annual, semi-permanent and permanent crops;
2. The modernization or termination of livestock grazing;
3. The promotion of forestry production in appropriate areas;
4. The reforestation and control of runoff in critical areas;
5. The stabilization of denuded areas associated with the construction of highways;
6. The consolidation of the system of protected areas;
7. The establishment and enforcement of regulations prohibiting illegal hunting, fishing, and capture of wild species and the introduction of exotic species;
8. The devolution of national authority for wildlife and wildlands management to a specific Bay Islands park authority that could develop co-management agreements with local NGOs and municipalities; and
9. The promotion of public participation in the development and implementation of the environmental management plan, not only through environmental education but also through the local population's participation in the economic benefits of tourism (Vega et al. 1993).

Despite a growing number of municipal ordinances and enhanced national recognition, attempts to manage conservation areas on the Bay Islands historically have met with little success. For example, one of the first areas to be protected was the Guanaja Forestry Reserve established in 1961. Vega et al. (1993, p. 63) report that at the time of their study in 1992 few local residents were even aware that these local forests had been protected. Moreover, a management plan had never been drafted, personnel had never been assigned and no research had ever been conducted. Likewise, on Roatán, the Port Royal Wildlife Refuge was established in 1979 via Acta No. 20 of the Municipality of José Santos Guardiola. Thirteen years later, in 1992, no management plan had been prepared for this protected area. According to the secretary of the Bay Islands Conservation Association: 'sure we've had two marine parks here since the 1980s . . . but as far as we're concerned they're just paper parks – no rules, no park rangers, not even a painted sign to tell people where they are' (Secretary of BICA; quoted in Gordon 1993, p. 78)

It is striking that over the years, an increasing amount of money has gone to fund an escalating number of consultants, environmental assessments and management plans for the Bay Islands. It remains to be seen if any will come to fruition or if they do, the effects they will have on the human residents as well as on the environment and natural resources of the islands. In any case, recent iniatives are steeped in so-called participatory approaches that urge or demand that community-based conservation and development be central to the efforts. For example, both the 1992 USAID/WCS conservation strategy and the IDB environmental management project proposal encourage a great deal of community involvement and local control. In 1997, BICA announced plans to implement management plans for the Sandy Bay–West End Marine Reserve on Roatán and the Turtle Harbour Wildlife Refuge on Utila. Financing for the three-year project was provided by Fundación Vida through funding by USAID and technical support from WCS. According to a BICA press release, the project's main objective is:

> . . . [T]o promote the conservation of the Bay Islands natural and marine resources in both protected areas. This will be achieved through the design and implementation of management plans for both areas, daily patrols by boat and on land, reef monitoring programs to identify problems and seek solutions. The installation of sediment traps . . . will minimize negative impacts in our marine environment . . . We aim to educate our people about the importance of our fragile resources and the need to protect, conserve, and manage in a sustainable manner. Our ecotourism program will help us educate our local and international tourist. Generating at the same time revenues that will help us cover operative costs (BICA 1997)

THE POLITICAL ECOLOGY OF TOURISM AND MARINE PROTECTED AREAS

The political ecology approach included determining the benefits and costs and the related winners and losers stemming from current trends in tourism and conservation. The Bay Islands' poor *ladinos*, poor islanders and women were receiving the least benefits from tourism as measured by levels of income, patterns of consumption, food security and nutritional status. It identified recently-arrived poor *ladinos* to be most in jeopardy in terms of these measures. Moreover, although all island residents as well as tourists currently face escalated risks from diseases associated with declines in the quality of fresh, brackish and sea water, the risks to recent *ladino* immigrants are the most serious. For poor *ladinos* and islanders, insufficient benefits from employment in the tourist sector have been exacerbated by reduced access to previously available natural resources through the establishment of protected areas such as the Sandy Bay–West End Marine Reserve. For some islanders the expansion of tourism has resulted in dispossession from their homes due to collusion between foreign developers, Honduran elites and government officials.

Understanding the relationships between tourism development and conservation efforts including MPAs requires understanding the interrelationships among diverse stakeholders. In the case of the Bay Islands, the GOH certainly is a major stakeholder, not only regarding its historical relationship to the Bay Islands but also in terms of the effects of its current incentives to promote tourism. Other important stakeholders include international donors, lenders and environmental organizations; foreign investors; government agencies and national NGOs; Honduran elites; extremely poor *ladinos* on the mainland; local non-governmental organizations; recently emergent, religiously based, grassroots organizations; the ethnically and economically diverse Bay Island population; and the escalating number of tourists. It is important to point out that the Bay Islands are not an example of the consequences of excessive foreign investment in the tourism industry. In fact, Bay Island elites contributed significantly to the current tourism boom on the islands. Moreover, in many instances, the interests of island elites are more akin to those of foreign investors than to those of their less affluent neighbors. Rather than being determined entirely by external forces, the present tourism sector has been shaped by a complex mix of local and extra-local forces and actors.

Many residents, especially those from predominantly Afro-Caribbean communities such as Flowers Bay, feel that they have been intentionally excluded from benefiting from tourism development by the GOH, international interests and island elites who control the development opportunities. Island elites and middle class business owners engage in environmentally destructive activities while they simultaneously extol the virtues of environmental conservation, attend international tourism conferences, and support the protection of marine reserves at the expense of poor *ladinos* and islanders. However, without the collaborative support of stakeholders, from the least to the most powerful, there is little chance that the existing reserves or the proposed Bay Islands National Marine Park will succeed in their conservation goals over the long-term. No single stakeholder or the various coalitions of actors are in complete control over all the forces and actors that are at play in the islands.

At present, unregulated tourist development appears to be accelerating through the construction of up-scale hotels and resorts by island elites, Honduran elites from the mainland and well-capitalized foreign investors; the expansion of small-scale hotels, rooms for rent, and other tourist-related businesses by middle class islanders and less-well capitalized foreigners; and the increased parcelization of remaining areas of tropical forests, upland areas, and prime beach property which is being sold principally to foreigners from the United States and elsewhere. The influx of a large number of less educated, less healthy and desperately poor *ladinos*, along with unbridled development and increased pressures on resources from tourists, affects the environmental quality of the islands, the environmental health of the population and the long-term viability of the tourism industry itself. The inability of the GOH, the IDB, the USAID, and the variety of NGOs to ameliorate the negative environmental effects and associated human costs of tourism command the meaningful involvement of local people in all facets of the tourism industry not just as workers at the lowest rung of employment. These failures are not merely problems of enforcement of existing environmental laws and regulations. This is one of the most important policy lessons to be learned from this case study. The emergence of the Native Bay Islanders Professionals and Labourers Association (NABIPLA) in the Afro-Caribbean community of Flowers Bay demonstrates that the less empowered on the islands want to share in the benefits of development and likewise are committed to sustaining the environment and natural resources on which an alternative vision or model of tourism development can be based. The expansion of NABIPLA beyond Flowers Bay to other parts of Roatán and the demands of the residents of West End to arrest control of their marine reserve are other examples. But according the members of NABIPLA: 'NABIPLA agrees with the world's environmental movement, but we need to fight the battle from the root. NABIPLA believes that our children are the Number 1 endangered species' (NABIPLA 1995, p. 3).

Obstacles to Community Participation, Development and Environmental Conservation

The uncontrolled growth of tourism that is occurring simultaneously with internationally funded environmental management plans and conservation initiatives emphasizes the underlying discord between the goals of economic development and environmental conservation on the islands. Even within the tourism sector, the Bay Islands present a case of unresolved contradictions between the desired models of tourism along with their respective environmental requirements – from mass tourism on the one hand to academic, adventure and ecotourism on the other. At the community level, effective community-based conservation and development also conflict with the interests of the state, the island elites and foreign investors. In this context, the coercive approach of the Sandy Bay–West End Marine Reserve may intensify with the creation of the Bay Islands National Marine Park. The integration of the Sandy Bay–West End Marine Reserve (as it is currently conceived and managed) with the Bay Islands National Marine Park may strengthen the GOH's control over the islands' natural resources and people. The mandate of the GOH to protect the country's environment and natural resources, along with its monopolization of legitimate force could combine to facilitate state control as well as exacerbate current levels of resistance, conflict and violence. The GOH in collaboration with unrepresentative NGOs such as BICA and island elites are likely to use conservation dogma to defend coercion in the name of conservation. Sanctioned violence in the name of resource defense also facilitates the control of people – especially less affluent black islanders, including members of NABIPLA, who challenge the state's claims to natural resources as well as its hegemony in other areas.

CONCLUSIONS AND RECOMMENDATIONS

The major objective of this chapter was to demonstrate the indispensability of integrating social, cultural and economic criteria into the design, management and evaluation of MPAs. It should be clear from the story of efforts at environmental conservation in the Bay Islands, whether terrestrial or marine, that the human dimensions (social, cultural, economic) are as crucial and perhaps more essential than biological criteria to the 'success' of MPAs and other conservation initiatives. Contrary to the recommendations made by conservationists and biophysical scientists that biological and biodiversity criteria should be paramount – there is little or no chance of conserving biological resources in locales such as the Bay Islands unless the human dimensions are given equal importance. Especially important is the first recommendation of the NRC – that meaningful participation of all interest groups (stakeholders in their terms) be included in all stages of project design, implementation, management and evaluation. That has yet to happen in the Bay Islands. Instead environmental conservation initiatives have exacerbated long-standing differences and tensions and created new ones. On the other hand, augmented conflict has also precipitated the emergence of NABIPLA, a grassroots NGO consisting of disenfranchised poor Afro-Caribbean Islanders, whose constituents were left out of earlier efforts but appear to be included in the most recent efforts of the IDB – PMAIB II. It remains to be seen how and if the emergence of this civil society group will affect further development or conservation initiatives on the islands. However, the success of future efforts is dependent on their meaningful inclusion in the process, as well as the participation of poor *ladinos* from the mainland who now comprise the majority of the Bay Islands' resident population, yet have not been represented in past initiatives.

A second major conclusion of this chapter is that it is impossible to separate environmental conservation measures, including the establishment of MPAs, from tourism development. From the scale of the Bay Islands National Marine Park to locally controlled MPAs like the Sandy Bay–West End Reserve, tourism development and environmental conservation are intimately connected in terms of objectives, goals and funding initiatives. While maintaining the Bay Islands' incredible biological diversity and environmental health are central objectives of most powerful stakeholders and the economic and environmental initiatives they promote, these are not goals for their own sake but only as a means to sustain and enhance tourism development. This basic linkage implies the necessity to understand the consequences of coupled tourism development and environmental conservation at all levels from individuals, to households, to diverse ethnic groups, to various socio-economic groups. Currently, the losers in terms of the establishment of MPAs are the same groups identified in previous political ecological analysis, which examined the effects of tourism development on ethnicity, household livelihood strategies, nutrition and food security, gender and human environmental health. Thus, vulnerability to MPAs is part of a larger set of vulnerabilities.

Finally, this chapter has also demonstrated the incredible degree of cross-scale linkages involved in the establishment of MPAs and other environmental conservation measures in the Bay Islands. A diverse array of international, national and local players have a stake in what happens in the Bay Islands, not least of which is the Honduran State. The Bay Islands are not among the group of small, independent nation states, such as those in the Eastern Caribbean that are dependent on tourism. Rather the Bay Islands are a formal department of the nation of Honduras and have been so for almost 150 years. The goals, objectives and power of the GOH have been fundamental in influencing the current conditions and future directions of the Bay Islands. It is clear that tensions between international institutions/donors, the state, and the local (in all its heterogeneity) must be addressed if any socially just and environmentally sound future for the Bay Islands is possible.

REFERENCES

Agardy, T. (2000), 'Information needs for marine protected areas: scientific and societal', *Bulletin of Marine Science*, **66** (3), 875–88.

Bay Islands Conservation Association (BICA) (1997), *Conserving Biodiversity in the Sandy Bay–West End Marine Reserve on Roatán and the Turtle Harbour Wildlife Refuge on Utila* [press release], Roatán: Bica.

Carr, M.H., J.E. Neigel, J.A. Estes, S. Andelman, R.R. Warner and J.L. Largier (2003), 'Comparing marine and terrestrial ecosystems: implications for the design of coastal marine reserves', *Ecological Applications*, **13** (1) Supplement, 90–107.

Gordon, D.G. (1993), 'An octopus' garden: a guide to the world's marine parks and reserves', *Hemispheres*, December, pp. 68–80.

Government of Honduras (GOH) (1997), *Executive Order: Bay Islands National Marine Park* (Executive Order Number 28279, 7 June), Tegucigalpa: Government of Honduras.

Halcrow and Partners (1983), *Plan de control ambiental de la Isla de Roatán*, Tegucigalpa, Honduras: Dirección General de Urbanismo.

Houlson, J.H. (1934), *Blue Blaze: Danger and Delight in the Strange Islands of Honduras*, London: Duckworth.

Inter-American Development Bank (IDB) (1994), *Bay Islands Environmental Management Project*, Washington DC: Inter-American Development Bank.

Inter-American Development Bank (IDB) (2002), *Bay Islands Environmental Management Project II*, available at: http://www.iadb.org/exr/doc98/apr/h011 13e.pdf.

International Monetary Fund (IMF) (2001), *Balance of Payments Statistics Yearbook*, Washington DC: International Monetary Fund.

Jones, P.J.S. (1994), 'A review and analysis of the objectives of marine nature reserves', *Ocean & Coastal Management*, **24**, 149–78.

Kelleher, G., C. Bleakley and S. Wells (1995), *A Global Representative System of Marine Protected Areas*, Washington DC: The Great Barrier Reef Marine Park Authority, the World Bank, and International Union for the Conservation of Nature and Natural Resources.

Lubchenco, J., S.R. Palumbi, S.D. Gaines and S. Andelman (2003), 'Plugging a hole in the ocean: the emerging science of marine reserves', *Ecological Applications*, **13** (1) Supplement, 3–7.

Mesoamerican Barrier Reef System Project (MBRS) (2002), *The Mesoamerican Barrier Reef System Project*, available at: http://www.mbrs.org.bz.

Native Bay Islanders Professional and Labourers Association (NABIPLA) (1995), 'The way we see things', *Bay Islanders' Echo*, **1** (1), 1-20.

National Research Council (NRC) (2001), *Marine Protected Areas: Tools for Sustaining Ocean Ecosystems*, Washington DC: National Academy Press.

Roberts, C., G. Branch, R.H. Bustamante, J.C. Castilla, J. Dugan, B.S. Halpern, K.D. Lafferty, H. Leslie, J.L. Lubchenco, D. McArdle, M. Ruckelshaus and R.R. Warner (2003), 'Application of ecological criteria for evaluating candidate sites for marine reserves', *Ecological Applications*, **13** (1) Supplement, 215–28.

Silva, M. and I. DeSilvestre (1986), 'Marine and coastal protected areas in Latin America: a preliminary assessment', *Coastal Zone Management Journal*, **14** (1), 311–47.

Stonich, S.C. (1998), 'Political ecology of tourism', *Annals of Tourism Research*, **25** (1), 25–54.

Stonich, S.C. (2000), *The Other Side of Paradise: Tourism, Conservation, and Development in the Bay Islands*, New York: Cognizant Communications.

Suman, D., M. Shivlani and J.W. Milon (1999), 'Perceptions and attitudes regarding marine reserves: a comparison of stakeholder groups in the Florida Keys National Marine Sanctuary', *Ocean & Coastal Management*, **42** (12), 1019–40.

Vega, A., W. Alevizon, R. Dodd, R. Bolauos, E. Valleda, C. Cerrato and V. Castro (1993), *Watersheds, Wildlands, and Wildlife of the Bay Islands: A Conservation Strategy* (Vol 1), Gainesville, Florida: Tropical Research and Development, Inc.

Western, D., R.M. Wright and S.C. Strum (eds) (1994), *Natural Connections: Perspectives in Community-Based Conservation*, Washington DC: Island Press.

World Tourism Organization (WTO) (1993), *Yearbook of Tourism Statistics*, Madrid: World Tourism Organization.

World Tourism Organization (WTO) (2002), *Yearbook of Tourism Statistics*, Madrid: World Tourism Organization.

6. Native Tourism, Natural Forests and Local Incomes on Ilha Grande, Brazil

Sven Wunder

INTRODUCTION[1]

Tourism on Ilha Grande is to an overwhelming extent nature-based and the attractiveness of the island as a tourist destination is neatly linked to its extensive forest coverage. But this is not yet another Costa Rica catering to high-income international tourists that admire the wonders of tropical rainforests, or another Seychelles that market the image of pristine beaches to developed-country tourists. At about 150 km from Rio de Janeiro and 400 km from São Paulo, Ilha Grande is close to two of the most populous cities in the southern hemisphere. It thus caters predominantly to native Brazilian tourists. This gives a focus that differs from other cases in this book.

Native tourism is of rapidly increasing significance in many developing countries, in particular middle-income countries with large urban populations, such as China, India, South Africa, Mexico, Thailand and Brazil. Statistics on domestic tourism in developing countries are weak, but WTO figures indicate that its volume grew by 22 per cent between 1991 and 1996; many specific sites are totally dominated by domestic visitors.[2] Until now, this trend has gone widely unnoticed by tourism researchers, planners and activists alike, who focus almost entirely on international tourism. One recent assessment of native tourism found that it often has positive effects on local livelihoods and strengthens local cultural traditions, but also often fosters environmental degradation, social differentiation or acculturation (Ghimire 2001). However, the case studies are still too few to make a consolidated evaluation.

Brazil has destinations of international fame like Rio de Janeiro, the Pantanal or Foz de Iguaçu, but in general national tourism is clearly dominating. In 1995, there were 1.99 million international visitors, more than half of which from the neighboring Mercosur countries. This compares to at least 40 million domestic tourists (Diegues 2001). In prime sun-and-beach holiday areas like the coastal areas of the northeast, the ratio of Brazilian tourists is even higher. In the case of the federal state of Ceará, only about 0.5 per cent of all arrivals are international tourists (Ghimire 2001, p. 14).

In Brazil, the main factors promoting native tourism's expansion have been a growing urban middle class with higher family income, a more extensive car park and better road infrastructure (Diegues 2001). However, in the 1990s growth was constrained by an economic policy leading to an overvalued currency. The grossly appreciated *real* vis-à-vis the US dollar also restricted domestic tourism; Brazilians often found it cheaper to go to Miami than to the prime Brazilian holiday spots. International arrivals also declined, except from Mercosur countries like Argentina or Uruguay with a similarly strong currency. This underlines the importance of price competitiveness for both international and domestic tourism.

Specifically for Ilha Grande, its key tourist attraction is its nature. While not a pristine environment – the landscape has been altered by humans for centuries and does not feature exceptional, charismatic fauna – tourist interviews confirmed that the integrity of forest cover is a crucial factor attracting domestic tourists. How important is such forest-based tourism throughout the tropics? Certainly, a number of prime international nature-tourism sites are ecosystems that are not dominated by forests, such as the African savannahs, the Nepalese trekking areas or the Ecuadorian Galápagos islands. In particular, fauna is viewed more easily in more open landscapes, and access tends to be easier than in tropical forests. However, forests occupy an important niche. One attraction is the remote and pristine frontier forests in all its abundant vegetation and ecological complexity, often combined with an 'ethno-touristic' element of indigenous people's traditional forest use. For example, this is the case of the Cuyabeno Reserve in Ecuador or Madre de Dios in Peru (BMZ 1995; Ceballos-Lascuráin 1993; Groom et al. 1991; Wunder 2000a). Another approach is to see a glimpse of rainforest in easily accessible remnant forest fragments and 'islands' of protected areas with good tourist infrastructure. Costa Rica practices this model with great success, in spite of accelerated deforestation (Boo 1992; Tobias and Mendelsohn 1991; Weinberg et al. 2002). A third approach focuses on the viewing of key charismatic species in the forest, for example gorillas in the mountain forests of Rwanda and Cameroon or orangutans near an Indonesian rehabilitation centre (BMZ 1995; van der Wal and Djoh 2001).

As we will see, the Ilha Grande case points to yet a fourth dimension: tourists who actually never set foot in the forest but appreciate the scenery from the sea – the aesthetics of an unbroken 'green carpet' breathing calmness and tranquility. Though some tourists on the island practice forest-hiking as a primary activity, not all forest-dependent tourism thus needs to occur inside the forest. Continuous forest cover is essential for the tourist's visual perception of landscape integrity, producing a hedonic non-use value that is a vital advantage of Ilha Grande over competing sites. In other words, had the island's vegetation been widely deforested or fragmented, it would probably receive far fewer tourists.

In economic terms, forest-based tourism is often supposed to help finance protected areas and to produce community benefits that strengthen local conservation incentives. There is some controversy to what extent that is actually the case. There have been raised doubts whether ecotourism is sufficient to justify the conservation of significant amounts of tropical forest (Southgate 1998). A common view on local benefits has been that 'relatively few local communities have realized significant benefits from nature tourism on their own lands or in nearby protected areas' (Wells 1997, p. iv). The typical developed-country ecotourist buys a 'package' where most of the value remains in developed countries, some is retained in the urban areas of the country of destination, while very little tends to trickle down to local communities (BMZ 1995; Gössling 1999). Yet, in some cases even these small shares of cash flows to local communities, related to direct access-right payments or derived local sales of goods and services, can be large relative to other cash income. Hence, they would have a weighty impact on local economies and land use (Lindberg and Enríquez 1994; Wunder 2000a; Landell-Mills and Porras 2002, ch. 6 for a review).

LAND-USE HISTORY ON ILHA GRANDE

Ilha Grande is a 180 km^2 island in the south of the Brazilian federal state of Rio de Janeiro (Figure 6.1). The northern coast is 15–20 km off the mainland port and municipal capital of Angra dos Reis. Abraão, the island's main port and tourist hub, connects to both Angra dos Reis and Mangaratiba by ferry (1.5 hours' ride). The second main settlement, the fishermen's town of Provetá in the west, has basically no tourism. In 1997, 4 697 persons resided on Ilha Grande (PMAR 1998), half of whom lived in Abraão and Provetá.

Ilha Grande has a colorful history, with shifting boom-and-bust cycles that continuously altered land-use patterns and vegetation cover (Wunder 2000b). Signs of occupation date back 3 000 years, with a population of primitive fishermen and clam gatherers. Later, the Tupinambá Amerindians brought in the widespread use of fire for slash-and-burn agriculture (Nesi 1990; Vieira de Mello 1987). Their habits and livelihood are well-described by Hans Staden, a contemporary German sailor who escaped the barbecue of the anthropofagist Tupinambá who had taken him prisoner (1999 [1548, 1555]). He describes them as skilful hunters, fishermen and cultivators of cassava. When local natural resources were exhausted, they would migrate to occupy a new place. As elsewhere in the Brazilian Atlantic forests, population densities likely reached levels that started to alter forest structure.

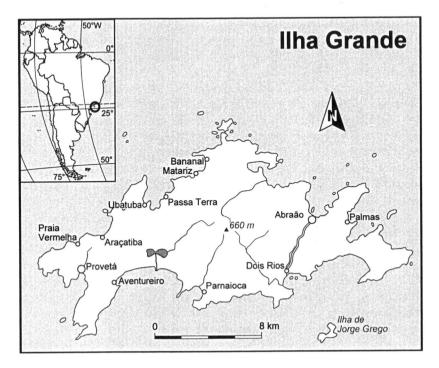

Figure 6.1   Ilha Grande, Brazil

In colonial times, the Portuguese developed nearby Angra dos Reis as an important continental port, and Ilha Grande thus had a strategically momentous location. As the Portuguese feared the establishment of hostile settlements on Ilha Grande, they prohibited settlement on the island until 1725. But in the 18th and 19th century, large plantations (*fazendas*) of coffee and sugar were established in Abraão, Dois Rios and Parnaioca. They were concentrated near the coast and in river valleys; thus cultivation never reached high and steeply sloped areas (PMAR 1998). This intensive farming led to lasting deforestation, while swidden farming simultaneously caused temporary deforestation (Ribeiro de Oliveira and Coelho Netto 1996; Ribeiro de Oliveira 1999).

In the late 19th century, the gradual opening of new and fertile agricultural areas on the continent, in particular in São Paulo State, reduced market prices for many crops. Ilha Grande, with its sloped topography and expensive boat transport, could not keep its plantations competitive. The construction of the coastal railway on the continent (opened in 1864) also pulled out much labor. Hence, agriculture on Ilha Grande suffered an irreversible decline. By the early 20th century, plantations had been widely abandoned. So, while the Brazilian Atlantic forest on the continent faced dramatic deforestation from originally about 1 000 000 km^2 to only 70 000 km^2, paradoxically the opposite occurred on Ilha Grande where forest cover recuperated considerably.

A number of other factors contributed to the island's economic marginalization. The old *fazenda* in Dois Rios was converted to a prison in the period from 1893 to 1903. In Abraão, a quarantine hospital was established for migrants from Europe suspected of being infected by contagious diseases. Obviously, this held back settlement on the island. For instance, it precluded road building, which implied a further disincentive to agriculture – though also to tourism development. The prison created a general law-and-order attitude and a tertiary-sector mindset that reduced forest-conversion pressures and was favorable to forest conservation (Prado 2000).

The booms and busts of Ilha Grande are also reflected in its shifting population size, rising from zero in 1725 to about 10 000 people at the peak of the plantation era. It then declined to its current levels, only interrupted by the 1950–80 fishing boom. At the height of that bonanza, 25 sardine factories were working on the island (Wunder 2000b). Condensing these historical cycles, three general land-use scenarios can be distinguished: ·

- *Land-intensive agricultural booms* (sugar, coffee) with site-specific, permanent forest conversion or degradation;
- *Extensive swidden agriculture* (by Amerindians and *caiçaras*) that modifies large areas, but allows for cyclical forest regeneration;
- *Forest-neutral cycles* (booms in fishing, tourism and other services – accompanied by agricultural busts) that enable the regrowth of natural vegetation and increases in forest cover.

Following the historical sequence of interventions, forest cover has today widely recovered, due to the predominance of forest-neutral cycles over the last century. According to the most recent data, 86.0 per cent of land area is covered by sub-montane forest, 6.6 per cent by montane forest, 0.6 per cent by restinga forest and 0.5 per cent by mangroves. Hence, 93.7 per cent of Ilha Grande is covered by forest. Two thirds of this is old secondary forest; the rest (high and inaccessible areas that have never been cleared or heavily intervened) is primary forest.[3]

The most important conservation areas on the island are the State Park of Ilha Grande (created in 1971) and the Biological Reserve of the Praia do Sul (created in 1981). Actually, the biological reserve was created as a direct response to the plans to create a large-scale tourism complex on the island, which would have included road building and multi-storey hotels. They limit the local exploitation of forest and marine resources and, more importantly, impose important restrictions on external commercial development and construction, though many speculators have bought up land in the hope that these restrictions will be eased in the future.

In terms of the island's biodiversity, large variations in floristic composition are found across sites and altitudes, as shown by the example of Praia do Sul (Dunn and Ribeiro de Oliveira 1988). Certain mammals normally found in continental Atlantic forests, such as tapir (*Tapirus terrestris*), capibara (*Hidrochoerus hidrochoerus*) or cayman (*Caiman latirostris*) are not found on Ilha Grande. Some of them may never have colonized the island, while others have become extinct because of excessive habitat loss and/or hunting (UFRRJ 1992). There are thus few endemic species, but a unique combination of landscapes. Ilha Grande is the only place in Rio de Janeiro state where five different ecosystems are still well-preserved simultaneously: *restinga* (coast-near) vegetation, mangroves, lagoons, rocky coast and hillside tropical forest (Maciel et al. 1982).

What is Ilha Grande's cultural heritage? The *caiçaras*, a post-conquest ethnic mix between Portuguese, Amerindians and Blacks, constitute the traditional rural population, as in large parts of Brazil's southeast coast. Between Rio and São Paulo, traditional *caiçara* communities have been widely replaced by construction and commercial development. On Ilha Grande, only a few genuine *caiçara* communities are left today – the case study village of Aventureiro (see below) is one of them. There has been much migration to the cities. Their culture and traditional livelihoods, based on swidden agriculture and artisan fishing, have rapidly eroded over the last half-century, a development that was already much advanced before the boom in tourism.

TOURISM ON ILHA GRANDE

The recreational vocation of Ilha Grande has long traditions. One source states that even the Amerindian Tupinambá used the island as a 'sanctuary', due to its healthy air and good climate (Nesi 1990). They named it *Ipaum poranga*, which in Tupi meant 'the beautiful island'. The Portuguese at some point called it Placentia (Latin: the Pleasurable) – a name that foreshadowed its current role. Prior to the quarantine hospital, the island had also been used as a reception center for slaves, allowing them to overcome the hardship of transport to and adapt to Brazilian conditions.

When the Rio-Santos road was paved in the 1980s, the region became accessible for weekend trippers from both Rio and São Paulo (Luchiari 1997). Tourism on Ilha Grande had remained obstructed by the negative image from the Dois Rios prison and by the additional transport time required (Quadros 1999; Ramuz 1998; Santos 1999). The abolition of the reformatory in 1994 much reinforced an expansion of tourism that was already underway. In the 1990s, tourism grew rapidly and spontaneously. Access to the island is decentralized. The ferry transports only about 15 per cent of tourists; the remainder arrives by small boats (PMAR 1998). The island-wide tourist survey showed that 95 per cent of tourists are Brazilians, with 53 per cent from Rio de Janeiro, 34 per cent from São Paulo and 9 per cent from Minas Gerais state.

Visitation to Ilha Grande is extremely seasonal, with peaks in the summer months (December to February) and public holidays. During these peaks, hostel prices rise to three times the corresponding low-season prices. Boat-transport prices also rise during peak season. One reason for seasonality is that air and water temperatures during much of the year are too cool for the typical Brazilian 'sun and beach' tourist. Another factor is that transport to the island, especially to its more remote beaches, still takes too much time to justify a visit during ordinary weekends.

Because of the decentralized, informal and seasonally-fluctuating visitation, the number of tourists and the length of their visit is unknown. Quadros (1999) estimated that Abraão is annually visited by about 97 200 tourists (of which 78 000 come in the three summer months), the northern beaches receive 9 300 visitors yearly, while the figure given for Aventureiro in the remote south is 17 200 (of which 7 600 visit in summer). The grand total would be 123 700 visitors, plus some day-trippers. The number of ferry passengers rose from 114 812 in 1992 to 168 865 in 1995, though this includes trips by resident islanders.

The most reliable indicator for tourism growth is the number and capacity of guesthouses. Informal camping sites and some privately rented rooms are not registered, but still Figure 6.2 gives a good reflection of the rapid increment in the 1990s in Abraão. The number of hostels (the lines in Figure 6.2) has been growing more rapidly over the last half-decade than the number of beds (expressed by the bars), indicating that many smaller hostels have emerged. Note that growth in the traditional tourist hub, Abraão, thus appears to follow an S-curve of gradual saturation, as predicted in Butler's (1980) resort life-cycle model. According to this model, Abraão would currently be in a tourism consolidation stage. However, bed capacity in the rest of the island is still growing at a fast pace.

The rapid, chaotic tourism growth in the 1990s has led to the unanimous verdict by the municipality (PMAR 1998), tourism consultants (Quadros 1999; Tangará 1998) and academics (Alves de Mello 1991; Ramuz 1998) that the island's carrying capacity has been surpassed. The 'Carrying Capacity Concept' (CCC) has normally four different dimensions (O'Reilly 1986):

1. *Physical* – limits beyond which environmental degradation arises;
2. *Social* – limits in the host population's willingness to tolerate visitors;
3. *Economic* – limits beyond which tourism displaces local activities;
4. *Perceptional* – limits beyond which tourists refuse to travel to an area affected by 'congestion'.

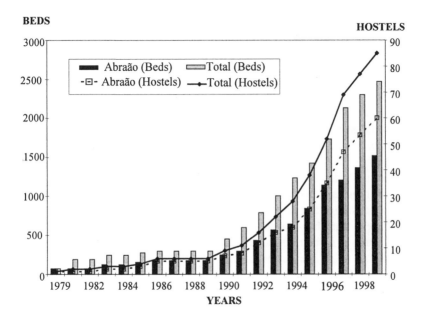

Note: 1998 figures are interpolated.

Source: Municipal data

Figure 6.2   Hostel and bed numbers on Ilha Grande

The first three CCC criteria refer to the traditional triangular dimensions of 'sustainability' vis-à-vis the tourism site; the fourth is a subjective indicator of emerging 'customer dissatisfaction'. An underlying assumption is that all four types of negative impacts are correlated to 'scale' – they rise with the number of visitors, and can be reduced by controlling access. It has been shown that perceptional degradation can be the first critical threshold to reach. This may have already happened at the consolidation stage of the resort's life-cycle, foreshadowing subsequent irreversible declines (Gössling 2000).

As will be shown in the following, the case of Ilha Grande exposes a series of ambiguities, inconsistencies and misperceptions related to the CCC, but the categories can help us to structure the discussion. Which are the scale-dependent limits that supposedly have been passed?

1. *Physical effects*: In the above-mentioned documents (and in interviews at the Municipality),[4] littering, sewerage and fresh water provision, trail erosion, dumping of motor oil into the bay, submarine harpoon fishing, jet-skiing and disturbance of dolphins' habitat are mentioned. Notably, none of the environmental impacts has been scientifically studied, so we do not know if any permanent damage is occurring. Still, in terms of the severity of effects, terrestrial effects are probably more benign than marine ones. For instance, a land-based effect like trail erosion has been painstakingly surveyed, and seems to occur in some places, but on a minor scale (Tangará 1998). Recreational hunting by tourists can threaten wildlife, but occurs very infrequently – much less than local subsistence hunting. Littering and beach pollution increases with visitor numbers, but often comes even more from the polluted bay (and from local residents) than from beach-visiting tourists. Regarding the marine environment, frequent oil dumping from schooners seems to be the most serious effect. In terms of 'scale', per-capita marine impacts seem more severe from boat-based luxury tourists than from land-based campers. Even so, industrial and artisan fishing combined constitute the main threats to the marine environment around Ilha Grande, not tourism.[5] Due to the lack of 'hard data', one can only speculate about the nature of potential damages, but most of the above-mentioned effects are strongly seasonal. For example, bay-water quality is compromised during visitation peaks, but judged from tourist and resident observations it recuperates during low season – except perhaps for the Abraão harbor area.

2. *Social effects*: A suggested fundamental impact is 'acculturation' of the island's *caiçara* population (Ramuz 1998) – a dubious argument, as *caiçara* culture had been eroded markedly already before tourism expanded. Yet, undeniable tourism-related social changes have occurred particularly in Abraão. Many outsiders have bought properties to establish guesthouses, meaning that the current population is highly mixed between natives and immigrants. That has also affected traditional values, for example, native residents state that now one mostly pays for the exchange of favors (Prado 2000). Abraão residents generally perceive the high-peak periods of tourist congestion as

stressful. There have been some reports about use of drugs and the emergence of prostitution, though both seem to occur on a very reduced scale.

3. *Economic effects*: Allegations have been made that traditional economic activities have declined from 'the growth of a predatory tourism that at the same time impoverishes the islander' (PMAR 1998, p. 10), creating 'large environmental and social impacts but little economic return' (PMAR 1998, p. 14), because 'it does not bring real benefits to the population – at least not financial ones' (Ramuz 1998, p. 117).[6] The island's tourism sector is said to be based on an unstable, seasonal economy, where a vicious circle is at work: environmental degradation diminishes product quality, which forces the lowering of prices, attracting more (and less-paying) tourists, who cause more degradation, and so forth (PMAR 1998; Tangará 1998). We will return to these claims in the Aventureiro case study below. Suffice here to note that most *caiçara* natives in Abraão have lacked the skills and capital to open guesthouses, but that many of them rent out rooms or camping grounds (catering to low spenders) or are employed in the tourism business.

4. *Perceptional effects*: The up-market tourist arrives at Ilha Grande by their own or chartered boat, develops most activities at sea level, eats in restaurants and sleeps in hostels, cottages or on their own boat. In peak season, some congestion of boats occurs around prime sites. However, the most critical perceptional effects are land-based, and relate to low-spending backpackers who arrive by ferryboat. They mostly camp, and bring along their food. Their large numbers during peak season cause an increasing amount of litter, waste water, noise, ill smell and other congestion symptoms in Abraão. With little environmental consciousness and no money to spend, it is argued that these people leave only litter behind on the island (PMAR 1998). Their massive presence induces the high-spending tourist to stay away in the peak season, a trend that has strongly alerted the owners of up-market hostels who have become prime agents pushing for access restrictions. [7]

How has the CCC been used in tourism planning discourses? As a first observation, arguments for access restriction (PMAR 1998; Quadros 1999) have focused on physical limits to environmental impacts – which have an appeal of objectivity. Yet, at this stage of tourism development and knowledge about environmental effects, the actual limits seem to be perceptional – which are clearly subjective. Obviously, it is more convincing to argue for the 'protection of the environment' than for the 'protection of the hostel owners' investments'. A first critique of the use of CCC on Ilha Grande is thus that CCC dimensions are being deliberately confused.

A second consideration is that the CCC's simple focus on 'number of visitors' misses out on the nature of environmental impacts on the island. As mentioned, per-capita impacts of backpackers are likely to be lower than those of luxury boat owners, yet it is telling that nobody has proposed to limit the access of the latter. Focus should thus rather be directly on impacts, and thus on 'limits of acceptable change' (Stankey et al. 1985).

A third critique is that none of the CCC dimensions justifies a fixed limit – all depend crucially on how visitation is managed. For instance, litter problems have been alleviated by raising consciousness of all stakeholders – and could basically be eliminated by devoting the necessary resources to rubbish collection. Likewise, the nuisance of sewerage and deficient water provision are in essence problems of under-investment in infrastructure. Until now, the municipality has failed to devise mechanisms on how to mobilize resources for local investments that are overdue.

Fourth, the recommendations for interventions put forward by CCC analysts have been simplistic and naïve. The island's Tourism Master Plan (see below) proposes a 'popular' zone (minimum 9 m^2 per tourist), a 'controlled' (25 m^2 per tourist) and a 'restricted' one (400 m^2 per tourist – see Tangará 1998, pp. 66, 105). As the authors of the Tourism Master Plan admit, it would be necessary to restrict tourist flexibility, selling exclusively fixed return tickets to pre-determined sites (Tangará 1998). On an island with multiple access points, weekly site-specific limits would have to be established, and one would have to 'control and discipline the attraction of tourist boats to the island and its surroundings' (Quadros 1999, p. 4). In addition, one would even have to limit the options of the islanders to travel between the different beaches, in order to avoid unauthorized tourist transfers (PMAR 1998). Knowing the pronounced individuality and liberal preferences of the average Brazilian tourist (and of local residents alike), such measures are indeed purely theoretical – they are confined to the imaginary world of tourism planners and environmental consultants.

TOURISM STAKEHOLDERS AND STRATEGIC CHOICES

After a decade of unplanned tourism growth, some contradictory interests have developed around what in the last section was called the 'perceptional limits' of Ilha Grande, in particular of Abraão as a resort. The main divide is between guesthouse owners and their up-market tourists on the one hand, and camping ground owners and their backpackers on the other. The up-market group is considerably more vocal and influential, and has gained the support of 'the environmentalists' – park authorities, NGOs and consultants who are worried (or paid to worry) about the dangers of degradation on the island. The group favoring low-spending tourism is small in Abraão, but prevails elsewhere (for example in Aventureiro – see case study below). In contrast to the up-market group, it is dominated by native islanders, and less well articulated. This group has an interest in maintaining high volumes of low-spending tourists. It actively opposes access restrictions – for example, Aventureiro residents did so in a June 2000 meeting, when environmentalists proposed to prohibit backpack tourism in the Biological Reserve (Prado 2000). From the case study below, we will understand what economic interests are at stake.

A third actor is the municipality in Angra dos Reis which, as locally argued, has benefited from the taxes paid by tourists but has been reluctant to recycle resources for investments on the island, thus exacerbating the conflict of interest between the two tourism groups. Finally, a fourth group – land speculators buying up property and hoping to build resorts – has until now been sidelined by regulations protecting most of the island's land area. However, they are wealthy and politically well-connected, and may at some point gain the upper hand in the struggle over the island's land use.

In 1997, a Tourism Master Plan was commissioned by the Ministry of the Environment and written up by a group of environmental consultants (Tangará 1998). The plan has until now not had a major impact on tourism on the ground. In part, this is due to a lack of resources to put it into practice; in part, it is because certain recommendations were unrealistic – such as the micro-level access restrictions discussed above. However, the participatory workshop carried out in 1997, prior to the elaboration of the plan, discussed four different tourism-development scenarios, which also give us a clear idea about the preferences of different local stakeholder coalitions:

1. Laissez faire (current default scenario).
2. Laissez faire with public investment (without access regulation).
3. Holiday resorts (including the elimination of caps on construction).
4. Ecotourism (investment with access regulation).

Due to the need for investments to meet the increasing influx of tourists, local stakeholders discarded the pure laissez faire (1) default scenario – although one can argue that this is de facto the strategy followed by the municipality. The resort option (3), pursued by investors and land speculators, proved detrimental to local people in coastal development on the mainland (Luchiari 1997), and was also locally rejected. The main choice thus came to stand between full-blown ecotourism with capacity restrictions (4) and laissez faire with increased public investments (2).

The consultants behind the Tourism Master Plan exhibited a strong preference for the 'ecotourism with regulation' scenario. As a rationale, 40 per cent of foreign visitors to Brazil enter the country through Rio de Janeiro International Airport, only a half-day trip away. The impressive global growth of ecotourism would thus endow islanders with a large income potential (high spending per visitor) that is compatible with nature conservation (restricted visitor numbers). 'Ilha Grande has one of the best tourist potentials in the world', it is stated immodestly in the document (Tangará 1998, p. 5) – based on its beaches, forests, underwater attractions, villages and local culture. It is thus being compared to the Virgin Islands, Bali, the Seychelles and Tahiti. According to the authors, ecotourism cannot be reconciled with a low-income 'sun and sea' campers' paradise.

Ecotourism had already before been recommended as a development option for Ilha Grande (Borges 1992), although with a devalued definition of the term, compared to that of Tangará (1998).[8] Beyond any doubt, the ecotourism potential of Ilha Grande is heavily underexploited at present. However, three qualifying statements seem necessary. First, as an international ecotourism site, Ilha Grande's potential is 'moderate' – certainly not 'exceptional'. Primary forests that would lend themselves to environmental interpretation for the experienced ecotourist are restricted to inaccessible areas at 300–400 m above sea level. Visible fauna attractions are rare, and the number of endemic species (for example of birds) is limited, compared to sites in the continental Atlantic forests. Snorkeling and diving are good by Brazilian standards, but mediocre compared to prime international sites such as Belize, the Red Sea or Thailand. Local traditional culture is in advanced stages of extinction, and neither as authentic nor as folkloric as that of the international comparisons made above. Ilha Grande's attractiveness thus rather lies in the integrity of its landscape, its 'peace of mind' – an observation that was confirmed by interviews of hostel proprietors.[9] Hence, Ilha Grande will necessarily continue to cater mostly to national tourists. The island does not have unique attractions to offer to compete for the attention of the targeted, selective international ecotourist with a high willingness to pay.

Second, the ecotourism option presents several social drawbacks, if the island were to be converted into an elitist, high-spending destination. Obviously, the ongoing exclusion and marginalization of native islanders from the tourism business would be accelerated, as they possess no skills to deliver a high-value ecotourism product. The option of 'laissez faire with investments' (2) thus also had considerable local support, recognizing that the degree of tourism sophistication was key: the more simple the type of tourism, the better the options for native islanders to participate.

Finally, the Tourism Master Plan may be too pessimistic about the compatibility of different forms of tourism. The island, as indicated by its name, is relatively large, and there seem to be no serious obstacles to the development of different types of tourism at different locations, for example through a zoning scheme. Also, as indicated by international experiences, ecotourism need not be for the well-to-do only.[10] Indeed, the average spending potential of international tourists on Ilha Grande may be over-estimated in the Master Plan, at least judged by the large group of price-conscious backpackers. The importance of this group outside peak periods is a main reason why guesthouse prices in Abraão drop to only one third during off-season (J. Coutinho 1999, local administrator of mid-range hostel in Abraao, personal communication).

On aggregate, authorities, consultants and activists may be excessively preoccupied with restrictive command-and-control measures. It seems more important to find means and ways to fund maintenance and investments in infrastructure to counteract the externalized costs of tourism, such as littering and water pollution. One way forward would be to levy a fee on the island's visitors, although creative thinking is required to implement a fair and efficient scheme.[11] Some crude calculations in this respect are made in Quadros (1999). This would only make sense if the generated funds were earmarked for spending on the island. A cost rise could also somewhat limit visitation, in a more acceptable way than access restrictions.

TOURISM IN AVENTUREIRO

The strong recommendations in the Tourism Master Plan on the need for access regulations on Ilha Grande are not backed by solid analysis of tourism impacts – in particular in the economic sphere. In this and the next sections, the socio-economic impacts of tourism on the island's local population will be quantified, using the example of Aventureiro.

This remote village is a traditional *caiçara* community in the extreme southwest of the island. The journey of about 2.5 hours from Angra dos Reis by local fishing boat in rough sea lives all too well up to the village's name in Portuguese, 'The Adventurer'. The scenic beauty of the surrounding landscape (beaches, hillside forest, restinga, large rocks, two lagoons) has since 1981 been protected in the Biological Reserve of Praia do Sul. About 90 persons live there today – less than decades ago when more swidden agriculture was practiced. The focus of the local economy during the 20th century has increasingly shifted towards fishery, and livelihood emphasis changed from the forested land to the sea. Just a decade ago, people lived more dispersed in the forest, cultivating subsistence crops such as cassava, beans, maize and bananas. Some cassava flour and coconuts were sold (Neiva and de Azevedo 1988). Artisan fishing was done near the village, and many men who participated in seasonal industrial sardine fishing along the Brazilian coastline would be away during the entire season (four to five months); they complained about the hard and often risky work. Remuneration on sardine boats depends on the catch, and is thus highly fluctuating, but at the time it was the major source of cash in Aventureiro.

When the protected area was created, two people were locally employed. Later, the municipality employed four additional people for maintenance activities (in particular of the trail to Provetá) and litter collection related to tourism. The salaries are low by urban standards (about US$130 monthly), but had an important local impact: in 1997, 6 out of 14 interviewed families reported salaries as their main cash income (Simão Seixas 1997). Since then, tourism has replaced both fishing and salaries as the main income source.

Tourism in Aventureiro is extremely homogenous: no hostels or other bed infrastructure exist; all tourists are campers. They stay in their own tents erected in the backyard of resident houses; camping on the beach is prohibited. Main attractions to visit are the beach and the surrounding landscape. Surfing, swimming, hikes to the lagoons of Praia do Sul, to Parnaioca and to a small waterfall are the most common activities, besides relaxing and sitting around on Aventureiro beach. Visits are extremely concentrated on peak periods, while it is close to zero during the rest of the year (see below).

The random tourist survey carried out in 1999 had a sub-sample (n = 74) from Aventureiro and the nearby Parnaioca, carried out on two occasions (high and low season). We used oral interviews for an on-the-spot questionnaire with both structured and open-ended questions; rejection rates on both occasions were below 5 per cent. This provides us with an approximate profile of Aventureiro visitors. Most are young people (average age 22.5), none traveled with children, and they stayed on average just over three nights. Seventy per cent were male, and no less than 60 per cent were students, predominantly university students with a completed secondary education. Weekly work time was 21 hours, a low average that was due to both the high general frequency of students and to fewer working hours even among the non-student Aventureiro visitors, compared to visitors to the rest of the island. In other words, people who make it out here like to spend time relaxing. Ample time is required for transport; on average, visitors spent 7 hours and 10 minutes to get from their home to Aventureiro. Average monthly income of respondents was US$488,[12] but their household income was US$2,240. This reflects the large number of part-time or non-working students with little own income, who come from middle- or upper-class households.

Current regulations do not allow tourists to hike inside the forest, with the (debatable) reasoning that visitation is not an appropriate activity for a Biological Reserve.[13] Few trails exist, and large posted signs presently prohibit the access to the forest, except for the main trail to Provetá. Staff from the Reserve claim that 'sun and sea' is all that counts for Aventureiro backpackers; allegedly they have no interest in forests. But our tourist survey contradicts that argument. Aventureiro tourists highly appreciate the presence and quality of the forest. Ninety-one per cent of the 74 interviewed judge forest quality as 'good'. Compared to the indices obtained for two other environmental dimensions (water quality – 2.81; litter collection – 1.84), forest quality had with 2.91 the highest score.[14]

Furthermore, tourists were asked to choose a maximum of three attractions (out of a list of nine) on Ilha Grande, which for them had been decisive in choosing to come to the island. Seventy-three per cent of the respondents gave one of their three votes to the category 'forests and green vegetation', ranking second on the list only to 'beaches' (85 per cent), but prior to factors such as 'peace and tranquility' (66 per cent) and 'the sea' (51 per cent). Other prospective assets of the island in general, and Aventureiro specifically, such as 'culture and local people' (11 per cent), 'low prices' (7 per cent), 'beauty of the villages' (1 per cent) and 'local cuisine' (0 per cent) had basically no importance in the perception of Aventureiro visitors. Part of the appreciation of the natural scenery is 'passive', in the sense of a visual recognition of landscape integrity from the distance. But, on average, Aventureiro visitors also hike 5 hours and 5 minutes per visit, which at an average stay of 3.3 nights comes out at about 1.5 hours per day; only 20 per cent do not hike at all. This hiking frequency is high, compared to all of Ilha Grande; some people tour the entire island.

The interest in greater access to forest trails is remarkable. Choosing three desirable improvements in tourist infrastructure among eight options, 'forest access and trails' ranked second (desired by 45 per cent of the tourists), only surpassed by 'sewerage' (47 per cent), but above factors such as 'better transport to the island' (44 per cent), 'better camping grounds' (41 per cent) and 'more tourist information' (30 per cent). Along with the example of Abraão, where forest hiking is probably the major land-based attraction,[15] these results show that there is a large potential to augment Aventureiro's attraction by increasing forest access. The decision on that lies in the hands of the park administration.

Finally, tourists were also asked the hypothetical question of how much they would be willing to pay as an obligatory entrance fee to Ilha Grande, provided that all the money were spent on an effective forest conservation project that would preserve the scenic beauty of the area. The default scenario was a tourism model with holiday-resort development, like on the continent.[16]

In spite of the low income of predominantly students in Aventureiro, the average 'willingness-to-pay' (WTP) was with US$5.21 only marginally lower than that of the average Ilha Grande tourist (US$5.61). An interesting feature is that the share of respondents who do not want to pay anything was about one third for all of Ilha Grande, but only 20 per cent for Aventureiro. In spite of low average incomes, the 'free-rider' mentality was thus less pronounced than in other parts of the island with wealthier tourists.

Information on tourism incomes was derived from two field visits (one in low, one in high season), including on-site observations, interviews with Aventureiro residents and the aforementioned tourist survey. No register of arrivals throughout the year exists. Table 6.1 provides figures based on interviews with residents, boat owners and park administration. Visits reach maximum capacity during Carnival and New Year (almost 1 800 visitors); other peaks are Easter and the local Santa Cruz festival. In addition, there are seven prolonged weekends. During these twelve weeks (or fractions thereof), there are more than 350 tents in the village, corresponding to 800 people or more. During the January–February and July school holidays, about half that number of visitors arrives (300 to 400). During December, March and the off-season (24 weeks), this is at least half of the year,[17] there are very few tourists in the village. The average weekly visitors in Table 6.1, 334 people, corresponds to 17 368 visitors per year. With an average visit length of 3.2 days, this adds up to a remarkable number of 57 314 bed nights per year.

Visitor numbers can now be related to income-generating activities in the village, in order to calculate the likely cash flows. Our interest is mainly in income net of external costs (gasoline, labor from outside, food items and equipment purchased in Angra dos Reis, etc.). This allows us to appreciate how much is left for the remuneration of local production factors.[18]

The single most important income source is clearly the rent of tent spaces. During carnival and the fortnight around New Year, tents cover almost every inch available. Rents had until recently been set collectively at a uniform rate of US$8.33 per tent per week (or fraction thereof), reflecting also an ability of the community to coordinate key tourism parameters. However, off-season discounts are now granted for short-staying visitors, especially by those 50 per cent of the hosting families who have not installed sanitary facilities (shower, toilet), and are thus unable to attract clients without lowering prices. Hence, an average off-season price of US$7.50 for the entire village is assumed. Due to the large number of visitors during peak seasons, aggregate tent-space rental income in the village is almost US$135,000. Of this income, some costs regarding the investments in showers and toilets have to be deducted, but as their total costs are less than US$1,000 per year,[19] net income is almost equal to gross income. Basically all camping cash flows end up in the village.

Table 6.1   Tourism cash flow in Aventureiro

Yearly gross and net income, in US$ (1)						
Period of the year (2)	Weeks	Average visitors	Camping rents (3)	Food sales (4)	Drink sales (5)	Boat trans- port (6)	Total gross income
Carnival	1	1 780	14 827	6 285	8 224	1 107	30 443
New Year	2	1 780	29 655	12 570	16 447	2 214	60 887
Easter	1	1 400	11 662	4 943	6 468	871	23 944
Santa Cruz festiv.	1	1 000	8 330	3 531	4 620	622	17 103
Long weekends	7	800	42 000	19 774	25 872	3 483	91 129
Jan./Feb.	6	400	18 000	8 474	11 088	1 493	39 055
July summer vac.	3	300	6 750	3 178	4 158	560	14 646
December	3	80	1 800	847	1 109	149	3 906
March	4	30	900	424	554	75	1 953
Rest of the year	24	5	900	424	554	75	1 953
Average/week	*	334	2 593	1 163	1 521	205	5 481
Gross income/yr	*	*	134 824	61 613	79 094	10 649	286 180
External costs (7)	*	*	990	36 968	59 321	6 389	103 668
Net income	*	*	133 834	24 645	19 774	4 259	182 513
Distribution (%)	*	*	73	14	11	2	100
Per family	*	*	7 435	1 369	1 099	237	10 140
Per inhabitant	*	*	1 487	274	220	47	2 028

Notes:
(1) 1 US$ = 1.80 R$ (August 1999).
(2) Carnival is assumed to fall in February; New Year fortnight is distributed equally between December and January.
(3) Average price of US$8.50 (US$7.50 off-season) for a maximum of seven nights.
(4) Calculated as the number of visitors times the number of weeks times the average length of 3.2 nights, times a 30 per cent rate of tourists who eat out. The same calculus was made for a 20 per cent share of tourists assumed to eat out for breakfast, at US$1.60 per meal. This sums up to food consumption of, on average, US$1.07 per person.
(5) Assuming a beverage consumption of US$1.40 per person.
(6) Assuming a 5 per cent participation of Aventureiro boat owners in all tourist boat transport (US$6.22 per one way trip).
(7) External costs (food, gasoline, canned and bottled beverages, etc.) are deducted from gross income using the following approximated external cost percentages: food 60 per cent, beverages 75 per cent, boat transport 60 per cent; the calculated cost for camping rent was 0.7 per cent of gross income.

Source: Field interviews and tourist questionnaire, August, October, November 1999

This situation is different for food sales. Aventureiro tourists typically bring their own noodles, soups and rice, and cook them over a camping stove.

Only about 30 per cent eat out standard meals (*prato feito*) prepared by nine small-scale, informal restaurants, at an average price of US$2.50. Similarly, breakfast and minor fast foods (at about US$1.60) is only consumed by around 20 per cent. On aggregate, gross yearly food sales remain more limited, at about US$62,000 per year. Unlike tent space, this is not a pure economic rent: except for some fish, cassava and other locally grown crops, foodstuff has to be transported from Angra dos Reis. In addition, during peak season food stall owners call in non-resident relatives and other labor from outside to help out with intensive kitchen work,[20] resulting in an additional 'leakage' of income. About 40 per cent of gross food sales (US$24,000) are estimated to stay in the village, basically for local labor remuneration.

Beverage sales create probably more gross cash flow than food sales: assuming an average purchase of one large beer per visitor (sold at US$1.39 in Aventureiro), the estimate in Table 6.1 is almost US$80,000 per year. The reason is that it is too heavy for a camper to bring along beverages for several days from the supermarkets – and even more difficult to keep them cold. A couple of bars in Aventureiro have invested in sizeable refrigerators to take advantage of the good market potential for chilled beers and soft drinks. During Carnival and New Year, entire boat trips are made to Angra dos Reis just to stock up on beverages. However, external costs (the bottled or canned beverage, boat transport/gasoline, refrigerator financial costs) are higher than for food sales: they were estimated at 75 per cent. Hence, net income per unit is reduced, though beverages require less local labor input than food.

Finally, boat transport to and from Angra dos Reis (2.5–3 hours) costs about US$13 for the return trip, but this business is dominated by the larger fishing boats from Angra dos Reis and Provetá, which diversify into the tourist business whenever demand is sufficient. The smaller fishing boats from Aventureiro take tourists on a more occasional basis. In Table 6.1, I have assumed a flat 5 per cent participation of Aventureiro fishermen in this activity, which results in a yearly gross income of US$10,649 and, discounting an estimated 60 per cent external costs, a net income of US$4,259.

The grand total of gross yearly income is estimated at US$286,180 in Table 6.1; net income is US$182,513 (63.8 per cent of the former). No less than 78 per cent of gross income is generated in 'high season': Carnival, New Year, Easter, Santa Cruz festival and seven long weekends. This marked seasonality also means that negative side-effects from tourism – heavy work load, congestion, and to a certain degree noise, pollution and some drug consumption[21] – are phenomena that are highly concentrated in time, while interfering little with villagers' life during the rest of the year.

Comparing the weight of different activities in total net income, camping rents are clearly dominating (73 per cent), while food sales (14 per cent), beverages (11 per cent) and boat transport (2 per cent) are complementary. What Aventureiro residents sell is 'access to a beautiful spot' – much aided by the park administration which, by prohibiting 'wild' camping on the beach, effectively protects the monopoly of Aventureiro residents in providing space to tourists. Leaving aside the inconvenience of literally living surrounded by backpackers during peak periods,[22] it is relatively 'easy money' to earn; it involves neither significant labor efforts[23] nor other notable costs – it is a rent transfer from young urban tourists to the *caiçaras* of Aventureiro.

LOCAL TOURISM IMPACTS

In general, there can be no doubt that tourism income, because of its remarkable size vis-à-vis all other local income sources, has had a revolutionary impact on the local economy. Table 6.1 reports a yearly tourism-derived net income of US$10,140 per family and of US$2,028 per capita. Considering that Brazil's overall per-capita income for 1999 was close to US$3,300, one cannot any longer refer to Aventureiro as a genuinely poor community – and it is tourism that has made the difference. Compared to traditional earnings within the local economy, the gap is striking. According to our interviews, traditional income is in the range of US$1,500–4,000 for a fisherman, and US$1,800 for a public employee (Park and Municipality). The rise of tourism has thus doubled or tripled the income for the average Aventureiro family. This certainly rejects the above hypothesis that 'backpackers leave no money behind'. Backpackers spend little per capita, but their large numbers trigger sizeable income flows to a small community with limited income sources. Hence, the poverty alleviation impact of tourism in Aventureiro stands beyond any doubt.

What about the environmental impacts? Again, these impacts have not been measured, but interviews and own observation in both high and low season indicate that the main impacts – from littering and wastewater – are of a temporary nature. They are not visible to an off-season visitor, nor do they seem to cause permanent damage to the environment or to local livelihoods. Most young tourists are aware of the aesthetic impact of throwing litter on the ground, in fact in the interviews many complained that more wastebaskets were needed. A number of villagers are externally paid to clean and maintain the area. Lacking sanitary facilities and sewerage is a main problem in peak periods, and was identified in the tourist questionnaire as the most needed improvement in tourist infrastructure. The main dilemma here is that some camping-ground owners under-invest; as we can see from Table 6.1, they could easily use part of their profits to pay for sanitary installations, but fail to do so. However, there is an increasing internal pressure inside the village for them to invest. Again, rather than reducing tourists' numbers and access to Aventureiro, as was proposed in June 2000 by environmentalist interests (and strongly opposed locally), one should strengthen intra-community organization so that under-investing 'free riders' among camping-ground owners are forced to comply with minimum sanitary standards.[24]

Are tourism incomes unequally distributed in the village, and do they cause social frictions? Certainly, camping rents – the principal source of tourism income – accrue unevenly, mainly because not all campsites are equally attractive. The factors determining the attractiveness of a specific camping ground (and thus the income differences between families) are, in the following order of importance: 1) closeness to the beach, 2) size of flat space available, and 3) the existence of sanitary installations.

This set of factors puts families in differentiated positions. Especially those houses that are situated in flat, beach-near areas with ample space attract basically all off-season and long-weekend tourists – except for a few that prefer the views from and solitude of the hillside areas that extend behind the beach-near belt, in an area dominated by crop cultivation. These hillside grounds thus mainly serve as buffers that fill up only during the four main tourism peaks, while visitor numbers remain very scattered during all the rest of the year. Nevertheless, it is worth stressing that all families participate to some extent in tourism income, so they feel they are better off than before tourism appeared. Even a remote hillside ground with little space suitable for camping and no sanitary installations still receives a benefit in the range of US$1,000–2,000 per year.[25] This can be further supplemented by selling beverages, cooking meals or working in neighbors' restaurants (the locally paid daily wage is US$8–14). Family ties within the village also imply some voluntary redistribution of income across households.

What have cash inflows over the last 3–5 years been used for? Three items stand out, construction, consumer durables and leisure. Economic progress is visible mostly in terms of the many new houses that have been, or are in the process of being built: traditional *caiçara* clay houses have either been replaced or stand beside new brick houses. Current consumption (foodstuff, clothing) does not seem to have been influenced much by tourism-generated wealth. But there has been a remarkable expansion in consumer durables, including gasoline-driven electricity generators, freezers, refrigerators, cooking stoves (partially as investments for food and beverage sales), washing machines, televisions, parabolic antennas and furniture. Third, people in Aventureiro have also used part of their new income to buy more leisure, specifically to reduce high-risk, strenuous or low-return activities, such as sardine fishing and slash-and-burn agriculture. For instance, various middle-aged fishermen say that they have now abandoned sardine fishing in order to spend more time with their family, and that this has been made possible by the money from tourism. Similarly, younger women express little interest in the *roça* (slash-and-burn agriculture) because, as one of them said, 'it does not reward the effort'. It is noteworthy that it is not necessity (such as tourism-induced labor shortages) that forces these productive changes, but rather a deliberate choice on behalf of Aventureiro residents. While one can discuss the sustainability of both slash-and-burn agriculture and sardine fishing (see references above), it should be clear that these income-led productive changes do not harm the environment, and most likely alleviate pressures on natural resources.

Finally, many of the academic scholars visiting Aventureiro focus on the cultural impacts that mass tourism in a tiny village is bound to cause: during Carnival and New Year, the ratio of visitors to residents is no less than 20 : 1. It is postulated that the loss of control over one's own space, tourists' lacking knowledge, interest and respect for the local culture, and the introduction of 'exotic' elements (notably, marijuana and other drug consumption) may cause a process of cultural erosion and loss of identity among the local population.[26]

Cultural aspects have not been the focus of this work, but a couple of observations can be made. First, the extreme over-crowding of the village is mainly restricted to four peak periods while, even during an average long weekend, daily life in Aventureiro seems largely to follow its usual rhythm. High seasonality can thus be an advantage in limiting direct cultural impacts. Second, the presence of and contact with the tourists and their (arguably) bad habits may actually constitute a less important cultural impact than the indirect effects, working through higher income and changing consumption patterns. The attitude that local dwellers develop towards the tourist is mostly indifferent – a necessary short-term companionship for which they have to set basic rules in order to protect their privacy. For comparison, the income-induced spread of television alone may have far more important cultural impacts than the occasional contact with marijuana-smoking city-slickers. This raises a broader question of the self-selected abandonment of certain *caiçara* traditions – perhaps these are empirically more important features than the externally induced changes.

CONCLUSION

Tourism on Ilha Grande constitutes the most recent chapter in a colorful island history from cannibals to pirates, slaves and escaped convicts, from hunters and gatherers to swidden cultivators, sugar barons and sardine industrialists. In terms of land use, tourism has tied in with a secular trend towards land-neutral activities (fishing, public services); indeed the fact that nature-based tourism has developed forcefully can be directly linked to the ample natural forest regeneration that occurred over the last century. Tourism could potentially result in land speculation and landscape fragmentation, as has occurred with the construction boom on the continental coast between Rio and São Paulo. Until now, two protected areas and a series of other restrictions on development, notably the lack of roads, have prevented that from happening. But it is important to consolidate this partnership between nature protection and tourism. This also means that protected-area managers have to realize that on Ilha Grande, parks are less justified by an 'abstract' preservation of species and habitats than by the thousands of urban, native tourists who come to appreciate and use this nature.

After the first decade of spontaneous tourism growth, the island is at a crossroad. In some key tourism spots, problems related to litter, sewage, fresh water and deteriorating tourist infrastructure multiply during peak seasons, creating perceptional degradation. Different tourism models that have coexisted until now start to develop mutual incompatibilities. Most tourism planners, consultants and influential operators on the island have argued that 'carrying capacity' has been surpassed and that low-spenders' access should be restricted. Otherwise, social, environmental and economic degradation would occur in a downward spiral.

The present chapter challenges this dominant view. There is no evidence to back up claims of lasting physical degradation of the island's environment or of social deprivation of its residents. Looking specifically at local incomes from low-income tourism in the case of the traditional fishermen's village of Aventureiro, the hypothesis that 'backpackers leave no money on the island' was clearly rejected. Campers spend little per capita, but their large numbers generate sizeable incomes: annual tourism income per family is over US$10,000, and per-capita income is over US$2,000. The main income-generating element is the rent of camping spaces, a de facto 'cost-free' financial transfer from tourists to residents. Food and beverage sales as well as boat transport are additional, complementary elements. Productive changes in response to tourism, for example in local labor use, occur only in peak periods. On the other hand, the large tourism incomes have been used for construction, consumer durables and to buy more leisure time at the cost of activities considered inferior (swidden agriculture), tough and risky (sardine fishery). Local people rightfully fear that external access intervention of the 'carrying-capacity' type, currently pushed by the municipality and by environmentalists, may deteriorate or even destroy their business.

Some think that Ilha Grande should be transformed into an exclusive, high-class international ecotourism destination with strongly regulated access. It has been argued in this chapter that this is not realistic, especially because of the type of attractions and due to the impossibility of implementing strong access restrictions. But it also seems strategically important that low-spending tourists are not ex ante precluded from the 'eco'-concept – this is that ecological tourism does not become for the elite only. One reason is that the native islanders, the *caiçaras*, have few options for participating in a highly sophisticated, elitist tourism product. For them, the 'tent-rental space' concept, practiced in Aventureiro as well as in Abraão, is the most realistic basis for making money from tourism. A second reason is the significant welfare loss that would occur to those urban low-spending tourists that are denied access to the island: their 'economic vote' may be quite limited, but there is clearly a social dimension that speaks against their exclusion.

This argument refers fundamentally to rights, fairness and egalitarian principles, but there is also a more visionary element to it. Many of those university-student campers that today consider every *centavo* that they spend on Ilha Grande will soon become professionals and decision makers, also in areas that involve natural resource-management decisions. As we have seen, access to the marvelous nature of a place like Ilha Grande also raises environmental awareness; it enhances the ability to appreciate and develop sensitivity towards nature. This 'positive externality' of visitation constitutes an investment in the ecological consciousness of the future generation. In times where the Amazon and Atlantic forests are increasingly threatened by rapid deforestation, it is important to build a future constituency in the Brazilian society for forest conservation. The well-preserved and accessible green forests on the 'Big Island' are thus not only assets for present-day cash-flow generation; they are also tools for affecting long-run attitudes.

DISCUSSION

To what extent could the findings of this study be upscaled to the whole Atlantic forest, to the rest of Brazil, or to other forest-tourism sites in developing countries? Obviously, the Aventureiro constellation of many tourists, few inhabitants, beautiful beaches and well-preserved vegetation is particularly favorable to a high per capita tourism income at the village level. In other parts of the island, several of those factors are less favorable (others – notably, access and transport time are actually more advantageous). For Ilha Grande in toto, the island's long periods of seclusion, high forest cover and closeness to urban markets constitute special features providing special opportunities. This scenario cannot directly be extrapolated for example to sites with intensive deforestation or with a very remote location. Cultural impacts from tourism could also be more detrimental in northern Brazil for indigenous populations with limited previous contact with the market economy, compared to the *caiçaras* in Ilha Grande.

However, many features sketched in this study are increasingly relevant, not only for natural sites in the developed coastal areas of the south and southeast of Brazil, but also for other middle-income countries with forests that are accessible from urban centers. For local people in those sites, income-generation options will often become available, although poverty-alleviation impacts may be less dramatic than in Aventureiro. Positive-evaluation case studies of tourism's local economic impact are still in the minority in the tourism literature, yet their number seems to increase (cf. Landell-Mills and Porras 2002; Weinberg et al. 2002). Too many studies have focused on the fairness of distribution of package-tour values, of which local communities usually receive only a small share; communities themselves tend to be much more interested in absolute tourism incomes, and what that means for their local economy.

What feedback does this case study provide on methods of tourism analysis, planning and regulation? How do the political-ecology concepts fit the case of Ilha Grande? Certainly, the study underlines the drawbacks of 'tourism carrying capacity' (CCC). The differential effect of low- and high-income tourists, with their land- versus sea-based activities, stressed that absolute numbers are not the crux of the matter. Problems like littering and sewage remained seasonal, and seemed much more related to under-spending on management and corrective actions than to be an inevitable consequence of excessive tourist numbers.

The discourse of the tourism planners on Ilha Grande generally was about environmental carrying capacity – 'degradation of the environment' – yet, as we have seen, the substance behind it was actually about perceptional limits. So, has perceptional carrying capacity then objectively been surpassed? Obviously not, since limits are subjective and differ enormously between, on the one hand, the low-spending students – and the camping ground owners catering to them – and, on the other, the higher middle-class tourist – and the up-market hostel owners with considerable investments at stake. By the end of the day, whose perception is it that counts?

The choice about what kind of tourism should prevail is ultimately a trade-off between different stakeholder interests. A concept like CCC can be (ab)used to strengthen one party's claim by creating a hallucination of scientific objectivity, but it cannot resolve the underlying dualism of interests. Even worse, it can distract attention from dynamic solutions to bridge the conflicts, either through planning tools (for example spatial zoning) or through market mechanisms. Regarding the latter, an interesting recent observation (March 2001) was that, in spite of sustained tourism growth in Abraão, the alleged 'downward spiral' did not seem to continue. 'Middle-class' hostels had clearly consolidated, while campers were increasingly being pushed out to peripheral areas, with rising property prices in central

Abraão as the main driver. This indicates that some local conflicts can be alleviated through economic mechanisms, without the necessity for tourism planners to intervene with command-and-control measures.

In relation to the social CCC dimension, a noteworthy observation from Aventureiro was that even a 'traditional' indigenous population may develop a significant tolerance to disproportionate tourist numbers if the economic incentives are sufficiently large. It may help that this traditional population is already linked to the external world by other ties, and that tourism remains highly seasonal. Seasonality is often criticized from the economic CCC angle, but from a social-resilience point of view it may be beneficial to be without too many tourists during most of the year.

This also provides a somewhat unexpected twist to the political-ecology approach, this is to 'the political dynamics surrounding material and discursive struggles over the environment' (Bryant 1998, p. 79). Tourism, which is normally carried forward by powerful international capital interests in conspiracy with the state, would typically cause 'increased social differentiation and a growing gap between rich and poor . . . reduced access for local people to the natural resources on which they depend for their livelihoods; . . . and deterioration of the biophysical environment' (Stonich 1998, p. 38). In this worldview, even ecotourism would just be a form of 'green greed', nourished by the neoliberal drive for globalization (Duffy 2002).

This is hardly a picture we can recognize from this chapter. On Ilha Grande, it is the less privileged who actually want more mass tourism, or at least preserve current numbers, while the more influential stakeholders try to restrict the destination to luxury tourists. The clashes between rich and poor concern what type of tourism should prevail, and the tourists themselves are legitimate stakeholders to be considered in the 'discursive struggles'.

Finally, 'economic carrying capacity' seems to be an even more dubious CCC sub-concept. For any conservationist-led ecotourism project, it certainly is the explicit objective to surpass economic carrying capacity limits, in the sense that these projects seek to actively change the local productive dynamics by substituting current pressures on natural resources for more benign activities (Wunder 2000a). In Aventureiro, tourism created little direct substitution. Yet, indirectly the large incomes from tourism substantially changed local production patterns by reducing swidden agriculture and sardine fishing. But that was because local people wanted to substitute these activities, even before tourism arrived. For them, passing economic CCC limits was an 'opportunity', rather than a 'pressure'. Moreover, tourism's impact tied into substantial past processes of change, this is the reduction of 'inferior' activities in the face of new sectors providing better alternatives.

Finally, in the face of multifaceted local development dynamics, we should be careful not to judge tourism exclusively on its absolute impacts. For instance, it is trivial to state that tourism has a negative environmental impact per se – almost any human production activity has. But what would people do for a living without tourism? Would these alternatives eventually be preferable in terms of social, environmental and economic effects? When using our analytical toolbox, we should be cautious not to romanticize about static patterns of 'traditional village life' in ways that come to glorify poverty and to deny local people their aspirations to improve livelihoods. Certainly, tourism can be one avenue to achieve these aspirations.

NOTES

1. The research included five visits to Ilha Grande during 1999 and one in 2001, with interviews of island residents, tourism operators, park authorities, boat and restaurant owners, and a 1999 survey of 357 tourists, supplemented by literature search in Angra dos Reis and in Rio de Janeiro.
2. Based on WTO statistics, Ghimire (2001, pp. 13–14) estimated a rise in developing-country domestic tourist nights from 624 624 in 1991 to 762 352 in 1996. He calculates that, for instance, national visitors to the sites of Agra (India) constituted about 7 million out of 8.4 million (83 per cent) and 4 million out of 5.4 million (74 per cent) per annum in the case of Chiang Mai (Thailand).
3. C. Athaide 1999, local administrator of the Biological Reserve in Aventureiro, personal communication
4. E. Dalboni de Souza 1999, Secretariat of Planning, Environmental Division, personal communication, Angra dos Reis, August 1999.
5. A participatory workshop confirmed the trade-off between recreational and artisan/comercial fishing (Tangará 1998, pp. 76–8).
6. All citations with my translation from Portuguese.
7. Interviews with hostel owners and the President of the Ilha Grande Hostel Association, Mr. Luis Fernando Medina, Abraão.
8. The 'eco-development' proposals in Borges (1992) include 'a few, non-paved roads, hydrofoil access, resorts, tennis clubs, bungalows, horse clubs and a health spa'.
9. 'Nature' was confirmed as an attraction by all guesthouse owners, 'peace and rest' by two thirds, while nobody mentioned the factors 'handicraft', 'local culture', 'climate' or 'cuisine' (Tangará 1998, p. 26).
10. For instance, trekking in the Annapurna area (Nepal) caters much to backpackers, but has been well organized in the ACAP project so as to minimize environmental impacts, and at the same time ensure significant income flows to the local population.
11. It can be difficult to distinguish clearly between locals (and their off-resident visiting families) and 'pure' tourists. Also, differential access by boat makes it hard to levy fees.
12. 1 US$ = 1.80 R$ (August 1999).
13. Notably, local extractive forest uses have a much higher biological impact than tourist visitation. Obviously, the more pragmatic motive is that tourists entering the forest on a large scale would put yet another task on the already limited capacity of the Reserve's administration.

14. The index is a simple average of the three possible answers ('good' = 3, 'ordinary' = 2, 'bad' = 1).
15. Another questionnaire by IEF among tourists in Abraão showed that 'hiking' was regarded the best recreational option among tourists (32 per cent), ranking even higher than 'swimming' (28 per cent) (UFRRJ 1992, p. 44).
16. We used photographs as a tool to visualize these different scenarios.
17. Most holidays and prolonged weekends occupy only a fraction of a week, typically four days.
18. Our net income figures are not 'pure profits' over and above an average local wage rate, but rather the implicit wage rate obtained from tourism-related activities.
19. Installation of full sanitary installations (a rudimentary toilet and shower) had an average cost of US$555, but only half of the owners (nine) had made such investments. The value of US$990 in Table 6.1 represents the annuity of a loan to finance this investment, at a 20 per cent real interest rate, thus approximating the opportunity cost of the investment in sanitary installations.
20. Several of the interviewed women who cook for tourists reported that they work in the kitchen up to 18 hours a day during the specific peak periods – but also that the effort is worthwhile in terms of good remuneration.
21. Some of the interviewed claimed that local residents are themselves involved in the trafficking of marijuana and other drugs, but as this was not possible to confirm, no local incomes from drug sales are included in Table 6.1.
22. One reason for investing in sanitary installations is that, in some cases, tourists are using family toilets *en masse* which creates a hygiene problem, especially for families with small children.
23. Basically, labor inputs are confined to the cleaning of private areas after the tourists have left.
24. Those who have invested in sanitary installations blame those who have not for excrement deposition in public areas or for tourists 'stealing their way' into their toilets.
25. For instance, an occupation of 15 tent spaces with 2.2 persons during the 5 peak periods yields, at the high-season rate of US$8.33, a total annual income of US$1,374.45.
26. For Aventureiro, D. Toffoli 1999, MA thesis researcher at the UFRJ University in Rio, personal communication. For tourism impacts on *caiçara* culture elsewhere, see Luchiari (1997) and Ramuz (1998).

REFERENCES

Alves de Mello, E. (1991), *Medidas, Procedimentos e Legislação Técnico Ambiental para uma Ocupação Turística na Ilha Grande*, Rio de Janeiro: Universidade do Estado do Rio de Janeiro.

BMZ (1995), *Ökotourismus als Instrument des Naturschutzes? Möglichkeiten zur Erhöhung der Attraktivität von Naturschutzvorhaben*, Munich, Cologne, London: Weltforum Verlag.

Boo, E. (1992), *The Ecotourism Boom, Planning for Development and Management*. Washington DC: World Wildlife Fund.

Borges, B. (1992), 'Um parque natural. Ecodesenvolvimento em Ilha modelo', *ECORIO*, **1** (6), Rio de Janeiro.

Bryant, R. L. (1998), 'Power, knowledge and political ecology in the third world: a review', *Physical Geography*, **22** (1), 79–94.

Butler, R.W. (1980), 'The concept of a tourist area cycle of evolution', *Canadian Geographer*, **24** (1), 5–12.

Ceballos-Lascuráin, H. (1993), *Promoción del ecoturismo dentro de la Reserva de Producción Faunística Cuyabeno*, Quito, Cooperación Ecuador-Alemania.

Diegues, A.C. (2001), 'Regional and domestic mass toursim in Brazil: an overview', in K.B. Ghimire, *The Native Tourist*, London: Earthscan, pp. 55–85.

Duffy, R. (2002), *A Trip too far: Ecotourism, Politics and Exploitation*, London: Earthscan.

Dunn, D.S. and R. Ribeiro de Oliveira (1988), 'Reserva biológica estadual da Praia do Sul (Ilha Grande, Estado do Rio de Janeiro): lista preliminar da flora', *Acta Botanica Brasilica*, **I** (2).

Ghimire, K.B. (2001), 'The growth of national and regional tourism in developing countries: an overview' in K. B. Ghimire, *The Native Tourist*, London, Earthscan, pp. 1–29.

Gössling, S. (1999), 'Ecotourism: a means to safeguard biodiversity and ecosystem functions?', *Ecological Economics*, **29** (2), 303–20.

Gössling, S. (2000), 'Tourism development in Sri Lanka: the case of Ethukala and Unawatuna', *Tourism Recreation Research*, **25** (3), 103–14.

Groom, M.J., R.D. Podolsky, et al. (1991), 'Tourism as a sustained use of wildlife: a case study of Madre de Dios, Southeastern Peru', in J.G. Robinson and K.H. Redford (eds), *Neotropical Wildlife Use and Conservation*, Chicago, London: University of Chicago Press, pp. 393–412.

Landell-Mills, N. and I.T. Porras (2002), *Silver Bullet or Fools' Gold? A Global Review of Markets for Forest Environmental Services and Their Impacts on the Poor*, London, International Institute for Environment and Development (IIED).

Lindberg, K. and J. Enríquez (1994), *An Analysis of Ecotourism's Economic Contribution to Conservation in Belize*, Washington DC: World Wildlife Fund and Government of Belize, Ministry of Tourism and the Environment.

Luchiari, M.T.D.P. (1997), 'Turismo e cultura caiçara no Litoral Norte paulista', in A. B. Rodrigues, *Turismo: Modernidade e Globalização*, São Paulo: Hucitec.

Maciel, N.C., D.S. Dunn, et al. (1982), *A Situação Ambiental da Reserva Biológica Estadual da Praia do Sul*, (Ilha Grande, Angra dos Reis, Rio de Janeiro), Rio de Janeiro, DECAM-FEEMA.

Neiva, A.M. and A. de Azevedo (1988), *O Povo do Aventureiro*, Rio de Janeiro: Fundaçao Estadual do Meio Ambiente.

Nesi, W. (1990), *Notícias Históricas de Ilha Grande (Rio de Janeiro)*, Juiz de Fora (MG): Esdava.

O'Reilly, A.M. (1986), 'Tourism carrying capacity – concept and issues', *Tourism Management*, **7**, 254–8.

Prado, R.M. (2000), *Depois que Entrou o Imbamba: Percepção de Questoes Ambientais na Ilha Grande*, Paper presented at the 22nd Meeting of Brazilian Anthropologists, Brasilia, 16–19 July 2000 (unpublished).

Prefeitura Municipal de Angra dos Reis (PMAR) (1998), *Base de Dados para Estudo de Análise Econômica do Ordenamento do Turismo na Ilha Grande - Angra dos Reis*, Secretaria de Desenvolvimento Econômico and Secretaria de Planejamento-Divisão de Meio Ambiente, Angra dos Reis: Prefeitura Municipal de Angra dos Reis.

Quadros, W.J. (1999), 'Relatório técnico final correspondente aos produtos 3.1. a 3.3.', *Relativos ao Estado do Rio de Janeiro*, Angra dos Reis: Programa Nacional de Meio Ambiente.

Ramuz, P.F. (1998), *Os caminhos do turismo na Ilha Grande*, Rio de Janeiro: Universidade do Estado do Rio de Janeiro.
Ribeiro de Oliveira, R. (1999), *O Rastro do Homem na Floresta: Sustentabilidade e Funcionalidade da Mata Atlântica Sob Manejo Caiçara*, Rio de Janeiro: Universidade do Estado do Rio de Janeiro.
Ribeiro de Oliveira, R. and A.L. Coelho Netto (1996), 'O rastro do homem na floresta. A construção do paisagem da reserva biológica estadual da Praia do Sul (Ilha Grande, Rio de Janeiro) a partir das intervenções antrópicas', *Albertoa*, **10** (4), 109–16.
Santos, M.S. (1999), *Projeto de Pesquisa: História e Memória das Instituções Carcérias na Ilha Grande*, Rio de Janeiro: Universidade do Estado do Rio de Janeiro.
Simão Seixas, C. (1997), *Estratégias de Pesca e Utilização de Animais por Comunidades Pesqueiras da Ilha Grande*, Campinas: University of Campinas.
Southgate, D. (1998), *Tropical Forest Conservation. An Economic Assessment of the Alternatives in Latin America*, New York and Oxford: Oxford University Press.
Staden, H. (1999 [1548; 1555]), *A Verdadeira História dos Selvagens, Nus e Ferozes Devoradores de Homems*, Rio de Janeiro: Dantes.
Stankey, G.H., D.N. Cole, R.C. Lucas, M.E. Petersen and S.S. Frissell (1985), *The Limits of Acceptable Change (LAC) System for Wilderness Planning*, Ogden, Utah: US Department of Agriculture, Forest Service, Intermountain Forest and Range Experiment Station.
Stonich, S. (1998), 'Political ecology of tourism', *Annals of Tourism Research*, **25** (1), 25–54.
Tangará (1998), *Ilha Grande. Plano Diretor de Turismo. Documento Base*, Angra dos Reis-Tangará: Serviços em Meio Ambiente e Turismo.
Tobias, D. and R. Mendelsohn (1991), 'Valuing ecotourism in a tropical rain forest reserve', *Ambio*, **20** (2), 91–93.
Universidade Federal Rural Rio de Janeiro (UFRRJ) (1992), *Plano Diretor do Parque Estadual da Ilha Grande*, Rio de Janeiro: Universidade Federal Rural.
van der Wal, M. and E. Djoh (2001), *Gorilla-Based Tourism: a Realistic Source of Community Income in Cameroon? Case Study of the Villages of Goungoulou and Karagoua*, network paper 25e, London: Rural Development Forestry Network, available at: http://www.odifpeg.org.uk/publications/rdfn/25/rdfn-25e-iii.pdf.
Vieira de Mello, C.E.H. (1987), *Apontamentos para a História Fluminense (Ilha Grande)*, Angra dos Reis: Edição do Conselho Municipal de Cultura.
Weinberg, A., S. Bellows, D. Ekster (2002), 'Sustaining ecotourism: insights and implications from two successful case studies', *Society and Natural Resources*, **15**, 371–80.
Wells, M.P. (1997), *Economic Perspectives on Nature Tourism, Conservation and Development*, Washington DC: World Bank.
Wunder, S. (2000a), 'Ecotourism and economic incentives – an empirical approach', *Ecological Economics*, **32**, 465–79.
Wunder, S. (2000b), *Big Island, Green Forests and Backpackers: Land-Use and Development Options on Ilha Grande*, Rio de Janeiro State, Brazil, Copenhagen: Centre for Development Research, available at: http://www.cdr.dk/working_ papers/wp-00-4.pdf.

7. The Political Ecology of Tourism in Zanzibar

Stefan Gössling

INTRODUCTION

Zanzibar comprises two islands, Unguja and Pemba, and is located 40 km off the Tanzanian mainland in the Indian Ocean. Zanzibar is one of the destinations in the tropics that have relatively recently established tourism as a sector of its national economy. For decades, the islands relied almost entirely on exports of cloves for their foreign exchange earnings. These also constituted the majority of government revenue. However, in the 1970s and 1980s, Zanzibar lost its dominating role in the international clove trade when other countries joined the production of the cash crop. World market prices fell drastically as a result of the growth in supply, with concomitant detrimental consequences for Zanzibar's economy. In response to these developments and facing pressure from the World Bank, the International Monetary Fund (IMF) and USAID for more liberal trade and investment policies, the government sought to establish new sources of income and focused on tourism (Honey 1999). In 1986, the Tourism Investment Act was established, encouraging foreign investors to make proposals for hotel constructions. Massive infrastructure development began to take place in the mid-1990s and still continues today. In 2002, there were about 6 640 beds in 190 hotels and guesthouses (Commission for Tourism 2002), and by 2015, a total of 15 000 beds are expected to exist in accommodation establishments in the islands (MWECLE 1993).

Despite the fact that the Zanzibar government has frequently expressed its commitment to ecotourism and even proclaimed it as the national tourism development strategy (cf. Khatib 2000), social and environmental concerns have largely been ignored in the infrastructure development process. Today, tourism is Zanzibar's second major foreign exchange earner, but this has simultaneously resulted in a multitude of land- and resource-use conflicts, contributed to resource depletion, increased the pressure on natural resources,

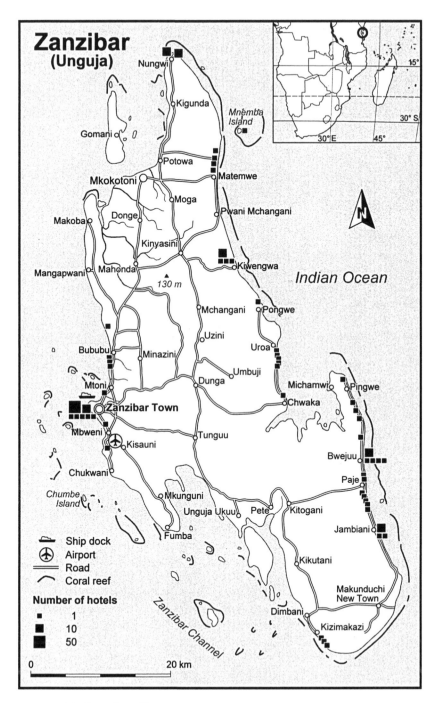

Figure 7.1   Zanzibar, Tanzania

changed human–environmental relations, caused the disempowerment of local communities and led to socio-cultural conflicts (Dahlin and Stridh 1996; Gössling 2001a; 2001b; 2002; Gössling et al. 2003; Honey 1999; Sulaiman 1996). In the light of these findings, this chapter seeks to describe the various actors in the interacting process of tourism development and environmental change, to evaluate their role and benefits in the observed developments, and to understand their views on the use of the environment. Focus is on Unguja Island, in this chapter also referred to as Zanzibar, where most of the tourist infrastructure developments have taken place.

HISTORY AND POLITICAL ECONOMY

For 2000 years, trade has been common along the East African coast, covering the northern Indian Ocean and the Red Sea, stretching as far as to China and Indonesia, and involving Assyrian, Sumerian, Egyptian, Phoenician, Indian, Chinese, Persian and Omani Arab traders (Sheriff 1987; Middleton 1992). The Omani Arabs were also the first to settle in Zanzibar, the most important trans-shipment market in the region. Over centuries, these merchants controlled the trade in the islands and along the East African coast. It was not until 1498 – the arrival of Vasco da Gama – that power relations changed. Within a few years, the East African coast came under control of the Portuguese, who stayed in power for 150 years. In 1650, the Arabs regained power over the city of Muscat (Oman) and subsequently won back hegemony over the East African coast, which they controlled again by 1698. In the following years, East Africa saw an intensification of the slave trade because cheap labor was needed for the date plantations in Oman. In Zanzibar, demand for slaves increased when cloves were introduced in 1812 and cultivation began subsequently in large plantations. During the 1840s, there might have been 60 000–100 000 slaves working in the clove plantations in Zanzibar and the archipelago had become both the world's largest producer of cloves and the largest slave trading center on the East African coast (Sheriff 1987).

The 19th century saw the arrival of new colonial powers. Great Britain and Germany both had a great interest in East Africa, and were soon in control of the region. In 1890, a contract between Great Britain and Germany turned Zanzibar into a British protectorate and made Tanganyika German territory (German East Africa). However, German colonial domination of Tanganyika ended after World War I, when control of the territory passed to Great Britain under a League of Nations mandate. British hegemony remained stable until 1950, when the first political movements came into existence in East Africa. Tanganyika declared itself an independent nation in 1961, followed by

Uganda in 1962 and Kenya in 1963. Zanzibar became independent in December 1963. At that time, two political parties had been founded, the predominantly African Afro-Shirazi Party (ASP) and the Arab Zanzibar Nationalist Party (ZNP). However, on 12 January 1964, the ruling ZNP was overthrown and the majority of the Arab elite killed in a violent uprising. The ASP took over power and its leader, Abeid Amani Karume, became president of the People's Republic of Zanzibar. On 26 April 1964, Karume and the new president of Tanganyika, Julius Nyerere, agreed upon the union of Tanganyika (Tan) and Zanzibar (Zan), which became the 'United Republic of Tanzania'. Defense, foreign policy, home affairs and monetary policy became union matters, even though the islands remained semi-autonomous with their own president, cabinet, legislature and judicial system. Furthermore, the government of Zanzibar kept control over all issues of development policy within the islands, including tourism. In 1977, the mainland Tanzania African National Union (TANU) and the Zanzibar ASP merged to form Chama Cha Mapinduzi (CCM), which continued to be the only party in Zanzibar. However, the World Bank pressed for multiparty democracy in the early 1990s, which resulted in the foundation of the opposing Civic United Front (CUF) in 1992. Since then, clashes between CCM and CUF have been the cause of many internal problems. These culminated in a violent uprising causing the death of 29 Zanzibari in January 2001, when the CUF refused to accept the results of the October 2000 elections, accusing the CCM of electoral fraud. In late 2002, the political situation appeared stable, with concessions made by the new president Amani Abeid Karume, son of Zanzibar's first president, to the CUF. There are now also several other minor political parties.

ECONOMY AND TOURISM DEVELOPMENT

The economy of Zanzibar consists of subsistence activities, particularly artisanal fisheries and agriculture, and a market sector based on the export of carrageenan-carrying algae, cloves and tourism. Artisanal fishing has traditionally mainly involved traps and nets (Jiddawi 1998). However, the collection of gastropods, bivalves and other marine organisms such as octopus has also been common in tidal zones. Subsistence economies also involve the production of cassava, maize, mango, papaya, coconut and bananas, and there are plantations of rice, cane, oranges, lemon, lime, tangerine, tamarind and spices. Carrageenan-carrying algae were introduced by the international pharmaceutical industry in 1989 and soon produced in virtually all villages on the east coast (Pettersson-Löfquist 1995). Farming of algae has now become an important cash income activity for the women in most families in coastal communities, even though subsistence production continues to be the basis of local livelihoods. Cloves are still the most important cash crop of the islands in terms of foreign exchange earnings. Tourism ranks second, contributing US$3.1 million to the Zanzibar economy in 2000 (ESRF 2002). Per capita, this amounts to roughly US$3.5, which can be compared to the Zanzibar per capita income of US$222 (in 2000; ESRF 2002). In 2003, there are 6 637 beds in 190 hotels and guesthouses – out of this 6 400 beds in 175 hotels and guesthouses in Unguja Island – with a planned capacity of more than 15 000 beds by 2015 (MWECLE 1993). The number of international tourist arrivals has increased from 8 967 in 1984 to 97 165 in 2000 (Commission for Tourism 2002). There were some 2 600 official jobs in Zanzibar's tourist industry in the late 1990s, most of them low-paid service positions in hotels (Honey 1999).

As pointed out earlier, Zanzibar's history of tourism development is rather recent. Plummeting clove prices, which fell from US$9,000 per ton in the early 1980s to US$600 in the mid-1990s, forced the government to identify new sources of foreign exchange earnings (Honey 1999). Simultaneously, the World Bank, IMF and USAID exerted pressure on the government to implement more liberal trade and investment policies. In 1986, the terms of an IMF structural adjustment loan dictated comprehensive economic liberalizations, including opening of the country to foreign investment, promotion of new exports, an easing of regulations on repatriation of profits, and abolition of duties and taxes on the import of raw materials for the industry. Several new laws were established during the same period. The 1985 Trade Liberalization Policy advocated diversification of the economy and a greater role for the private sector (Honey 1999), and the 1986 Tourism Investment Act encouraged foreign investors to make proposals for hotel constructions (Khatib 1999). This was followed by an amendment of the 1989 Investment Protection Act, so that tourism became qualified for an array of investment incentives. In 1992, the Zanzibar Investment Promotion Agency (ZIPA) was established and in the same year, the Commission for Tourism was created to promote Zanzibar as a tourist destination. In 1994, the World Bank started to support Tanzania and Zanzibar with a several million dollar tourist infrastructure project aimed at improving roads, electricity and water facilities (Honey 1999).

Investment approval procedures on the basis of the 1986 Tourism Investment Act worked on a 'first-come first-served' basis, with the effect that the government did not choose between competing investment proposals (Sulaiman 1996). Very few applications were rejected and investment was encouraged before either a tourism policy or a land-use plan had been developed. In 1993, when the Tourism Zoning Plan was finally published (MWECLE 1993), a total of 86 hotels and guesthouses had already been approved by ZIPA (Sulaiman 1996). Nearly all approved applications came from independent companies, more than half of them from foreign investors (Honey 1999). In 2003, virtually all large hotels in coastal areas are run by the international tourist industry, and by Italian and South African companies in particular.

In 1994, an International Workshop on Ecotourism and Environmental Conservation was held in Zanzibar. According to Honey (1999, p. 267), the aim of the conference was to review ecotourism experiences in other countries, give government officials and tour operators a practical introduction to ecotourism, discuss plans to establish nature conservation areas and to examine the benefits of local community involvement in tourism. The conference also set forth a blueprint for future tourism development in Zanzibar, based on 16 recommendations addressing, in particular, social and environmental aspects of tourism development. However, the theoretical insights of the conference largely remained free of practical consequences. Sulaiman (1996, p. 35) remarked:

> The national tourism policy is still being formulated. In theory, it will advocate low-volume, high-class, culturally and environmentally sensitive tourism. In practice, there is still no agreement on either the desired quality or the volume of approved hotel application, nor a formalized system of environmental impact assessment that would give environmental considerations their appropriate weight in a fragile, small-island ecosystem.

Eight years after the conference, in 2002, consideration of environmental measures by hotels was still voluntary, including such issues as proper garbage disposal, careful fresh water use and adequate sewage treatment. Environmental legislation regarding tourist infrastructure does not exist or is not enforced, and there are no guidelines or monitoring procedures. For example, Environmental Impact Assessment (EIA) is part of the Environmental Management for Sustainable Development Act of 1996 as a process to be carried out by any person to 'undertake any activity which is likely to have a significant impact on the environment' (House of Representatives 1996b, p. 71). Taking the vulnerability of island environments into consideration, this would in practice apply to almost all constructions. In reality, however, there have been less than ten EIAs since 1996, and these seem to have remained without practical consequences (H. Rijal 2002, Dept. of the Environment, personal communication). It is known, on the other hand, that hotels are constructed without EIA in non-tourism zones or too close to the high-water line (A. Khatib 2002, Commission for Tourism, personal communication). It should also be noted that there are a number of publications and reports that have described the economic, social and ecological consequences of tourism development and made recommendations for improvements (cf. Dahlin and Stridh 1996; Gössling 2001a, 2001b, 2002; Honey 1999; Sulaiman 1996). However, these have remained unnoticed. The same is true for critical remarks from the side of the Commission for Tourism: 'we have a problem with the perception of the politicians. We are aware [of the problems], we know what to do, but for the politicians it seems to be different' (A. Khatib 2002, Commission for Tourism, personal communication; cf. also Khatib 1999, 2000). Honey (1999, p. 288) summarizes: 'so far, Zanzibar has failed to formulate and then stay the course on a new model that encompasses ecotourism instead of merely . . . upscale, foreign-owned conventional tourism'.

ENVIRONMENTAL AND SOCIAL CHANGE

Zanzibar's major ecosystems comprise coral reefs, tidal zones, coral rag (fossilized corals with bushy vegetation), mangroves and forests. With the exception of three marine protected areas (Mnemba Island, Mafia Island and Chumbe Island) and one terrestrial protected area (Jozani Forest, soon to be extended to Chwaka Bay Conservation Area), most of these ecosystems have in recent years been under increasing pressure through coastal development and global environmental change. The latter includes sea-level rise and increasing water temperatures through El Niño Southern Oscillation phenomena. Even though most of the population is dependent on agriculture, the most important ecosystems in terms of protein sources are coral reefs, which are the habitat of most of the fish species used for local consumption. Fisheries are also important in terms of job generation. It is estimated that there are 23 000 full-time fishermen in Zanzibar (Lyimo et al. 1997, quoted in Jiddawi and Öhman 2002), which represents 2.5 per cent of the total population of 907 400 (in 2000; ESRF 2002). There is evidence that artisanal fisheries are in decline as a result of overexploitation. The total annual catch in Zanzibar was 20 000 tons in 1988, but it had dropped to less than 15 000 tons in 2000. There is also a reported decline in fisheries of crustaceans, sea cucumber, gastropods and sharks (Bakari 1998; Johnstone et al. 1998). For example, due to an intensive trade in lobsters and crabs to tourist hotels, restaurants and cruise liners, these crustaceans show signs of depletion (Jiddawi and Öhman 2002). This is also reflected in Zanzibar's export statistics, which indicate a decline in lobster exports from 23 tons in 1993 to 0.7 tons in 1997. While the overall amount of harvestable marine resources appears to be declining, demand for marine sources of protein has substantially increased, both as a result of population growth and an increase in tourist arrivals. Even for other ecosystems such as mangroves and tidal zones a critical ecological situation has been reported (cf. Muhando 1998).

With respect to social aspects, the islands have gone through a process of change in recent years. Zanzibar's ethnic composition includes African, Arab, Hindu and Indonesian elements, and is 90 per cent Muslim with respect to religion (Middleton 1992). This is primarily a result of the islands' mercantile history, which has made the population 'one of the most cosmopolitan in the World' (Ingrams 1931 [1967], p. 28). The meeting of different cultures over centuries might have made Zanzibar open towards visitors from other cultures and relatively resistant to the adoption of elements of these cultures. Nevertheless, the islands now see themselves confronted with new lifestyles of both tourists and a large number of migrants from the Tanzanian mainland. Their lifestyles may often be perceived as superior because they are orientated towards leisure, pleasure, consumption and individualism, and thus contradict local lifestyles, which are oriented towards work, religion and kinship (cf. Gössling 2002). The local younger population in particular is often mesmerized by the 'lightness of being' implicit in tourist lifestyles, which has led to profound changes in the culture of Zanzibar. As will be shown, such changes also include human–environmental relations and are thus important factors in environmental change.

TALES OF CONFLICT

Tourism development has caused major changes in Zanzibar, which will be evaluated in the following by a description of the conflicts that have occurred between the different actors involved in these changes. Basically, these can be divided in place-based actors (local communities, migrants, hotel managers, tourists) and non-place based actors (World Bank/IMF, government, tourist industry) (cf. Blaikie 1995). Conflicts caused on account of tourism development have occurred between the main political parties CCM and CUF; the government and the tourist industry; the government and international organizations; the government and local communities; local communities and the tourist industry; local communities and tourists; and between other actors such as migrants or investors. As will be shown, these conflicts involve dimensions of power, identity, entitlements and resources (financial or natural); they are violent or peaceful, open or hidden, and they may or may not be perceived by the actors.

Chama Cha Mapinduzi–Civic United Front

Since multiparty democracy was established in 1992, Zanzibar has been going through a difficult political situation, including frequent clashes between the main political parties CCM and CUF. This conflict was especially brought to light with the last national elections held in October 2000, which resulted in violent outbursts between members of the two rival parties. Generally, CUF believes in the ideology of *Utajirisho* (enrichment), rejecting the 'negative features of Capitalism and Socialism' (Mmuya 1998, p. 20). Tourism has for this reason been one of the subjects of political dispute, with some CUF politicians voting against this economic activity (cf. Honey 1999). In fact, whereas CCM clearly outlines the contributions of tourism to economic development, including the promotion of services, the use of environmental resources as tourist attractions and the participation of Tanzanians in tourism activities, CUF makes no mention of this sector under its major policy concerns, and instead focuses on agriculture, education and infrastructure as the objectives of a sound development (Kisembo 2001).

Particularly in the more traditional Islamic village of Nungwi, a CUF stronghold, which has mainly been visited by a rather hedonistic backpacker type of tourist, tensions have arisen on account of tourism. Alcohol consumption, drugs and the beachwear of (female) tourists, all brought to the formerly remote village by several hundred visitors at any one time, have been observed with anger by part of the village population. Tourism also brought Tanzanians from the mainland to Nungwi, who work in hotels, restaurants or the informal sector. These are frequently blamed for 'taking the jobs of the locals', and are generally made responsible by the local population for the cases of robbery, theft and rape of tourists that have occurred in the village. Women from the mainland, in some cases prostitutes, may also have brought a different, 'liberal' lifestyle to Nungwi. These developments, all of which have taken place within a few years, are reported by villagers to have resulted in disputes. In September 2002, eight small hotels burnt down in Nungwi, the fires officially having been caused by an electric spark. However, there are also rumors that the fire might not have been an accident at all, but rather a logical consequence of the local tensions. Honey (1999, p. 282) remarks in a more general context:

> Whereas elsewhere, increased tourism has frequently led to liberalization of social mores and strengthening of movements of women, gays and lesbians, and other oppressed groups, Zanzibar's tourism boom coincides with a rise in conservative Muslim practices. This marks a shift from the island's tradition of religious moderation and tolerance stemming from its location as a cultural, commercial, and intellectual crossroads.

Over the years, there have been several acts of violence in Zanzibar against places serving liquor and tourist facilities deemed offensive to Islamic law (Honey 1999). Today, alcohol consumption might be tolerated, but insensitive tourist behavior continues to be a source of anger among locals in many areas visited by tourists. A particular problem is walking in beachwear through villages or in public places. With CCM and CUF seeking to politicize tourism for their respective political goals – jobs and income versus traditional Islamic life – tourism continues to be a source of internal conflict (see also Myers 2002 for the degree of politicization in the villages).

Government–Tourist Industry

There are also numerous conflicts between the tourist industry and the government, which mainly concern the smooth running of businesses. Hotel managers' complaints include the difficulty of employing better-educated staff from outside Zanzibar, the poor condition of the roads, insufficient security, and unsatisfactorily provision of electricity and water. However, beyond these tensions there is a mutual dependence. The government ensures that gains made by the international tourist industry remain satisfactory to investors and that new construction sites are made available – generally without consultation of local communities. In return, the government receives foreign exchange earnings from the tourist industry. Little of this money seems to be reinvested in the development of the island. In 1993, it was agreed that 9 of the 15 per cent VAT paid by hotels (the VAT has now increased to 20 per cent) would go to the treasury, while the Commission for Tourism should receive 5 per cent for promotional purposes, and the Tourism Training School at Maruhubi, intended to teach basic skills in hotel management, another 1 per cent. However, neither the school nor the Commission for Tourism have ever received financial support (A. Khatib 2002, Commission for Tourism, personal communication), and it thus remains an open question where the financial resources vanished. More generally, it also remains questionable if official figures on income. from tourism are correct. Considering the fact that hotels alone may annually pay at least US$5 million in VAT, which excludes licenses for boutiques, bars and diving centers, as well as import, fuel and airport taxes, the official figure of US$3.1 million in tourism revenue (in 2000) seems heavily understated. Rumors of corruption can be heard anywhere on the islands, and one manager suggests that 'much money has disappeared with the last government [of former president Salmin Amour]'. Even though there is no proof for these accusations, it is worth noting that Tanzania is listed in the Corruption Perceptions Index with a rating of 2.7 on a scale of 10, indicating a highly corrupt state (Transparency International 2002). It should also be noted that much power is allocated to the president of Zanzibar, who appoints, for example, the chairman, executive secretary and all directors of the Commission for Tourism (House of Representatives 1996a, p. 137), as well as the director of the Department of the Environment (House of Representatives 1996b, p. 60).

Government–International Organizations

International organizations such as the World Bank, IMF and United Nations Development Programme (UNDP) have played an important role in the post-independence history of Zanzibar. When Julius Nyerere stepped down from presidency in Tanzania, the new government embarked upon a World Bank/IMF sponsored Economic Recovery Programme (ERP) that lasted for three years (Ahluwalia and Zegeye 2002). The ERP was aimed at correcting external imbalances, reducing budget deficits and inflation, providing incentives to producers, adjusting exchange rates, liberating the trade and reducing the public sector. However, when the ERP ended in 1989, wages and social services decreased, while inflation and unemployment increased and income distribution became more unequal. The negative effects led to a growing opposition towards the government and demands for political liberalization within the country. However, Ahluwalia and Zegeye (2002, p. 6) remark that:

> The impetus for liberalization came not only from opponents of the ERP who blamed the one-party state for the country's economic woes, but also from the fatigued international donor community under the aegis of the World Bank which advocated good governance as an essential part of the reform process.

In the following years, the World Bank pressed for multiparty democracy, blaming the CCM for the failure of the ERP. However, what seemed rational from a democracy perspective had complex consequences in local communities in Zanzibar, where power structures changed rapidly. For example, coastal villages were in theory under national legislation since independence, but local rules and laws regulated everyday life in reality, particularly the use of natural resources.

There are many examples of local resource use legislation. Tobisson et al. (1998), for instance, describe the prawn (*kamba*) management system in Mapopwe Creek, which was characterized by closure periods during hatching, and locals on the east coast explain that in the villages of Paje, Bwejuu and Jambiani, elders used to stop octopus hunting in intermediate periods of three months. In these villages, there were also protected marine spots (*shimoni*), where nobody was allowed to fish. Such local systems ensured the recovery of certain species, and offenders were punished. Nowadays these systems have disappeared and the reasons for this may ultimately be of a political nature. The *kamba* system in Mapopwe Creek, for instance, collapsed because migrants moving to the Creek disregarded the closure period. Traditionally, village elders had been in a position to punish violations of the local regulations, but the government's classification of the area as common property undermined local control (Tobisson et al. 1998). A similar case occurred in Bwejuu and other villages on the east coast, where multiparty democracy led to the collapse of mechanisms of self-regulation and control. One local woman explains:

> When the multiparty system came in, people argued 'you stop me for political reasons', and the local laws disappeared. Elders belonged to the CCM, and when the multiparty system was introduced, all local laws were broken down because they [the villagers] said 'it is this party, let's not do it'.

The degree of politicization in local communities is also reflected in Myers (2002, p. 156), who quotes a local in the village of Chwaka in the context of lacking social cooperation: 'multipartyism makes everything political, even garbage'. Even western residents of Zanzibar critically remark that the World Bank's good intentions have resulted in no improvements of local livelihoods, but caused politically motivated clashes and deaths. One respondent critically remarks that democratic societies have to evolve and cannot be imposed: 'maybe we need to realize that there are countries that are not ready for multiparty systems'.

The involvement of international organizations in the development of Zanzibar has also provoked much discontent among the employees of government departments. For example, one ecologist at the Department of the Environment describes how Zanzibar's environmental legislation was written by a US lawyer and financed by the World Bank. The Department of the Environment was financed by the Finnish International Development Agency, Finnida, which also financed the Tourism Zoning Plan. Finally, the implementation of protected areas was planned by foreign researchers and financed by UNDP. In the ecologist's opinion, the use and conservation of Zanzibar's environment was turned into a western action plan, largely ignorant of local legislation, knowledge systems, property rights, wants and needs: '... they all suggest ways of how to develop, and as they come with a lot of money, these paths are accepted. However, this leaves little room for our own ways' (interview October 2002).

Government–Local Communities

When independence was declared in Zanzibar in 1963, all lands were turned into government property and fell under national legislation. This represented a major change for local communities in many areas, which had developed their own legislative, administrative and authoritative structures based on a committee of elders and each village's head (*sheha*). With the advent of tourism in the early 1990s, the government needed to allocate lands for hotel constructions, thus forcing local communities to give up their lands in return for financial compensation. The latter was paid by the tourist industry to the traditional owners of coconut trees on the respective lands, the only resource with a local market value (the beaches themselves were village property). Local communities had no power to negotiate the conditions of tourism development, to identify the areas that in their eyes should be made available for constructions or to block development per se (Sulaiman 1996). Payments per coconut tree were in the order of TSh1 000–20 000 (US$2.5–55) in 1990, which was a fair price in the eyes of many locals. In fact, as most villages along the coast still lived largely outside cash economies, the amount of money obtained by individuals for selling a number of trees often seemed to correspond to a small fortune. However, in the course of the coastal development process, the value of land increased continuously. In 2002, the amount of money paid for plots of land was already in the order of TSh0.4– 1.5 million (US$410–1 545) per tree, a sum far beyond local purchasing power. Even though communities appeared ready to sell their land use rights in the early 1990s, they were little informed about the consequences or adequate levels of compensation:

> It is common now to hear the lament of villagers who, attracted by the apparently high prices offered for their coconut trees or other assets, rushed to sell them and now regret their decision. The money that they received has been dispersed among their wide, extended family and they are left with nothing – not even the land that previously provided their financial security. Other villagers, who initially looked with approval on such sales, thinking that hotels would bring jobs for the many underemployed young people in their village, now regret that such transactions ever took place as the jobs have not materialized, yet local access routes have been closed, the prices of local raw materials, such as coconut fronds (the typical roofing material), have risen or water sources have become saline through over-exploitation (Sulaiman 1996, p. 42).

One local respondent hints at the underlying problem, which is of a more fundamental cultural nature: 'If you give me money, I will forget everything because I have money. He [a man selling his coconut trees] lost the money without understanding what was happening. People look at now. They don't look forward.' Coastal communities in Zanzibar live in the present, being less aware of the long-term effects of their decisions. There were no systems to save or re-invest the money received for the trees, and local communities were unaware of the fact that the seemingly high compensation paid for the trees (representing the net present value of the resource), was extremely low for the foreign investors. Villagers have realized that 'now they sell the land with the trees, not the trees'. However, most of the lands of any value for tourist infrastructure development have already been sold, and all along the east coast community-owned lands have become private lands, mostly owned by foreigners.

In order to understand the dimensions of this change in land-ownership, one needs to recall the government's driving role in this process. Based on the argument that lost foreign exchange earnings from the export of cloves had to be replaced, tourism development was encouraged. Tourism was also promised to bring benefits to coastal communities, which, as should be noted, were poor in relative, not in absolute terms. However, most of the benefits went to the government, which receives an annual rent of US$1,500–2,000 per hectare of land (Sulaiman 1996). As local tree owners were compensated only once, this development represents a process of long-term financial empowerment of the government. These findings confirm that tourism can be a centripetal, state-enhancing force (cf. Weaver 2000). Local communities, on the other hand, go through a process of financial disempowerment, which is a result of increasing prices for land and other resources important for local livelihoods, such as fish. Furthermore, common property (land) has been turned into a commodity, which has contributed to the commercialization of local relationships, even this with concomitant consequences for the social, political and authoritative structures in the villages (cf. Gössling 2001a). From a more abstract point of view, villagers not only lost resources such as coconut trees, but also entitlements to these resources, including access to the coral rag area, the beach and the tidal zone. All of these were traditionally the basis for local livelihoods. As pointed out earlier, hereditary rights to land were turned to the government with independence, but it was with the advent of tourism that this shift in ownership became perceptible. As land entitlements are now gradually shifted to the government (land lease contracts usually expire after 33 years), and as the administrative and procedural forms, which regulate bureaucracies in the institutional center, now also become applicable to the formerly independent periphery, this process represents an allocation of power to the government.

Local Communities–Tourist Industry

On a legislative or authoritative level, conflicts over land occur between local communities and the government. Physically, they take place in tourism development areas. In total, 0.3 per cent (435 ha) of Zanzibar's land area is designated as future tourist area (MWECLE 1993). On top of this, land requirements by migrants have to be added, which are also substantial. As virtually all hotel constructions are located along the northern and eastern coast, conflicts over land concentrate in these areas. For example, Mnemba Island, today the site of Zanzibar's most expensive hotel (which also won, among others, the British Airways and Green Globe's ecotourism awards), used to be an important landing site for fishermen. When the hotel was built in 1988 with permission probably obtained through corruption (Honey 1999), fishermen were excluded from their traditional fishing grounds and camps. Even though fishermen are now allowed to fish around Mnemba, they are still denied the right to land on the island. Compensation for this loss of entitlements was never paid (Honey 1999). In other areas, scuba diving and snorkeling have been reported to conflict with local fishing activities (Johnstone et al. 1998), and in other cases, it has been reported that locals had to refrain from the use of the tidal zone (Tobisson et al. 1998). This is problematic particularly in the case of villagers farming algae in the tidal zone, an activity particularly important for women. It has also been reported that fishermen had to move their traditional landing sites or were kept away from the hotel area, even though this is not legal (Sulaiman 1996). Some hotels run by the international tourist industry even re-located local access routes along the beach, which not only resulted in longer travel times, but also physical hardship because the new roads were built through the extremely hot and humid coral rag. In the village of Kendwa in northern Zanzibar, locals tore down the jetty of a new five-star hotel under construction in late 2002, which they believed would damage the coral reef.

Conflicts between local communities and the tourist industry also include natural resources. Due to its high nutritional value and protein content, the most important resource in Zanzibar is seafood. With the advent of tourism, the demand of seafood, including marlin, sailfish, tuna, red snapper, kingfish, barracuda, shrimps, crabs and lobster has increased substantially. A survey in the Kiwengwa area found, for example, that resource use had almost tripled through the additional demand of the tourist industry (Gössling 2001a). Migrants, moving in substantial numbers to the tourist development areas, also increase the demand for fish, and may use particularly unsustainable fishing techniques not adapted to the local environment, such as nets with very small mesh sizes. Tourist demand for fish is also reflected in prices, which have, for example, increased by several hundred percent in the Kiwengwa area in the period 1993–1999. Prices for prawns are reported to have fallen from TSh3,000 (US$3.7) per kilo in 2000 to TSh1,000 (US$1.1) in 2001, when tourist numbers declined as a result of the events of 11 September. When tourist arrivals resumed in 2002, prices went up again (H. Rijal 2002, Department of the Environment, personal communication). The tourist industry is also reported to pay the highest prices for seafood. Seafood prices thus seem to be coupled with tourist demand, which needs to be seen in the light of declining fisheries. In the long run, this may lead to nutritional problems. For example, in Bwejuu, some fish species are reported to have disappeared and most species have become scarce, forcing locals to turn to the commercially least important species (cf. Sulaiman 1996). Similar developments are reported from other villages such as Chwaka (Myers 2002).

Tourism has also led to the commoditization of marine resources, as virtually all marine species have become valuable with the advent of tourism, including fish, crustaceans, sharks, corals and shells. For example, shark jaws and teeth have become sought-after souvenirs, the latter being sold for about US$1.5 each in Zanzibar Town. This has raised the market value of sharks by 10 per cent within a few years. Gastropods, for example the giant triton shell, helmet shells or the CITES-enlisted *Tridacnidae*, are now sold for substantial amounts of money in all tourist areas (Gössling et al. 2003). In some areas, they are reported to have disappeared as a result of the tourist-related curio trade. Even though the consequences of these developments to the ecosystem are unknown, it seems clear that they add on environmental stress such as increasing water temperatures, physical reef destruction and water pollution.

Tourism has also increased the demand for other resources. The east and north of Zanzibar, where most of the large hotels have been built, is characterized by water scarcity. Tourism has substantially increased water demand in the area, with per capita uses ranging between 100–2 000 liters per day (Gössling 2001b). The weighted water consumption in hotels and guesthouses was calculated at 685 liters per tourist per day, which compares unfavorably to recommended consumption guidelines of 200 liters per tourist per day (Halcrow 1994). Water scarcity was of particular concern in Nungwi, where angry villagers cut off a hotel pipeline tapping water from the main pipeline supporting the village. Groundwater has also been recognized as an important source for nutrient influx to coastal marine ecosystems and it is likely that poor sewage treatment (deposition in former wells or caves, non-concreted septic tanks and so on) has increased the nutrient content of the groundwater (Gössling 2001b).

Other important ecosystems such as mangroves and coral rag vegetation are also under pressure due to constant and high demands for building materials. For example, each of the resort hotels using traditional building materials such as *makutis* (coconut fronds) needs several ten thousand units to cover a single one of the spacious roofs. *Makutis* need to be replaced after seven years. Roof constructions also require substantial numbers of stems and branches, mostly taken from mangroves. Sand quarrying for constructions has also been reported as an environmental threat. Tourism has thus substantially increased the overall demand of natural resources in Zanzibar, often to the detriment of the environment.

From a human–environmental point of view, tourism development has fundamentally influenced traditional resource use systems in coastal communities. Economic activities such as fisheries have traditionally been characterized by high degrees of risk and uncertainty in terms of personal safety, amount of catch and income, which led to cooperative behavior and the establishment of share systems built on kinship (Andersson and Ngazi

1998). Kinship also secured access to resources because the right to use reef areas or tidal zones was exclusive to certain families (Jiddawi 1998; Tobisson et al. 1998). As described earlier, many of these characteristics of traditional resource use systems may have vanished when local communities became politicized in the early 1990s. However, there is also a strong trend towards abandoning traditional activities in favor of tourism, particularly among the younger population, which can be seen as part of a broader pattern of modernization. For example, in Kiwengwa, a village located adjacent to a number of resort hotels, it was found that within less than five years, 36 per cent of the working population above 14 years old had focused on tourism as the main economic activity (Gössling 2001a). Other consequences of altered resource use systems include selective fishing to meet the specific demands of the tourist industry (Bakari 1998). In Chwaka Bay, the crab (*kaa*) management system restricted crab hunting to low water during spring tide. This system collapsed when tourism development brought snorkels and masks to the villages, which allowed for more efficient hunting (Tobisson et al. 1998). In this case, technological innovation (snorkels and masks) caused a disruption of the traditional management system, because crabs could now be hunted throughout the day, instead of being restricted to low water during spring tide, as was formerly the case. Tourism is also a major transformer of human–environmental relations. This is reflected, for example, in the statement of a local working in the tourist industry: 'I cannot go fishing, because it is hard work and little pay. It's better to stay home'.

In many areas, tourism has also created an attitude of expectation. The tourist industry is expected to provide jobs and income, to establish electric power supplies and supply piped water, to support schools and health centers. Even projects like the Matemwe Bungalows, attempting to bring benefits to the villages in an integrated way, see themselves confronted with continuous new claims from the side of the village. The manager explains that 'managing this place is more like political bargaining. Half of my time goes to this'. From the locals' point of view, tourism may often be understood as a superior industry with infinite financial resources, potentially able to solve any problem. From a socio-cultural perspective, donations and jobs 'given' to locals have turned formerly self-sufficient villagers into passive beneficiaries. This is also illustrated by the case of children that have stopped going to school in order to beg for presents and money, or to sell souvenirs to the tourists. These children will lose access to knowledge resources, a process likely to lead to their future disempowerment.

Conflicts also include the traditional role of women. For example, women looking for employment opportunities in hotels, restaurants or the informal sector have met negative reactions, especially from members of the older generation, and specifically in the more traditional rural areas. The reason for this may ultimately be a perceived empowerment of women, achieved through the availability of financial resources and increasing self-confidence, fostering fears that the women's role in society will change.

Tensions on account of tourism seem generally to increase. There are now an increasing number of cases of robbery and rape of tourists reported, reflecting changes in a society traditionally known as peaceful and safe. Fires have been reported in several hotels, often with contradicting reports on the causes, and a large number of hotels have been subject to violent attacks. Violence has also reached new dimensions, as a bomb recently exploding in the toilet of a popular tourist bar indicates. As with other cases of such violence, it is not known whether locals or immigrants are responsible for these actions, and if they are against tourism development in general or happening for other reasons.

Despite these conflicts, tourism may often be perceived as contributing positively to local communities, a result of its job- and income-generating effects. For example, one case study in Kiwengwa found that for households involved in tourism, the average annual income (US$2,000) was 43 per cent higher than for those not involved (US$1,175) (Gössling 2001a). Financial advantages may thus contribute to creating a certain willingness to accept developments perceived as negative.

Local Communities–Tourists

There are also conflicts between tourists and locals. Often, these concern Muslim traditions, which are contradicted by the tourist lifestyles. One hotel employee from the Tanzanian mainland suggests that: 'the Zanzibari don't like tourism because the tourists eat pig meat and they go naked'. Even though the eating and drinking habits of the tourists now seem to be accepted, tourists in beachwear still cause irritations. Prostitution and the 'sex-oriented' lifestyle of part of the younger population in villages adjacent to the large hotels continue to be a source of anger (cf. Gössling 2002). There might also be local conflicts, such as one case in Bwejuu, where tourists were found taking pictures of a child that they had paid for posing half-naked. Generally, it is felt by most islanders that tourism changes local lifestyles and identities (for a more comprehensive discussion see Gössling 2002).

Conflicts between other Actors

In interviews with hotel managers, it becomes clear that there is strong competition between the hotels, which sometimes try to attract tourists from the same source countries. This competition is primarily one for uniqueness: each additional bed in new hotels makes it more difficult to sell Zanzibar as a unique and exclusive destination in international markets. However, large hotels also compete for scarce resources, including sites for hotel construction, seafood, water and building materials.

Tourism has initiated migration on a substantial scale as Tanzanians move to Zanzibar in order to earn money. In the tourist areas, they compete with locals for jobs, and they are also an important factor in the increasing demand of resources. Migrants have also been a source of social conflict because they frequently have the best positions in the souvenir trade and earn substantially higher incomes than locals engaging in this business. In Stone Town and other tourist areas, 'beach boys' (*papasi*) have become a common phenomenon. The majority of these come from Tanzania. As *papasi* often engage in illegal markets, hassle tourists and are made responsible for the majority of cases of theft, they are now largely perceived as a problem. The Commission for Tourism reports that 95 per cent of all complaints of tourists are on account of *papasi* (A. Khatib 2002, Commission for Tourism, personal communication).

POWER, IDENTITY, ENTITLEMENTS, RESOURCES

The political ecology of tourism development in Zanzibar is not only a conflict about the alteration of the environment, entitlements and resources. Ultimately, it also involves dimensions of power and identity. It has also been shown that conflicts are not always obvious. For example, few locals may be aware of the relationship between increasing resource requirements, largely caused by the growing tourist industry, and increasing resource prices. This is also true for the process of ecosystem change caused by selective fishing and the commercial use of marine resources with formerly no or little economic value, such as shark teeth, bivalves and gastropods. Most locals will not be aware of the detrimental long-term consequences of these activities. Ecosystem change is also a result of changing human–environmental relations and as such is part of a broader process of modernization. This has been shown to create new identities and to lead to the loss of indigenous knowledge systems, resource use strategies, efficient property rights and diversified production strategies.

The World Bank has been a powerful international actor putting the socialist government of Zanzibar on a neoliberal economic track, and its influence on tourism development has been substantial. However, the World Bank failed to take into consideration Zanzibar's Muslim traditions, the need of community involvement, the structure and complexity of local economies, the role of local resource use systems, and the importance of entitlements and property rights. Its engagement in Zanzibar's economic development became just another example of development imposed, which has had detrimental consequences for the environment of the country.

Conflicts also indicate that there might be winners and losers in the process of tourism development. Generally, there are two groups of actors that could be seen as winners, the government and the tourist industry. Not surprisingly, these are identical with the driving forces in tourism development. The government profits primarily from foreign exchange earnings, as the money is directly available to the government, largely beyond democratic control. However, these financial resources have been generated on the cost of environmental change, which has accelerated with tourism. This needs to be seen in the light of the fact that tourism contributes a meager 1.5 per cent to per capita income (given the correctness of official figures). Tourism may thus be important in terms of foreign exchange earnings, but it contributes little to the livelihoods of most of the local population. Quite the contrary, as local communities remain dependent on agriculture and fisheries, the continued degradation of the environment will instead severely affect their livelihoods.

With respect to natural resources and entitlements, tourism has been the major factor turning marine species and beaches, traditionally only exploited for subsistence, into commodities. Natural resources are now increasingly subject to transactions operating outside the pre-existing tradition-based systems and local legislation fails to control and manage their exploitation. Local legislation is also replaced by national law, which mirrors a shift in power relations. Tourism is also a direct agent in the degradation of local ecosystems through buying and collecting marine species and its high demand for fish, building materials and other resources. However, tourism does not only change access to and availability of resources. Alterations of human–environmental relations and local identity need to be seen in themselves as important determinants of environmental change as they lead to the loss of indigenous knowledge and resource use strategies. In the light of these findings, it may thus seem surprising that developments take place with little resistance of local communities. The reason may be that the loss of power, identity, entitlements and resources is often complex and beyond the understanding of local residents. Shifts in power relations, for example, are abstract in time and space, as they occur over rather long periods. Furthermore, financial benefits received from tourism development might have increased the local communities' willingness to accept the occurring changes.

TALES OF CHANGE

Tourism development in Zanzibar has so far largely been without consideration of socio-cultural, economic and ecological issues. However, there are signs of change. Local communities and a number of hotel managers seem to be increasingly aware of the negative impacts of tourism. For example, in Bwejuu and Jambiani, there are now initiatives towards 'community-based' tourism, with organized village tours inviting tourists to experience village life. It seems that such initiatives in theory can raise an interest in local lifestyles, traditions and rules, and create a climate of mutual respect. This needs to be seen in contrast to conventional mass tourism, which seems to deepen the cultural conflicts involved in the meeting of the different cultures (cf. Gössling 2002 for Zanzibar). Within the villages, there also appear to be more debates on the benefits and disadvantages of tourism development. Such local debates often involve a large number of stakeholders, and are thus important instruments in solving tourism-related conflicts. Even hotel managers show concern about the conflicts that tourism development has caused in Zanzibar, and there are calls for stronger environmental regulations. A number of hotels have also started to inform their guests about appropriate behavior in local villages, the importance of saving fresh water and the problems associated with buying marine artifacts. There are now even plans for the foundation of a hotel association to address these issues.

Tourism has also brought some benefits. For example, income from tourism has made a contribution to conservation in Zanzibar. The protected area Jozani Forest (soon to be extended to the Jozani–Chwaka Bay Conservation Area, proposed as Zanzibar's first National Park) was also implemented to create a tourist attraction, and is largely financed with money from tourists. Part of the money earned from entrance fees is forwarded to the surrounding villages making up the Jozani Environmental Conservation Association, where it has for example been invested in schools and health centers (for a more controversial discussion of environmental planning in this area see Myers 2002). There are also four marine protected areas: Mnemba Island, Mafia Island, Chumbe Island and Misali Island in Pemba. Chumbe Island, a privately managed nature reserve, can today be seen as Zanzibar's most successful ecotourism project. The reserve was officially gazetted in 1994 as the 'Chumbe Reef Sanctuary' to protect a biodiversity-rich coral reef system. The protected area was established after a three-year period of political struggle between the initiator, who had earlier worked as an aid project manager, the government and local fishermen. It was largely financed with private money as well as funds from the European Union, the German aid agency GTZ (*Gesellschaft für Technische Zusammenarbeit*) and several other donors. The running costs are now covered by a small-scale ecotourism project. A maximum of 14 visitors can be accommodated on the island, with prices per bed per night being in the order of US$200 during the tourist season. Local rangers control nature trails and swimming activities in the reef and a range of research projects ensures the monitoring of the ecosystem. School excursions are part of the island's educational program. Chumbe Island has also won a number of prizes, including the UNEP Global 500 Award for Environmental Achievement and the British Airways Tourism for Tomorrow Southern Regional and Global Awards.

In the future, some fundamental issues need to be considered in order to establish a more sustainable tourism. First, western conceptions of time, work and development need to be adjusted to local conceptions. For example, from today's point of view, it was wrong to compensate local people for their coconut trees by paying one lump sum (corresponding to an arbitrary net present value). Instead, an annual rent should have been paid, which would have been better adapted to the cultural characteristics of life in coastal communities where it is rather unusual to have money in excess that needs to be saved or re-invested. Second, the tourist industry needs to respect the ecological limits of the islands. For example, it may be easy for hotels to overcome the scarcity of resources by purchasing at higher prices or turning to imports. Obviously, these are not alternative solutions for the local population. Furthermore, even though there are now some environmentally aware hotel managers, the majority of the tourist industry seems to ignore environmental issues – despite the fact that the existence of the hotels is ultimately based on pristine, intact environments. There may be two major reasons for this: (i) the unstable political situation of the past, which resulted in low investor confidence in the long-term economic viability of this destination and (ii) the frequent changes of the management of most large hotels (usually at least once a year). Under such circumstances, it is unlikely that managers are concerned with sustainability, which can only be achieved through a long-term interest in the place as well as a profound understanding of the processes that have a negative impact on the environment. Finally, and overcoming these fundamental problems, the government's officially proclaimed, but non-existent commitment to ecotourism needs to be put to practice. Given the dependence of the government on foreign exchange earnings and the likelihood of corruption, this will not be an easy task. Tourism development thus needs to become a public debate to raise awareness of the environmental and social changes caused by this activity, and to exert pressure on the government to seriously address negative developments. This needs to go along with more transparency concerning the spending of foreign exchange earnings. Within the villages adjacent to the large hotels, there need to be debates on the benefits and disadvantages of tourism, too. The ecological limits to the use of ecosystems are usually well known in these areas (cf. Msuya 1998), and the mechanisms that traditionally governed resource use need to be re-established.

REFERENCES

Ahluwalia, P. and A. Zegeye (2002), 'Multiparty democracy in Tanzania. Crises in the Union', *African Security Review*, **10** (3), 1–16.
Andersson, J. and Z. Ngazi (1998), 'Coastal communities production choices, risk diversification, and subsistence behavior: responses in periods of transition', *Ambio*, **27** (8), 686–93.
Bakari, R. (1998), *Factors Determining the Exploitation of Crustacean Resources in Tanzania: an Application of Fisheries Model*, Paper presented at the Workshop on Valuation of the Marine and Coastal Resources and the Environment, Zanzibar, Tanzania, 6–9 December 1997.
Blaikie, P. (1995), 'Understanding environmental issues', in S. Morse and M. Stocking (eds), *People and Environment*, Norwich: School of Development Studies, University of East Anglia, pp. 1–30.
Commission for Tourism (2002), *International Tourist Arrivals by Nationality 1998–2001*, Zanzibar, Tanzania.
Dahlin, P. and P. Stridh (1996), *Huts or Hotels? A Minor Field Study on Land Management within the Tourism Sector in Unguja Island*, M.Sc. Thesis, Stockholm: Royal Institute of Technology, Department of Real Estate and Construction Management.
Economic and Social Research Foundation (ESRF) (2002), *Zanzibar Investment Development Policy (ZIDP)*, Draft Version 06, Zanzibar, Tanzania.
Gössling, S. (2001a), 'Tourism, environmental degradation and economic transition: interacting processes in a Tanzanian coastal community', *Tourism Geographies*, **3** (4), 230–54.
Gössling, S. (2001b), 'The consequences of tourism for sustainable water use on a tropical island: Zanzibar, Tanzania', *Journal of Environmental Management*, **61** (2), 179–91.
Gössling, S. (2002), 'Human–environmental relations with tourism', *Annals of Tourism Research*, **29** (2), 539–56.
Gössling, S., T. Kunkel, K. Schumacher and M. Zilger (2003), 'Use of marine species by tourism', *Biodiversity and Conservation*, submitted.
Halcrow, W. (Sir William Halcrow & Partners Ltd) (1994), *The Development of Water Resources in Zanzibar*, Final Report (Draft), and Appendices to Final Report, Wiltshire, England.
Honey, M. (1999), *Ecotourism and Sustainable Development*, Washington DC: Island Press.
House of Representatives (1996a), *The Promotion of Tourism Act, 1996*, Zanzibar, Tanzania.
House of Representatives (1996b), *The Environmental Management for Sustainable Development Act, 1996*, Zanzibar, Tanzania.
Ingrams, W.H. (1931) [1967], *Zanzibar. Its History and its People*, London: Frank Cass & Co. Ltd.

Jiddawi, N. (1998), 'The reef dependent fisheries of Zanzibar', in R.W. Johnstone, J. Francis and C.A. Muhando (eds), *Coral Reefs: Values, Threats, and Solutions*, Proceedings of *the National Conference on Coral Reefs*, Zanzibar, Tanzania, 2–4 December 1997, Zanzibar: Institute of Marine Sciences, pp. 22–36.

Jiddawi, N. and M.C. Öhman (2002), 'Marine fisheries in Tanzania', *Ambio*, **31** (7–8), 518–27.

Johnstone, R.W., C.A. Muhando and J. Francis (1998), 'The status of the coral reefs of Zanzibar: one example of a regional predicament', *Ambio*, **27** (8), 700–707.

Khatib, A.H. (1999), 'The importance of tourism to coral reefs on Zanzibar', in R.W. Johnstone, J. Francis and C.A. Muhando (eds), *Coral Reefs: Values, Threats, and Solutions*, Proceedings of *the National Conference on Coral Reefs*, Zanzibar, Tanzania, 2–4 December 1997, Zanzibar: Institute of Marine Sciences, pp. 36–8.

Khatib, A.H. (2000), 'Ecotourism in Zanzibar, Tanzania', in P.U.C. Dieke (ed.), *The Political Economy of Tourism Development in Africa*, New York: Cognizant Communication Corporation, pp. 167–80.

Kisembo, P. (2001), 'Major policy concerns of a selected number of political parties', *Political Handbook and NGO Calendar 2001*, Friedrich Ebert Stiftung, Tanzania.

Lyimo, E., B.A. Juma, I. Bhai and A.H. Juma (1997), *Report of the Fisheries Frame Survey Conducted in Unguja and Pemba*, Small Holder Support Project Report, Zanzibar.

Middleton, J. (1992), *The World of the Swahili. An African Mercantile Civilization*, New Haven: Yale University Press.

Mmuya, M. (1998), 'Tanzania: political reform in eclipse, crises and cleavages in political parties', *Handbook for Election Observers October 2000*, Tanzania: Friedrich Ebert Stiftung.

Msuya, F.E. (1998), 'Socioeconomic impacts of coral destruction on Unguja Island, Zanzibar, Tanzania', in R.W. Johnstone, J. Francis and C.A. Muhando (eds), *Coral Reefs: Values, Threats, and Solutions*, Proceedings of *the National Conference on Coral Reefs*, Zanzibar, Tanzania, 2–4 December 1997, Zanzibar: Institute of Marine Sciences, pp. 52–62.

Muhando, C.A. (1998), 'The status of coral reefs around Zanzibar and the general environmental services they provide', in R.W. Johnstone, J. Francis and C.A. Muhando (eds), *Coral Reefs: Values, Threats, and Solutions, Proceedings of the National Conference on Coral Reefs, Zanzibar, Tanzania, 2–4 December 1997*, Zanzibar: Institute of Marine Sciences, pp. 15–22.

MWECLE (Ministry of Water, Energy, Construction, Lands and Environment) (1993), *Tourism Zoning Plan*, Zanzibar, Tanzania.

Myers, G.A. (2002), 'Local communities and the new environmental planning: a case study from Zanzibar', *Area*, **34** (2), 149–59.

Pettersson-Löfquist, P. (1995), 'The development of open-water algae farming in Zanzibar: reflections on the socioeconomic impact', *Ambio*, **24** (7/8), 487–91.

Sheriff, A. (1987), *Slaves, Spices, and Ivory in Zanzibar. Integration of an East African Commercial Empire into the World Economy, 1770–1873*, Eastern African Studies, Nairobi: Heinemann.

Sulaiman, M.S. (1996), 'Islands within islands: exclusive tourism and sustainable utilization of coastal resources in Zanzibar', in L. Briguglio, R. Butler, D. Harrison and W. Leal Filho (eds), *Sustainable Tourism in Islands and Small States: Case Studies*, London and New York: Pinter, pp. 32–49.

Tobisson, E., J. Andersson, Z. Ngazi, L. Rydberg and U. Cederlöf (1998), 'Tides, monsoons and seabed: local knowledge and practice in Chwaka Bay, Zanzibar', *Ambio*, **27** (8), 677–85.

Transparency International (2002), *Transparency International Corruption Perceptions Index 2002*, available at: http://www.transparency.org/pressreleases _archive/2002/dnld/cpi2002.pressrelease.en.pdf.

Weaver, D. (2000), 'Tourism and political geography in Southern Africa', in P.U.C. Dieke (ed.), *The Political Economy of Tourism Development in Africa*, New York: Cognizant Communication Corporation, pp. 52–61.

8. 'High-value Conservation Tourism': Integrated Tourism Development in the Seychelles?

Stefan Gössling and Oliver Hörstmeier

INTRODUCTION

The Seychelles, a republic of 115 coralline and granite islands comprising 455 km² of land and a surrounding exclusive economic zone of almost 1.4 million km², is a unique destination with respect to a number of aspects. Like no other country in the world, the Seychelles have committed themselves to environmental conservation. The first environmental management plan for the islands was presented in 1990 (RoS 1990), world-wide one of the first of its kind. Its successor, the 'Environment Management Plan of Seychelles 2000–2010' (MET 2001) was presented almost simultaneously with the tourism management plan 'Vision 21 – Tourism Development in Seychelles 2001–2010' (MTCA 2001a). Both documents aim at achieving environmentally sound development in the islands, with tourism holding a key position in this process.

Environmental achievements can already be seen as remarkable. Half of the terrestrial surface of the islands is preserved in protected areas, proportionally more than in any other country in the world. Monitoring programs and the eradication of alien species have ensured the survival of threatened species and those 1 500 species endemic to the islands (Shah 2001; 2002). Environmental impact assessments are regularly carried out before new tourist infrastructure can be built, and programs are aimed at restructuring particularly those economic activities that need to be seen as harmful to the environment. The Seychelles have also hosted a number of international conferences on the environment, and they are at the forefront of initiatives such as 'Small Islands' Voice' (SIV). SIV was launched by UNESCO in 2002 as an attempt to achieve cooperation on environmental policies by the 42 of the 189 member states of the UN that fall under the category 'small islands'.

All these activities have made the country a pioneer in environmental conservation and have contributed to its image as an eco-destination. This image helps to attract a particularly wealthy tourist clientele expecting to experience unique, pristine and unsullied environments. In return, these visitors finance protected areas through governmental revenue, entrance fees and donations. In 2000, tourism ranked second to fisheries in the national economy, contributing about 20 per cent to GDP and 60 per cent to foreign exchange earnings (Shah 2002). In contrast to most other tropical destinations, the Seychelles have been able to attract an up-scale segment of international tourism, with prices per bed-night reaching from US$40 in guesthouses to US$2,040 in one of the most exclusive hotels in the world, Frégate Island Private. Tourism has also contributed to making the Seychelles one of the wealthiest nations in Africa with a per capita GDP of US$12,508 in 2000 (PPP US$), ranking 47 in the United Nations' Human Development Index (of 174 nations; UNDP 2002).

In summary, the Seychelles have managed to achieve a sound balance of environmental preservation and tourism development, or what could be termed 'high-value conservation tourism'. Accordingly, this contribution raises the question as to whether or not the islands can be considered an ideal-typical model for tourism development for other tropical islands.

TOURISM DEVELOPMENT

Tourism in the Seychelles began in the late 1960s, when visitors still arrived exclusively by ship. It was not before the international airport in Mahé opened in 1971 that tourist arrivals rose significantly, increasing from 1 600 in 1970 to 15 300 in 1972. In the years before independence in 1976, the British government sought to further intensify tourism with the primary goal of reducing the islands' economic dependency (Wolf 1983). This resulted in a period of intense tourist infrastructure development, during which a number of large hotels, an extended road system, and a water- and electricity supply system were built. By 1978, there were five large and several small hotels as well as some guesthouses.

On 5 June 1977, President James Mancham, who joined a Commonwealth Conference in London, was overthrown in a *coup d'état* and could not return to the country. The initiator of the coup, France Albert René, declared himself President and introduced a one-party system oriented towards socialism (cf. Därr 1996). Despite the unstable political situation, tourist numbers continued to grow and in 1980, almost 71 800 tourist arrivals were accounted for.

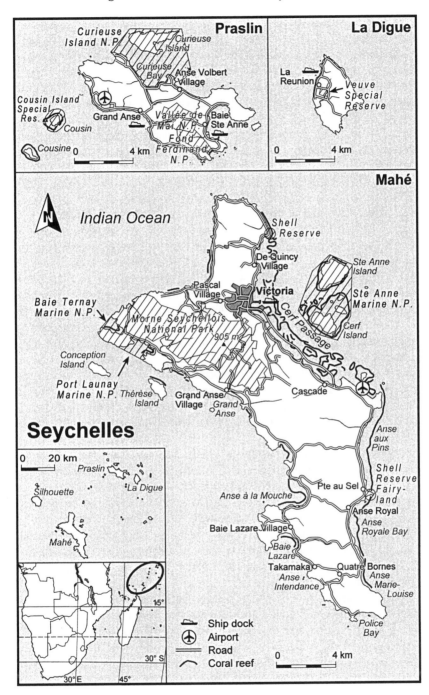

Figure 8.1   Seychelles

However, the situation changed when South African mercenaries engaged in an attempt to restore Mancham in November 1981, which was thwarted by René with the help of Tanzanian troops. This incident, followed by an army mutiny in 1982 and several attempted coups, spread the news of political instability and made the safety situation unbearable. Tourist numbers declined sharply in the following years. This negative trend was enforced further by economic recession in the European source markets, rising oil prices and airfares, the revaluation of the Seychelles' rupee, the introduction of a departure tax, poor marketing and increasing competition from other tropical destinations (Gabbay and Ghosh 1997; Wolf 1983).

The government, realizing its dependency on factors beyond its control, established a national airline, and in 1983 Air Seychelles operated its first flight (Vorlaufer 1991). The islands were now in the position to control tourist flows better and to actively open up new markets. Within the country, the government initiated an upgrading of the existing tourist facilities. In addition, new up-market hotels were built to attract wealthy tourists. Inter-island traffic connections were improved and marketing in the source countries intensified. As a result, growth resumed in 1983, and tourist numbers exceeded 100 000 in 1990. In the following year, René had to restore multiparty democracy, possibly in response to pressure from foreign creditors and aid donors such as France. Despite the short-term detrimental effects of the Gulf War, visitor numbers continued to increase. Pushed by marketing campaigns focusing on so far underrepresented source countries, international tourist arrivals climbed to 130 000 in 2000. On top of this, some 10 000 cruise ship passengers on day tours visited the islands in 2000 (MISD 2001a).

Politically, the situation in the Seychelles has now been stable since the mid-1980s, with René winning presidential elections in 1993, 1998 and 2001. Visitor numbers stagnated in 2001, a result of the situation following 11 September 2001 (Seychelles Nation 21.02.2002), but arrivals are expected to reach 180 000 in 2005 and 195 000 in 2010 (MTCA 2001b). Simultaneously, a major program is underway to upgrade accommodation establishments and to turn the Seychelles into a 'three to five star destination' (A. Volcere 2001, Director General of the Ministry of Tourism and Civil Aviation, personal communication).

The structure of the Seychelles' tourism industry consists of a mixture of large hotels and small guesthouses, including a broad array of ownership. When the islands became independent in 1976, most of the existing hotels were run by foreign investors (Vorlaufer 1991). However, the government also owned a number of accommodation establishments itself. In order to manage these, the Compagnie Seychelloise de Promotion Hotelière (COSPROH) was founded in 1980. In 1985, hotels were re-organized under the newly founded Seychelles Hotels, which in 1986 administered and managed 1 404 (58 per cent) of the 2 414 beds existing in the islands (EIU 1992, Gabbay and Gosh 1997). Financial losses made it necessary to privatize hotels, though, and by 1996, the share of state-owned bed capacity had decreased to 27 per cent, further declining to less than 17 per cent in 2001 (corresponding to 892 of the 5 378 beds) (Gabbay and Gosh 1997; Hörstmeier 2003, unpublished data; MTCA 2001b). Of the newly approved hotels to be built until 2007, less than 14 per cent (280 of 2 054 beds) will be state-owned. By 2007, the overall number of beds is expected to total 7 400 (MISD 2001b). In order to distribute the increasing number of visitors, part of these beds will also be located in formerly uninhabited and remote islands such as North, Coetivy, Silhouette, Farquhar, Poivre, Assomption, Rémire and Platte (MISD 2001b). It is also planned to make use of a growing number of yachts and catamarans to reduce the demand of land for hotel constructions (Seychelles Nation 26.12.2001).

The structure of accommodation establishments is well mixed. Three quarters of the existing hotels and guesthouses have fewer than 25 beds, 18 per cent have 25–99 beds and 7 per cent have 100 or more beds. The distribution of beds is shown in Table 8.1.

Table 8.1   Distribution of beds in accommodation establishments

	Mahé		Praslin		La Digue		Other islands		Total	
Beds	beds	%	beds	%	beds	%	beds	%	beds	%
< 10	118	2.2	44	0.8	58	1.1	0	0	220	4.1
10–24	650	12.1	348	6.4	174	3.2	58	1.2	1 230	22.9
25–49	218	4.0	150	2.8	68	1.3	120	2.1	556	10.2
50–99	50	0.9	468	8.7	0	0	100	1.9	618	11.5
100–199	124	2.3	496	9.3	120	2.2	0	0	740	13.8
> 200	2 014	37.5	0	0	0	0	0	0	2 014	37.5
Total	3 174	59.0	1 506	28.0	420	7.8	278	5.2	5 378	100

Source: MTCA 2001b

It should be noted, though, that the structure of the size of accommodation establishments in the Seychelles is changing, with foreign-owned chains gaining control over an increasing number of beds. For example, the Berjaya group alone manages 18 per cent of all beds, and the recently opened Ste. Anne Resort with 176 beds is run by the foreign-owned Beachcomber group, which is also involved in a number of other large projects. However, establishments with fewer than 50 beds are, with a few exceptions, entirely in local ownership.

The distribution of income from tourism is skewed. For example, working in the lower positions in hotels and guesthouses might provide an income of less than one third of the average income. Another aspect is that even though any Seychellois can theoretically participate in tourism development, this might be very difficult, in reality. For example, one guesthouse owner in Praslin describes his struggles to acquire a piece of land, to apply for a bank loan, to import building materials and to deal with the government. Building the guesthouse took him nine years. He remarks: 'I was angry, I was mad. In the end, when it was finished, I did not feel any satisfaction any more' (interview April 2001). There is also evidence that the government supports large hotels, which generate higher revenue in tax. For example, in mid 2001, local guesthouse owners were angry with the government, which had promoted the Seychelles as a tourist destination in a spot broadcast on CNN. In this spot, only the two most expensive hotels, Frégate Island and Lémuria Resort, had been shown. Comments made to Small Islands' Voice point in a similar direction:

> I for one believe that the current tourism policy in Seychelles, which is pitched at the higher end of the market, is short-sighted and misguided. . . . We ought to encourage tourism which not only benefits the large industries and corporations but . . . will also cascade to other small businesses around such as guesthouses, local shops, taxis, restaurants, etc. . . . In my view, the smaller projects will have a less destructive impact on our environment and will also spread the benefits of tourism to all parts of the country thus giving rise to a local supply and demand chain, a vital ingredient for job creation (Albert 2003).

However, tourism development goals will be repositioned in the future. Focus will be on the promotion of eco- and community tourism, environmentally better integrated development and increasing yield per tourist. With respect to the latter, tourist expenditure per day is expected to rise from US$102 per tourist in mid 2002 to US$150 by 2010. In the upper tourism segment, the number of tourists spending more than US$500 per day is expected to more than double by 2010 (MTCA 2001).

ENVIRONMENT AND DEVELOPMENT

Efforts to become a sustainable nation have sparked many debates in the Seychelles, and the conservation of the environment is a subject addressed by various groups. In contrast to developments in Europe and the USA, where a broad public movement pressed for stricter 'green' legislation, environmental laws in the Seychelles have been implemented in a top-down process under the one-party state of president France Albert René in the mid-1970s. This policy continued even after the turn to democracy in the early 1990s. To create public awareness of environmental issues, the government started a range of campaigns such as litter clean up and tree planting programs. Public support was also sought through popular campaigns such as 'Miss World for the Environment'. In 1997/98, the contestants planted trees at Anse Intendance (Mahé) to popularize the government's coastal management program.

Many Seychellois seem to have a profound knowledge of environmental issues. For example, one local, discussing the impacts of El Niño phenomena and drift-net trawling, concludes that 'I want to show nature to my children, so it should not be destroyed' (interview April 2001). However, there is also evidence that environmental awareness does not always translate into more environmentally friendly behavior. For example, in his contribution to SIV, one Seychellois claims that '99 per cent of all litter on beaches is deposited by locals, not tourists, [and] 100 per cent of turtle deaths are perpetrated by locals . . .' (Alphonse 2003). Governmental efforts to raise awareness of the environment thus continue, including radio programs, spots and reports on TV, articles in the national newspaper Seychelles Nation and educational programs in schools (RoS 2001). The SIV initiative also has the aim of awareness building, particularly among the younger population. The project also aims at promoting the participation of locals in environment and development issues, and is to ensure that environmental activities and decisions are 'even more in tune with community wishes and concerns' (Jumeau 2002). One of the first activities in each of the constituting islands of this initiative (St. Kitts and Nevis, Seychelles and Palau) was to carry out an opinion survey to determine how residents 'view the past and future changes in their island and their individual role in development' (De Comarmond 2002). Another recent initiative is the implementation of Wildlife Clubs to create environmental awareness through conservation projects, tree planting and field trips to protected areas. There are now 30 clubs with about 20 members each (Seychelles Nation 25.04.2002).

Tourism may foster the environmental awareness of both tourists and locals. Currently, about 80 per cent of all visitors to the Seychelles are from European countries, where conservation issues have a high social value. Tourists could raise environmental awareness through their euphoria for the Seychelles' environment and through their interest in ecologically sound economic designs. Several hotels reported, for instance, that German tourists had separated their garbage, even though there is virtually no recycling of wastes in the Seychelles as yet. However, their behavior might have contributed to a first project to separate paper, plastics and biodegradable garbage that has now been initiated in Mahé (Seychelles Nation 05.03.2003). Tourists may also influence conservation priorities. For example, the protection of marine turtles has received much attention in recent years (cf. Shah 1997), which may partly be a result of the attractiveness of these animals to visitors. Traditionally, turtles have been highly esteemed by the

Seychellois for their meat (FLS 1985). A visit to the Seychelles may also foster the tourist's interest in the environment. Tourists may see tropical environments as an attraction in itself, including spectacular landscapes, colorful fish species, or tropical plants and foods, such as orchids, sugar cane, coffee, tea and tropical fruits. Festivals such as SUBIOS, the annual underwater festival, offer opportunities to explore marine ecosystems. Renowned experts take part in the event and contribute with presentations to a better understanding of tropical ecosystems and their functions (Rowat 2000; Seychelles Nation 05.11.1999; Seychelles Nation 12.10.2001). There are also many kilometers of nature walks through all kinds of ecosystems, with detailed descriptions of the flora and fauna available from the Ministry of Tourism. The Botanical Garden already receives some 40 000 visitors annually, and a new Biodiversity Centre will be opened in Barbarons Bay in Mahé, both as an information and research centre (MTCA 2001a; RoS 2001). Even other, more unusual measures might raise interest in the environment. For example, it is possible to dive in a submarine in the Ste. Anne National Park to observe marine life. In summary, tourism may foster environmental interest and awareness, and could thus be an important incentive to preserve the environment, both for its amenity and economic values.

From a legal point of view, 'the state recognizes the right of every person to live in and enjoy a clean, healthy and ecologically balanced environment' (Constitution of the Seychelles, § 38; quoted in MET 2001, p. 15). The institutional framework for environmental conservation was established with the implementation of the Department of the Environment (DoE) in 1989. As early as in 1990, the DoE presented the first environmental management plan for the Seychelles (RoS 1990). The plan was followed by the Environment Management Plan of Seychelles (EMPS) 2000–2010, which provides guidelines for all activities related to the environment (RoS 2001). As a tool for planning and coordination, the plan defines political goals and suggests ways to realize these. The EMPS has three priorities, including the (i) implementation of environmental legislation, (ii) awareness building among the local population and (iii) the promotion of sustainable economic activities. These are to be achieved in cooperation with private enterprises and with the support of international and non-governmental organizations (NGOs) (RoS 1990; RoS 2001).

One example for the involvement of NGOs is Cousin Island, home to several endemic and endangered birds, which was bought in 1968 by BirdLife International (United Kingdom). Cousin Island has been described as 'a unique island ecosystem that offers a richness of biodiversity that needs protection under all circumstances and at all cost' (Shah 2002, p. 188). In 1998, management was passed on to BirdLife Seychelles, a locally registered NGO (now Nature Seychelles). BirdLife Seychelles turned to a policy of opening the island for paying tourists. The 11 000 tourists visiting the island in 1999 paid over US$200,000 in entrance fees, a sum large enough to finance management and even to generate surpluses (Henri 2001, Nature Seychelles, personal communication). Even other attempts to collect revenues through entrance fees have been successful. The Vallée de Mai, for example, generates enough revenue to also finance a research station in Aldabra. Conservation is nevertheless still largely dependent on external funding. For example, a recent survey (1999/2000) on the potential of several islands for 'ecosystem restoration' was funded by the Global Environment Facility and administered by the World Bank (Seychelles Nation 19.12.2002).

Overall, the Seychelles have systematically and actively explored the possibilities of international funding. The EMPS 1990–2000, for example, was presented to donors in 1990 and raised pledges of US$40 million (Dogley 2001). However, the country also devotes a substantial part of its national budget to environmental conservation.

The major strategy to preserve ecosystems in the Seychelles has been the creation of protected areas. The National Parks and Nature Conservancy Act from 1971 (amended in 1973 and 1982) distinguishes National Parks, Strict Natural Reserves, Special Reserves and Areas of Outstanding Natural Beauty. Since 1966, when the first National Park was implemented (Vallée de Mai), new protected areas have been established on a regular basis. For example, the first Marine National Park, Ste. Anne, was inaugurated in 1973 (Nevill 2001), and Aride and Cousin Island – now Special Reserves – were established in 1973 and 1975, respectively. Morne Seychellois, the largest National Park in the Seychelles followed in 1979. Aldabra became a World Heritage Site in 1982 (Därr 1996), and the Fond Ferdinand National Park in Praslin is expected to be opened in 2003. In total, about 50 per cent of the land area of the Seychelles (230 km^2) are now contained in protected areas (RoS 2001).

Even though the overall integration of environmental concerns into planning is remarkable, critics point to a number of deficits. For example, it has been criticized that conservation efforts have been slowed down because of the involvement of a great number of different actors, whose coordination and cooperation has been insufficient (MET 2001). Several marine protected areas are legally implemented, but have remained unmanaged due to the lack of financial means and qualified, motivated staff (cf. Shah 1995; Shah 1997; see also Lindén and Lundin 1997). Poaching is a problem in some areas such as Aride Special Reserve (Shah 2002). With respect to the tourism industry, a French consultant (Blangy 2001) points out that few hotels have taken steps to cut down resource use (particularly fresh water) and become more environmentally friendly with respect to sewage treatment, waste disposal and the use of renewable energy sources. Energy use is particularly high in upscale hotels. For example, the 240-bed five-star Lémuria Resort in Praslin uses more energy than the rest of the island with its 6 500 inhabitants and its more than 1 500 beds in hotels and guesthouses (Gössling et al. 2002). The expectations of luxury-oriented up-scale tourists also make it necessary to import a vast array of goods and products. As imports are based on the use of fossil fuels – vegetables, for instance, are imported by air – this has also enlarged the ecological hinterland of the islands and contradicts efforts to become sustainable. With respect to area use, 110 hectares of land were converted to build the Lémuria Resort alone (including an 18-hole golf course). Area requirements in this hotel are more than 4 580 m^2 per bed, compared to, for example, 60–200 m^2 per bed in guesthouses. For irrigation of the golf course, 2 million liters of water are used every day. This needs to be seen in the light of water availability because fresh water has become such a scarce resource in Praslin that guesthouses have access only during one hour per day in the dry season (this is 3–4 months of the year). Tourism is responsible for 10 per cent of all water use in Mahé, 30 per cent in Praslin and 25 per cent in La Digue (MTCA 2001a). The government is thus poised to solve fresh water problems by building energy-intensive desalination plants on all three main islands (MTCA 2001a), which will increase emissions of greenhouse gases. Overall, development towards a three to five star destination is likely to increase the relative and absolute use of water and other resources.

Other consequences of tourism include the generation of solid or fluid wastes, and increasing levels of traffic and noise, as well as the consumption of marine resources for food and souvenirs. The latter include shark jaws and teeth, corals and ornamental shells. As the collection or hunting of some species is now prohibited by national legislation, they are imported from the Philippines, Madagascar and Kenya (Därr 1996; F. Dogley 2001, Ministry of Environment, personal communication), creating 'souvenir hinterlands' (Gössling et al. 2002). Until recently, parts or even whole tortoise shells were also sold to travelers. However, the selling of species protected by the Convention on International Trade with Endangered Species (CITES) had a negative effect on the green image of the islands. All trade in tortoise shell was therefore banned in 1998 (Seychelles Nation 21.10.1998) and legislation foresees a general ban on the trade with marine species by 2010 (MET 2001). The illegal collection of plants and seeds is another tourist activity difficult to control. For example, there is evidence that the endemic and protected Coco de Mer, the world's largest nut, is collected and illegally sold to tourists (Seychelles Nation 24.05.2002; Wilson 1994). Visitor pressure on certain areas is currently addressed by temporarily closing down damaged areas for the public. Nevertheless, plans for continued development might collide with environmental conservation in the future. For example, it might prove difficult for the Marine Parks Authority to control the behavior of the tourists in the 82 new villas located in the Ste. Anne Marine National Park (cf. Quod 1999; Seychelles Nation 11.06.2001).

The Seychelles are also vulnerable to environmental change beyond their influence. For example, the 1997/98 El Niño Southern Oscillation (ENSO) had detrimental consequences for marine ecosystems. In March and April 1998, seawater temperatures increased on average by 1.5°C above values measured during the same period in 1997. Following the event, coral mortality ranged from 50–90 per cent over extensive areas of shallow reefs in the Seychelles. In some areas around Mahé, mortality was even close to 100 per cent (Lindén and Sporrong 1999). Climate change is also likely to lead to substantial sea-level rise in the future (IPCC 2001). More generally, the environment of the Seychelles has already been fundamentally altered in colonial times, when trees were cut down in substantial numbers to build ships and houses. Only very little of the Seychelles' ecosystem has not been transformed by human activities.

TOURISM, ENVIRONMENT AND POWER

Undoubtedly, the government of the Seychelles is seriously committed to environmental conservation, and harmful economic activities and developments have often been abandoned in favor of preserving areas in their original state. The argument becomes more complex, though, if the value of these decisions for the economic and political elite of the country is considered. As one recent quote of the president reveals, a pristine environment is understood as the precondition for attracting wealthy tourists:

> We have many success stories. We are dedicating more of our limited land area to national parks and reserves. More species are getting our special attention as we do the inventory of our flora and fauna. We are investing millions in projects to limit the impact of human activities on the environment. We have amassed plenty of experience in finding the right balance between economic development and environmental protection. We are proud to have given our people a high standard of living, and at the same time feel greatly satisfied that we have kept our hillsides green, the water clear, the sand sparkling white, and the surroundings pleasant to life. After having jealously guarded our environment we are now opening up more of our natural treasures to eco-tourists from all over the world (René 2001, cited in MET 2001, p. i).

As stated earlier, the benefits from tourism are more equally distributed in the Seychelles than in other countries. All small accommodation establishments are in private ownership, mostly by Seychellois, and a large share of the local population is involved in tourism. However, governmental revenue may be primarily generated from the large hotels and there is also evidence that many key enterprises in the periphery of the tourism industry are controlled and managed by the islands' economic and political elites. For example, the President is also the chairman of the Seychelles Marketing Board (SMB), a state-owned company controlling virtually all imports and exports. His wife Sarah René is the vice-chairman of the Seychelles Broadcasting Corporation, comprising the only national TV station and the two national radio stations. Three children of the President's former wife hold important positions: Francis Savy is the CEO of the Seychelles Tourism Marketing Authority (STMA), David Savy is the CEO of Air Seychelles and Glenny Savy is CEO of the Island Development Company (IDC) (Därr 2002, Honorary Consul of the Republic of Seychelles, personal communication). A friend of the president, Gregoire Payet, is the owner of several exclusive hotels (La Digue Lodge, Félicité Island Hotel, L'Union Estate Hotel). Rolph Payet is both Director General of the Islands Conservation Society and Director General of the Policy, Planning and Services Division under the Ministry of the Environment. These examples illustrate the narrow political and economic relationships existing in the Seychelles, and the concentration of power in a few hands. As Benedict (1967) noted, kinship ties and face-to-face personalism in small societies render objective decision making difficult. Quite the contrary, decisions may be made in a way supportive of individual interests in what could be termed economic and political elitist networks. Consequently, environmental conservation aimed at attracting particularly wealthy tourists can be seen as a mechanism to stabilize the position of the local elites and to increase their power, influence and wealth. It has been pointed out that the nationalization of natural resources, for example through the establishment of protected areas, has since historical times been a means to allocate authoritative power and entitlements to the government. Conservation could thus be seen as a means to increase state control (Krings 2003).

National elites in the Seychelles are also at the core of larger networks, involving external actors such as the World Wide Fund for Nature, World Bank, Global Environment Facility and BirdLife International. Their interaction could be explained in terms of a 'network of interest' because there are mutual interests beyond the goal of safeguarding ecosystems. As pointed out earlier, the government may be rewarded for environmental conservation with increasing numbers of 'high-value conservation tourists', with a growing number of protected areas also representing the ethical foundation and justification for growing tourist numbers. Furthermore, it becomes easier to apply for international funding on the basis of the mediated image of conservation efforts and environmental goodwill. The implementation of parks and protected areas is thus an important factor –

environmental progress is both visible and measurable – which makes it possible to draw in financial resources (cf. Bates and Rudel 2000). In fact, given the high standard of living in the Seychelles, environmental conservation may be the only remaining option to receive financial support from international donors. In summary, the successful cooperation with international donors and organizations contributes to a positive image of the Seychelles, which is important for a government that was not democratically legitimized from the beginning and still exerts control over media and imports. For the donors themselves, it is important to present positive results to their clients or supporters. Cooperation for the purpose of preserving species or ecosystems is efficient and almost free of problems in the islands, and the Seychelles are thus popular for such projects.

Another group of actors worth mentioning are tourists, tour operators and accommodation establishments. For the tourists, the pristine environment is a primary travel motive (Hörstmeier 2003) and they thus share the government's interest in preserving the environment. Given the upscale character of this destination, conservation creates 'exclusive environments' accessible for only a few, wealthy tourists. Environmental conservation inherently presents a justification for their stay in such exclusive environments, which needs to be seen in light of the fact that travel to the Seychelles and staying in luxury hotels is characterized by over-proportionally high energy and resource use (Gössling et al. 2002). Obviously, tour operators also have an interest in unsullied environments. However, their interest is primarily economic and they may agree to national policies as long as they are not in conflict with economic considerations. For example, the government's Gold Card campaign (launched in 1998) was opposed by the tourism industry and finally not implemented. The program had the aim to collect a levy of US$100 from each tourist for the management of protected areas. The tourism industry rejected the plans because it was feared that increasing prices would lead to decreasing tourist numbers. As stated earlier, only few hotels have taken serious steps towards ecologically sound management (Blangy 2001). The ecological image of hotels and guesthouses promoted by the government is thus often based on portrayals of Bird and Frégate Island. Both islands have monitoring and awareness programs, they have taken steps to become autonomous in their resource requirements, particularly fresh water, and to cut down energy requirements. As a winner of the British Airways for Tomorrow Award and the Green Planet Award by the Kuoni Group, Bird Island in particular has been used to create the image of 'green' accommodation establishments, which in reality applies to a minor percentage of the existing hotels and guesthouses. However, it is planned to introduce an eco-label and environmental performance indicators (Jones 2002), which may lead to the involvement of a larger number of hotels in environmentally sound management. In this context, it is interesting to note that an opinion survey on the importance of engagement in activities for the protection of the environment by accommodation establishments found that the large hotels had a tendency to be in favor of these, while smaller establishments gave it a low priority (Hörstmeier 2003). As mentioned above, large hotels are usually foreign-owned, while guesthouses are in the hands of Seychellois, indicating a divide with respect to pro-environmental activities.

Finally, the question arises of how the Seychellois perceive environmental conservation programs. In fact, there seem to be conflicting attitudes. Basically, the government seems to see the local population as a rather passive factor in the development process which needs to be educated and managed. For example, the former Director General of the Ministry of Tourism and Civil Aviation claimed that 'people need to be educated not to throw garbage away because this disturbs the tourists' (A. Volcere, personal communication 2001). A similar view is expressed by Shah (2002, p. 194):

> Many communities and people still view the islands with a frontier mentality, i.e., environmental resources are boundless and can be used by anyone for any purpose. Because of this, compliance to environmental laws in the Seychelles has been historically poor. In addition, enforcement has been weak, complicated by a small island mentality and society 'where everybody knows or is related to everyone else'.

As in many tropical countries such as the Dominican Republic, Sri Lanka, the French Antilles or Madagascar (cf. Bates and Rudel 2000; Burac 1996; Ghimire 1994), protected areas are implemented as tourist attractions. Even in the Seychelles, this means that locals are excluded from the use, though generally not access, of those areas deemed valuable for conservation. Compensation is indirect, often stemming from tourism-related activities leading to increasing income levels. Access to land may nevertheless be lost through strictly protected areas and resort development, which fosters local resentment. Contributions to Small Islands Voice read:

> Access to some of our beaches is restricted by buildings and resorts. While resorts provide employment and dollars for the economy, sometimes too they deprive the communities of their relaxation activities (Savy 2003).

> . . . [A]s an example, let us look at St. Anne. Here we have a large island, close to the main island of Mahé that could have been developed to provide homes for a new community of about one hundred families of Seychellois. This would have released some of the pressure on trying to find suitable building land on Mahé. . . . Such a housing project on St. Anne would also have created a local economy for goods and services. In the midst of this community, small tourism establishments could have been accommodated providing jobs for the inhabitants. Instead of all

these possible benefits, the bulk of this large island is tied up for the next 99 years because St. Anne now has a hotel owned by a large foreign company (Albert 2003).

Even though environmental organizations argue that conservation is supported by locals, this may primarily be for economic reasons. Shah (2002, pp. 192, 196) reports on Cousin:

In general, these groups strongly supported tourism operations on Cousin as conservation values were apparently well understood and benefits flowing to local business and communities were perceived.

On the other hand, any perturbation in the tourism industry in the Seychelles will probably have an impact on Cousin. A decline in tourism in the Seychelles may lead to a concomitant decline on Cousin. A down-turn in tourism revenues may mean that biodiversity management is affected. It behoves the authorities, therefore, to preserve a high-quality tourism product so that the current level of biodiversity conservation on Cousin and other similar sites in the Seychelles are maintained, or even enhanced.

This clearly highlights the interdependence of tourism and conservation and the interconnection of government and international organizations or NGOs.

In summary, most actors involved in tourism development in the Seychelles directly or indirectly profit from tourism development, and campaigns of the government to increase the share of protected areas, to draw in donor money for conservation and to attract high-value tourists might have been successful because they have been built on one mainstream conservation discourse. This discourse involves and suits all groups of actors and has ultimately become a 'truth system' (Adger et al. 2001, p. 685) through its homogeneity in message – with the notable exception of the perception of those locals cited above. It is not known, though, which percentage of the Seychellois is of a similar opinion.

A MODEL FOR OTHER DESTINATIONS?

Most tourism is somehow based on environmental assets, and the interest in nature and the natural increases in modern societies. Upmarket tourism in tropical islands in particular is based on unsullied, pristine environments (cf. Hörstmeier 2003, WTO 2001). In the Seychelles, conservation of the environment might have been a process in its own right in the 1970s, but it is today an important part of the islands' successful marketing strategy. For destinations wishing to attract wealthy tourists, the minimization of negative environmental impacts and the preservation of the environment thus seems of primary importance. However, while it is generally not known if international markets cater for an increasing number of high-value tourists, the Seychelles also have a number of other advantages over tropical destinations with similar environmental features. Crime is virtually absent, there is no begging, and tourists are neither confronted with extremely poor people nor with hassling in shops or on the beaches. Tropical diseases like malaria do not exist, the climate is stable and seasonality low, there are no tropical storms, and the great number of small bays and beaches makes it possible to distribute the tourists in a multitude of locations. The economy is diversified, also building on a strong fisheries industry, and the culture seems resistant to the tourist's cultural influences (Hörstmeier 2003; cf. Wilson 1994). The tourist infrastructure is mixed, consisting of large hotels and guesthouses in local ownership, which leads to the more even distribution of the monetary benefits derived from tourism. Finally, the natural beauty of the island, the great number of endemic and/or unique birds and plants, and the variety of possible activities (big game fishing, snorkeling, scuba diving, etc.) make the islands attractive even from this point of view. With respect to environmental conservation, the constellation of actors involved in planning and development and their mutual interest in preservation have made it possible to achieve development and conservation as simultaneous goals. It should be noted, though, that the costs of safeguarding ecosystems are substantial, both economically (external funding) and ecologically (contribution to global warming) (cf. Gössling et al. 2002).

It should also be noted that the Seychelles have wisely used the wealth generated from tourism to strengthen their position in international markets and to create a society that can compete in a globalized world economy. There are many aspects to this. For example, the preservation of the environment has been an early priority, based on integrated development plans. This will in future help to attract particularly wealthy tourists, who are less affected by factors beyond the Seychelles' control, such as rising oil prices. Tourist revenues have also contributed to creating a socially stable society with health care and social security systems. Furthermore, financial resources are invested in schools and education, and many young locals are sent abroad to study in industrialized countries. Finally, most guesthouses have invested part of their income in technical infrastructure such as internet connections. This opens up new opportunities for marketing. In consequence, it will be difficult for other destinations to copy the Seychelles' strategy.

Overall, the government-led, conservation-based development approach of the Seychelles has been very successful. Up to now, there are still substantial social costs involved, but a number of programs are underway to improve integration of local needs and wants.

REFERENCES

Adger, N.W., T.A. Benjaminsen, K. Brown and H. Svarstad (2001), 'Advancing a political ecology of global environmental discourses', *Development and Change*, **32**, 681–715.
Albert, T. (2003), *Let's Rethink Our Tourism Strategy*, available at: http://www.sivglobal.org/?read=20.
Alphonse, T.T. (2003), *Providing Public Access to the Beach*, available at: http://www.sivglobal.org/?read=16.
Bates, D. and T.K. Rudel (2000), 'The political ecology of conserving tropical rain forests: a cross-national analysis', *Society & Natural Resources*, **13**, 619–34.
Benedict, B. (1967), *Problems of Smaller Territories*, London: Athlone.
Blangy, S. (2001), *Les Seychelles: une Destination Écotouristique? Bilan et Recommendations*, presented during the Conference on Sustainable Development and Management of Ecotourism in Small Island Developing States (SIDS) and other Small Islands, Mahé, Seychelles, 8–10 December 2001.
Burac, M. (1996), 'Tourism and environment in Guadeloupe and Martinique' in L. Briguglio, R. Butler, D. Harrison and W. Leal Filho (eds), *Sustainable Tourism in Islands and Small States Case Studies*, New York: Pinter, pp. 63–74.
Därr, W. (1996), *Richtig Reisen. Seychellen*, Cologne: Du Mont.
De Comarmond, A. (2002), *Small Islands Voice at the Local Level*, available at: www.unesco.org/csi/smis/siv/civil.htm.
Dogley, F. (2001), *Environment Management Plan for the Seychelles (EMPS) 2002– 2010 – Sustainable Tourism in Seychelles – are We on the Right Track?*, presented during the Conference on Sustainable Development and Management of Ecotourism in Small Island Developing States (SIDS) and other Small Islands. Mahé, Seychelles, 8–10 December 2001.
Economist Intelligence Unit (EIU) (1992), *International Tourism Reports*, No. 4, London.
Fisheries Legislation in Seychelles (FLS) (1985), *SWIOP/WP/21 – Fisheries Legislation in Seychelles*, available at: www.fao.org/docrep/field/254701.htm.
Gabbay, R. and R. Ghosh (1997), *Tourism in the Seychelles*, Discussion Paper 97.08, Perth: The University of Western Australia, Department of Economics, Centre for Migration and Development Studies.
Ghimire, K.B. (1994), 'Parks and people: livelihood issues in national parks management in Thailand and Madagascar', *Development and Change*, **25**, 195– 229.
Gössling, S., C. Borgström-Hansson, O. Hörstmeier and S. Saggel (2002), 'Ecological footprint analysis as a tool to assess tourism sustainability', *Ecological Economics*, **43**, 199–211.
Hörstmeier, O. (2003), *Wettbewerbsbedingungen kleiner Inselstaaten im internationalen Tourismus – untersucht am Beispiel der Seychellen*, Paderborn: Paderborn University, Department of Economic Geography and Tourism Research (unpublished).
Intergovernmental Panel on Climate Change (IPCC) (2001), '*Climate Change 2001: the Scientific Basis*', edited by J.T. Houghton, Y. Ding, D.J. Griggs, M. Noguer, P.J. van der Linden, X. Dai, K. Maskell and C.A. Johnson, Contribution of Working Group I to the Third Assessment Report of the Intergovernmental Panel on Climate Change, Cambridge: Cambridge University Press.

Jones, T. (2002), 'National development policies and strategies in the Seychelles', *Vision 21: Tourism Development in the Seychelles 2001–2010*, presented during the Conference on Sustainable Development and Management of Ecotourism in Small Island Developing States (SIDS) and other Small Islands, Mahé, Seychelles, 8–10 December 2001.

Jumeau, R. (2002), 'Minister launches Small Islands Voice 2004 project for Seychelles' *Small Islands Voice*, available at: www.unesco.org/csi/smis/siv/ioarticle.1htm.

Krings, T. (2003), 'Politische Ökologie', in D. Böhn (ed.), *Handbuch des Geographieunterrichts*, Vol 8, 'Entwicklungsräume', Cologne: Aulis Verlag, forthcoming.

Lindén, O. and C.G. Lundin (eds) (1997), 'The Journey from Arusha to Seychelles. Successes and failures in integrated coastal zone management in Eastern Africa and island states', Proceedings of *the Second Policy Conference on Integrated Coastal Zone Management in Eastern Africa and Island States*, Seychelles 23–25 October.

Lindén, O. and N. Sporrong (1999), *Coral Reef Degradation in the Indian Ocean*, status reports and project presentations, SAREC Marine Science Program, Department of Zoology, Stockholm University.

Management and Information Systems Division (MISD) (2001a), *Seychelles in Figures*, Victoria, Seychelles.

Management and Information Systems Division (MISD) (2001b), *Visitor and Hotel Statistics*, Victoria, Seychelles.

Ministry of Environment and Transport (MET) (2001), *Environment Management Plan of Seychelles 2000–2010*, Victoria, Seychelles.

Ministry of Tourism and Civil Aviation (MTCA) (2001a), *Vision 21, Tourism Development in the Seychelles 2001–2010*, Victoria, Seychelles.

Ministry of Tourism and Civil Aviation (MTCA) (2001b), *List of Establishments and Future Projects*, Victoria, Seychelles.

Nevill, J. (2001), *Integrating Biodiversity in the Tourism Sector, A case study on the Republic of Seychelles for the UNDP/UNDP biodiversity planning support programme*, March 2001, available at: http://www.unep.org.

Quod, J.P. (1999), 'Consequences of the 1998 coral bleaching event for the islands of the Western Indian Ocean', in O. Lindén and N. Sporrong (eds), *Coral Reef Degradation in the Indian Ocean,* status reports and project presentations 1999, SAREC Marine Science Program, Department of Zoology, Stockholm University, Sweden, pp. 53–9.

Republic of Seychelles (RoS) (1990), *Environmental Management Plan of Seychelles (EMPS) 1990–2000, Achieving Sustainable Development,* Victoria, Mahé, Seychelles.

Republic of Seychelles (RoS) (2001), *Environment Management Plan of Seychelles (EMPS) 2000–2010, Managing for Sustainability,* Victoria, Mahé, Seychelles.

Rowat, D. (2000), 'SUBIOS, The Indian Ocean underwater festival', in Ministry Of Tourism And Civil Aviation (MTCA) (eds), *Tourism in Progress,* Tourism week 2000, Victoria, Mahé, Seychelles, pp. 14–6.

Savy, N. (2003), *Sharing Beach Resources*, available at: http://www.sivglobal.org/?read=19.

Seychelles Nation (21.10.1998), *Protection of Hawksbill Turtles*, Mahé, Seychelles, available at: http://www.nation.sc.

Seychelles Nation (05.11.1999), 'SUBIOS launch tonight', *The Oceans – Our Heritage, Our Future*, Mahé, Seychelles, available at: http://www.nation.sc.

Seychelles Nation (11.06.2001), *Environment Week. Exhibition showcases 300-year History of St. Anne*, Mahé, Seychelles., available at: http://www.nation.sc.

Seychelles Nation (12.10.2001), *Official Opening Thursday of SUBIOS 2001*, Mahé, Seychelles, available at: http://www.nation.sc.

Seychelles Nation (26.12.2001), *Luxurious Catamaran to Ply Seychelles' Waters*, Mahé, Seychelles, available at: http://www.nation.sc.

Seychelles Nation (21.02.2002), *Jan–Nov 2001 Hotel Statistics*, Mahé, Seychelles, available at: http://www.nation.sc.

Seychelles Nation (25.04.2002), *Wildlife Clubs of Seychelles to Set Up Centre in Victoria*, Mahé, Seychelles, available at: http://www.nation.sc.

Seychelles Nation (24.05.2002), *Minister Lanvironnman i Demann Plis Proteksyon pour Koko-d-Mer*, Mahé, Seychelles, available at: http://www.nation.sc.

Seychelles Nation (19.12.2002), *Biological Surveys of Seychelles Islands*, published scientific work by a Seychelles NGO receives international recognition, Mahé, Seychelles, available at: http://www.nation.sc.

Seychelles Nation (05.03.2003), *Sélection des Ordures Ménagères Star/Swac Lancent une Opération Pilote à Roche Caïman*, Mahé, Seychelles, available at: http://www.nation.sc.

Shah, N.J. (1995), 'Managing coastal areas in the Seychelles', *Nature & Resources*, **31** (4), 16–33.

Shah, N.J. (1997), 'Integrated coastal zone management in the Seychelles', in O. Lindén and C. Lundin (eds), *The Journey from Arusha to Seychelles. Successes and Failures in Integrated Coastal Zone Management in Eastern Africa and Island States*, Proceedings of the Second Policy Conference on Integrated Coastal Zone Management in Eastern Africa and Island States, Seychelles 23–25 October 1996, pp. 135–49.

Shah, N.J. (2001), *The Cousin Island Reserve Visitation Programme*, presented during the Conference on Sustainable Development and Management of Ecotourism in Small Island Developing States (SIDS) and other Small Islands, Mahé, Seychelles, 8–10 December 2001.

Shah, N.J. (2002), 'Bikinis and biodiversity: tourism and conservation on Cousin island, Seychelles', in F. di Castri and V. Balaji (eds), *Tourism, Biodiversity and Information*, Leiden, The Netherlands: Backhuys Publishers, pp. 185–96.

Small Islands Voice (SIV) (2002), available at: http://www.unesco.org/csi/smis/siv/sivindex.htm.

United Nations Development Programme (UNDP) (2002), *Human Development Reports*, available at: http://hdr.undp.org/reports/global/2002/en/indicator/indicator.cfm?File=cty_f_SYC.html.

Vorlaufer, K. (1991), 'Die Seychellen, Tourismus als Entwicklungsoption für einen insularen Kleinstaat', *Afrika Spectrum*, **26**, 221–55.

Wilson, D. (1994), 'Unique by a thousand miles. Seychelles tourism revisited', *Annals of Tourism Research*, **21**, 20–45.

Wolf, H. D. (1983), *Tourismus und Verkehr auf den Seychellen*, Doctoral thesis, Frankfurt am Main: Frankfurter Wirtschafts- und Sozialgeographische Schriften.

World Tourism Organization (WTO) (2001), 'Tourism market trends', *World Overview & Tourism Topics*, Madrid: World Tourism Organization.

9. Human Resources Development for Tourism in a Peripheral Island: Hainan, China

Abby Liu and Geoffrey Wall

INTRODUCTION

Tourism is wishfully used in many developing countries to help to overcome hardships through the contributions that it can make to economic growth and diversification. As a development strategy, tourism is manipulated and institutionalized predominately by bureaucratic initiatives, since the local people in such situations are generally unfamiliar with the workings of a services economy. However, a supply-oriented development approach to tourism, focusing primarily on the provision of up-market hotels, often does not seem to be in the best interests of the hosts. In the tourism planning process, emphasis is largely placed on the creation of a tourism industry through meeting the perceived needs of the tourists. The issue of human resources needed to deliver the tourism services appropriately and effectively has often been given a lower priority and, in some cases, has been totally neglected (Echtner 1995). This has resulted in serious staffing problems in the tourism industry and, more importantly, has precluded the participation of the host populations in the economic activities associated with the tourism development. Consequently, there are significant debates concerning the use of tourism as a means to achieve a wider economic prosperity because of a frequent neglect of local considerations and, thus, a minimal share of benefits to the original residents of destination places.

Using the People's Republic of China's Hainan Province as an example, this chapter will examine the nature of local involvement in tourism, the status of tourism employment and the availability of human capital in a peripheral island location. A broad perspective will be taken on tourism's human resources needs to encompass entrepreneurship and the informal sector as well as training in hospitality services. To illustrate the common oversight of human resources issues in tourism, the policy, cultural context and content of education and training will be considered as revealed in the priorities of national government as well as the involvement of ethnic minority peoples.

It will be argued that much tourism planning on national and provincial scales has concentrated primarily on the provision of infrastructure to the relative neglect of human resources development. Furthermore, where human resources development has been considered, it has often been viewed from a narrow perspective with a focus upon the needs of large companies in the hospitality industry and the provision of a product that meets international standards. This emphasis may not address the needs of the domestic market and, furthermore, may work to the disadvantage of residents of domestic tourist destinations who may lack the background to benefit from such education and training opportunities. Thus, local involvement in tourism is frustrated and job opportunities in tourism bypass those with the greatest need to benefit from tourism employment.

CHINA'S CHANGING INVOLVEMENT IN TOURISM

China is a late entrant in the world tourism and travel market, although blessed with abundant tourism resources including a long history, a civilization with notable achievements, varied natural endowments and diverse ethnic cultures. Tourism was formerly taboo in the communist government's national policies because of the preceding domestic turmoil and national security concerns. Neither international nor domestic tourism were encouraged in China until the late 1970s. This retarded China's development of tourism as an economic sector. Tourism was initially resumed on a small scale through the leadership's pursuit of diplomatic exchanges and cultural propaganda but growth has become substantial since the introduction of the 'open door' policy in 1978. The promotion of tourism has become increasingly prominent in the central government's development policies and initiatives, with the main efforts directed to the promotion of international tourism to earning foreign currencies.

Chinese tourism development has tended to focus on the construction of physical infrastructure targeting a foreign clientele. Over the expansionary period of the 1980s and 1990s, most investments by governments were allocated to physical improvements in proximity to cultural and historic sites. Foreign capital was pursued zealously to increase the number of establishments aspiring to an international standard. Domestic tourism was not of much concern. The domestic leisure needs of China's large population were not seriously considered until recently when the Chinese, particularly in the eastern cities, started to enjoy more discretionary income with a rapidly improving national economy and greater freedom to travel with gradually relaxing controls. Levels of development contrast markedly between the coast and interior regions and most foreign visitors concentrate in the metropolitan areas seeking heritage and cultural attractions. While the central government has lacked a thorough, comprehensive, approach to the development of tourism, it also limited the ability of lower-tier bodies to give due consideration to the needs of the domestic market and, most significantly, has been little concerned about the dearth, in both numbers and abilities, of adequate personnel to engage in tourism.

HAINAN

Hainan (Figure 9.1) is a tropical island in the South China Sea with a substantial tourism industry. While foreign tourists typically flock into the mainland coastal regions and major metropolitan areas (Qiao 1995), Hainan has become a centre of attraction for millions of affluent Chinese. Almost all visitors come from mainland China, most on package tours. Although it is a special economic zone (SEZ), the island is quite poor even in Chinese terms and unemployment rates are high, especially among the ethnic minority peoples whose cultures are one of the tourist attractions. Tourism, along with tropical agriculture, constitute substantial growth opportunities, but the potential of local people to take advantage of these opportunities has yet to be fully realized and many jobs are taken by immigrants from the mainland. Using examples drawn from Hainan, this chapter will examine the status of tourism employment in a peripheral island location. It will also demonstrate the problem of weak local involvement that has emerged as a result of inadequate attention being accorded to the human resources aspects of tourism planning practices.

TOURISM PLANNING IN HAINAN

Hainan is an island province of China which is geographically peripheral, economically disadvantaged and historically and politically inferior (a place of exile in the imperial era) in comparison to mainland regions. Located in the South China Sea, Hainan is blessed with oceanic endowments and tropical exoticism that have contributed to its status as one of the twelve national resort destinations in China. The prospects for tourism development in Hainan were first raised officially in 1983 and were centrally directed by the Chinese State Council, aiming to use tourism as a tool to achieve higher levels of development. In 1986, Hainan was designated as one of the seven major tourist areas in China.

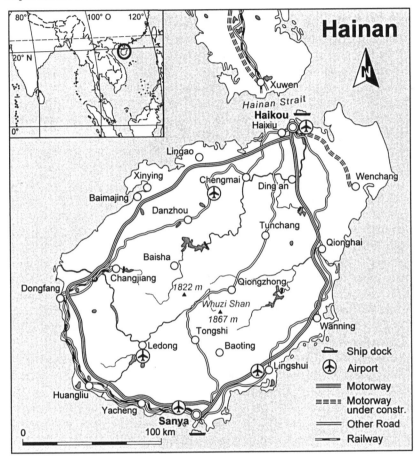

Figure 9.1   Hainan, China

In 1989, Hainan was upgraded to provincial status from being an offshore part of Guangdong Province, having been designated as an SEZ in the previous year. It was intended that considerable industrial development would occur, but this strategy has met with only mixed success. Population growth, fueled by immigration from the mainland, coupled with slow economic growth has resulted in a shortage of employment opportunities. Nevertheless, a substantial tourism industry has been established based on both natural and cultural resources, albeit with low occupancy rates in hotels and questionable profitability in commercial accommodation. Entry formalities have also been eased in that landing visas were made available at the entry points to spur the growth of visitor arrivals, and the requirement was eliminated entirely in 2001 for visitors from some countries.

Tourism development in the 1980's and early 1990's was undertaken without appropriate guidance. It was not until October 1993 that 'an outline of the Planning of Hainan Provincial Tourist Development' was promulgated by the Tourism Administration Bureau of Hainan Province (HPTA) as a measure for approving and implementing development programs to guide tourism investment and management, and to serve as a guide for decision making. Although with relatively low industrialization and urbanization, the Hainan tourist system was depicted under the provincial tourism development guidelines as of international standard. It was expected to be an up-market destination, catering to tourists with high expenditure. Indeed, the same strategy has been suggested in the unpublished plans prepared by the tourism planners of the World Tourism Organization tabled in 2002.

Although tourism has expanded rapidly, as has already been indicated, it caters primarily to visitors from mainland China (over 85 per cent throughout the 1990s). However, the enhancement of the quality and variety of tourism offerings that occurred in the 1990s and continues today has been achieved through an extremely complex ownership structure. For example, the number of hotels increased from 31 in 1987 to over 250 in the late 1990s. Luxurious establishments (4 five-star hotels, 9 four-star hotels and 31 three-star hotels in 2000) are operated by private proprietors, sino-foreign joint ventures, and foreign and overseas Chinese enterprises.

On a macro-scale, Hainan's role as an international tourist destination in China is still modest relative to its mainland counterparts. Hainan accounts for less 1 per cent of the total overseas tourists received by the designated hotels in China. Similarly, while total foreign currency earnings from tourism have amounted to over US$12 billion in China, Hainan received only about US$0.1 billion. Nevertheless, tourism in Hainan has risen to be an important economic sector but it has done this to date by serving a domestic clientele. Tourism is featured in the provincial statistical yearbooks. The emergence of Hainan Airlines as the fourth largest and most profitable carrier in China is another indicator of tourism's economic significance to Hainan island (Dolven 2002). Other indications of the growth of tourism in Hainan and its contribution to regional development include tourism's contribution of approximately 15 per cent of Hainan's Gross Domestic Product in recent years. Although agriculture is still the dominant sector, tourism has diversified Hainan's economic base through a growth in services. Future prospects for tourism in Hainan are expected to be congruent with current initiatives to establish Hainan as an 'eco-province' and to grow along with other industries which are deemed to be environmentally friendly.

STATUS OF TOURISM EMPLOYMENT AND HUMAN CAPITAL

Hainan has to create substantial employment opportunities to meet large job demands from its massive workforce of 3.4 million, or nearly half of its total population (7.2 million). However, while the labor participation rate is relatively high, employment available other than agriculture is rather limited: only 30 per cent of total employment, this is 1.1 million, jobs are non-agriculture (Liu and Wall 2000). Tourism, if properly planned, might be an ideal means for alleviating employment shortages through the generation of jobs in the services sector. Hainan's tourism industry, in fact, demonstrates remarkable employment absorption, due to the dominance of state and collective corporate ownerships that generally have large numbers of employees. Cheap labor costs (annual average labor wage was RMB7,408 or US$896.8 in 2000; HPBS 2003) are another major factor encouraging a high employment capacity of tourism. According to the data available in 1992, the ratio of employees to rooms in Hainan was equivalent to 1.9 jobs which is much higher than ratios produced in Asia (1.14), the Caribbean (1.15) and worldwide (1.02) (Baroncini 1982; Liu 1998; UNEP 1996). Furthermore, a census undertaken by Hainan Provincial Tourism Administration (HPTA) showed that direct employment in tourism doubled from 20 000 jobs in 1992 to 40 000 jobs in 1997. Adding the multiplier effects of tourism employment, HPTA claimed that tourism contributed to the creation of 160 000 jobs in 1997.

Structurally, the high share of tourism in total employment resulted in a significant change in the overall labor force composition – an 8.8 per cent growth in the tertiary sector and a 12.7 per cent decrease in the primary sector over the last decade. An ambitious estimate by HPTA (1993) indicated that jobs created in tourism were expected to continue to grow between 16.7 per cent and 17.9 per cent per annum between 1995 and 2010 (Table 9.1) and, by 2010, direct employment in tourism was expected to reach 80 000 to 100 000 jobs.

In terms of the quality of tourism personnel, tourism appears to capture the relatively well-educated when taking into account the local education standards – the students constituted only 20 to 22 per cent of the total population in the last decade and approximately three-quarters (about 74 per cent) of these were in elementary schools. According to HPTA, in the tourism sector, workers with high school diplomas (60 per cent) were in the majority and the rest were secondary school (23 per cent) and college graduates (17 per cent). Significantly, while much employment in tourism is often considered to be suitable primarily to socially marginalized people, women, the young and minorities, data from 114 state-owned hotels indicate that in

Hainan, access to tourism jobs is very competitive, particularly for women and minorities. In 1998, 57.2 per cent of the 11 654 jobs were taken by females and as few as 5 per cent were taken by minority people. Also, children, as young as 6 or 7 years old, are involved in both the formal and informal sectors to help supplement their family income. In the cultural parks, little girls of Li or Miao ethnic groups, wearing their traditional costumes for photograph-taking by the tourists, earn US$0.12–0.24 per photograph. Similarly, at the popular scenic spots, children gather in small flocks trying to tout tourists with coral, shell-made souvenirs and other small craft items.

Table 9.1   Estimation of required tourism workforce by sectors 1995–2010

	Hotel	Tour operators	Other tourism agencies	Total
1995	25,000 – 29,200	3,000 – 3,500	2,000 – 2,300	**30,000 – 35,000**
2000	41,700 – 45,900	5,000 – 5,500	3,300 – 3,600	**50,000 – 55,000**
2005	54,200 – 62,600	6,500 – 7,500	4,300 – 4,900	**65,000 – 75,000**
2010	66,700 – 83,400	8,000 – 10,000	5,300 – 6,600	**80,000 – 100,000**
Change % **1995/2010**	266.8 – 85.6	266.7 – 285.7	265.0 – 87.0	**266.7 – 285.7**

Note: Unit: 10 000 people

Source: HPTA (1993)

Unfortunately, tourism has not been properly manipulated to alleviate prevailing unemployment problems in the island. Despite the fact that tourism offers job possibilities, new jobs have not been created sufficiently quickly and unemployment is a serious concern in both rural and urban areas. The slow recognition of the need to develop locally the human resources required for tourism has also reduced tourism's employment effects. Balancing the supply of and demand for tourism, human capital has become a complex issue in Hainan, as generalized by HPTA (1993) in the following observations:

- The shortage of qualified tourism workers, particularly for the higher level positions that require skilled workers;
- The tourism industry's limited capacity to absorb college graduates from tourism programs;
- The lack of systematic institutional systems for the cultivation of tourism manpower at all levels; and
- The absence of a match between the supply and demand in the middle and higher level managerial positions of the tourism workforce.

In spite of a high unemployment rate and a significant growth in tourism employment, difficulties have been experienced in balancing supply and demand in the workforce because of a mismatch between industry needs and available skills and experience. In some instances, people residing in the rural areas are not even aware of the employment opportunities available in tourism. The recruitment dilemma can be illustrated by quoting the frustrated statement of a General Manager from the hotel sector: 'When we opened our four-star hotel in 1994, we had serious problems in meeting our employment demands; the newly recruited were predominately from agricultural work. Virtually, all of our staff only knew rice plantations'.

Similarly, Hainan's Li, Miao and Hui minority groups, who are mainly located in the vicinity of the southern resort areas, do not have a substantial involvement in tourism, especially in the formal sector. Li and Miao cultures are promoted as part of Hainan's attractions by the provincial tourism agency and local collective bodies, and some job opportunities are available to the Li and Miao minorities who work as cultural performers, vendors and services personnel in the cultural parks. Folk villages provide a variety of positions to Li and Miao minorities but their viability has been precarious, particularly in the centre of the island (Xie and Wall 2001). The Hui group, however, can only intercept tourists on their travel circuits to sell souvenirs as the culture of this Moslem group is not manipulated as part of a tourism part product. Lack of vision and inadequate institutional capacities obstruct the utilization of tourism as an employment generation strategy.

TOURISM EDUCATION AND TRAINING

The availability of tourism education and training has increased substantially over the last decade in Hainan. The field of 'tourism study' has emerged as a result of increased recognition of the income potential that tourism brings as discerned by the public sector, of more secure employment prospects as perceived by prospective students, and of increasing demands and opportunities as responded to by education institutions. Hainan's tourism operators also exhibit a considerable positive inclination for hiring workers endowed with a tourism background. This suggests that tourism education not only helps students enhance their employment potential, but also is a base on which to build a career with good prospects for advancement for the tourism graduates.

Hainan University was the first institute of its kind that innovatively introduced tourism education into the university sector. Tourism-related courses were introduced in 1992 and a tourism program was initiated in 1996 and, in 1999, almost 300 students, perhaps excessive, were enrolled in two, three and four-year programs. In 1999, four out of five universities in Hainan offered tourism courses/programs that largely emphasized hospitality management. At the secondary level, six out of 45 vocational schools had a tourism program. More recently, with a goal to meet the current and projected tourism workforce requirements, the Provincial Government of Hainan has taken some important steps to integrate the cultivation of human resources into tourism development. The establishment of a hospitality vocational high school in Haikou, the provincial capital, along with plans to collaborate with other tourism centers on the Chinese mainland, is expected to improve the tourism labor supply.

Curriculum design stresses industrial relevance, with some incorporation of local social and cultural concerns. Industrial placement is an integral part of much tourism training. The mandate of such hospitality programs is to prepare students with necessary managerial skills and knowledge, to help them to get acquainted with actual work situations and to develop their real-world, problem solving capabilities, with an emphasis on the needs of the social market economy. While most universities suffer funding retrenchment from the public sector, the provision of the tourism programs has contributed significantly to university finances and, at the same time, has helped them to achieve the targeted number of students. The provincial tourism authority, the HPTA, however, has reservations about the expansion, primarily because of the flimsy faculty base for high quality tourism and hospitality education. Nevertheless, the provision of tourism education at the tertiary level has been beneficial in:

- Raising government and the industry's willingness to invest in tourism education/training;
- Providing prospective participants and existing tourism employees with means to further their tourism education;
- Increasing the number of students at the higher education level; and
- Contributing to sustainable tourism development in Hainan with academia's involvement in tourism planning projects.

The tourism programs that have emerged in Hainan focus upon technical and operational competence and, as such, they are very much in line with the majority of institutes involved in tourism training. An emphasis on hospitality is commonly found in higher education institutes for tourism in Hainan. This is perhaps because of demands from both employers and students for an emphasis on job training. Based on results derived from a questionnaire survey of 136 respondents, students choose to enroll in tourism programs because of personal interests, because they regard jobs in tourism as challenging, and also because they believe that the employment prospects are good. At the same time, they acknowledge that the pay and benefits as well as job status are likely to be less than those in some other fields. Employment security appears to be students' main reason for enrolling in a tourism program. Students choose security over status and high remuneration, believing that job opportunities are more likely to be available in tourism than in other economic sectors in Hainan (Liu and Wall 2000). Students generally expect the curriculum content to concentrate on industrial applications with vocational courses and practical training in order for them to be well trained and ready for a post within the industry. Perhaps this explains the tourism institutes' narrow approach to tourism studies and students' main concerns regarding the acquisition of operational skills at the expense of a broader education. The accumulating supply of high caliber personnel is then likely to be cornered by the more renowned and prestigious employers.

Considering the relatively low education levels of many employees in Hainan, the tourism industry's in-house training in Hainan generally emphasizes skill competence with prominent requirements for solid services techniques. Similarly, the drive for HPTA's training efforts is invigorated by 'Chinese Hawaii' aspirations leading to a desire for high, international-standard, quality but ignoring alternatives and the needs of less sophisticated operations. As well, when considering the high unemployment rate, apart from the jobs created by tourism in the formal sector, self-employed operations and the enhancement of entrepreneurship are also vital to the generation of employment opportunities. However, little attention has been directed to these needs. The problem is further compounded by the complex corporate governance system; even non-starred lodging houses are typically operated under collectivism. It is unfortunate that tourism's capacity to generate jobs in the informal sector is underestimated and, in fact, such jobs are often despised by the powerful as being detrimental to the development of a sophisticated tourism industry in Hainan. Legal powers are used to crack down on the expansion of the informal sector. Training, thus, has no role in breeding entrepreneurs, nor does it match the service expectations of the dominant domestic market segment.

A survey undertaken by the first author of 61 vendors in major scenic spots in Hainan demonstrated that they rely heavily on a job in the informal tourism sector for their livelihood, because they generally have underprivileged living and socially disadvantaged lifestyles. Since there are limited sources of employment and few alternatives, they exhibited a high rate of stability in retaining their jobs. The respondents were generally depressed about their situation with feelings of inferiority because of poor remuneration, an unpredictable work environment and the very long work hours involved. The vendors did not see their employment as being well paid, stable, secure, or socially desirable. Thus, there is an urgent need to tackle the problem of lack of expertise and innovation that makes the vendors' operations precarious and of marginal profitability.

There should be a better appreciation of the mix of tourism employment and this should be used to inform program directions. Thus, it is appropriate to consider the perceptions of students; the expectations of the industry; as well as the relatively disadvantaged who strive for basic sustenance by grasping at peripheral opportunities adjacent to deluxe tourism enclaves when investing in tourism training and education endeavors.

POLICY IMPLICATIONS

Tourism studies and training programs are in great demand in Hainan due to the fact that tourism offers better employment prospects than any other economic sector. Unemployment rates are extremely high in Hainan and, although tourism positions are not highly remunerated, tourism employment is still an attractive option where paid employment of any kind is in short supply. The economic importance of tourism is well acknowledged by the HPTA, whose efforts have been apparent in raising tourism awareness and the overall local capacity to better respond to the commercial opportunity provided by tourism. However, the oversupply of tourism graduates with a tertiary educational background is an indication of lack of systematic planning for the tourism workforce. While nearly all the universities in Hainan offer tourism or hospitality programs, the trained personnel output from vocational schools is comparatively insignificant and certainly insufficient to fully satisfy the industry's workforce demands. Because of the difficulties in employing the tertiary-level graduates, tourism employers are blamed by the public sector for their failure to absorb the proliferation of students emerging with tourism or hospitality qualifications.

Key policy decisions made in an authoritarian manner have immense influences but exert disturbing effects on the development of education and training infrastructure. Fundamentals of workforce training deployed by the HPTA, in adherence to the stipulations of the Chinese National Tourism Administration, are imbalanced with excessive concerns to inculcate political doctrines, to reinforce workers' obedience of socialist tenets so that they will behave correctly as disciplined tourism professionals. Some industry informants suggested that such a scheme does not best suit their specific interests or requirements. Recent reinforcement of licensing measures and the mandatory training hours involved for senior management personnel have aggravated the irritations: the manager of human resources of a four-star hotel indicated that 'good sum was paid over to HPTA for practitioner admission' but 'the quality of training programs and training staff was not very elaborate'.

Attitudes to tourism in Hainan are profoundly affected by an aspiration that Hainan will become the 'Chinese Hawaii', although very few have actually been to Hawaii. Even the taxi drivers are capable of expressing this image by alerting tourists' to their impression that 'Hainan is like the Hawaii island, very beautiful'. Tourism students are trained to describe the geographic and climatic similarities to Hawaii. Tour guides can even go further to demonstrate Hainan's superiorities over Hawaii: Hainan has longer coastlines of natural white sandy beaches and the transparency of the sea water reaches 7 to 9 meters with a pleasant all-year-round water temperature at 25° Celsius. The attributes that make Hawaii an internationally famous destination are vague notions that cannot be fully appreciated by the locals with their limited exposure to, and even alienation from, places other than Hainan. Therein lies the paradox of using a Hawaii image to promote Hainan as a comparable product. Adherence to socialist tenets but adoption of an international tourism paradigm both tend to subdue individualism and personal initiative. Concurrently, tourism personnel are required to be familiar with an 'ultra-sophisticated western custom' (a mandatory change of mentality as expected by the foreign visitors; Oudiette 1990, p. 128), but remain in adherence to socialist dogma. Somewhat similarly, even when confronted by high unemployment, the public sector simply does not appreciate the range of employment effects that tourism brings. Among most such informants, antagonism was voiced against the petty traders, fearing that they would jeopardize the tourism enclaves that reflect the modern facet of the Hainan SEZ and many other tropical island destinations.

Although the need for a competent workforce has been recognized as being fundamental to Hainan's tourism industry, the full implications of this are not widely understood. Too often, aspirations to replicate a Hawaiian image have led to an approach to tourism education and training that does not fit well with cultural norms of hierarchy, subservience and collectivism and neither of these perspectives may be in the best interests of local residents who wish to participate in tourism. Thus, the types, levels and expected outputs of tourism programs remain a matter of considerable concern that need to be dealt with to suit the specific situation in Hainan.

CONCLUSIONS

In a relatively brief period of little more than two decades, China's policies towards tourism have changed drastically. With its SEZ status and peripheral location, Hainan has greater flexibility in policy spheres compared with other regions on the Chinese mainland. Nevertheless, designated as one of the national tourist destinations, the Hainan situation not only mirrors general trends in tourism policy directions elsewhere in China, but also exhibits interesting tourism complexity characterized by its historical backwardness, island peripherality and market-oriented policy.

Tourism initiatives in Hainan provide examples that illustrate efforts to improve a peripheral region's marginal economic status. Most importantly, tourism is a promising sector for economic development that provides employment alternatives that are often preferable to those in traditional occupations, such as agriculture, because of higher rates of remuneration, access to foreign currency, relatively limited physical demands and better working conditions (Liu and Wall 2000). However, with planning efforts now directed towards meeting the tastes of an international clientele, the resultant priorities and allocation of resources have left very little room for the local Chinese to become involved in the expanding tourism commerce. In addition, the ongoing prominence that is placed on socialist doctrines and communist ideological tenets has led to a situation in which tourism policies and planning, as well as the contents of tourism training and education programs, are highly circumscribed in that individualism and local participation are not fostered. Hence, even though education and training provision relating to tourism have been portrayed as being required in the tourism plans, the fragmented characteristics of tourism that necessitate the inputs of a wide variety of employment types across many economic sectors have not been differentiated by the policy makers. Such an omission has hampered China's ability to transform its economic base from a former agricultural and, more recently, a manufacturing dominated economy to a services-oriented one. Few mechanisms have been deployed to support tourism employment opportunities for the many people who seek work in tourism for a livelihood.

As evidenced from the Hainan case study, among major issues identified are the shortage of qualified candidates, particularly for higher-level positions requiring skills and experience, the lack of a well-organized institutional system for the education and training of tourism personnel at all levels, and the inability of the tourism industry to absorb the college graduates that are currently being produced. At the same time, the marginal incomes of vendors from their employment in tourism's informal economy also signify that additional training is essential. This is required to facilitate entries for those who depend on tourism for their livelihood and, through the provision of training, to improve the quality of their operations for higher profits.

To summarize, Chinese tourism authorities' approaches to tourism workforce development have suffered from inappropriate organization. An ideological emphasis has often overridden what is required by the industry, as tourism education and training have been used for propaganda purposes.

Perhaps this explains the organization of tourism training and education which neglects the industry's diverse requirements but reflects, to some extent, students' concerns about acquiring operational skills at the expense of a broader education. Tourism studies are generally quite narrowly defined. Also, while many students are attracted to tourism studies because of the relatively high probability of acquiring a position and job security, many also perceive it as a glamorous industry providing opportunities for adventure – notions that may be misplaced (Liu and Wall 2000). At the same time, tourism employers have reluctantly embraced their responsibility to deal with the transformation of labor from unskilled agricultural work to semi-skilled and skilled tourism employment. They have done this mostly through on-the-job training, since governmental (including the tourism administrative body) and educational authorities have not given sufficient priority to employment issues (Liu and Wall 2001).

REFERENCES

Baroncini, G.L. (1982), 'Tourism manpower development in Asia: problems and managerial responsibilities', *Journal of Travel Research*, **21** (2), 19–21.

Dolven, B. (2002), 'The best little airline in China', *Far East Economic Review*, 17 January, 32–6.

Echtner, C.M. (1995), 'Entrepreneurial training in developing countries', *Annals of Tourism Research*, **22** (1), 119–34.

Hainan Provincial Bureau of Statistics (HPBS) (2003), *Annual Statistics of 2000*, available at: http://www.statistic.hainan.gov.cn/yearbook/2001nj/ind ex.htm.

Liu, A. and G. Wall (2000), 'Tourism training and employment: student perspectives from Hainan, China', *Proceedings of the Asia Pacific Tourism Association Sixth Annual Conference*, Phuket, Thailand, pp. 243–48.

Liu, A. and G. Wall (2001), 'Hainan tourism employers expectations and responses', *Proceedings of the Asia Pacific Tourism Association the Seventh Annual Conference*, Manila, The Philippines, pp. 240–43.

Liu, Z. (1998), 'Tourism and economic development: a comparative analysis of tourism in developed and developing countries', in C.A. Tisdell and K.C. Roy (eds), *Tourism and Development: Economic, Social, Political and Economic Issues*, New York: Nova Science Publishers, pp. 21–37.

Oudiette, V. (1990), 'International tourism in China', *Annals of Tourism Research*, **17** (1), 123–32.

Qiao, Y. (1995), Domestic tourism in China: policies and development, in A. Lew and L. Yu (eds), *Tourism in China: Geographic, Political, and Economic Perspectives*, Boulder, Colorado: Westview Press, pp. 121–40.

United Nations Environment Program (UNEP) (1996), 'Sustainable tourism development in small island developing states', report of the Secretary-General, Addendum to the 4th Commission on Sustainable Development, 18 April–3 May 1996, *Progress in the Implementation of the Programme of Action for the Sustainable Development of Small Island Developing States*, available at: http://www.unep.ch/islands/d96-203a.htm.

Xie, P. and G. Wall (2001), 'Cultural tourism experiences in Hainan, China: the changing distribution of folk villages', *Tourism*, **49** (4), 319–26.

10. Community-oriented Marine Tourism in the Philippines: Role in Economic Development and Conservation

Alan T. White and Rina Rosales

INTRODUCTION

The Philippines is endowed with a wealth of coastal natural resources that are the delight of many foreign and national visitors. White sand beaches, diverse coral reefs, wetlands with endangered birds and an extensive tropical shoreline provide the basis for the potentially largest marine tourism industry in the world. Marine tourism has expanded rapidly in the 1980s and 90s in the Philippines and much of the increase is attributed to these tropical coastal assets that are very appealing to vacationers from temperate places. Increasing numbers of middle and upper income Philippine people are also engaging in scuba diving, snorkeling and beach visits for recreation and relaxation, and are adding to tourism revenues and demand. Visitor numbers declined somewhat in 2000 and 2001 due to perceived peace and order problems in the southern part of the country but 2002 again had increased arrivals approaching 2 million visitors annually (Figure 10.1). Although coastal and marine tourism is growing in the Philippines, it has not reached its potential and is threatened with stagnation if new opportunities and directions are not tested.

Tourism overall in the Philippines accounts for 8.7 per cent of the Gross Domestic Product and generates approximately 5 million jobs within its 80 million population. The Tourism Secretary sits on the National Cabinet and tourism is seen as a means to assist with national objectives of poverty alleviation, employment generation and infrastructure strengthening (DOT and DENR 2002). A 'National Ecotourism Strategy' has recently been endorsed at the national level which further focuses tourism development along sustainable and environmentally beneficial lines (DOT and DENR 2002).

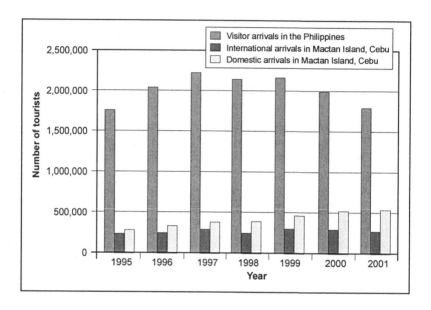

Source: Department of Tourism (2002)

Figure 10.1   Trends in tourist arrivals from 1995 to 2001 for the Philippines and Cebu[1]

The 18 000-kilometer Philippine coastline is endowed with a wealth of natural tropical resources that provide numerous benefits to local residents and to the economy in general. Coral reefs alone cover about 27 000 square kilometers of area and provide about 15 per cent of annual fish catch to the country. Coral reefs are also an increasingly valuable asset for the tourism industry. Recent valuation studies indicate that reefs in the whole country are contributing a conservative US$1.35 billion to the national economy (White and Trinidad 1998). Locally, one square kilometer of healthy coral reef with some tourism potential produces net revenues ranging from US$29,400 to US$113,000 (White and Trinidad 1998; White et al. 2000a). These revenue potentials are realistic since a large proportion of visitors to the Philippines spend time on a beach or swim or dive in a coral reef environment. Others come for more specialized activities such as bird watching in wetlands, recreational fishing or even to assist with coral reef research or conservation. Thus, the Philippine coastal environment through tourism generates significant revenues from marine recreation and the associated hotels, food and purchases. In selected tourism areas where studies have been conducted, the economic benefits from tourism far surpass those derived from traditional fishing and other livelihoods (White et al. 2000a). Yet, the question arises about who receives the benefits and how sustainable are these benefits?

The socio-cultural setting in the Philippines is quite favorable to tourism for several reasons. English is commonly spoken around the country, the level of education is high by developing country standards and people are naturally friendly and outgoing. Also, Filipinos travel and work in many countries, and are thus quite international and adaptable in their experiences and can relate well to outsiders to the Philippines. One result is that coastal tourism is thriving in the Philippines in various locations (Figure 10.2).

The political setting, although not directly contrary to the development and success of tourism, tends to work against a well-managed and smoothly functioning tourism industry. Politicians often vie for tourism development in their areas thus creating many small, poorly planned tourism development areas with little or no central planning to prevent the usual environmental and social pitfalls of tourism enclaves (Huttche et al. 2002). Obstacles to large-scale tourism development in terms of hotels and beach resorts mostly pertain to the faulty infrastructure. Roads are not well maintained, there are few sewer facilities, planning is weak and corruption of government or private company officials sometimes detracts from a smooth development. The cases of pollution, building on the beach, sex industry operation and others are well documented in the country, and will probably not go away soon. Nevertheless the tourism industry is growing and the potential is large.

The peace and order situation has taken its toll recently because of all the international attention on several kidnapping cases in the southern Philippines and because there are travel warnings in effect for parts of the country issued by the United States and several European countries. Media reports about events in one location tend to be generalized and scare travelers just by mention of the Philippines. Such reports have deterred visitors who are not familiar with the country. The reality, though, in a country that stretches more than 1 200 miles from north to south, is that a problem in Basilan Island, in the far south, does not affect the rest of the country.

In spite of the problems, the country is dotted with various forms of tourism enclaves mostly occupied by small scale and locally owned tourism establishments that assist to varying degrees with rural economic development (Figure 10.2). Many contribute significantly by providing jobs and stimulating development and conservation in areas that would have few other viable economic and environmentally aware alternatives.

This chapter highlights the potential for a much larger contribution of tourism in the Philippine economy and to coastal conservation, if certain obstacles are overcome. It stresses the growing role of marine tourism in coastal conservation in the country, and how conservation is also extremely important for the economy and the well-being of coastal communities. Four

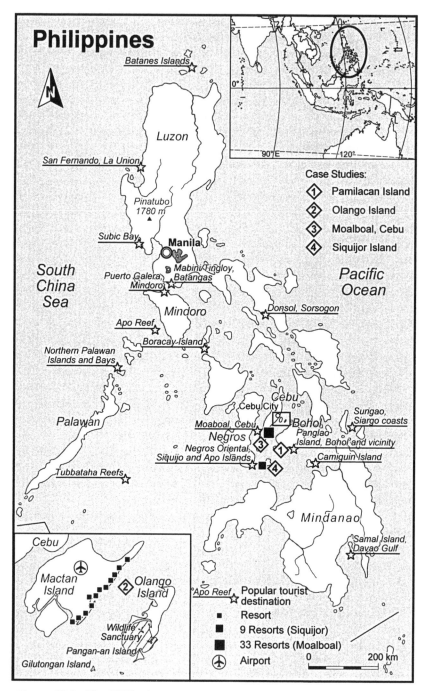

Figure 10.2   The Philippines

'ecotourism' case studies provide insights into local stakeholder dynamics, politics and economic recovery options for local resource management. They also highlight the difficulty of setting up such programs through institutions that do not exist or are weak. The classic tourism model of enclosed resorts is present in the Philippines but does not dominate and thus the potential for involvement of local people through community-models is starting to thrive. How to scale up models to support more rural development is explored. Finally, the critical need to conserve coastal resources that attract tourists is highlighted and analyzed with respect to localized sustainable financing mechanisms and the implementation of integrated coastal resource management.

MARINE TOURISM IN THE PHILIPPINES

The Philippines has a diverse coastal environment with a variety of ecosystems, and an extremely rich biodiversity and productivity. Sandy beaches, coral reefs, rocky headlands, mangroves, wetlands, estuaries, lagoons and seagrasses are typical (White 2001). Each ecosystem plays a critical role in maintaining the health of the coastal zone as well as in maintaining the health of people that depend on them for sustenance. This interdependence makes the coastal zone one of the most sensitive and dynamic geographic areas. Damage to a coral reef, for example, will allow greater wave action on shore, causing beach loss. Alteration of one ecosystem in the coastal zone usually causes damage to another, either directly or indirectly.

Maintenance of coastal ecosystems in the Philippines is important in sustaining the tourism industry because a large proportion of visitors, national and international, relax and recreate in coastal and marine areas. Some of the direct conflicts of tourism and other development with maintenance of coastal ecosystems in the country include (Huttche et al. 2002):

Affecting beaches:
- Sand and coral mining in coastal areas (for example, from dredging of boat channels and mining of sand for construction or beach replenishment);
- Building structures which inhibit long shore sediment transport such as jetties, airport runways into the sea, port facilities and others;
- Construction of groins and seawalls that adversely affect adjacent coastal areas which is the common practice of some beach resorts to protect their own beaches while disturbing adjacent beaches.

Affecting coral reefs:

- Increased sedimentation from dredging, filling or coastal construction, all of which can be the result of resort or harbor construction;
- Pollutants and excess nutrients from waste disposal and sewage discharge that is commonly associated with small scale resorts;
- Over-fishing and blast fishing to provide fish for local tourist restaurants; and
- Coral breakage from guests exploring the reef, anchor damage or collection of organisms for sale or souvenirs or for recreation such as by spear fishing.

Affecting wetlands (mangroves and estuaries):

- Removal of mangrove habitat for resort construction;
- Disposal of sewage and solid waste into wetlands; and
- Construction of obstructions to the natural water movement within or between wetland water bodies.

All of the above impacts related to tourism development are quite common in a localized context in the Philippines. Mactan Island, near Cebu City, known for its marine-based tourism industry, has all of the above problems in various forms (Huttche et al. 2002; Wong 1999) (Figure 10.2). Nevertheless, there, as in other areas in the country, it is recognized by the tourism industry that the coastal resources are a prime attraction for visitors. But, these occurrences continue primarily because of relatively low awareness among developers, planners and local government bodies. Also, although all such activities are illegal and coastal resources and habitats are protected or limited in use by various laws, these pertinent laws are often not enforced. In addition, the awareness of legal mandates by local government about how to implement the laws is limited (DENR et al. 2001).

To address these issues of coastal resource degradation, the Philippine government, with assistance from various donors, is pursuing coastal resource management with the objective of reversing downward trends in the condition and productivity of its coastal ecosystems (DENR et al. 2001). Legislation in 1991 and 1998 supports devolution of authority to local government units in natural resource management so that the common planning unit is the municipal and city governments. These local government units are beginning to seriously consider the plight of their coastal resources and are developing coastal resource management plans (Courtney et al. 2002). These plans require budgeting and support from the municipal or city councils but often lack economic justification to help the decision-makers appreciate what they are supporting. Such economic information is needed to justify investments in management and protection at a level of government that is directly concerned with its natural resource base.

One strategy being used to counteract the continuing degradation and destruction of coastal resources from development and from everyday actions of many people is to inform people about the economic value of the resources being lost. In the Philippines, the economy, until very recently, was largely based on the exploitation of natural resources such as forests, minerals, land for agriculture and fisheries. Now that the forests are nearly depleted, mining is declining and agriculture is a steady but not a growing contributor to the economy and food production, the coastal environment is increasingly being recognized as having a very important role in national economic development (DENR et al. 2001). The coastal and marine resources include the extensive fisheries it harbors and the various coastal habitats that support most of the tourism industry (White et al. 2000a). But these resources are fast being depleted and it requires sizeable investments to stabilize fisheries and coastal habitats. To make a good case for these required investments, economic valuation studies and cost-benefit analyses have been conducted to show policy makers, industry and government officials and other stakeholders the value of protecting and managing these resources (Arin and Kramer 2002; Cesar 1996; White and Trinidad 1998).

A study of the benefits and costs of coral reef and wetland management for Olango Island, Cebu (near Mactan Island and Cebu City) revealed substantial annual net economic revenue (direct) per square kilometer of coral reef, wetlands with mangroves, and estuary and associated habitat. When aggregated for the entire island area which includes about 4 000 hectares of coral reef and about 1 000 hectares of wetland, all with some tourism potential, the annual net revenues were impressive. The annual (1999) net revenue from fisheries, tourism, seaweed farming on the coral reef and from fisheries, wood and tourism uses of the wetland amounted to US$2,423,000. It was also shown that, with an investment of US$100,000 per year for management and conservation, the annual revenue from the natural resource base through improved fisheries and tourism would be US$3,871,000 after five years (White et al. 2000b). The analysis showed that the local and national government together with the tourism industry could justify larger allocations of their annual budgets in managing coastal resources.

Olango Island is a microcosm of the Philippines where the coastal natural resource base holds much potential to improve the incomes and quality of life of people if only it is protected and managed for sustainable use (Figure 10.2). Favorable benefit : cost returns of about 15 : 1 from a small marine sanctuary within the larger Olango Island and about 30 : 1 for the whole of Olango Island have attracted the attention of local officials and tourism operators (White et al. 2000b). These benefit–cost ratios assume increasing investment in management of coastal resources. Unfortunately such management is not immediately forthcoming and requires expertise, dedicated people and programs. These costs can all be justified in economic terms as for Olango Island where the annual incremental benefits from coral reef and wetland-generated fisheries and tourism of US$1.4 million are much more than the associated costs.

The economic benefits from coastal resource management in Olango almost all accrue to the residents and businesses based in nearby Mactan Island. Although some benefits from reef conservation and tourism accrue to the community on Olango Island as explored later, the weak link is that tourism operators on Mactan Island are not usually willing to pay a tax to conserve the coral reefs and wetlands and to promote more marine sanctuaries for scuba divers who are the core of their tourism businesses. There are exceptions but this is changing slowly.

The efforts to manage coastal resources and tourism development in the Philippines are also being aided by the substantial legal and institutional system that is in place. Although not all laws are enforced, as mentioned, the laws tend to be comprehensive and provide much guidance to protection of coastal resources and in the development of tourism facilities. To the credit of the Departments of Tourism and Environment and some local government units, all new large beach resorts are required to follow environmental impact assessment requirements. Increasingly there are model resorts in the country that are truly sensitive to their local coastal environments and use 'green technology'. More of a problem are the numerous small-scale resort complexes that develop without much area-wide or local planning and minimal investments in water treatment facilities or other considerations to limit impacts (Huttche et al. 2002; White and Dobias 1991; White et al. 1991).

The negative impact of coastal tourism development in the Philippines reached the general public through media coverage of one recent near-environmental disaster. In July 1997, the headline: 'Boracay Water Unsafe for Bathing' shocked tourists, developers and operators of one of Philippines' most famous resort destinations, once voted the 'world's most beautiful beach' (Trousdale 1997). Boracay waters were allegedly unsafe for swimming and other recreational activities due to high levels of coliform bacteria, indicating the presence of other microbes more harmful to human health. These organisms can cause cholera, typhoid fever and skin disorders.

The contamination of Boracay was the result of untreated or insufficiently treated wastewater from the countless small-scale septic tanks seeping into the water table or being flushed directly into the sea via beaches or streams. With its skyrocketing popularity as the major beach destination in the Philippines, the discharge of wastewater had soared to unmanageable levels during peak seasons. The Department of Environment and Natural Resources (DENR) was the agency that insisted on the public notice of contamination to the displeasure of the Department of Tourism.

Boracay's tourism industry and the provincial government had to learn the hard way: sensational newspaper headlines almost ruined the local tourism industry. The Philippine Tourism Authority is now working on Boracay's water system, aided by Japan's Overseas Economic Co-operation Fund. The project includes setting up a system to transport fresh water from the mainland to Boracay, as well as the installation of a sewage treatment plant.

If proper planning and effective environmental management practices were in place in Boracay, the risk of losing important coastal tourism business would have been avoided. The lesson seems to be sinking in since sincere efforts are now underway to improve water quality in Boracay. But, there are still many other locations in the Philippines that have not yet heeded this call of preventive action. The bottom line is lost or improved revenues that might stimulate the private sector to act sooner.

In addition to environmental considerations of tourism development in the Philippines are the social, equity and employment issues for local communities. The many small-scale resorts and various tourism development areas (Figure 10.2) provide rich study sites for these complex issues. And even with the substantial local ownership and control of tourism revenues in the country, one has to look at the many poor communities completely left out of the tourism-generated wealth in rural areas. Olango Island, described above, is an example of poverty in the midst of a healthy tourism industry. The island population of about 23 000 is extremely poor, comprised of traditional fisher families and those without any livelihood (Santos et al. 1997; Sotto et al. 2001). Scuba divers may visit a coral reef in front of a poor Olango Island fishing community where no benefit accrues to the community. Only the boat operator and the hotel on Mactan Island, where the diver is staying, benefit. This scenario, typical of most of the developing world, is beginning to change in the Philippines and is the substance of the case studies below. Through the cases, we explore options for addressing the social, equity and employment issues inherent in Philippine tourism development, and determine who are some key actors.

CASE STUDIES IN REALITY

The thrust of the type of tourism development in the following four case studies is that the environment is actively conserved and that tourism revenues accrue directly to the communities of fishers, farmers and residents of the place where the tourism attraction or activity is located. The cases illustrate how the tourism enterprises were organized to create tangible incentives for resource dependent people to conserve their resources. They also highlight the willingness-to-pay of visitors to an area for conservation through community and local government-based management. The important non-monetary benefits such as food from fishing, and the social and cultural values of the community are noted as the direct by-products of such tourism enterprises.

Whale Watching in Pamilacan Island, Bohol: A Community-based Tour

Pamilacan Island is approximately 700 kilometers southwest of Manila just off the southern shore of Bohol Island, accessible by boat either from Cebu or Bohol Island. Its land area of 135 hectares includes 22 hectares of sandy white beach, and the island is fringed by coral reefs covering 180 hectares (Savina and White 1986). There are about 250 households on the island.

The waters around Pamilacan are one of the most critical habitats of marine mammals in the country. Locals have traditionally been hunting whales, dolphins, manta rays and whale sharks for decades and selling them at lucrative prices. Unsustainable catching has allegedly caused two whale species (Minke whale and Bryde's whale) to become locally extinct, and has caused a severe decline in the incidence of manta rays and whale sharks (Green et al. 2002).

To counteract the alarming rate of hunting, whale watching was introduced as an alternative means of livelihood in the 1990s. Whale and dolphin watching is undertaken best during March to August, with the peak season coinciding with the summer months of April and May. This form of recreation is fast gaining local and international attention, as the waters surrounding the island serve as refuge for these marine animals. Aside from dolphin and whale watching, Pamilacan Island is also a favorite destination of scuba divers originating from Panglao, Bohol. A marine sanctuary established in 1985 was opened for scuba divers in 2002. Large marine life, such as napoleon and bumphead wrasses can be sighted.

A recent study determined the recreational values for dolphin and whale-watching activities as part of a project to encourage improved conservation of island and coral reef ecosystems through marine protected areas (MPAs). This willingness-to-pay study determined values that visitors place on the resources (Rosales 2003). A short history of the area and problem sets the context for the study results.

In the late 1990s, awareness about the alarming rate of extraction of marine mammals from Pamilacan Island led to the formation of the Inter-agency Task Force on Marine Mammal Conservation. Furthermore, the Bureau of Fisheries and Aquatic Resources (BFAR) banned the capture of manta rays and whale sharks in 1998 while whales and dolphins have been protected since the 1970s in the country. However, such efforts were not enough to effectively protect these animals and indeed whale sharks and manta rays have been the subject of controversy because they are claimed to be part of a 'traditional' fishery. Thus, in 2002 the ban on catching manta rays was lifted whereby fishers in the vicinity of southern Bohol were given a six-month reprieve by the BFAR. The lifting of the ban was intended to establish the level of sustainable catch of the marine animals although no definitive outcome has yet resulted.

Meanwhile, in 1997, the World Wildlife Fund (WWF) implemented a Marine Resource Conservation Project called the Pamilacan Island Dolphin and Whale Watching Village Integrated Development Program, which lasted for three years and was co-sponsored by the Department of Tourism (KKP 2000). In 1998 a people's organization, 'Pamilacan Island Dolphin and Whale Watching Organization' was formed with over 100 members (Green et al. 2002). The program also refitted seven whale-hunting boats into whale-watching tour boats. In 2002, three boats were operating.

In the willingness-to-pay sample survey of island visitors conducted by Rosales in 2002, the unique characteristic of the recreational activity was the primary reason why visitors chose Pamilacan. Diversity of underwater wildlife and cleanliness of the environment followed (Rosales 2003). The study showed that Pamilacan visitors were highly satisfied with the hospitality accorded to them by the local residents. The ambience and cleanliness of the environment were likewise rated very highly, followed by the high level of satisfaction with visitors' personal safety.

A 79 per cent majority of the respondents expressed their willingness-to-pay entrance fees for whale and dolphin watching in Pamilacan. Among these, Filipinos made up the larger percentage and were willing to pay as high as US$3.51 per person per visit. Foreigners' bids, on the other hand, averaged US$1.80. This discrepancy between Filipinos and foreigners reflects the relative value that Filipinos place on this unusual nature tourism opportunity. In contrast, most foreigners come to scuba dive on the reefs and not for marine mammal watching. Respondents preferred to make their entrance fee payments as part of their tour payments. The least preferred option was paying through the Municipal Hall because that would be logistically complicated for visitors.

Contrary to survey results in Moalboal, Cebu discussed below, Pamilacan tourists preferred a community-based organization to handle the funds coming from entrance fees. The local government was the least preferred means of managing the funds although usually, the most viable funds manager is the local government because of its legal mandate to collect and manage fees and resource rents for its area of jurisdiction.

The whale watching enterprise on Pamilacan Island is thriving albeit at a lower level than originally envisioned. It is gaining momentum in terms of lowering the desire among traditional fishers to continue targeting these and related animals for capture (Moral 2003). It is also interesting that the tour is more frequented by Filipinos than foreigners thus indicating the potential for nature-based tourism in the country. Also, the direct actors and beneficiaries of this enterprise are the people on the island who charter the boats as part of the island-based organization. Others who also benefit and assist include the resorts on nearby Panglao Island, the municipal and provincial governments concerned and of course the marine life being conserved.

Olango Birds and Seascape Tour: A People-Oriented Ecotourism Venture[2]

The Olango Birds and Seascape Tour (OBST) is an ecotourism business venture in the island of Olango, Cebu Province, discussed above. Residents of Suba, a fishing village in Olango Island, own and operate it. The business successfully integrates the elements of full community benefit and participation, contribution to environmental conservation and education, product differentiation and marketability, economic viability, and promotion of local culture. OBST started in March 1998 and was made possible through the Coastal Resource Management Project (CRMP) supported by the United States Agency for International Development. The goals of the project were to:

1. Develop environment-friendly livelihood alternatives for resident fishers;
2. Model sustainable tourism development in islands as a strategy for improving coastal management by local stakeholders; and
3. Promote local cooperation in the conservation of natural protected areas.

The ecotourism venture is built around the unique environmental attributes and serene beauty of Olango Island's coast, seas, reefs and bird life (Sotto et al. 2001). Bird watching, coastal trekking, canoe paddling, snorkeling, swimming, visiting seaweed farms and island hopping are among the low-impact recreational activities offered. The tour promotes and showcases local conservation of threatened coastal habitats and marine and bird life in particular. Tourists can also snorkel and witness the abundance of fish in a protected coral reef that has been declared by the local government, and is managed by the community, as a marine sanctuary. Community members help monitor the reef, and boat and dive operators pay user fees and observe user guidelines. The high level of participation seems to pay off in terms of better regulation of human activities, generation of tourism revenues, and improved regeneration of marine life. The project showcases the potential, viability, and benefits of full community participation in the ownership and operation of ecotourism ventures. By actively managing the protected area, the community has gained substantial economic benefits through entrance fees and provision of multiple services. The people have also gained a growing sense of pride, technical skills, and confidence in their ability to provide a better future for themselves and their children.

Olango is near Mactan Island, the second largest tourist area in the Philippines (Figure 10.2). Mactan has an international airport, five-star resorts and numerous tourism businesses. Olango's proximity to Mactan and Cebu City adds to the island's potential as a tourism destination. Mainland Olango's flat and elongated dry land measures about 1 000 ha. The intertidal wetland, known as the Olango Island Wildlife Sanctuary (OIWS), extends the island further south by 904 ha. The OIWS is the first area in the Philippines to be declared as a RAMSAR site, recognition of its international importance as a wetland for birds belonging to the East Asia Migratory Flyway. An extensive, submerged reef that connects the island to other islets, surrounds Olango. One of these islets is Gilutongan Island, with a protected reef that serves as a strategic spawning ground for marine organisms, and an increasingly popular destination for diving, snorkeling and swimming.

Of Olango's 23 000 residents, 75 per cent are dependent on fishing and related activities such as harvesting of shells, starfish, sea cucumbers, sea urchins, tropical aquarium fish, live food fish, corals, mangroves and others. Olango's fisheries have declined considerably due to over-fishing and the destruction of coastal habitats by cyanide and dynamite fishing. Declining resources, high population density, and insufficient basic service delivery all contribute to the low income, low education and low occupational mobility of fishing families in Olango (Sotto et al. 2001). Earlier initiatives in coastal tourism development marginalized the community in terms of participation in decision-making and benefit-sharing.

CRMP saw in Olango the challenge as well as the opportunity to assist the community and key public and private stakeholders in the island by introducing sustainable tourism and participatory development. OBST went through five stages of development prior to becoming functional in 2000:

Stage 1. *Assessment.* A rapid survey of Olango's resources determined product options for enterprise development, including ecotourism products that had low environmental impact, marketability and community benefit.

Stage 2. *Participatory ecotour product development.* Meetings and workshops were conducted with community members interested in the project to orient them on the nature of and potential benefits, constraints and problems related to tourism and ecotourism development.

Stage 3. *Development of linkages*. Linkages were established with public institutions and tour companies for marketing, policy, program and promotional support.

Stage 4. *Capability building*. Community capacity was strengthened in tour operations and business development.

Stage 5. *Transfer of business administration to community*. Two years after the project started, the community assumed full control of the administration of tour operations and formalized collective ownership of the business.

Factors that have contributed to the success of the OBST are strategies of implementation that considered the socio-cultural, marketing, environmental and stakeholder participation needs and aspects of the tourism enterprise.

Key socio-cultural strategies consisted of:
(a)   Orientation of the product around the use of local skills, everyday activities, local crafts/arts and music;
(b)   Community ownership of the tour product;
(c)   Participatory processes and mechanisms;
(d)   Implementation of a training strategy of 'learning by doing';
(e)   Delivery of immediate economic returns;
(f)   Spreading benefits through local sourcing of services and goods;
(g)   Support of community organization to influence planning and policy development through a high media profile, generation of multi-institutional support and endorsements by visitors;
(h)   Managing the number, frequency and behavior of visitors; community users of the natural resource; and other development interests within the locality.

Marketing strategies included:
(a)   Tapping the development sector as the primary market to jumpstart and test-run the tour;
(b)   Developing a tour product to capture tourist segments from resorts and hotels in nearby Cebu City;
(c)   Designing the tour product to capture niche markets;
(d)   Making the OBST different from existing tours by providing expert interpretation, interaction with coastal villages, visit to a marine sanctuary and other nature- and culture-based activities;
(e)   Making the OBST the country's leading community ecotourism product.

Environmental strategies consisted of:

(a) Promotion of shoreline management among landowners, residents and public resource managers;

(b) Implementation of participatory resource assessment, integrated coastal management and ecotourism planning;

(c) Formulation and implementation of resource use guidelines;

(d) Designing the tour as a low-impact itinerary;

(e) A training and accreditation system with strong emphasis on environmental consciousness and practice.

To ensure sustainability, during OBST's second year of operation, CRMP established marketing support and environmental management systems, and began preparations for its exit from the project. Mechanisms were developed for booking services under co-management by the community and its partners outside the island; networking with tour operators, guides, hotels and resorts; and building community capability in and understanding of the marketing of the product. Primary emphasis was given to coastal resource management as a motive and tool for sustainability. A proposal was presented to the government agency in charge of managing OIWS, seeking to deputize the cooperative to assist in protection, rehabilitation and research activities at the sanctuary. CRMP saw that the long-term sustainability of the OBST depended on its integration into OIWS's comprehensive management plan, enforcement of environmental laws outside the sanctuary boundaries and harmonization of land use practices in adjacent villages. CRMP phased out from providing technical assistance to the community tourism project in December 2000, allowing the community and local institutions to begin to manage the enterprise on their own. CRMP monitored the project briefly before fully leaving its management to the community and sharing lessons with a broader audience. The OBST has prospered under its own management and generated substantial income for the participating community. It has been able to do this within the legal context of a national park under the direction of the DENR. An important factor in the ongoing success of the OBST organization is having a good rapport with the nearby resorts on Mactan Island that promote the tour among their guests. The resort managers are proud they can send their guests to a well-managed tour run by the local community. Through this collaboration with the local resorts, the OBST is providing one of the few viable options to redistribute wealth directly from the larger resorts and their occupants on Mactan Island to the Olango Island community.

Marine Sanctuaries Attract Divers in Moalboal, Cebu

The municipality of Moalboal, 93 kilometers from Cebu City on the west side of Cebu Island, is reputed to be one of the prime scuba diving destinations in the country (Figure 10.2). Recreational activities are mostly centered on scuba diving, although a few tourists go there for snorkeling, swimming and beach relaxation. Four marine sanctuaries in the area are the primary attraction: Saavedra and Tongo Sanctuaries which were established in 1987 through the efforts of the Central Visayas Regional Project, a World Bank project; Pescador Island Sanctuary, which was initiated in the early 1980s and made legal by municipal resolution in December 1995; and Colase Marine Sanctuary.

The main attraction is tiny Pescador Island, 2 km offshore from the village beach of Panagsama Beach. The sanctuary portion of the island reef covers 4.5 hectares and is off limits to all forms of fishing. It has been rated as a five-star diving and snorkeling destination (Jackson 1995).

The other three sanctuaries do not equal Pescador Island's clear water and attractive reef but by any standards are still very nice dive sites and attract many visitors. Saavedra Marine Sanctuary covering 8 hectares is generally classified as a 4-star diving and snorkeling destination, a close second to Pescador. Aside from the four sanctuaries, there are other dive sites frequented including reefs fronting the numerous resorts. The majority of the scuba divers who visit Moalboal are foreign, although a significant number of local divers visit the area.

Up until 1984, Moalboal, particularly Panagsama Beach, was also known for its white sandy beaches and clear waters that were even being compared to Boracay, discussed above. However, due to a devastating storm in 1984, subsequent erosion of major portions of the beachfront occurred. The construction of man-made structures such as dikes, seawalls and cottages on the beachfront areas compounded the beach erosion situation. Currently, the sandy portions of Panagsama Beach have almost completely disappeared except for small stretches north of the village. There, many local residents still frequent the area for swimming, beach combing and picnicking. Most of these beach visitors stay for a day, particularly during weekends in the summer time.

Infrastructure development in Moalboal is ribbon-like, whereby resorts have sprouted and located right next to each other during the past 20 years. To date, there are 33 resorts in Moalboal, 25 of which are in Panagsama, five in Saavedra and three in Tongo. The maximum capacity of all resorts is 636 visitors, with a total of 301 rooms. Moreover, there are ten dive shops and 22 restaurants operating in the area; again most are located along Panagsama Beach (Rosales 2003). The fishing and agricultural communities are poor by

Philippine standards and the only real influx of investment and alternative income is associated with the beach and coral reef recreation activities.

As part of a marine protected area valuation study by Rosales, almost all local divers, and around 79 per cent of foreign respondents, expressed their willingness to pay user fees for being able to dive at Moalboal dive sites. Among the foreigners who were unwilling to pay a fee, their reason was not for lack of financial resources but based on the lack of trust in the fee system, linked to mistrust in government. Nevertheless, there is a great potential for a fee system to be implemented in Moalboal given the high approval rate of the users themselves.

About 70 per cent of the respondents indicated a preference for a one-time fee to be paid, which would allow them access to all dive sites for one trip. The average amount for such bidders was US$1.25 per person per trip. For foreigners, only 36 per cent indicated preference for such a system, but the average bid was high at almost US$9 per person per trip. On a per site basis, Pescador Island had the highest figure at US$1.27 per local per trip and almost US$5 per foreigner per trip. For beachfront improvement, around two-thirds of locals and half of foreign respondents indicated positive bids for fees. Locals were willing to pay US$0.43 on average, while half of the foreign respondents were willing to pay US$5.80 for beach improvement.

The most preferred option for respondents in general was for the fees to be incorporated in their resort bills, while the least preferred option was for tourists to pay to the boat operator or boatman. Meanwhile, NGOs are preferred to handle the funds, rather than government bodies. A local tourism association was the second most preferred option.

The overall outcome of the study on coastal tourism in Moalboal was that a significant majority was willing to pay over and above the entrance fees, for specific types of improvement, foremost of which is regular monitoring and evaluation of coral reefs and beaches in the area. This finding highlights the value that visitors place on the area for marine tourism and also how much local visitors place a premium on this recreation outlet. It also highlights the need to develop efficient mechanisms for fee collection to channel the funds into the deserving recipients at the community level.

One of the thorny issues to be resolved in Moalboal and other similar areas is the effective sharing of a portion of the user fees with the local stakeholder community. The mechanism for doing this in the Philippines, if the revenues are collected and managed by the local government, is for the community through the official 'barangay' unit, to apply for a grant to accomplish a specified community project that utilizes the allotted funds. Revenue generated funds can be earmarked by the municipality or city, through the ordinance that establishes the marine protected area, user fee system or other financial management tool (DENR et al. 2001).

The Municipality of Moalboal is now actively supporting the implementation of a user-fee system in Pescador and Saavedra Sanctuaries that will be used for maintenance and conservation of the areas concerned, and to provide some direct revenue to the fishing communities associated with the sites. In the case of Saavedra, the sanctuary is managed entirely by the local village fronting the area while offshore Pescador Island is under the management of the municipal government. The fee collection systems, in both areas, are ordained by the municipal government. Thus the actual management of the funds is through the Moalboal Municipality. The tricky aspect of this arrangement is that the community has to keep tabs on the municipal government financial manager to ensure that their share is available and tallied accurately. Experience around the country indicates that some municipal governments are fully capable of this degree of transparency and honesty with their respective communities while others are not.

Siquijor Island Makes Transition from Witchdoctors to Marine Tourism

Declared as a full province in 1971, Siquijor is an island just south of Bohol and Cebu Islands (Figure 10.2). There are some 80 000 people living in six small towns. It is an economically poor province with one of the lowest average family income levels of the 72 Philippine provinces (Shields and Thomas-Slayer 1993). The prevailing reputation of the province is primarily based on its inhabitants' practice of 'witchcraft', locally known as *barang*. During Holy Week, numerous tourists visit the island and seek practitioners who come out and display their 'healing powers', or simply entertain people with their famous dancing paper dolls. The power center is on Good Friday, when the influence of good and evil allegedly come together. At the core of the belief system is deep respect for the sacred, as well as selected plants and animals. Most of the ingredients for potions are plants and sea life from cliffs, ravines and deep water, which are believed to contain more power than cultivated organisms (Rocamora 2002).

Aside from the practice of witchcraft, Siquijor is slowly gaining another reputation, that of being a prime scuba diving destination in the Visayas. At the time of the survey in 2002, there were five diving spots that were being frequented by tourists and locals. Resorts and scuba diving facilities have likewise sprouted all around the island. Unlike Moalboal though, these resorts are located far away from each other, hence there is much more space for tourists to relax and recreate. Furthermore, there are a larger percentage of non-divers in Siquijor compared to Moalboal. To date, there are nine resorts offering accommodation and lodging facilities, and three dive shops operating on Siquijor, which can accommodate a maximum of 159 visitors a day (Rosales 2003).

The valuation study revealed that among Siquijor divers, a high percentage were willing to pay entrance fees. In particular, 87 per cent of locals and 83 per cent of foreigners, or 84 per cent of the sample, signified a positive bid for diving fees in Siquijor. The average amount was also very high at US$4.62 for locals and US$17 for foreigners, for all dive sites per visit. Local bids ranged from US$1.51 per site, and foreigners bid between US$12–13 per site. These are higher than the bids made for Moalboal dive sites. But since there are fewer divers who frequent Siquijor as compared to Moalboal in the end, higher values per person do not necessarily mean a higher total value for the site, if the population of users is small.

In terms of hypothetical improvements presented in the survey, a large majority of local respondents were in favor of all situations presented to them, while a significant number of foreigners supported some of the improvements. Amounts ranged from US$0.50 – 1.10 and US$7 – 14 for locals and foreigners, respectively. Again, these are much higher than the amounts stated for the Moalboal survey. This may be partly due to the higher average household incomes of Siquijor divers. In fact, Siquijor foreign divers had much higher personal incomes compared to their counterparts in Moalboal, thus the higher bids for both current and improved levels of services.

With respect to the manner of payment, respondents preferred to pay their fees as part of their dive tour fees or resort bill. The least preferred was paying the fees through the boat operator or boatman. A multi-sectoral group was preferred to handle the funds, followed by an NGO. And like the Moalboal survey, the least preferred organization to handle the funds, from the visitors' view, was a community-based organization.

Siquijor is included as a case study because it points to some new directions in development of tourism from the perspective of an entire island province. Although historically poor, there is a strong bias towards truly sustainable development in Siquijor as reflected in the provincial, municipal and national government agency policies for Siquijor (Siquijor Province 2002). Second, unlike many other tourism development areas in the Philippines, there is still time for planning of infrastructure to avoid crowding and building directly on the beach. Good roads exist and the local governments appear to have a major role in planning development in consultation with private sector developers, so far.

DISCUSSION AND CONCLUSIONS

The Philippines is actively promoting tourism and has earmarked 2003 as 'visit Philippines year'. Not only does the country want tourism, it needs it for economic development since the society is service oriented and indeed has the capacity to manage visitors. It is easy for Filipinos to accept and accommodate tourists and given the opportunity, people will gravitate towards tourism as an enterprise with the hope of improving their incomes. Nevertheless, there are those individuals and organizations who recognize the pitfalls of tourism as discussed in this chapter and elsewhere, even though there are few that aggressively resist tourism development. The main concerns about tourism development in rural areas stem from the potential negative social and cultural impacts. Traditional and conservative elements of a Catholic society, as in the Philippines, can point out numerous incidents of changing values in areas where tourism is thriving and where sex, drugs and other lax values seep into adjacent communities. Although there is no denying that this does occur, similar problems are somewhat pervasive in the society as a whole among certain sectors and it can not be blamed directly on tourism. Because the Philippines is very media and communication oriented, the exposure of people to new and not so savory values is very common. The proponents of tourism suggest that visitors can also stimulate more positive value formation and indeed cite the case of environmental conservation, that more often than not, is encouraged by recent trends in marine tourism development in the country (Huttche et al. 2002).

The generally favorable attitude of Filipinos towards tourism, as explained, stems from the open nature of the culture and its ease in speaking English among other factors. The society is also very adaptable in looking for livelihoods and there exists an ease of transition from one occupation to another. But, the question remains to be answered about what type of tourism will most benefit the society and its economy. The case studies highlighted in this chapter attempt to answer this question through their bias towards community level involvement and responsibility in managing attractive ecologically friendly marine tourism enterprises.

Whale watching through the community-based organization of Pamilacan Island is a first glimpse of how a tradition of whale, dolphin, manta ray and whale shark harvesting can be turned into an ecotour that conserves these animals for viewing instead of capture. Although there are conflicts within the island community about preferences for traditional fishing versus tourist viewing, popular opinion is turning towards that of tourism because of its more sustainable nature as evidenced by the shift in community attitude during the last two years (Moral 2003). The potential revenues are not very large from whale watching on Pamilacan but over time they will continue to accrue to the community. They are also within the law in conducting this activity as opposed to receiving attention from the notoriety of being the marine mammal hunters of southern Bohol Island. National and local media have played a role in this positive progression. And, as awareness increases, the desire among the island community to promote other marine recreation activities, such as scuba diving and snorkeling in their marine sanctuary, is also prospering and generating additional revenue.

The Bird and Seascape Tour of Olango Island, Cebu is a different example of a community-based ecotour that is thriving. A unique feature of the OBST is that it is managed to be a locally constituted corporation comprised of island residents who, before the tour was started, had few productive livelihood opportunities. Surprisingly, in the context of various environmental and social problems on the island of Olango related to poverty, this tour is doing well and appears to be sustainable and growing. As on Pamilacan Island, the tour is providing a strong incentive to protect the island biodiversity resources of birds, mangroves and coral reefs because of the attraction they offer to Filipino and foreign visitors alike. Such monetary incentives have never existed in the past. It is also an opportunity for islanders to share their traditional knowledge, thus adding to their pride. For those who have participated in this tour, a lasting memory is the pride displayed by the tour creators manifested as part of the tour. The OBST corporation is functioning well but time will reveal its durability given the vagaries of managing money through a locally constituted organization.

The case of Moalboal highlights the potential for scuba diving to catalyze the stewardship of the coral reefs. Traditionally, Moalboal coastal residents were almost entirely dependent on the relatively rich fishing grounds of the fringing reefs and offshore waters. By 1980, the reefs were already severely depleted and being destroyed by destructive uses. Diving tourism began and was uncontrolled for many years, and not much benefit accrued to the residents except for those who worked directly in the dive shops or resorts. Now the realization that visitors are willing to pay for entrance to their reef sanctuaries is a revelation that can build financial sustainability into the protection of the coral reefs and enhance the incomes of traditional fishers in an historically poor setting. The study of Rosales reveals a substantial potential for income generation not only limited to Moalboal. Other areas in Cebu Province have an equal potential and interest, and are beginning to establish similar mechanisms through marine sanctuaries and better management of their beaches through a simple 'user-fee' system that covers management costs which directly adds wealth to the local context.

Siquijor Island is notable in that an entire island province has now opted to promote nature-based tourism as its primary means of development beyond traditional fishing and agriculture as well as its historical image of witchcraft tourism. Siquijor residents want to preserve their environment and peaceful atmosphere by avoiding the frenzied development of other localities. And, they want to project an image of value as reflected by the high (US$25 per visit) willingness-to-pay of visitors. A recent ecotourism and community enterprise development-planning workshop underscored the need to build on quality destinations that utilize the uniqueness of the island province and its environment, culture and people (Siquijor Province 2002).

The four case studies contain a strong presence of the local government in the management of their respective marine sanctuaries, the collection of user fees and in planning for tourism development. This prominent role of the local government may be an advantage relative to the pre-1990s control by the national government, and can encourage more eager support and appropriate planning for tourism in diverse settings. A comparison of marine protected areas (MPAs), for example, being managed by national government, local governments and community-based organizations shows that local government and non-government managed sites performed best (Javier 2002; White et al. 2002). The role of the local government was deemed vital for an effective implementation of a management plan, given that it is the administrative arm of the community where the MPA is located. Hence, if local governments continue to take on an active role in managing their respective MPAs, beaches and coral reefs, the potential of realizing the economic values of such can be more easily translated into better conservation and management practices through local stakeholders (Courtney et al. 2002). This, in the end, will result in a higher social welfare for the users and managers of these resources as explored in the case studies above.

The total revenue potential for the sites of the four case studies is substantial if sustained with good management. Table 10.1 indicates the large willingness-to-pay of visitors in each site on a per day basis. The overall present value of the MPA areas (coral reefs and beaches) under management is indicated in Table 10.2. These significant amounts will make local and national government decision-makers realize that there are ways to help finance the tremendous marine conservation needs in the country and at the same time generate rural wealth in impoverished communities. The case studies point to the most appropriate means for channeling and managing revenues that are not centralized through local resource and financial management mechanisms controlled by local stakeholders. In all cases, there are strong preferences for collecting user fees and distributing them through local government channels, but with the assumption that credible personnel and accounting practices are utilized. It is fortunate that there are good precedents in the Philippines for managing revenues locally without corruption such as in the Olango Bird and Seascape Tour and the user fees from Saavedra Marine Sanctuary managed by the Municipality. There are also precedents for poor management in areas with less informed local governments.

Table 10.1   Potential user fees for marine tourism activities

Site/Type of user	Recommended fee per visit (US$)
Moalboal scuba divers	1.60 (local); 4.00 (foreigner)
Moalboal beach visitors	0.80 per person
Siquijor scuba divers	4.00 (local); 25.00 (foreigner)
Pamilacan whale & dolphin watchers	5.00 per person

Source: Rosales (2003)

Table 10.2   Present values of coral reefs, beaches and marine waters for marine protected areas

Location	Resource area	Present value (US$) per hectare *
Moalboal	Coral reefs in sanctuaries	11,658 to 17,956
Moalboal	Beaches	2,685 to 8,260
Siquijor	Coral reefs in sanctuaries	10,655 to 14,225
Pamilacan	Marine waters around island	2 to 5

Note: * Present value discount rate is 15 per cent for a time horizon of 50 years

Source: Rosales (2003)

The national objective of increasing rural wealth can be substantially assisted by more locally operated nature based tourism opportunities since they are win–win situations that bring wealth and encourage conservation (DOT and DENR 2002). This appears to be obvious but what happens when tourism fails or overdevelops as in so many places around the world? In the Philippines, there are many cases of poorly planned and managed tourism development areas that have created more problems then they have solved. The boom and bust cycles in other Asian counties such as Thailand's Pattaya and Sri Lanka's Hikkaduwa can be seen in Boracay Island, Puerto Galera, Mindoro and other Philippine sites (Sullivan et al. 1995). One response is that the country needs moderate-scale tourism facilities that are well planned in terms of infrastructure and area development. Although not a model for area-wide planning, Mactan Island, Cebu has quality resorts with manageable impacts (Martinez 1997). These resorts make the community-based operations on Olango Island possible because it is not desirable for visitors to stay on Olango since it could not withstand the impacts of resort development. In Moalboal, the resorts are small and need to improve their shoreline management practices, but here again, they bring visitors willing to pay to access and utilize the community managed marine sanctuaries for diving. This localized tourism contributes directly to maintenance of the sanctuary, coral reef or beach while providing a livelihood for the fishing community through the legal and institutional support of the local municipal government. Even Boracay is now actively implementing an island-wide management plan that includes its coastal and marine waters (Trousdale 1997). In addition, the Philippines can build on its large potential for national tourism among Filipinos, which it is already doing.

A thread through our discussion is that successful Philippine tourism examples all represent partnerships among local governments, resorts and the communities living adjacent to the resources of tourism interest. This situation is not unique in the world but so often the partnerships are not working as they could to benefit all the parties in a harmonious manner. If this model can thrive in the Philippines, it might offer some hope for coastal conservation and livelihood generation that is sustainable. Indeed, based on the examples discussed above together with other similar developments in the Philippines, we are optimistic that community-based and local government facilitated tourism development in coastal areas of the country will thrive in the coming years and contribute more to both environmental sustainability and the generation of rural wealth.

ACKNOWLEDGMENTS

This chapter is possible because of support to Alan White from the Coastal Resource Management Project supported by the United States Agency for International Development under the terms and conditions of Contract No. AID-492-0444-C-00-60028-00 and support from the Pew Fellows Program in Marine Conservation, a Program of the Pew Charitable Trusts. The Coastal Conservation and Education Foundation, Inc. of Cebu, Philippines supported Ms. Rina Rosales in her research.

NOTES

1. Cebu is included because most of the tourist arrivals to destinations discussed in this chapter pass through Cebu and are reflected in this data.
2. This section is adapted from Flores (2001).

REFERENCES

Arin, T. and R.A. Kramer (2002), 'Divers' willingness to pay to visit marine sanctuaries: an exploratory study', *Ocean and Coastal Management*, **45**, 171–83.
Cesar, H. (1996), *The Economic Value of Indonesian Coral Reefs*, Washington DC: Environment Division, World Bank.

Courtney, C.A., A.T. White and D. Deguit (2002), 'Building Philippine local government capacity for coastal resource management', *Coastal Management*, **30** (1), 27–45.

Department of Environment and Natural Resources, Bureau of Fisheries and Aquatic Resources of the Department of Agriculture, and Department of the Interior and Local Government (2001), *Philippine Coastal Management Guidebook Series*, Cebu City, Philippines: Coastal Resource Management Project of the Department of Environment and Natural Resources, Books 1–8.

Book 1: Coastal Management Orientation and Overview
Book 2: Legal and Jurisdictional Framework for Coastal Management
Book 3: Coastal Resource Management Planning
Book 4: Involving Communities in Coastal Management
Book 5: Managing Coastal Habitats and Marine Protected Areas
Book 6: Managing Municipal Fisheries
Book 7: Managing Impacts of Development in the Coastal Zone
Book 8: Coastal Law Enforcement

Department of Tourism and Department of Environment and Natural Resources (2002), *National Ecotourism Strategy*, Manila: Department of Tourism, Department of Environment and Natural Resources and the New Zealand Agency for International Development.

Flores, M.M.M. (2001), 'Olango birds and seascape tour: a people-oriented ecotourism venture', *Tambuli: A Publication for Coastal Management Practitioners*, Vol. 4, Cebu City, Philippines, Coastal Resource Management Project, 23-5.

Green, S.J., R.D. Alexander, A.M. Gulayan, C.C. Migriño III, J. Jarantilla-Paler and C.A. Courtney (2002), *Bohol Island: Its Coastal Environment Profile*, Cebu City, Philippines: Bohol Environment Management Office, Bohol and Coastal Resources Management Project.

Huttche, C.M., A.T. White and M.M.M. Flores (2002), *Sustainable Coastal Tourism Handbook for the Philippines*, Cebu City, Philippines: Coastal Resource Management Project of the Department of Environment and Natural Resources and the Department of Tourism.

Jackson, J. (1995), *The Dive Sites of the Philippines, Comprehensive Coverage of Diving and Snorkeling*, London: New Holland Publishers Ltd.

Javier, E. (2002), *Analysis of Institutional Arrangements in Selected Marine Protected Areas in the Philippines: Impacts on Biodiversity Conservation*, research paper presented to the Economy and Environment Program for Southeast Asia.

Kabang Kalikasan ng Pilipinas (KKP) (2000), *Life of the Project on the Pamilacan Island Dolphin and Whale Watching Village Integrated Development Program*, Quezon City, Philippines.

Martinez, O.Y (1997), *The Impacts of Coastal Tourism in Maribago*, Lapu-Lapu City Master's Thesis in Environmental Studies, University of the Philippines, Los Banos.

Moral, C.V. (2003), 'Whale of a difference', *Philippine Daily Inquirer*, 11 February 2003.

Rocamora, J. (2002), *Siquijor On My Mind*, (unpublished)

Rosales, R.M.P. (2003), *A Survey to Estimate the Recreational Value of Selected Marine Protected Areas: Moalboal-Cebu, Siquijor and Pamilacan Island-Bohol*, Report for MPA Project of Coastal Conservation and Education Foundation, Inc., Cebu City, Philippines.

Santos, L.C., F.B. Sotto, T. Heeger and S.D. Albert (1997), *Livelihood and the Environment: Inextricable Issue in Olango Island*, Cebu City, Philippines: University of San Carlos.

Savina, G.C. and A.T. White (1986), 'A tale of two Islands: some lessons for marine resource management', *Environmental Conservation*, **13** (2), 107–13.

Shields, M.D. and B.P. Thomas-Slayer (1993), *Gender, Class, Ecological Decline, and Livelihood Strategies: A Case Study of Siquijor Island*, The Philippines, Ecogen Case Study Series, Clark University.

Siquijor Province (2002), 'Enhancing community and conservation-based enterprise development and ecotourism potentials, Siquijor Province, Central Philippines', *Proceedings of the Forum on Ecotourism and Enterprise Development*, Siquijor Province and the Siquijor Coastal Resources Enhancement Project, Siquijor.

Sotto, F.B., J.L. Gatus, M.A. Ross, M.F.L. Portigo and F.M. Freire (2001), *Coastal Environmental Profile of Olango Island, Cebu, Philippines*, Coastal Resource Management Project, Cebu City, Philippines.

Sullivan, K., L. de Silva, A.T. White and M. Wijeratne (1995), *Environmental Guidelines for Coastal Tourism Development in Sri Lanka*, Colombo, Sri Lanka, Coastal Resource Management Project and Coast Conservation Department.

Trousdale, W. (1997), *Trouble in Paradise: A Survey and a Discussion of Solutions, Boracay Island, Philippines*, Canadian Urban Institute, Philippines and Department of Tourism.

White, A.T. (2001), *Philippine Coral Reefs: A Natural History Guide*, Manila: Bookmark Inc. and Sulu Fund for Marine Conservation Foundation Inc.

White, A.T. and A. Trinidad (1998), *The Values of Philippine Coastal Resources: Why Protection and Management are Critical*, Cebu City, Philippines: Coastal Resource Management Project.

White, A.T. and R.J. Dobias (1991), 'Community marine tourism in the Philippines and Thailand: A boon or bane to conservation?', in Marc L. Miller and Jan Auyong (eds), *Proceedings of the 1990 Congress on Coastal and Marine Tourism: A Symposium and Workshop on Balancing Conservation and Economic Development*, National Coastal Resources Research and Development Institute.

White, A.T., V. Milan and D. Corpuz (1991), 'Community-based marine tourism in the Philippines: A case study of Anilao, Batangas', *Proceedings of the Third Global Congress*, Honolulu, Hawaii, 3–8 November 1991.

White, A.T., H. Vogt and T. Arin (2000a), 'Philippine coral reefs under threat: the economic losses caused by reef destruction', *Marine Pollution Bulletin*, **40** (7), 598–605.

White, A.T., M.A. Ross and M.M.M. Flores (2000b), 'Benefits and costs of coral reef and wetland management, Olango Island Philippines', in H.S.J. Cesar (ed.), *Collected Essays on the Economics of Coral Reefs*, CORDIO, Department for Biology and Environmental Sciences, Kalmar University, Kalmar, Sweden and Coastal Resource Management Project, Cebu City, Philippines, pp. 215–27.

White, A.T., A. Salamanca and C.A. Courtney (2002), 'Experiences with marine protected area planning and management in the Philippines', *Coastal Management*, **30** (1), 1–26.

Wong, P.P. (1999), 'Adaptive use of a rock coast for tourism – Mactan Island, Philippines', *Tourism Geographies*, **1** (2), 226–43.

11. Tourism Development and the Coastal Environment on Bintan Island

Poh Poh Wong

INTRODUCTION

Southeast Asia with its warm climate, abundance of islands, beaches, and coral reefs, and sometimes coupled with cultural attractions, provides suitable conditions for the development of coastal and island tourism. Although Hua Hin in southern Thailand is the region's first seaside resort dating from the early 1900s, the majority of the resorts are from the 1960s (Franz 1985). Much of the region's coastal tourism development has been unplanned leading to environmental degradation in the major resorts, Pattaya (Charoenca 1993), Penang (Hong 1985; Smith 1992a; Tan 1992), Boracay (Smith 1992), Phuket (Bunapong and Ausavajitanond 1991) and Kuta (Hussey 1989). Various alternative development strategies have been taken to reduce the environmental degradation.

One strategy is the integrated resort model first used in Kaanapali Beach on Maui, Hawaii, and adapted by the rest of the world. The integrated resort model caters to a number of resorts within a planned area that benefits from the synergy in terms of a variety of activities for the tourists, a critical mass in terms of infrastructure, amenities and marketing, and control by a master developer to ensure compatible and complementary land uses. The controlled development of the environment is to minimize environmental degradation (Stiles and See-Tho 1991).

In a worldwide review of six integrated resorts in countries without previous experience in developing such resorts, Inskeep and Kallenberger (1992) found that such balanced development brings substantial economic and social benefits while minimizing problems associated with uncontrolled tourism development. Indonesia was the first in Southeast Asia to employ the integrated resort model in Nusa Dua (Smith 1992b) and this has been applied elsewhere in the country (Indonesian Commercial Newsletter 1996) and in Southeast Asia with varying success (Smith 1992b). To date, the biggest integrated project is on the north coast of Bintan (Figure 11.1).

This chapter uses a modified political ecology approach (Bryant 1992; Bryant 1998) to examine the integrated resort development on the north coast of Bintan with attention to its geographical scale, major actors and the importance of government. In particular, it focuses on environmental aspects related to this approach and how the development by those in control of the environment is not necessarily always negative as illustrated by the marine water quality data. It also examines what other issues of environmental equity and inequity can be learnt from this modified political ecology perspective.

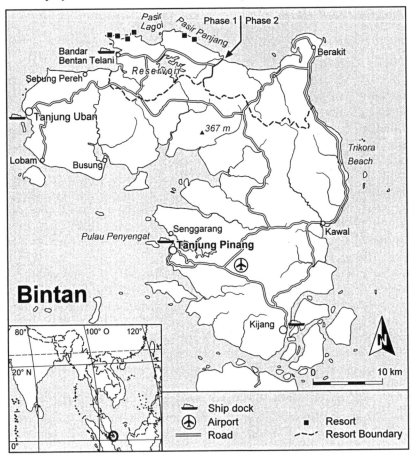

Figure 11.1   Bintan Island, Indonesia

Also, Bintan provides an ideal situation for comparison with unplanned tourism development which continues to develop outside the integrated resort area.

POLITICAL ECOLOGY PERSPECTIVE

For environmental research in Third World countries, Bryant (1997) shows how the control of environment can be conceptualized as a political ecology approach. For tourism, Stonich (1998, p. 29) identified the essential elements of political ecology analysis for which the corresponding features of integrated resort development in Bintan can be tentatively identified:

- *The ideologies that direct resource use and influence which social actors benefit and which are disadvantaged*: the rationale for the growth triangle and the integrated resort;
- *International interests, such as donor agencies or private investors that promote particular patterns of natural resource use*: the state-linked companies, government agencies and private sectors from Singapore and Indonesia involved in the integrated resort;
- *The function of the global economy in promoting particular patterns of resource use*: heavy dependence of the integrated resort on the international tourism industry;
- *The role of the state in determining and implementing policies that favor the interests of certain social actors over those of others*: implementation of policies for the success of the integrated resort by both Singapore and Indonesian governments;
- *The relationship of class and ethnic structures to conflicts over access to productive resources*: the displaced farmers and the ensuing land issue;
- *The interrelationships among local resource users and groups of society who affect resource use*: tourism development inside and outside the integrated resort and the relative access to available resources and facilities;
- *Diversity in the decisions of local resource managers*: the unclear decision in the land issue.

The above features have been re-cast into three main thrusts in a modified political ecology approach to examine the integrated resort of Bintan:

1. *Integrated resort development as planned environmental change*. As the public sector plays a significant role in integrated resort development,

the political ecology approach is considered suitable for examining the various actors of the public sector and their relationship to the geographical scale and national/international, island/resort, and the resort interests. Contrary to many large-scale businesses (Bryant 1997, p. 5), the integrated resort cannot be an example of the 'business-as-usual' on environmental matters. Further to the three dimensions of the politicized environment (Bryant and Bailey 1997, p. 30), the integrated resort can be considered as a planned dimension, which carries attendant conditions such as high investment costs and centralized control.

2. *Environmental control and responsibility.* Attention is given to environmental control and responsibility in the integrated resort in terms of the application of environmental impact assessment and maintenance of environmental quality. In contrast to the normal political ecology approach where the control over the environment is reflected in the power to pollute the environment (Bryant 1997, p. 11), here, the power is to eliminate the negative impact. Earlier experience with coastal tourism development in Southeast Asia shows that legislation without enforcement led to environmental degradation. Continuous monitoring and enforcement are carried out in the integrated resort to ensure that environmental quality is maintained. Specific data on coastal water quality will illustrate this point and comparison will be made with other Southeast Asian resorts.

3. *Environmental equity and inequity.* The environmental responsibility and control of integrated resorts has overlooked or not factored adequately the local human–environmental equation, thus affecting certain local resource users negatively. In dealing with such environmental 'results' of these interactions and unequal power relations (Bryant 1997, pp. 12, 13), the land issue and aspects of tourism development outside the integrated area will be examined. The subsequent measures taken by the integrated resort and local authorities in the light of the land issue are analogous to the power actors seeking to build a long-term stake in a given locale (Bryant 1997, p. 14).

This study is based on a combination of qualitative and quantitative data from various sources. Published and unpublished reports including my own work with the integrated resort, and various field trips provided much of the familiarity with the island. The marine water quality and visitor data were supplied by Island Leisure International, formerly Bintan Resort Management. Discussion was also held with a number of professionals working in Bintan.

BINTAN

The political ecology approach inevitably requires a historical perspective of the environment (Bryant 1998, p. 85). Here, it has been modified to provide a geographical brief on the environment, the population and the economic activities for understanding tourism development on the island, including the integrated resort development on the north coast. Due to the focus on coastal tourism, more attention is given to the coastal resources and environment.

Geographical Background

Bintan is located just 1° N and 104° 30' E or about 45 km southeast of Singapore and has an area of 1 140 km² (Figure 11.1). It is one of more than 3 000 islands comprising the Riau archipelago and it has a rolling topography with the highest elevation at 376 m. It has a tropical monsoon climate with two seasons, a wet northeast monsoon from November to March and a dry southwest monsoon from June to October. Its annual rainfall varies from about 2 500 to 3 000 mm. As a result of its insular character, daily temperatures are generally constant with an average of 26°C and highs reaching 31°C.

Historically Bintan was part of the Johor-Riau kingdom dating from the mid-sixteenth century in which the Sultan of Johor moved his residency repeatedly between Johor, Riau and Lingga. The territory was divided by a complex process of dynastic quarrels and Anglo-Dutch competition for dominance of the region at the beginning of the 19th century. Eventually, the Riau-Lingga kingdom with its capital at Bintan came under the Dutch while Singapore was ceded to the English in 1819 (Colombijn 1997). Bintan remained part of Netherland East Indies until the independence of Indonesia in 1945.

Biophysical Resources

Primary forests covered only a small area on the highest elevated area of Bintan. The original vegetation was cleared largely for the cultivation of gambier (*Uncaria gambieri*) and for the firewood required in the processing of the gambier leaves. Each gambier plantation of 30 ha required an equal amount of forest for the firewood. After 12 years of production it was abandoned as the search of new stocks of firewood continued (Colombijn 1997). Gambier eventually gave way to rubber in the 20th century. Today, much of the abandoned rubber land on higher grounds not subject to water-logging has reverted back to secondary forests or used for other land uses.

In terms of coastal resources, Bintan has more than 720 km of coastline, 12 200 ha of mangroves, 16 800 ha of coral reefs and 8 800 ha of sea grasses (Iswahyudi 2000). Mangroves are mainly along the sheltered southern half of the island and in estuaries in the northern half. Coral reefs, much of which have been damaged, are mostly on the east and north coasts. Along the north coast are seasonally inundated mixed swamp forests, flooded during the northeast monsoon. A number of sandy beaches are on the north and east coasts and the longest beach is at Pasir Panjang.

As a result of considerable land clearing and burning by farmers, the overall environmental impact is severe deforestation, soil erosion and loss of soil fertility. During the dry monsoon, a common practice is to burn the vegetation as preparation for cultivation. If unutilized, bare areas are quickly replaced by lalang (*Imperata cyclindrica*).

Settlements

Bintan had an estimated population of 135 000 in 1995 with a fairly distinct geographical pattern of settlements corresponding to the two major ethnic groups, Malays and Chinese. The Malays are mainly in the villages and the typical coastal village is built on stilts and characterized by boardwalks (*pelantar*) over the water. Examples include Sebung Pereh, Busung and Berakit. Economic activities and population growth in the villages have put a strain on coastal and marine resources. Many villages share the common problems of access to clean water supply, and sewage and solid waste disposal. The Chinese are concentrated mainly in the towns of Tanjung Pinang and Tanjung Uban for trade and commerce, and in some villages. The Chinese population in Tanjung Pinang is confined to the seaward side of the town built out on stilts over the mudflats. They are also in Senggarang, an old Chinese village, and Kawal, a fishing port.

The capital of Tanjung Pinang has a dispersed layout influenced by the topography and connected by winding roads within a 10 km radius of the ferry terminal. Its land use is rather haphazard without proper town planning. For example, local government offices are scattered among mixed residential and commercial sectors. Like many villages and Tanjung Uban, the coastal environmental degradation is evident – full of litter, rat-infested, foul-smelling and no proper or inadequate sewage treatment.

Economic Activities

Bintan's major economic activities are fishing, agriculture, export of rubber and bauxite mining. Coastal and marine resources traditionally support the livelihood of coastal villages which evolves around the fishing industry. The local fishermen use traditional methods and a large percentage of the boats are non-motorized. Dynamite fishing is widespread, spurred by lucrative demand for specific species sold to fish traders from Hong Kong and Singapore (Antara 2000). Overexploitation by dynamite and poison fishing has destroyed much of the reefs. Kawal is a fishing port for the large boats and it exports fish to other parts of Indonesia and Singapore.

Bintan has a relatively important mining industry. Tanjung Uban serves as an offshore oil terminal where tankers take oil and gas from the Natuna field in the South China Sea. Indonesia's only bauxite mine is on Bintan. It commenced operation in the mid-1930s around Tanjung Pinang and Kijang. The Kijang concession produces chemical grade bauxite for export to Japan and China, increasing its production from 0.84 million tons in 1996 to 1.24 million tons in 2001 (USA Embassy 2002). It has almost reached the end of its economic life but the re-granting of lapsed license areas has extended the operation for four more years.

The bauxite industry causes substantial environmental damage around the mining and shipping areas. The bauxite ore is barged to the main stocking and loading facility at Kijang where a jetty and load-out facilities are available. The environmental damage comes from the open pit mining, the runoff of soil and bauxitic clay, spillage into the sea, and local oil and fuel spillage around the workshops. Nine islands near Kijang are badly silted from bauxite mining. In 1997 an estimated 570 ha were to be rehabilitated, involving regrading and revegetation (IMC Mackay and Schnellmann 1999).

Pineapple is cultivated commercially on 2 700 ha by a private Indonesian company for the export of pineapple juice. Increasing areas of old rubber land are being converted by the local farmers for crops of commercial value, such as vegetables and fruits, in particular, pineapple.

Prior to the integrated resort, tourism development was only confined to Tanjung Pinang and the east coast. Within the capital, there were few hotels near to the ferry terminal. The tourists were drawn to cheap shopping in the town, the historical attractions at Pulau Penyengat, Senggarang and seafood restaurants along the coast. Several small-scale tourist establishments were at Trikora Beach. Except for one small hotel, the rest were mainly guesthouses with simple structures.

With the eventual cessation of mining at Kijang, Bintan would have remained economically dependent on agriculture and fishing with commerce and services in Tanjung Pinang and small-scale tourism on the east coast. This economic structure was to be changed with the industrialization and large-scale tourism development, precisely what was proposed by the Indonesian government for the modern development of Bintan.

INTEGRATED RESORT DEVELOPMENT AS PLANNED
ENVIRONMENTAL CHANGE

The integrated resort development project in Bintan has its origin in the concept of the Singapore-Johor-Riau (SIJORI) growth triangle mooted about 20 years ago. The triangle would serve as an economic zone creating mutual benefits for participating members with the advantage of easy access to financial and commercial services from Singapore, relatively cheaper labor provided by the Riau islands and natural resources suitable for tourism development. The integrated resort project is one of four flagship cooperation projects between Singapore and Indonesia to promote investment and tourism in Riau. The other three are the Batamindo Industrial Park on Batam, the Bintan Industrial Estate at Lobam and the marine and industrial complex in Karimun.

Geographically, the integrated resort project occupies 23 000 ha on the northern coast of Bintan and is equivalent to about one-third the size of Singapore island. Its southern boundary line is approximately 3–5 km inland and runs along a ridge approximately 100 m above sea level. The western half of the project has beaches in bays between rocky headlands while the eastern half is more low-lying with fewer beaches. The project enjoys the advantages of large land size, available beaches, clean sea water and cheap labor suitable for the service industry. Its distinct drawbacks were remoteness and the need for expensive infrastructure and facilities.

The governments of Singapore and Indonesia determine and implement the policies favoring their interests in the integrated resort project. Both signed an agreement on August 1990 for the establishment of Bintan Beach International Resort (BBIR) to be marketed and managed by Bintan Resort Management Pte Ltd (BRM), a Singapore-based company for and on behalf of the master-planner, Bintan Resort Corporation (BRC). Sixty per cent of the resort is owned by an Indonesian consortium led by the Salim Group and the rest is owned by a Singapore consortium consisting of eight companies. The resorts will enjoy duty free status, quick customs and immigration procedures and have a land tenure initially of 30 years with a possible extension for another 20 years, and then 30 years (Business Times 1991). The integrated resort is in fact the largest of its kind in Asia with about 65 land parcels ranging from 30–300 ha. It is to be connected by a green zone to include the reservoirs, flora and fauna. Currently, six groups of resorts with a total of 1 400 rooms have been completed in Phase 1, and Phase 2 is yet to be implemented. Singapore's total investment in the project is about US$500 million.

The project bears the features of a large planned environment coordinated by the various departments of BRM to serve the investor developers in resort planning, investor services, and marketing and resort operations. Modern infrastructures costing a total of US$170 million were started in 1991 (Business Times 1991). By 1992, the ferry terminal at Bandar Bentan Telani was completed. By 1996, 12.5 km of the east–west arterial road of 35 km were built and connected by sub-arterial roads to land parcels. Within each land parcel, the resorts have their own distributor roads. A potable water system is supplied from a water treatment plant drawing water from a reservoir with yield of 5 million liters per day and a service reservoir of 1.5 million liters. Power is generated by a 18 MW plant with the capability of upgrading to 24 MW. The water and power supply is brought to the parcels for connection to the resorts and the potable water conforms to World Health Organization standards. All resorts have modular sewage treatment plants and the recycled effluent is used for irrigation purposes. Solid waste is collected daily from the resorts and disposed of in a centralized sanitary land-fill site.

The integrated resort is highly dependent on the international tourism industry. Despite some overall negative trends, tourist arrivals and hotel occupancy have been promising. Based on data supplied by Island Leisure International (2003), tourist arrivals during the period 1996–2001 increased from 113 494 to 340 465. They registered a double digit growth from 1996–2000, then dropped to a single digit due to the 11 September 2001 event, and a slight negative growth in 2002 due to the Bali bomb blast on 12 October 2002. The annual overall resort occupancy has increased steadily from 40 per cent in 1996 to 60.5 per cent in 2001. The mix in tourists, dominated initially by Singaporeans, has improved to a broad base with Singaporeans accounting for 30 per cent, Japanese and Koreans more than 16 per cent each, Europeans another 16 per cent, and tourists from Oceania 6 per cent.

The development of the project was affected by a number of factors, some beyond the control of the master-planning of BBIR. The factors included the economic downturn in 1997, the change in political leadership in Indonesia in 1998, and subsequent political, economic and social crises in the following three years, which have a negative impact on both investments and tourist travel. Other problems were the haze arising from agricultural burning in Sumatra and malaria cases in the integrated resort (Straits Times 1997). To make the project more attractive to investments, smaller parcels were to be introduced in the future, and these include plans for an urban beach center with smaller-type accommodation and a wide range of retail, recreation, food and beverage facilities, services and offices.

ENVIRONMENTAL CONTROL AND RESPONSIBILITY

The Bintan integrated resort project pays attention to environmental control and responsibility, and environmental impact assessment approval is required before each individual development project can take place. The basis of such assessment is in a decree from the Indonesian Ministry of the Environment (March 1994), which provides the guidelines for the preparation of the environmental impact statement and the environmental impact assessment. Individual developers need to obtain approved terms of reference before proceeding with the assessment process which includes an environmental inventory, management plan and monitoring plan.

The Regional Environmental Impact Assessment for the integrated project requires individual development projects to compile individual environmental management and monitoring plans while the Regional Environmental Management Plan and the Regional Environmental Monitoring Plan act as guidelines. BRM acts as the supervisor in the implementation of the environmental management and monitoring plans in conjunction with the Indonesian authorities. At the integrated resort level, BRM sets the environmental guidelines based on international best practices, and these resulting standards become part of the design and development guidelines and approved in the Regional Environmental Impact Assessment.

When each development project is completed, environmental monitoring ensures that standards are maintained. From the perspective of environmental control and responsibility, the process is of implementation, enforcement and monitoring by BRM at all phases of the project. In a number of instances, monitoring carried out at the construction phase has prevented spillage of material into the coastal water, the unnecessary clearing of the natural vegetation, and so forth. The author has been involved in this process by providing specific advice relating to the removal of vegetation, coral boulders and rock outcrops, construction on specific coastal features and the determination of a setback line. Such advice has minimized the negative impact to the coastal environment, but has caused the developer to change the plans for construction.

Marine Water Quality

The quality of the coastal water on the north coast of Bintan is dependent on prevailing wind and wave conditions and local conditions, such as stream discharge. During the northeast monsoon, increased turbidity is associated with river and stream outlets after heavy rains. The resorts along the coast are expected to generate some erosion and runoff from land, effluent discharge from sewage treatment plants, fertilizers and pesticides washed from landscaped areas and golf courses, oil spillage from boats, as well as industrial wastes outside the resort area.

The primary objective of monitoring the marine water quality is to ensure that the water is suitable for swimming and for marine ecosystems. A secondary objective is to assess the efficiency of the resort sewage treatment plants within the discharge/mixing zone. Currently, four sewage treatment plants have overflow discharge points to the coast. Sampling of marine water is carried out at nine sites, representing developed sites, sites under construction and undeveloped sites. With the completion of the resorts, there will be eight resort sites and one undeveloped site (control area). Water samples are normally taken at 1 m from the surface and at a depth of 3 m or less and also at the mixing zone where potentially contaminated stream discharge is suspected. Up to nine parameters are monitored (Table 11.1).

Table 11.1   Explanation of water quality parameters

Parameter	Explanation
Salinity	Measure of all salts dissolved in water. Average ocean salinity is 35 ppt (parts per thousand) average river water salinity is 0.5 ppt or less.
pH	Measure of acidity (values < pH 7) or alkalinity (values > pH 7) of a solution, with pH 7 considered as neutral. Ideally, a value of about pH 7.4 is the same as the lachrymal fluid of eyes; values outside range of 6.5–8.5 are expected to cause eye irritation.
Biochemical Oxygen Demand (BOD)	Measures the amount of oxygen consumed by bacteria as they decompose the organic wastes. Widely used indicator of water quality. Higher values reduce the dissolved oxygen concentration in water for fish and other water life.
Chemical Oxygen Demand (COD)	Represents the measure of amount of oxygen required to destroy all the pollution in the water. An alternative measure to BOD.
Total Suspended Solids (TSS)	Amount of suspended material in water; solids may indicate inorganic inferior water quality from pollution.
Nitrate	Used in inorganic fertilizers. More commonly found in water than nitrite.
Nitrite	Intermediate form in oxidation of nitrogen, found in wastewater treatment plants.
Phosphate	Widely used in fertilizer and major constituent of detergents.
Fecal Coliform	Type of bacteria used as indicator of extent of sewage contamination.

Source: Orange County Government 2003

Two sets of marine water quality data are available. The first shows the average values of six parameters from all nine locations from May 1996–November 2000 (Figure 11.2), with the first bar of each parameter indicating the environmental guideline. More details from the resorts or developed sites are shown by minimum and maximum values for nine parameters from April 2001–October 2002 (Table 11.2). Both data sets provide some idea of the quality of the coastal water resulting from integrated resort development.

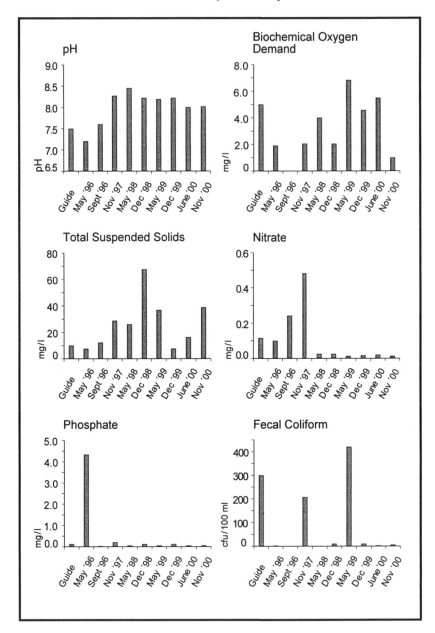

Source: Island Leisure International (2003)

*Figure 11.2   Average marine water quality of Bintan Beach International
Resort, May 1996–November 2000*

*Table 11.2   Marine water quality of the resorts on the north coast of Bintan,
April 2001–October 2002*

Parameter	Unit	Guide-line	April 2001	September 2001	March 2002	October 2002
Salinity	ppt	n.a.	17.6–27.8	13.7–14.8	36.3–36.7	28.9–31.1
pH	pH	6.5–8.5	8.0–8.3	7.8–8.2	8.0–8.3	8.1–8.5
BOD	mg/l	5	1–11	1–4	2–4	5–11
COD	mg/l	n.a.	20–46.5	166–266	292–295	215–298
TSS	mg/l	10	1–27	0.2–3.8	2–4.8	<1–13.9
Nitrate	mg/l	0.11	0.01–0.03	n.a.	0.2–0.4	0–0.2
Nitrite	mg/l	n.a.	0.0002–0.0006	n.a.	n.a.	n.a.
Phosphate	mg/l	0.1	0.006–0.12	0.06–0.15	0.05–0.08	0.01–0.22
F. Coliform	cfu/100 ml	300	1–10	2–27	0–5	3– >600

Notes: n.a.: not available

Source: Island Leisure International (2003)

Salinity is affected by the seasonal factor and locally by fresh water discharging from streams. Values of pH have remained within the acceptable range. BOD and COD values have increased but are generally acceptable. Values of TSS are higher than the standard as expected in tropical waters. Except for isolated values, phosphates are also within the limits. Nitrate values generally reflect an overall improvement in the maintenance of sewage treatment plants. High values of fecal coliform are associated with the operation of a specific sewage treatment plant. For example, in October 2002 there was a single value of >600 cfu/100 ml when the rest showed 3–87 cfu/100 ml.

There is a wide variation in both sets of environmental data due to seasonal fluctuations, site factors and spot values. But the overall quality of the coastal water has been maintained within the guidelines since the coast was opened to resort development. In some cases, the quality has improved with the completion of all construction activity and more efficient operation of the sewage treatment plants of the resorts. Future analysis for cadmium, copper and lead will be carried out if heavy metal pollution becomes apparent.

In contrast, poor marine quality seems to plague spontaneous coastal resort development in other areas of Southeast Asia. From 1989–1990, the total coliform bacteria at Pattaya beach exceeded the standard seawater for swimming (more than 1 000 MPN/100 ml) (Thongra-Ar and Poonpium 1992) and worsened in 1991 (Thongra-Ar and Mokkongpai 1992). The situation deteriorated and Pattaya was declared a pollution control area. With the provision of facilities to treat wastewater in late 2001, the situation had improved and total coliform counts at Pattaya decreased from 1 300–52 600 MPN/100 ml in 1997 to 240–550 MPN/100 ml in 2001 (Tour East Newsletter 2002). From 1986–1989, the coastal communities and resorts were major sources of marine water quality for the western coast of Phuket where the coliform content was higher than the norm for swimming (Bunapong and Ausavajitanond 1991). Before the availability of centralized sewage treatment facilities for the hotels at Batu Ferringhi in Penang, the marine water quality was also unsuitable for swimming (Hong 1984).

ENVIRONMENTAL EQUITY AND INEQUITY

Within the project area, BRM's control over the environment and resource use, planning, management and conservation is evident. Its spatial control has made the integrated resort development into a distinctive enclave. However, the extent of local environmental 'results' and how the local human–environmental equation has worked out is less evident. At the island level, there are some issues relating to local resource users, relocated villagers and the unused land in phase II. As the integrated resort has an impact on tourism development outside its boundaries, it stands to reason for each form of tourism to establish or find more beneficial links between them.

Blurring the Boundaries of Tourism Development

Integrated resort development has brought economic benefits to Bintan. The resorts employ about 3 300 Indonesians, a large proportion from Bintan itself. Many are resettled in new homes in the form of cluster housing and dormitory accommodation. The resorts inject about US$6 million annually into the local economy through the purchase of goods and services to support the resort operations (Tan 2002a). They contribute another US$1.5 million annually to the provincial government in the form of various taxes (Kompass 1998). Within the integrated resort, a shopping village with more than 20 outlets has attracted some locals from Tanjung Uban and Tanjung Pinang to set up shops, although the business is not very good (Tan 2002b). More successful is the supply of fresh produce from the villages of Bintan and other Riau islands to the resorts, using the domestic ferries to Tanjung Uban. Transport and other basic services have also developed immediately outside the integrated resort on the main road to Tanjung Pinang, reminiscent of the unplanned development reported by Smith (1992b) in Nusa Dua.

The development of the integrated resort, the overall increase in tourism, and the availability of regular and better ferry service to Bintan including Tanjung Pinang have provided a stimulus to tourism in Tanjung Pinang, Tanjung Uban and other small-scale or less formal resorts. Since 1990, Tanjung Pinang has grown rapidly as a tourist destination with more than 20 small hotels. It is also known for its sex tourism. Although officially denied, the brothels moved out of town to certain villages. The private sector has acknowledged that the sex trade has actually been a shot in the arm for Bintan tourism, creating many jobs for taxi drivers, in hotels, restaurants and karaoke bars, and for food sellers (Inter Press Service 1998). Tanjung Uban, the nearest town to Bandar Bentan Telani ferry terminal, has seen the construction of a few hotels and is expanding north along the main road to cater to the needs of the integrated resort and tourists on tours.

Tourism has stimulated the growth for cheaper accommodation and a range of other smaller resorts outside the integrated resort. A number of cheap resort accommodation establishments with a rustic setting appealing to budget travelers have been set up on the Trikora coast. Some are getting specialized to meet increasing demand from different travel sectors and are not necessarily on the coast. An agro-resort has been built near to the mangroves in southeast Bintan. Another is an adventure resort with more than 10 years of experience in offering cycling, tracking and boating around Bintan and other islands. A number of *kelongs* (traditional fishing traps with live-in facilities) operate more as 'floating resorts'. One 5-ha island, 3 km off the south coast of Bintan is available for rent as a resort island (Straits Times 2000b).

Tourism development outside the integrated resort has distinctive features. It tends to offer a wider variety in tourism experience, has a stronger local participation, non-enclave in character and readily accessible to the locals. But such development has some negative environmental impacts, such as pollution, littering and others, arising from a lack of enforcement, reminiscent of the unplanned development in other parts of Southeast Asia.

From the mid-1990s, the integrated resort tried to develop various one-day tours to the mangroves, old rubber estates, coastal forest and secondary forest, but without much success. A mangrove tour for Sungei Sebung launched in February 2001 received better response with 10 000 visitors after one year. It also has a night component to observe the fireflies in the mangroves. A full day tour is being developed for tourists from the integrated resort, bringing them to Senggarang, Pulau Penyengat and Tanjung Pinang. This is a new beneficial link between tourism inside and outside the integrated resort.

The Land Issue

Several thousand Indonesians from different islands had settled and farmed the north coast before it was acquired for tourism development. They were supposed to be compensated adequately. An indication of the insufficient compensation surfaced in early 1995 when some farmers sought help from the National Commission on Human Rights in Jakarta (Jakarta Post 1995). This was followed by two peaceful demonstrations in November 1998 and in December 1998. In the latter, the demonstrators delayed tourists in getting into their hotels and blocked the access road to one resort (Business Times 1998).

The extent and seriousness of this human–environment equation in the integrated resort was only realized when on 15 January 2000, about 200 villagers and students took temporary control of the power station and the Bandar Bentan Telani ferry terminal. They shut down the power for two days, and blocked the entrance to the integrated resort for eight days before Indonesian police and military personnel put an end to the blockade (Straits Times 2000a).

The main issue in this human–environment equation is over the payment of land. The villagers demanded at least US$1.17 per m^2 for the land acquired for the integrated resort project. Several sources point to the unclear circumstances surrounding the compensation process (Matrix-Batam 2003; Kompass 1998; Jakarta Post 2000). The villagers claimed that compensation was arbitrary and inadequate, as many received US$0.04 per m^2 while others received US$2 per m^2. They blamed the military and the government in forcing them to leave their land. Ten per cent of the compensation plan was not finalized and this was complicated by speculators and new arrivals claiming to be inhabitants. Salim's subsidiary, which coordinated the land acquisition with the local government bodies, had claimed it paid the full amount. The regional government claimed that the compensation was carried out fairly. Bintan Resort Corporation and Bintan Resort Management were never involved in the dispute over the resettlement issue (Business Times 1998).

Strengthening Stakeholders

The land issue and environmental inequity show the importance of building up long-term stakes with the local population. Community projects involving the local government, the resorts and the NGOs have been implemented to provide support and assistance to the local community living below the poverty line, especially to the villagers who are affected by the Bintan integrated resort project. Since 1998, these have included an education assistance program with scholarships and bursaries given to students, dental and medical care and *gotong royong* (mutual-help) projects (Bintan Resorts 2003). The locals are also encouraged to set up shops and services in the Bintan Industrial Estate (Tan 2002c).

The Singapore Chapter of UNIFEM Singapore (United Nations Development Fund for Women) also spearheaded a community project to render medical and dental care to the villages of Busung, Ekang, Teluk Sasah and Air Rajah. Educational assistance was given to some children to continue with their education (UNIFEM Singapore 2003).

In the long term, the stability of long-term stakes with the local population has to progress from the provision of community projects to more sustainable development. In the aftermath of the demonstration in 2002, the local government has set aside US$1 million per year over a 4–5 year period for a building project that would benefit local farmers and fishermen. This has resulted in better accessibility with Tanjung Uban which has since developed rapidly. Local residents are increasingly involved in economic activities related to the integrated resort, such as making available vegetables and chickens to the hotels (Jakarta Post 2000). A project on community-based ecotourism to create job opportunities for the locals is currently developed with partial support from overseas funding.

CONCLUSIONS

The Bintan integrated resort project shows that the public sector has a significant and effective involvement in environmental control and responsibility. It has since developed to combine the advantages and potential of Singapore professionals and Indonesian participation instrumental in attending to indigenous problems. Environmental degradation has been prevented by environmental impact assessment and proper enforcement and monitoring. The problem of wastewater treatment in unplanned tourism development is no longer an issue.

But the powers behind the integrated resort project still have to learn that corporate relationships are not confined within the project but also extend to the outside. The land issue is outstanding and efforts have to be made to resolve it. The project has not fully utilized phase I land and it will be a long time before phase II land is likely to be used.

The author proposed that phase II land of the integrated project be considered for a new dimension of planned tourism development that can bring benefits to all stakeholders. This will be planned small-scale tourism development involving the locals and the master developer with the participation of the local government and the NGOs. Perhaps, one could look to the experience of planned small-scale tourism development in Gili Trawangan, Lombok, where the local tourist operators were resettled in a small area provided with proper infrastructural facilities. The environmental degradation is minimized and the welfare of the local communities improved (Soemodinoto and Wong 2000). Where necessary, the implementation of the planned small-scale tourism can be carried out in phases and integrated with coastal zone management in Bintan.

REFERENCES

Antara (2000), *Napoleon fish in Bintan on verge of extinction*, 3.3.2000, Jakarta.
Bintan Resorts (2003), 'Community development programmes', available at: http://www.bintan_resorts.com.
Bryant, R.L. (1992), 'Political ecology: an emerging research agenda in third-world studies', *Political Geography*, **11**, 12–36.
Bryant, R.L. (1997), 'Beyond the impasse: the power of political ecology in Third World environmental research', *Area*, **21**, 5–19.
Bryant, R.L. (1998), 'Power, knowledge and political ecology in the third world: a review', *Progress in Physical Geography*, **22**, 79–94.
Bryant, R.L and S. Bailey (1997), *Third World Political Ecology*, London: Routledge.
Bunapong, S. and S. Ausavajitanond (1991), 'Saving what's left of tourism development at Patong Beach, Phuket, Thailand', in O.T. Magoon, D. Clark, L.T. Tobin, V. Tippie and H. Converse (eds), *Coastal Zone '91*, New York, American Society of Civil Engineers, pp. 1685–97.
Business Times (1991), *Giving Nature and History a Helping Hand*, 20.11.1991, Singapore.
Business Times (1998), *Villagers Block Briefly Roads to Bintan Resorts*, 22.12.1998, Singapore.
Charoenca, N. (1993), 'Tropical coastal pollution: a case study of Pattaya', in J.E. Hay and L.M. Chou (eds), *Contributions to Training in Coastal Zone Management in the Asia-Pacific Region and Report of the First NETTLAP Resources Development Workshop for Education and Training at Tertiary Level in Coastal Zone Management*, UNEP/ROAP Network for Environmental Training at Tertiary Level in Asia and the Pacific, Bangkok, Publication No. 7, pp. 123–42.
Colombijn, F. (1997), 'Of money and trees: a 19th century growth triangle', *Inside Indonesia*, edition 49, Jan–March 1997, available at: http://www.insideindonesia.org/edit49/freek.htm.
Franz, J.C. (1985), 'The seaside resorts of Southeast Asia (Part one)', *Tourism Recreation Research*, **10**, 15–23.
Hong, E. (1985), *See the Third World While It Lasts: Penang*, Penang, Consumers' Association of Penang.
Hussey, A. (1989), 'Tourism in a Balinese village', *Geographical Review*, **79**, 311–25.
IMC Mackay and Schnellmann (1999), *Independent Review of Mineral Resources and Ore Reserves*, available at: http://www.antam.com/News/Publications/IMC/Mineral%20Reserves%201999.htm.
Indonesian Commercial Newsletter (1996), *Indonesia has an Additional 9 Tourist Resorts Including Bintan Beach International Research*, 23.12.1996, Jakarta.

Inskeep, E. and M. Kallenberger (1992), *An Integrated Approach to Resort Development*, Madrid, World Tourism Organization.

Inter Press Service (1998), *Indonesia: Sex Industry is Island's Tourism Lure*, 4.6.1998, available at : http://194.183.22.90/ips%5Ceng.nsf/vwWebMainView/3C FDFCA8910EE37380256A070053736F/?OpenDocument.

Island Leisure International (2003), available at: http://www.bintan-resorts.com.

Iswahyudi, Y. (2000), 'Economic valuation in integrated coastal zone and marine biodiversity resources management in Barelang (Batam, Rempang, Galang) and Bintan Islands', presented at *International Conference on Sustainable Development of Coastal Zones and Instruments for First Evaluation*, 23–27 Oct 2000, Bremerhaven, available at: http://www.rabbigraph.de/cdg/p_iswhud.htm.

Jakarta Post (1995), *Displaced Bintan Farmers Seek Rights Commission Help*, 4.2.1995, Jakarta.

Jakarta Post (2000), *Occupation of Bintan Estate Starts to Scare off Investors*, 20.1.2000, Jakarta.

Kompass (1998), *Islanders Intercepted Foreign Tourists in Bintan*, 21.12.1998, Jakarta.

Matrix-Batam (2003), *Land Rights Demos in Bintan*, available at: http://matrix-batam.hypermart.net/demos.htm.

Orange County Government (2003), available at: http://www.onetgov.net/topics/ Lakes/Parameter_Definitions.pdf.

Smith, R.A. (1992a), 'Conflicting trends of beach resort development: a Malaysian case', *Coastal Management*, **20**, 167–87.

Smith, R.A. (1992b), 'Review of integrated beach resort development in Southeast Asia', *Land Use Policy*, **9**, 209–17.

Smith, V.L. (1992), 'Boracay, Philippines: a case study in 'alternative' tourism', in V.L. Smith and W.R. Eadington (eds), *Tourism Alternatives*, Philadelphia: University Press of Pennsylvania, pp. 135–57.

Soemodinoto, A. and P.P. Wong (2000), 'Small scale tourism and community development: the case of Gili Islands in Lombok, Indonesia', presented at *WTO/UNEP International Conference on Sustainable Tourism in the Islands of the Asia-Pacific Region*, Sanya, Hainan, 6–8 December 2000.

Stiles, R.B. and W. See-Tho (1991), 'Integrated resort development in the Asia Pacific region', *EIU Travel & Tourism Analyst*, **3**, 22–37.

Stonich, S. (1998), 'Political ecology of tourism', *Annals of Tourism Research*, **25**, 25–54.

Straits Times (1997), 'Malaria scares bite into Bintan tourist arrivals', 15.12.1997, Singapore.

Straits Times (2000a), *Life is Returning Normal to Bintan*, 1.2.2000, Singapore.

Straits Times (2000b), *Rent an Atoll for $1350 a Night*, 4.3.2000, Singapore.

Tan, F. (2002a), 'The Riau islands – spotlight on Bintan Part 1', *Radio Singapore International*, 6 February 2002, available at: http://www.rsi.com.sg/en/assignment/ articles/Bintan/Bintan01.htm.

Tan, F. (2002b), 'The Riau islands – spotlight on Bintan Part 5 ', *Radio Singapore International*, 6 March 2002, available at: http://www.rsi.com.sg/en/assignment/art iclesBintan/Bintan05.htm.

Tan, F. (2002c), 'The Riau islands – spotlight on Bintan Part 6', *Radio Singapore International*, 13 March 2002, available at: http://www.rsi.com.sg/en/assignment/a rticles/Bintan/Bintan06.htm.

Tan, P.K. (1992), 'Tourism in Penang: its impacts and implications', in P.K. Voon and T. Shamsul Bahrin (eds), *View from Within: Geographical Essays on*

Malaysia and Southeast Asia, Malaysian Journal of Tropical Geography, Kuala Lumpur, pp. 263–78.

Thongra-Ar, W. and P. Mokkongpai (1992), *A study on coastal water quality in the swimming zone at Bangsaen, Pattaya and Jomtien beach, Chonburi Province in 1991*, Institute of Marine Science, Burapha University, available at: http://staff.buu.ac.th/~academic/research1/abstracts/content/marin/2535.html.

Thongra-Ar, W. and P. Poonpium (1992), *A study on coastal water quality in the swimming zone at Pattaya and Jomtien beaches, Chonburi Province in 1989-1990*, Institute of Marine Science, Burapha University, available at: http://staff.buu.ac.th/~academic/research1/abstracts/content/marin/2535.html.

Tour East Newsletter (2002), *Situation of Coastal Water Quality in Pattaya During the Past Decade*, September/October 2002, available at: http://www.google. com./search?q=cache:_DscWNcmmLIC:www.toureast.net/newsroom/newsroom.ht ml+%22Situation+of+coastal+water+quality+in+Pattaya+during+the+past+decade %22&hl=en&ie=UTF-8.

United Nations Development Fund for Women (UNIFEM) (2003), *Humanitarian Projects*, available at: http://www.geocities.com/RainForest/Jungle/8728/uhuman itarianindex.html.

USA Embassy (2002), 'Recent economic reports: march mining update', March 2002, available at: http://www.usembassyjakarta.org/econ/miningupdate03-02. html.

Index

11 September 2001 96, 97, 112, 192, 272
3S tourism 41

actor analysis 12
actor groups 12
admission fees 10
Afro-Caribbeans 126, 127
Afro-Creole elites 69
aid programs 94
amenity values 19, 70
anchor damage 46
Anglo-Caribbeans 126, 127
Arawak tribes 67, 88

backpackers 167
Bay Islands
    Commission for Development 132
    Conservation Association 130, 132
    Department of Protected Areas
        and Wildlife 131
    Development Promotion
        Association 132
    Garifuna 126
    Honduran Institute of Tourism 132
    Ladinos 126, 127, 128, 129
    Ministry of Culture and Tourism
        131
    Native Bay Islanders Professionals
        and Labour Association 143
    Wildlife Conservation Society 134
    Wykes-Cruz Treaty 127
beach boys 196
Beachcomber group 206
Berjaya group 207
Bintan
    Bintan Beach International Resort
        271
    integrated resort development 271
    Marine Resource Conservation
        Project 247

National Commission on Human
    Rights in Jakarta 279
biotic isolation 6
bird extinctions 7
BirdLife International 214
bottom-up tourism 29
Brazilian Atlantic forest I152
British Airways for Tomorrow Award
    199, 215
British West Indies Airways 41
Brundtland report 51

Caribbean Coastal Marine
    Productivity Program 30
Caribbean Conservation Association
    113, 114, 115
Caribbean Development Bank 71,
    111
carrying capacity 20, 26, 155, 170,
    172
Cayman Islands
    Anglo-American Commission 39
    bank and trust companies 44
    Central Planning Authority 48
    Coastal Works Advisory
        Committee 50
    Draft Tourism Policy Framework
        52, 53
    Environmental Charter 57
    Environmental Protection Fund 50
    Hotel Aid Law 41
    Land Development Law 48
    Marine Conservation Law 48
    money laundering 56
    Mosquito Research and Control
        Unit 44
    Multilateral Environmental
        Agreements 52
    National Planning Committee 53
    National Trust 50, 51
    offshore finance 43

Partnership and Prosperity White
    Paper 51
Planning Appeal Tribunal 50
Protocol Concerning Specially
    Protected Areas and Wildlife
    18, 57
Replenishment Zones 49
Tourism Association 51
Tourism Management Policy 52
Tourist Board 48
UK Overseas Territories
    Conservation Forum 52, 57
user quotas 55
Central American Commission on
    Environment and Development
    134
coastal ecosystems 241
coastal zone management 115
colonialism 7
commodity values 19, 70
common property 75, 191
Commonwealth Development
    Corporation 102
communication 18, 26
community projects
    management 246
    conservation 144
    institutions 72
    organization 256
    tourism 198
compensation 71, 279
conflict 11, 25
Convention on Biological Diversity
    57
Convention on International Trade
    with Endangered Species 212
Cook, James 2
coral reefs 23, 46
    damage 23, 224, 195
    management 243
corruption 239
Court Lines 94, 97
cruise ships 7, 46, 50, 53, 77
cruise tourism 19, 64
Cunard Lines 94, 95
currency exchange rate fluctuations 6

dairy industries 6
de Bougainville, Louis Antoine 2
decision-making 19, 28, 115
deforestation 88

desalination 8
discourse 20, 26
disempowerment 19
diversified production strategies 9
domestic tourism 22, 24
Dominica
    Black Power Movement 69
    Carib territory 19, 68, 71, 73
    Caribs 67, 88
    ecological and social systems 64
    economic citizenship 79
    Hotel Owners Association 75
    Kalinagos 67
    marginalization 60
    Maroons 68
    National Biodiversity Strategy and
        Planning 72
    National Development
        Corporation 65
    Ortoroid people 67
    Taxi Drivers Association 75
    Treaty of Aix-la-Chapelle 68
    Treaty of Versailles 68
    women's network 75
dredging 19, 45

ecological and social systems 64
ecological footprints analysis 8
ecological identity 9, 10, 27
ecological modernization 15, 17
economic citizenship 79
economic diversification 29
Economic Recovery Programme 188
economic transformation 39
ecotourism 160, 173, 199, 249
efficient property rights 9, 196
El Niño Southern Oscillation 8, 213
elites 26, 138, 142, 213
employment 5, 100, 227
endemic species 6
energy use 7, 8
entitlements 18, 19, 26, 185
entrance fees 25
environment
    degradation 28
    quality 267
Environment Coordinating Unit 73
environmental impact assessment
    115, 183, 273
environmentalists 53, 54, 159
epidemics 6

erosion 7, 23, 66, 79, 102
European Union 5, 198
expatriate workers 46, 51
external actors 28
externalized costs of tourism 161

financial capital, lack of 3
Finnish International Development
    Agency 189
foreign aid 20
foreign capital 4
foreign currency earnings 20, 39, 197
foreign developers 138
foreign development aid 4
foreign investment 77, 94
fresh water 7

Gauguin, Paul 2
Gesellschaft für Technische
    Zusammenarbeit 198
Global 500 Award for Environmental
    Achievement 199
Global Coral Reef Monitoring
    Network 30
Global Environment Facility 134, 211
global warming 8
grass-roots initiatives 76
Green Planet Award 215
guest-host relations 20

Hainan
    human resources 222
    minority groups 229
    Tourism Administration Bureau of
        Hainan Province 226, 232
hedonic non-use value 149
high-density Tourism 115
high-value tourists 217, 218
high-volume tourism 29
Holiday Inn International 94
hospitality management 230
Human Development Index 4, 204
human-environmental relations 12,
    27, 61, 185
human resources 3, 222
Hurricane Allen 92, 95

identity 5, 26, 76, 185, 196
Ilha Grande
    Caiçara 153, 157, 161, 167, 169
    Tourism Master Plan 159, 161

tourist survey 162
Tupinambá Amerindians 150
immigrants, s. migrants
increasing water temperatures 8
indigenous knowledge systems 196
information technologies 29
infrastructure development 4, 7
integrated resort development 271
Inter-American Development Bank
    134, 136
International Monetary Fund 15, 20,
    178, 182, 188
International Union for the
    Conservation of Nature 139
International Whaling Commission
    80

Japan's Overseas Economic Co-
    operation Fund 21, 245

kinship ties 18

land ownership 3
land reclamation 45
land-tenure 75
leakages 5
Lesser Antilles 61, 66
limitations on growth 29
limits of acceptable change 158
livelihoods 19, 39, 197, 245
local agro-industries 6
local and national law 27
Local Area Management Authorities
    30
local communities 189, 190
local economy 167
local resource use legislation 188
localization policies 77
low-density tourism 23, 113
low species diversity 6

mangroves 7, 19
marginalization 27, 60
Marine Protected Areas 19, 121, 198,
    211, 246, 258
Marine Reserves 123, 129
marine water quality 275
market-oriented policy 234
market values 19, 71
Matisse, Henri 2

Mesoamerican Barrier Reef System
    126, 134
Mesoamerican Biological Corridor
    24, 133, 134
migrants 23, 185, 195, 224
money laundering 56
mono-structured economy 3
multinational companies 17, 18, 94,
    97, 117
multiplier effect 78

narratives 11
national law 27
native tourism 148
natural capital 63, 72
natural disaster 6
natural hazards 66
neoclassic development paradigm 15
network of interest 214
networks 19
non-market contributions to welfare
    61
non-market forms of capital 71
non-monetary benefits 246
non-self governing territory 2
non place-based actors 12

offshore finance 43
oil price 6
Organization of Eastern Caribbean
    States 80
ornamental shells 23
overseas aid 3
overseas territory 3

Paradise on Earth 2
pelagic fisheries 6
Philippines
    Bureau of Fisheries and Aquatic
        Resources 246
    Coastal Resource Management
        Project 248
    Department of Environment and
        Natural Resources 244
    Department of Tourism 245
    National Ecotourism Strategy 237
place-based actors 12
plantation economy 39
plantation tourism model 4
political instability 6
polluter-pays 52

population growth 93, 225
positive externalities 63, 171
poverty 61
power 18, 26, 74, 185, 197
pre-paid package tours 100
property tax 47
protected areas 10, 203

remittances 3
Replenishment Zones 49
resort life-cycle model 154
Romanticism 2

sand mining and dredging 7
sand quarrying 23, 193
sea level rise 8, 9, 213
sedimentation 7, 45
service industries 9
sewage 7, 23
Seychelles
    Compagnie Seychelloise de
        Promotion Hotelière 206
    Department of Environment 210
    Environment Management Plan of
        Seychelles 203, 210
    Gold Card campaign 215
    Islands Conservation Society 214
    National Parks and Nature
        Conservancy Act 211
    Policy, Planning and Services
        Division 214
    Tourism Marketing Authority 214
shifting cultivation 68
slash-and-burn agriculture 150, 169
slavery 90, 180
slow-growth approach 56
small domestic markets 3
Small Island's Voice 29, 203, 209
small islands developing states 60
small-scale tourism 23, 29
social capital 74
social costs 76
social networks 75
socialist political worldview 20
South Pacific Regional Environment
    Programme 30
souvenir hinterlands 23
St Lucia
    British/American Lend-Lease
        Program 91
    Caribs 88, 90

Ciboney 88
Development Control Authority 106
Development Cooperation and Programme Planning Division 111
Heritage Tourism Programme 110, 116
Hotel Trade School 105
Land Development Act 103
Ministry of Commerce, Tourism, Investment and Consumer Affairs 101
Ministry of Planning, Personnel, Establishment and Training 103
Ministry of Trade, Industry and Tourism 109
National Development Plan 116
National Land Policy Committee 112
National Tourism Policy 112, 116
Physical Development Strategy 106
Tourism Advisory Council 110
Tourism Development Study 105
Tourism Hospitality and Development Act 103
Tourism Incentives Act 103
Tourist Board 94, 111
Treaty of Paris 90
Steigenberger AG 94, 95
Structural Adjustment Programs 5
subsistence
economies 9, 181
farming 7
sustainable development 15, 16
sustainable tourism 16, 28, 29

tax
exemptions 79
holiday 103
incentives 94
terrorism 6
top-down
conservation 24
tourism 28
tourism-related imports 5
traditional economic activities 9, 29
traditional resource management systems 72, 193
travel choices 6

Treaty of Aix-la-Chapelle 68
Treaty of Paris 90
Treaty of Versailles 68
tropical paradise 2

UK Overseas Territories Conservation Forum 52, 57
unemployment 61, 93
United Agency for International Development 248
United Nation Conference on the Law of the Sea 18, 57
United Nations Development Programme 5, 134, 189
United States Agency for International Development 20, 134, 139, 178, 182
user quotas 55

war 6
waste and wastewater 78
water consumption 193
wetlands
management 243
draining 23
whale watching 21, 78, 246
willingness-to-accept Z195
willingness-to-pay 163, 246, 247, 253, 258
Windward Islands 60, 88
Wise Coastal Practices for Beach Management 18
Wise Coastal Practices for Sustainable Human Development 30
World Bank 5, 15, 20, 134, 178, 182, 188, 189, 196, 211, 214, 252
World Development Index 63
World Heritage Site 134
World Tourism Organization 5, 226
World Trade Organization 64
World Wide Fund for Nature 134, 214, 247

Zanzibar
Chama Cha Mapinduzi 181, 185
Civic United Front 181, 185
Commission for Tourism 182, 187
Department of the Environment 189

Environmental Management for
    Sustainable Development Act
    183
Investment Promotion Agency 182

Tourism Investment Act 178, 182
Tourism Training School 187
Tourism Zoning Plan 182
Trade Liberalization Policy 182